Second Edition

Children
in Canada Today

Patrizia
Albanese

OXFORD
UNIVERSITY PRESS

OXFORD
UNIVERSITY PRESS

Oxford University Press is a department of the University of Oxford.
It furthers the University's objective of excellence in research, scholarship,
and education by publishing worldwide. Oxford is a registered trade-mark of
Oxford University Press in the UK and in certain other countries.

Published in Canada by
Oxford University Press
8 Sampson Mews, Suite 204,
Don Mills, Ontario M3C 0H5 Canada

www.oupcanada.com

Library and Archives Canada Cataloguing in Publication
Albanese, Patrizia, author
Children in Canada today / Patrizia Albanese. – Second edition.

(Themes in Canadian sociology)
Previous edition published by Oxford University Press, 2009.
Includes bibliographical references and index.
ISBN 978-0-19-901913-7 (paperback)

1. Children–Canada–Social conditions–Textbooks. 2. Family–
Canada–Textbooks. I. Title. II. Series: Themes in Canadian sociology

HQ792.C3A43 2015   305.230971   C2015-904246-1

Cover image: © iStock/BankPhoto

Oxford University Press is committed to our environment.
This book is printed on Forest Stewardship Council® certified paper
and comes from responsible sources.

MIX
Paper from
responsible sources
FSC
www.fsc.org   FSC® C103567

Printed and bound in Canada

1 2 3 4 — 19 18 17 16

Contents

Preface

Shanahan (2007: 407) reflexively noted that social scientific research on childhood is "oddly ambivalent" and that despite some theoretically and creatively innovative work, the sociology of childhood, in particular, is often uncomfortable with its own object of inquiry. Truth be told, for a number of years I taught a sociology of childhood course without a textbook, using a repro text or collection of readings instead, as no Canadian texts had been written in this area for years. For the most part, instructors teaching sociology of children and childhood courses have been forced to use American or British textbooks, or textbooks that have a psychological or social work orientation. None of these options, to my mind, are adequate as Canadian trends, policies, programs, and research are quite different from American and European ones, and a sociological approach or orientation is considerably different from a psychological one.

Not unlike Shanahan (2007), Stearns (2005: 3) noted that research on the history of childhood "receded during the 1980s," but is "now reviving strongly." With recent changes in government policies and growing public interest in children's rights, child poverty, child care, declining fertility rates, changing trends in divorce, and other family issues has come a shift in academic research and writing on children and childhood. Academics and policy-makers have been relying on data from the National Longitudinal Survey of Children and Youth (NLSCY), as well as the National Population Health Survey (NPHS), Youth in Transition Survey (YITS), General Social Survey (GSS), and the Longitudinal Survey of Immigrants (LSI) to better understand the lives of children in Canada. There has also been a rise in insightful qualitative studies involving children. As a result, we have seen a growing number of publications, mostly research articles and policy papers, on, about, and with children. This text synthesizes some of these important research findings on Canadian children and childhood in Canada into material accessible to undergraduate students in their second, third, and fourth years of study.

Overview of the Book

The status and lives of children in Canada have changed considerably over the past century. In fact, childhood as a discrete life stage has been understood differently by different people at various points in time. As the study of families has changed from treating families as monolithic units of consumption, so has the study of the status, role, lives, and perception of the children within them.

Children have become a nexus of family aspirations for higher social status, among other things. Since the 1950s and 1960s a great deal of emphasis has been placed on "proper" parenting and child-rearing, attested to in the popularity of parenting manuals, journals, books, and websites. We will explore the process through which children become members of our society. We will consider the roles played by various "agents of socialization" and the locales in which socialization takes place. In other words, we examine how, where, when, and with whom children grow up to be socially "functioning" adults. We emphasize the amount of work that goes into making children into consumers, workers, masculine and feminine beings, and, otherwise, members of society. At the same time, we explore the diverse and changing roles that children play in shaping their own complex social worlds, as social agents or "doers" of childhood.

Part I opens with a chapter on the history of thinking and theorizing about childhood, followed by a chapter on theories of child development and socialization, with an overview of new sociological theories of childhood. Chapter 3 outlines ways of doing research on, for, and with children and is followed by three chapters on various agents or locales of socialization: the home (Chapter 4), schooling and peer groups (Chapter 5), and the mass media (Chapter 6).

The second half of the book (Chapters 7 through 13) explores select Canadian social policies and practices that affect and are affected by children. We have been told that Canada's most precious resource is children. Part II evaluates aspects of Canadian society and social policies to determine if indeed we "practise what we preach." This second edition includes significant updates in data and research, with more attention to better understanding the unique circumstances and outcomes of children with disabilities, and a new chapter on Aboriginal children and the policies that affect them.

Over the past decade or two, we have seen significant growth in the number of Canadian policies and programs with the word "child" or "children" in them (Jenson, 2004). We also have seen shifts in the underlying assumptions driving some of the new policies. Recent changes have not always resulted in significant improvements in the lives of children, but they mark a shift in thinking and theorizing about children. This part of the book includes a critical examination of national and provincial policies touching the lives of children, including Canada's policy responses to issues such as child care (Chapter 7), immigration (Chapter 8), Aboriginality (Chapter 9), poverty (Chapter 10), divorce (Chapter 11), and child abuse (Chapter 12). While presenting past practices and recent trends, we scrutinize the assumptions underlying these programs and policies and evaluate them in relation to how inclusive and effective they are in achieving their stated goals.

Policies might be analyzed from the point of view of governments, from the point of view of families, and increasingly, from the point of view of children. We evaluate policies and programs in relation to how they are administered, from the standpoint of their outcomes and impacts on the well-being of children and their families and from the lived experiences of children. To do this, each of these chapters includes an overview of statistics and trends, a presentation of Canadian research in the area, and—where possible and appropriate—actions and insights from and by children. We also include recommendations for improvements.

Finally, in Chapter 13, we consider the future of childhood, looking at the debate on the "disappearance" of childhood. In assessing whether, indeed, childhood in Canada is doomed, the last chapter reminds us that childhood is a social construct, and, as adults working with and for children, there is much important and rewarding work yet to be done.

Acknowledgements

Revising this book proved to be as fun as writing the first edition. It was a very busy period in my life, as I held the presidency of the Canadian Sociological Association, so I counted on the generous support of many around me. My parents helped feed me as they enthusiastically counted down chapters as I revised them. I have enjoyed working with Darcy Pepper and Tanuja Weerasooriya at Oxford University Press. Special thanks to Tasleen Adatia for her meticulous copy-editing. My gratitude also goes out to the anonymous reviewers of the first and second editions, who provided valuable suggestions for improvements. Thanks to all of you!

This book is dedicated to my late husband, Slobodan Drakulic, who passed away suddenly and unexpectedly in 2010, and to Canada's children—may your voices be heard, especially when we forget to listen.

1 Histories of Childhood

Learning Objectives

◎ To see contemporary examples of how our definition of "child" varies depending on the context in which it is used.

◎ To discover what makes concepts like "child" and "childhood" social constructs.

◎ To learn about some of the challenges associated with the study of children in history.

◎ To understand competing theories and explanations of the "discovery" and "emergence" of childhood in history.

◎ To examine competing philosophical approaches to understanding childhood.

◎ To explore some historical variations in the understanding and treatment of children.

◎ To briefly assess a contemporary example of ongoing challenges associated with how "child" is defined.

Introduction

Children exist in every society, of course. But the meaning of the term *child* or *children* and the age or time at which "childhood" is believed to begin and end vary from culture to culture, across time, and among organizations and institutions within any one society. For example, consider the following questions: At what age can parents legally leave a child home alone? At what age can children legally work for pay? When can a young person legally consent to have sexual relations? Who does child pornography legislation protect? When can a noncustodial parent stop paying child support? At what age do children stop being eligible to receive the Canada Child Tax Benefit? What about the Universal Child Care Benefit? At what age can a young person skip classes without parental consent or choose to drop out of school?

The fact that the answers to these questions vary across provincial and national borders and over time are indications that the concepts of child and childhood are **social constructs**—social creations subject to redefinition by the society or culture that attempts to define them (Danby, 2009). According to Oswell (2013), childhood assumes multiple emergent forms within diverse social, economic, historical, and cultural contexts. Furthermore, Shanahan (2007) makes an important distinction between the study of children as members of a particular society and the study of childhood as a set of cultural ideas. In this chapter we will begin by discussing various contemporary defin-itions of the term *child* and some of the reasons for their variation. We will also learn about how these and other types of variations in the definition of child lead us to the conclusion that ideas about children and childhood are social constructs. We will explore what is meant by this and by some of the dif-ferent forms, meanings, and experiences these concepts can encompass. We will do this by looking at the changing notion of childhood across history, by learning about different and competing ways of studying and understanding the evolution of childhood. We will see that even within a given time period and geographic region, there are differing philosophical approaches to under-standing children and childhood and that children of different genders, races, and social class backgrounds will experience childhood differently. In order to critically assess some of these competing theories and approaches, we also will look at how childhood varies cross-culturally. This chapter concludes by bringing the debate back to current and ongoing challenges when defining who and what makes up childhood through a brief look at the current debate about so-called child soldiers.

Defining Children and Childhood Today

There is little consensus in how child, children, and childhood are defined, even among some of Canada's contemporary official or legal documents. For example, according to the 2011 Canadian Census Dictionary, **children** refers

> to blood, step or adopted sons and daughters (*regardless of age* or marital status) who are living in the same dwelling as their parent(s), as well as grandchildren in households where there are no parents present. Sons and daughters who are living with their married spouse or common-law part-ner, or with one or more of their own children, are not considered to be members of the census family of their parent(s), even if they are living in the same dwelling. In addition, the sons or daughters who do not live in the same dwelling as their parent(s) are not considered members of the census family of their parent(s). Sons or daughters who study or have a summer job elsewhere but return to live with their parent(s) during the year are con-sidered members of the census family of their parent(s). (Statistics Canada, 2012; emphasis mine).

Here, we see that in helping to define a census family, Statistics Canada takes the term *children* to mean offspring of any age, residing with their parents (or grandparents)—with a qualification: the offspring's children and their spouses or partners cannot be living in the same (parental) home. In this case, in other words, being a child has nothing to do with physical mat-uration, chronological age, or level of maturity. Instead, it has to do with the nature of the living arrangement, which perhaps, and clearly not in all cases, has something to do with (inter)dependency. It seemingly has its origins in the notion that economic adulthood (Stearns, 2005) begins with moving out of one's parental home and/or having and residing with a partner and/or child of one's own.

Other variations in the definition of child can be seen in the Criminal Code of Canada. For example, Sections 150.1, 151, and 152 of the Criminal Code of Canada protect anyone under the age of 16 (up from age 14 in 2007) from sexual exploitation; effectively, with some exceptions, children under the age of 16 cannot legally consent to sexual activity (more on this in Chapter 12). Except for a narrow exception (if the two individuals are close in age), all sexual activity with a child under the age of 16 (up from age 14 in 2007) is a criminal offence, regardless of the child's ability or willingness to consent (Department of Justice, 2007a; MacKay, 2005). According to this section of the Criminal Code, a child is anyone under the chronological age of 16. Interestingly, although normative trends in physical maturation and age at puberty have been declining (Sorensen et al., 2012), age of legal consent has gone up with the passing of Bill C-22 (Parliament of Canada, 2007). This obviously reflects political rather than physiological motivations for how child is defined.

In another section of the Criminal Code (163.1), child pornography refers to any written, audio, or visual representations of "a person who is or *is depicted* as being under the age of *eighteen* years and is engaged in or is depicted as engaged in explicit sexual activity" (Department of Justice, 2007b; emphasis mine). In this case, the definition of child has to do with chronological age (or *appearing* to be younger than a certain chronological age), and not necessarily physical maturation or level of maturity—because, as we have just noted, someone who is between 16 and 18 years of age could legally engage in sexual acts (except with a person in a position of trust or authority), yet persons within that age range cannot create, sell, or distribute representations of such acts—for the sake of protecting the child. This point is made not to defend or dispute the law, but to demonstrate the variability of definitions.

Many of our current definitions of child have to do with parental rights and obligations towards their children, and on this front, things should be clearer—parents are responsible for their children until they reach the age of 16? 18? 19? Even this definition varies. On the Citizenship and Immigration Canada (CIC) website, a section on children's rights in Canada states that "[p]arents in Canada have a legal duty to provide their children with the necessities of life until they reach age 16" (CIC, 2014a). However, the Ontario Child and Family Services Act defines child as "a person under the age of eighteen years" (Government of Ontario, 2014). Similarly, Manitoba's Child and Family Services Act defines child as "a person under the age of majority," which in that province, like in Alberta, Ontario, Saskatchewan, Quebec, and Prince Edward Island, happens to be the age of 18 (Government of Manitoba, 2014). British Columbia's Child, Family and Community Services Act defines child as a person under 19 (Government of British Columbia, 2014), given that its age of majority—as well as that in New Brunswick, Nunavut, the Northwest Territories, Nova Scotia, Yukon, and Newfoundland and Labrador—happens to be 19. Much of this variation reflects the fact that child and family services in Canada fall under provincial jurisdiction, a factor with consequences that we will encounter time and again (and will discuss in more detail) throughout this book.

Like Prince Edward Island, Quebec, Ontario, Manitoba, Saskatchewan, and Alberta, the United Nations (UN) Convention on the Rights of the Child aims to protect children under the age of 18 (more on this in Chapter 6), which some have argued reflects the largely Western ideal of childhood as a time of play and training for adulthood (Bentley, 2005).

What does all this tell us? It tells us that the term *child* varies depending on the context in which it is used, the purpose it is intended to serve, and the type and nature of interactions it involves. What *child* means varies based on chronological age and level of maturity (in reference to physical maturation or economic dependency) and according to political interests. At the same time, our definitions largely reflect Western assumptions about ability, power, autonomy, and dependency (Bentley, 2005). Definitions also tell us that the larger or narrower slice of time over the life course that has come to be known as childhood is socially constructed, and the experiences, behaviour, and expectations attached to this life period come to be seen as characteristic of childhood in ways that also vary over time and across cultures.

Understanding Variations in Childhood over Time

Stearns (2009: 35) noted, "different societies, as anthropologists well know, carry different conceptions of childhood, which in turn influence the experience of children themselves." In fact, childhood has almost always and everywhere taken on distinct forms, with sets of expectations and experiences that depend on the economic organization of the society (hunting and gathering, agricultural, or industrial), the socioeconomic class and the social status of the families under study, and the historical period or epoch of the society under study (classical, postclassical, premodern/modern). Stearns (2009: 35) declares that "culture counts." For example, you would expect the experiences of children living in ancient Greece to differ from those of children living in contemporary, economically struggling Greece. You would expect those differences to appear along gender and possibly ethno-racial lines, not to mention other social locations, intersections, and variations. Before investigating some of these variations and the theories and explanations connected to why they are believed to exist, let us consider some of the ways in which childhood has been studied and some of the challenges associated with these diverse approaches.

A great deal of research on children and childhood focuses on the experiences and treatment of children in particular societies, during specific periods in time. For example, Haas (1998) writes about childhood in Renaissance Florence, Hsiung (2005) focuses on late imperial China, and Kojima (1986) studies children and childhood in seventeenth-century Japan. While having a clearly defined historical focus is seemingly advantageous in understanding childhood at a particular point in time, comprehensive studies of this type recognize and point to diversity of childhood experiences within the time period, along class, family status, and gender lines. For example, think about how different are the lives and experiences of girls and boys in the (sub)culture in which you were raised.

Other researchers, like Stearns (2005, 2006), have taken a "world history approach" when studying childhood, meaning they try to capture the "big picture" by paying attention to the major changes and continuities in the concept of childhood. This second approach is particularly challenging, as it requires awareness of commonalities and differences across societies and a relatively wide understanding of both global and regional trends and details, which are necessary to avoid making sweeping overgeneralizations. Another potential problem with this type of approach is that all too often, the "big picture" history of childhood takes on a Western European and/or North American focus, treating these as universal and ignoring the vastly diverse experiences found in the rest of the world.

Regardless of the general approach, the historical study of children and childhood remains difficult. Think about how we come to know what we know about people who lived in the past. Many historians reconstruct history through the analysis of personal documents (letters, diaries, photographs and paintings, autobiographies, oral narratives recorded by someone else, etc.), official and unofficial records (court records and laws; religious documents and records; coroner's reports; church registries of births, marriages, and deaths; wills; ship's logs; etc.; see Stearns, 2014, for an analysis of the use of the term *obedience* in manuals and texts from the 1800s), and by studying social artifacts or material objects people and groups leave behind (buildings, eating utensils, garbage, newspapers, toys, etc. [see Montgomery, 2009]). Children themselves leave behind comparatively few direct records (Stearns, 2006).

Like many adults living in the past, "average" children for the most part were illiterate, and so could not write about their own experiences. They tended to live less public lives and were much less likely than adults to appear in court cases, newspaper accounts, or other public documents. Some of their material culture (toys, games, cribs, clothing) survived, depending on the period of study, but may also have been misinterpreted, misread, or misunderstood (e.g., "is this a cornhusk doll or a remnant of dinner?"). Furthermore, while we may know about how particular individuals and groups in societies disciplined children (through laws, religious teachings and documents, court cases, letters, and coroners' reports), we know little about how children themselves experienced it. When we think we know something, it often involves recollections by adults about how discipline was believed or remembered to have been experienced, which is considerably different from how that person as a child *actually* experienced it (Stearns, 2005; Janovicek, 2003; Sutherland, 2003).

In addition, while some—often affluent, literate, and powerful—adults have written about their childhood in letters, diaries, and autobiographies, these accounts tend to reflect specific memories or events, and even these (knowingly or unknowingly) may not be completely accurate. What and how they choose to retell may actually reflect more about their adult life than about their childhood. You may have experienced such "distortions" yourself when hearing your parent or sibling talk about what you were like as a child. Therefore, much of what we know about children is filtered through the images, experiences, and ideas of adults. As a result, most children living in the past were silent, or silenced by history and circumstance, and we are left with a considerable amount of speculation about the "true lives" of children. This, in turn, has sparked theoretical debates about children and childhood, with one of the greatest debates starting in the 1960s when Philippe Ariès published his book, *Centuries of Childhood*. In it he argued that until medieval times, societies did not recognize childhood as a distinct period in the life course. Only with the passage of time and significant changes to the social order did we see the emergence of "childhood." In response, some have argued that the beginning of the historical study of childhood, often attributed to Ariès's work, involves a "false start" of sorts (Stearns, 2005). Let us see how this came to be and what it involved.

Philippe Ariès's "Discovery of Childhood" and His Critics

Philippe Ariès, French scholar and demographic historian, has been recognized by many as one of the "pioneering" (Stearns, 2006), best-known (deMause, 1974), and most influential (and controversial; Classen, 2005; Archard, 2004) historians of childhood in the twentieth century. Ariès (1962: 33) argued that "there was no place for childhood in the medieval world." In his book *Centuries of Childhood* (1962), he explained that he was not arguing that children were neglected or despised in the medieval world, nor that they lived lives devoid of affection, but rather that in the past people lacked the awareness of the distinctiveness of childhood apart from adulthood. He noted that this was evidenced by their absence, marginalization, and adult-like depictions in portraits, and by their absence from the focus of religious festivals and celebrations. Children, he added, were not given special emotional or legal allowances and were depicted clothed as mini-adults or mingling with adults in everyday life for the purposes of work, relaxation, and sport (Ariès, 1962: 37). An interesting outcome of this supposition of the medieval world's "indifference" towards childhood was that it gave children more latitude, less monitoring, and more autonomy.

Ariès noted that at about the thirteenth century, images of children become available that are closer to the modern concept of childhood (ibid., 34). As a result, Ariès declared that "no doubt, the discovery of childhood began in the thirteenth century, and its progress can be traced in the history of art in the fifteenth and sixteenth centuries. But the evidence of its development became more plentiful and significant from the end of the sixteenth century and throughout the seventeenth" (ibid., 47)—a period that he called the "development of childhood." He explained that changes were first seen among the upper classes, among whom there was a growing recognition of children's special need for attention, nurture, and guidance accompanied by an increased attention to schooling. Birth rates began to drop, allowing parents the resources to pay more attention to individual children.

While many, such as Classen (2005) and Stearns (2005, 2006), note that Ariès's work exerted a vast influence on historiography, and was foundational in kickstarting the historical study of childhood, they also note that a growing body of research indicates that Ariès's thesis was not always substantiated. Many have tried to prove, contrary to Ariès's views, that some medieval societies did have a view of childhood as unique and special. Others have criticized Ariès for generalizing, overemphasizing, and misinterpreting on the foundation of a limited and select amount of evidence. For example, Koops (2003) critically reassesses Ariès's thesis on the images of adult-like children in early paintings (and increased infantilizing of images with the passing of time). Koops (2003), who was prepared to dismiss Ariès's evidence, conducted a very time-consuming analysis of a random (scientific) sample of Dutch and Flemish paintings, and to his surprise found evidence supporting Ariès's thesis—children did appear more childlike in later paintings. Others, drawing on evidence from medieval letters and diaries (Pollock, 1987, 1983), and conducting historical analyses of the abuse of children (deMause, 1974), point to more continuity than change in the treatment of children over time. Interestingly, Pollock (1983) notes that in the Middle Ages and early modern period children were more loved and kindly treated than the Ariès thesis implies, while deMause (1974) supplies evidence that they were less kindly treated.

Heywood (2001: 32) shows that at any given point in time one can find competing themes in the treatment and understanding of childhood. For example, children have at concurrent times been written about as both innocent and depraved (wicked), as products of both nature and nurture, as both needy and dependent and unsupervised and independent. He contends that our historical understanding almost always involves variable views on the treatment and experiences of children along age and gender lines. Heywood also points to considerable variations in perceptions of childhood within Europe, at about the same periods in time, as we will see in the work of Locke and Rousseau.

For some, the "inventor" of the concept of childhood was Jean-Jacques Rousseau (1712–78). The French philosopher, some argue, pushed the concept of childhood to mean something that was not only quantitatively different (children having lived fewer years) from adulthood but qualitatively different as well (Jalongo, 2002). Others point, instead, to the work of John Locke (1632–1704), the English philosopher, for his pioneering work on childhood (Archard, 2004). Let us briefly look at what each has contributed to our current notions of childhood.

Competing Turning Points in European Thought

In *Some Thoughts on Education* (1693), John Locke, the "father of English liberalism," is believed to have provided Europeans with the first treatise or manifesto on a scheme for child-centred education (Archard, 2004). Even earlier, his work on governance refers to childhood as a distinct and unique period in the life of a person; writing on "paternal power" in *A Treatise on Civil Government* (1937 [1690]: 35), Locke explains that children are not born in a "full state of equality," as their parents have "a sort of rule and jurisdiction over them when they come into this world," even if this is only temporary. He added that "the power . . . that parents have over their children arises from that duty which is incumbent on them, to take care of their offspring during the imperfect state of childhood" (ibid., 37). While this may not seem especially significant to readers today, it was revolutionary for his time, when it was commonly believed that children were born either good or bad ("born of original sin" [Heywood, 2001]), a concept that could be twisted to relieve parents of a sense of responsibility—except that parents had the right and duty to "beat the sin" out of them (see Chapter 12).

Locke wrote about children as "citizens in the making" or incomplete versions of their future adult selves (Archard, 2004). This was especially significant as it highlighted his view that children have needs and interests different from those of adults, and because of this require special attention and proper upbringing. He argued that children are born free of reason—as blank slates (*tabula rasa*)—and that experience alone, slowly acquired, stocked the mind. In other words, with proper education, children, who were not yet fully rational, were brought gradually to reason. Most significantly, and contrary to popular views of the time, he argued that children should not simply be driven into conformity and "good behaviour" by being beaten or coerced (Locke, 1964 [1693]). For Locke, education formed a child's ability to reason and fully function as a free and equal adult (Locke, 1937 [1690], 1975 [1697]).

In contrast to Locke, as Rousseau expressed in the first sentence of his most famous work, *Social Contract* (1762), "Man is born free but everywhere is in chains." Rousseau's political statement also expresses his views on childhood. First, it implies that a child is born (care)free and innocent, but not "blank" and unequal, as Locke believed; and not "of sin," as many, but especially priests and educators, believed. In another of his famous works, *Emile* (1762: 5), Rousseau exclaims, "God makes all things good; man meddles with them and they become evil." For Rousseau, childhood was uniquely a time of innocence and honesty (in sharp contrast to Locke's view of childhood as an "imperfect state"). Some note, building on and in response to the philosophies and writings of Augustine (Duschinsky, 2013), Rousseau believed that children had their own way of seeing, thinking, and feeling apart from adults; and while they did not reason as adults do (intellectual reason), they had their own form of sensitive or puerile (silly/infantile) reason, which they should be free to explore and enjoy (Heywood, 2001). He condemned Locke's advice that we should reason with children, explaining that they should be left alone to "be children," as nature intended. His philosophy of education is built on the premise that there are natural stages of development for different periods in the life cycle: infancy (from birth to age two); childhood (2–12 years of age); boyhood or preadolescence (12–15 years of age); adolescence or youth (15–20 years of age, or the age of marriage); and manhood (from age 20 or marriage and beyond)[1]—each period requiring its own distinct pedagogical approach (see Sahakian and Sahakian, 1974).

Rousseau explained that children would eventually become stifled by life experiences, but for the time being they should be left to enjoy and freely explore their social worlds.[2] In fact, he blames educators and other adults for much of the stifling. For example, he states

> children's lies are therefore entirely the work of their teachers, and to teach them to speak the truth is nothing less than to teach them the art of lying. In your zeal to rule, control, and teach them, you never find sufficient means at your disposal. You wish to gain fresh influence over their minds by baseless maxims, by unreasonable precepts; and you would rather they knew their lessons and told lies, than leave them ignorant and truthful. (Rousseau, 1762: 66)

It is no wonder that Rousseau and his *Emile* were severely criticized and condemned at the time (Jimack, 1974). His views were highly controversial but extremely significant in challenging and transforming past European views on childhood.

Although these two philosophers' views on childhood seem very different—for Locke, childhood was an imperfect state and education built upon the blank slate, whereas for Rousseau childhood was carefree and special, and education stifled and detracted from a child's freedom and humanness—they both had profound social consequences because their views placed on parents and educators the responsibility for how children "turn out." Although they did not agree on the type of attention needed by the child, both recognized childhood as unique and distinct from adulthood. Both philosophies expressed an underlying need for more adult attention to identifying and addressing children's needs and concerns, by either securing them the space and time to explore their natural world (Rousseau) or educating them by using developmentally appropriate, noncoercive methods (Locke). They also show us that in Europe there was no single, unified view on what childhood was or how it should be treated.

In focusing on the work of these two philosophers and not on the work of others like the Confucian Kaibara (who published his book in 1710, advising that formal teaching should begin at age six or seven; see Kojima, 1986), I, like Ariès, may be criticized for being Eurocentric in my writing. To counter this, let us consider how the concept of childhood varies along cultural lines.

Cross-Cultural Similarities and Variations

When we look back in time, across borders and within cultures, we see oscillations in the notion of childhood caused by social, cultural, economic, and political diversity and change. In fact, anthropologists hold that there are multiplicities of childhoods, each culturally codified and defined by age, ethnicity, gender, history, location, etc. (Rosen, 2007). We even see transnational variations in such taken-for-granted things as the structuring of age categories and the way chronological age has been counted. For example, writing on the Japan of the 1700s and 1800s, Kojima (2003) explained that in this older Japanese reckoning system, which had its roots in China, every newborn was reckoned to be one year of age, and on the next New Year's Day (usually in late January, early February by the Gregorian calendar) those born in the previous year became two years of age regardless of the month in which they were born. Clearly, the culture, nature, and economic organization of any given society shape how childhood is measured, understood, and xperienced.

Some, who like Stearns (2006, 2005) have taken a "world history approach," look at how the economic organization of diverse societies (hunting and gathering versus agricultural versus industrial) affects how childhood is understood and experienced. For example, he explains that nomadic peoples in hunting and gathering societies, with more temporary settlements and travelling distances for food and other resources, represent childhood as a period of dependency that potentially burdens the group. He sites archaeological and anthropological evidence from the Americas, Australia, and India to show that in hunting and gathering societies birth rates were intentionally kept relatively low through prolonged lactation (breastfeeding for up to four years or longer), by abortion through the use of abortifacient plants, by infanticide, or by regulation of sexual contact in order to minimize the group's burden on its scarce food supplies on account of too many mouths to feed. Disease and malnutrition also kept birth rates down. While some children could help with food-gathering, their work at times actually reduced the productivity of others, was supplemental at best, and often could not cover their own maintenance (Stearns, 2005). Because such groups were nomadic, too many children slowed the group and acted as economic liabilities rather than as assets in foraging (hunting and gathering) economies.

In contrast, Stearns (2006) notes, in agricultural societies children of different ages quickly come to be seen as part of an essential labour force. With an expanded food supply, and in light of this realization, birth rates begin to grow. When there are more children in the society, they gain attention in legal codes, have more people their own age to interact with, and begin to be thought about as a distinct group. Their increased numbers and visibility, Stearns points out, give rise to superstitions about children. He notes that some "African groups"[3] believed that twins carried evil spirits and often were put to death, and that children in the early Harappan civilization (along the Indus River) had their ears pierced to ward off evil spirits. In agrarian societies, it was important that children be "protected" in this way and kept well enough to work.

Having said this, we should be careful not to overgeneralize. Here microhistories provide interesting examples of variations that emerged from unique economic and political circumstances. For example, during the fur trade in territories governed by the Hudson's Bay Company (later part of Canada), Pollard (2003) states that wives, particularly Aboriginal wives, were deemed an asset, while children, in contrast, were seen as a liability, at a time when in other parts of the country (in farming communities) and in parts of Europe from which these settlers came, children were an economic asset, as they served as a source of labour on farms or of income in factories. Interestingly, in contrast to European views and those of North American settlers, girls were the preferred sex when children were born to unions of European fur traders and Aboriginal women. In the absence of European women, "mixed-blood" daughters were the most desirable marriage partners because mixed-race women became strategic resources when their male partners were working across two cultures (ibid.). In other words, there were economic benefits to alliances with Aboriginal families through marriage to their daughters and through their mixed-race granddaughters.

Other macrohistorians, like Colón and Colón (2001), have uncovered interesting information about the treatment of children and about childhood in early civilizations. They write about the first "four great civilizations" that emerged between 10,000 and 5000 BCE, close to large rivers: the Tigris and Euphrates Rivers in Mesopotamia (the Middle East); the Nile in Egypt; the Hindus River in Indus; and the Yellow River in China. They explain that while we are extremely limited in what we can know and can assume about these societies, all four provide us with examples of the treatment of children that counter Ariès's thesis that childhood did not exist as a concept before medieval European times. For example, some of the earliest codes of law known to us, dating back to 4,000 years ago in ancient Sumer in Mesopotamia, make reference to the concept of parental responsibility towards children (ibid.). Similarly, in the same region, around 1792 BCE, the famed ruler Hammurabi created a comprehensive code of 282 laws, of which 16 directly mentioned children. Some of these laws protected children from abduction (punishable by death), and from loss of rights resulting from a loss of one parent (through remarriage) or of both parents (ibid.). Colón and Colón also point to archaeological evidence of toys that were buried with their affluent, young, prematurely deceased masters.

Similarly, they present archaeological evidence that Egyptian tombs contained colourful wall paintings of life events, including children at play and scenes of affection between parents and children. And while Egypt had no legal codes protecting child welfare like those of Hammurabi, there is documentation of laws that protected legitimate and "illegitimate" children, as well as the unborn. For example, a pregnant Egyptian woman convicted of a crime could not be punished for that crime until the child was born. And while a parent (anyone who had given life) was not sentenced to servitude or death for taking the life of a child, historical evidence reveals that he or she was required to embrace that murdered child in his or her arms for three days and three nights and face the scorn and anger of the community (ibid.). The Egyptian *Book of the Dead* listed 36 incantations, of which two were "I have not had sexual relations with a boy" and "I have not taken milk from the mouths of children" (ibid., 28).

One could go on and on citing interesting and unique examples of the existence of childhood in diverse societies across time and space, but the point is simple and brief: the notion of childhood oscillated, taking on a more significant/discernible or less significant/indiscernible place within the life cycle depending on the economic, political, and cultural composition of any given group at any point in time. Childhood also varied along social class and gender lines, among other variations, as we will see in more detail throughout this book.

One final point that should be made in regard to attempting to identify "a starting point"—"the birthplace" or "discovery" of childhood—is that this quest not only proves to be difficult, but also often implies that the treatment of children has progressed or developed from a difficult past towards a decent or better present. And there have been researchers and historians who have talked about a series of increasingly triumphant gains over time, and those who have made proclamations that "the twentieth century is the century of the child" (Key, 1907) and that our recent age has witnessed "the ascendancy of childhood." But we should be cautious of such generalizations; it is not often or necessarily the case that they can be supported. To the previous triumphant assertions we must add that we also have examples of widespread, institutionalized, and state-sponsored cultural genocide and abuse of Aboriginal children, throughout the twentieth century, in residential schools in Canada (see Chapter 9) that were unheard of and would have been strongly condemned by Aboriginal communities hundreds of years ago. We cannot assume there has or will be progress in the understanding of childhood and treatment of children as unique or special simply because of the passage of time. Let us consider an example that demonstrates both continuity and change in our understanding of childhood, but at the same time highlights the complexity of how *child* is defined both in Canada and abroad.

Child Soldiers—Past and Present

Children, especially boys, of different ages have participated in wars and armed conflict throughout history and across continents. Ariès (1962: 71) wrote that the "Caravagesque painters of the seventeenth century often depicted bands of soldiers gambling excitedly in taverns of ill fame: next to the old troopers one can see some very young boys, twelve years old or so, who seem to be enthusiastic gamblers." Widespread evidence from other sources, times, and places confirms the role children played, again, especially boys, in armed combat and war.

Today, while some national and international bodies treat the use of child soldiers as a modern international humanitarian and human rights issue or violation,[4] the issue is not resolved nor are we even close to consensus on the matter. In fact, the issue embodies some of the interesting challenges we have encountered in this chapter when it comes to current historical and cross-cultural variations in the notions of child and childhood. As we have seen, age categories are used differently by local, national, and international actors, by members of different cultural groups, and at different points in time. At the moment, in Canada, children between the ages of 12 and 18 can enrol in Canada's sea, army, or air cadets, a federally funded program run for those, in the case of army cadets, "craving exciting outdoor activities where their personal limits as individuals and team-members will be tested" (Canadian Cadet Organizations, 2013). Could this be considered recruitment or training of child soldiers? Some, certainly, would say yes, even though none of these children will likely ever experience combat or war.

Advocates from a number of international organizations, including Human Rights Watch, Amnesty International, Save the Children International, the International Committee of the Red Cross, Child Soldiers International, and the Coalition to Stop the Use of Child Soldiers actively work to put a stop to the use of child soldiers in armed conflicts throughout the world. The UN Convention on the Rights of the Child (1989/1990; see Chapter 2), the Optional Protocol to the Convention on the Rights of the Child on the Involvement of Children in Armed Conflict (2000), parts of the 1989 Rome Statute of the International Criminal Court, and the 1949 Geneva Conventions (and their more recent supplements) all have criticized and condemned the use of child soldiers.

Many child advocates support the "Straight-18" position (see Box 1.1), which seeks to prevent the recruitment and use of children younger than 18 years of age into armed forces and to bar the criminal prosecution of children for war crimes. Furthermore, many argue that adults who recruit children into the armed forces and armed conflict should be held criminally responsible and prosecuted for war crimes.

Some, like Rosen (2007) and Bentley (2005), have noted that at the heart of the Straight-18 position is the requirement that existing and competing definitions of childhood be abandoned for a single universal and international standard. This would force every government around the globe to agree to one clear-cut definition of child—anyone under the age of 18—denying and negating historical, cross-cultural, and institutional variations in the definition of child, at least for the purpose of training for or participation in combat. While this may appear to be suggested as a solution for child protection, questions remain. For example, should there be only one universal, international standard? What would be gained? What would be lost in doing this (think about cross-cultural diversity, national autonomy, etc.)? Will "powerful" nations end up imposing their definition, in order to fulfill their own interests and needs at the expense of less powerful ones? Should one universal approach to children's rights be the approach we take? While we will take up some of these issues in Chapter 2, I leave you with this potentially uncomfortable and difficult challenge because the debates around the definitions of child and childhood remain serious, significant, and unresolved. Despite the fact that most children's rights activists and some government legislation consider a child as anyone under the age of 18, there are significant similarities and differences in the experiences of those persons above the age of 12—teenagers or adolescents—and those below that age. The remainder of this book, for the most part, focuses on the experiences of persons under the age of 12.

**Box
1.1**

Child Soldiers International—Straight-18

Established in 1998, Child Soldier International, (formerly known as the Coalition to Stop the use of Child Soldiers) is a coalition of human rights and humanitarian organizations that includes, among others, Amnesty International, Defence for Children International, Human Rights Watch, International Save the Children Alliance, and World Vision International. Its purpose was to campaign for a human rights treaty to prevent the military recruitment of children in conflict zones. Their Straight-18 initiative aims to protect children from military recruitment by armed forces or groups involved in armed conflict. The following is an excerpt from their website:

> There is wide acceptance that the minimum age at which an individual should be permitted to join government armed forces is 18 years. Today, almost two thirds of UN member states have established in law or otherwise committed to a minimum military recruitment age of 18 years. With very few exceptions, states have adopted 18 years as the minimum age for conscription.
>
> There are, however, a diminishing number of states which, contrary to best practice, still permit the voluntary recruitment of under-18s. According to the latest available information 17 year olds can enlist in the armed forces of *Algeria, Australia, Austria, Azerbaijan, Bolivia, Brunei, Cape Verde, Chile, China, Cuba, Cyprus, France, Germany, Israel, Jamaica, Lebanon, Malaysia, Malta, Netherlands, New Zealand, the Philippines, Sao Tome and Principe, Saudi Arabia, and the USA.*
>
> States which continue to permit the voluntary recruitment at the lower age of 16 years are: *Bangladesh, Brazil, Canada, Egypt, El Salvador, India, Iran, Ireland, Jordan, Mauritania, Mexico, Pakistan* (with exception of aero-technicians, see below)*, Papua New Guinea, Singapore, Tonga, Trinidad and Tobago, the United Kingdom, and Zambia.* In a few states there is no minimum age or it has been set below 16 years. Such states include *Barbados, Guinea Bissau, Guyana, Pakistan* (aero-technicians only)*, and the Seychelles.*
>
> States which permit under-18s to join their armed forces, even if only for training purposes, put in jeopardy the well-being of children and deny them rights to which they are entitled. Critically, they also put them at increased risk of use in armed conflict: as our research shows, where states recruit individuals below the age of 18 years, prohibitions on participation in hostilities (even when supported by systems to screen troops prior to deployment) do not constitute an effective guarantee against child soldier use.

Continued

Our work aims to:

- Build increased momentum towards 18 as the universal minimum age for conscription and enlistment by state armed forces.
- Bring about change in selected countries, beginning with the United Kingdom, through campaigns for legal reform to raise the age of voluntary recruitment to a minimum of 18 years.
- Provide research, analysis and concrete recommendations to states and other key stakeholders on practical measures needed to enforce minimum recruitment ages, including effective age verification procedures and independent monitoring regimes.

Source: Child Soldiers International (2014).

Summary

Since the beginning of the historical studies of childhood, whether one attributes this to Ariès or not, many debates, diverging themes, and competing schemes and explanations have surrounded the definition of childhood, its geographical origins, and "starting point." We see that even in Canada today, the official definition of child varies across institutions and jurisdictions because of variations in the purpose it is intended to serve and the type and nature of interactions it involves. We also briefly looked at different ways of studying children historically, and some of the challenges posed in doing this, including the predominating silence of children themselves as subjects of and in history. Despite this, many, like Ariès, have attempted to describe what life was like for children at various points in time. The competing philosophies of Locke and Rousseau arose to shape and change parents' and educators' understanding of their own roles vis-à-vis children. We also see that Europeans of the seventeenth and eighteenth centuries did not "invent" the notion of childhood and child protection, as archaeological evidence suggests that early civilizations, thousands of years before that period in Western thought, distinguished childhood in some of their codes and practices. We considered an ongoing challenge to our current definition of child as it applies to child soldiers. What rises above the questions about what life was *really like* for children "then and there" or about what life *should be like* for children "now and here" is that opinions in our day and age remain varied—a debate about what childhood has encompassed in the past continues because people today question what childhood should encompass.

Questions for Critical Thought

1. How similar or different do you think childhood is today, compared with when you were a child? How about differences between your childhood and that of your parent(s)? What do you think accounts for the similarities? What accounts for the differences? How might your current and future work, and your interaction with children, be affected by your acknowledgement of these similarities and differences?

2. If you were asked to design an early childhood education program premised on Locke's views, how would it look? How would it compare with a program built on Rousseau's views? Which do you believe would yield the "best" results for our society? Why?

3. If we have so many diverse definitions of child and childhood, can there be such a thing as universal children's rights, such as the UN Convention on the Rights of the Child? Do these types of documents impose culturally imbued notions of one or more dominant groups at the expense of all others, especially minority views? Should we safeguard universal children's rights? How? How do we make sure we are not perpetuating inequality by imposing one set of expectations about childhood?

Suggested Readings

Ariès, Philippe. 1962. *Centuries of Childhood: A Social History of Family Life.* New York: Alfred A. Knopf. First published in 1960 as *L'Enfant et la vie familiale sous l'ancien régime.* This is Aries's groundbreaking and highly debated book on the "discovery" and development of the concept of childhood in history. Using examples of vocabulary, literary scenes, manners of dress, types of games, visual images, education, and family structure in European history, he reconstructs the evolution of childhood.

Janovicek, Nancy, and Joy Parr, eds. 2003. *Histories of Canadian Children and Youth.* Toronto: Oxford University Press. This Canadian collection includes 28 essays arranged in an overlapping chronological and thematic fashion. The book includes sections on colonial childhood (1700–1880); young workers (1841–1923); schools and schooling (1850–1923); "bad homes" and delinquent children (1890–1955); residential schools (with a focus on 1938–49); children's rights in war and peace (1940–60); immigrant children in the late twentieth century; and learning about sexuality (1950–84).

Koops, Willem, and Michael Zucherman, eds. 2003. *Beyond the Century of the Child.* Philadelphia: University of Pennsylvania Press. This collection of papers brings together authors who present historical perspectives on children of diverse nations, including Kloek on children of The Netherlands, Calvert on children of America, Kojima on children of Japan, and Nylan on children of China.

Montgomery, Heather. 2009. *An Introduction to Childhood: Anthropological Perspectives on Children's Lives.* West Sussex, UK: Wiley-Blackwell. This book provides a critical examination of childhood in anthropological research. She focuses on how anthropologists have studied children's lives while she deconstructs the history of cultural anthropology.

Stearns, Peter. 2005. *Growing Up: The History of Childhood in a Global Context.* Waco, Texas: Baylor University Press. This very short book contains two provocative essays that challenge historians and students of the history of childhood to think seriously and globally about the history of childhood through the transitions from hunting and gathering societies to agricultural and industrial economies. It traces the distinctive ways that diverse civilizations and religious traditions approached childhood.

Websites

Child Soldiers International
www.child-soldiers.org/

Child Soldiers International is an international human rights research and advocacy organization that seeks to end the military recruitment and the use in hostilities, in any capacity, of any person under the age of 18 by state and non-state armed forces or groups.

H-Childhood History of Childhood and Youth
www.h-net.msu.edu/~child/

H-Childhood is an edited electronic network on the history of childhood and youth from Michigan State University, which also publishes the *Journal of the History of Children and Youth*. The site contains links to conferences and book reviews. It also contains an international Syllabus Exchange and newsletter.

Images Canada
www.imagescanada.ca/r1-220-e.html

Images Canada provides central search access to the thousands of images held on the websites of participating Canadian cultural institutions. Through Images Canada, you can find images of the Canadian events, people, places, and things that make up Canadians' collective heritage. You can search many collections by typing in a keyword in the search box at the top right of each page. The keyword search for "children" results in more than 6,000 images of children throughout Canadian history.

Society for the History of Children and Youth (SHCY)
shcyhome.org/

The SHCY was founded in 2001 to promote the study of the history of children and youth. Its goals are to support cross-disciplinary research and scholarship about childhood, youth cultures, and the experience of young people across diverse times and places.

United Nations Human Rights—Optional Protocol to the Convention on the Rights of the Child on the Involvement of Children in Armed Conflict
www.ohchr.org/EN/ProfessionalInterest/Pages/OPACCRC.aspx

This protocol, by the Office of the High Commissioner for Human Rights, includes an important resolution on the involvement of children in armed conflict. The Optional Protocol was adopted and opened for signature, ratification, and accession by members of the UN General Assembly (General Assembly resolution A/RES/54/263) on 25 May 2000, and entered into force 12 February 2002.

Social Theories of Childhood

Learning Objectives

◎ To consider the virtual absence of childhood in Canadian sociology until relatively recently.

◎ To survey the changing landscape of theorization of childhood.

◎ To consider what past theories of childhood assumed about children.

◎ To understand the paradigmatic shift in thinking about children, particularly in light of changing international and national approaches to children's rights.

◎ To map what has been happening to what were once called the "new" social theories of childhood.

◎ To see what theories of childhood dominate in Canada today.

Introduction

In 1988, Leena Alanen wrote that the study of children is "either totally absent in sociology or is treated within very limited contexts which are considered marginal for sociological theory and research" (Alanen, 1988: 53). Only recently has sociology as a discipline begun to take children seriously as subjects, actors, and objects of social inquiry. To underscore the point, Corsaro's (2015) *Sociology of Childhood* has a section of an opening chapter titled "Sociology's Rediscovery of Childhood." Even then, the uptake has been uneven; in some parts of the world, including the United Kingdom, Australia, Germany, and Scandinavia, we have seen children and childhood taken more seriously within sociological studies (Mayall, 2013; Moran-Ellis, 2010). In Canada things have been somewhat slower. For quite some time, the sociology of childhood has remained on the margins of the discipline, with few sociology departments offering courses directly on or about children. That said, a body of research on children in Canada is growing, though children remain, for the most part, as "add-ons" to courses on parenting, families, and related subfields. For example, children are often mentioned in chapters and courses on socialization, gender, and education—but rarely in their own right, as the main focus of attention. Bühler-Niederberger (2010a) noted that sociologists always *thought* they were including children, but in actuality only touched upon children as they related to other research and writing on families or education.

We should not underestimate the importance of including children and childhood in sociological theorizing and research. In fact, in places (particularly in the United Kingdom, Australia, Germany, and Scandinavia) where sociology has made the shift, universities have found that the inclusion of children as a focus of study has transformed important aspects of the discipline (King, 2007; Wyness, 2006) as well as educational policy and practice (Smith, 2007; Danby and Farrell, 2004). As Mayall (2000: 243) noted, proper understanding of the social order requires consideration of all its members and all social groups.

While this chapter will include a relatively large number of names and theories that may seem daunting at first sight, it may be useful to think about the development of theorizing about children as following a path similar to that trod by feminists in theorizing about women in earlier decades. For example, women in the past, like children more recently, were excluded from both theory and research in sociology. Both were slowly "added" into the discipline. As they received attention, a large part of our earliest theorizing on women and, later, on children included primarily biologically based theories and explanations (e.g., women are biologically different from men and unfit to rule or hold paying jobs, etc.). Another body of theorizing on women, and (later) children, embraced a social constructionist approach, arguing that women and gender differences are "made" and imposed, ignoring women's agency or voice. These two opposing approaches—biological versus radical social constructionist or behaviourist—are clearly seen and articulated in the nature–nurture debate, presented below, which often dominated sections of introductory sociology textbooks. This chapter will show that while some sociologies of childhood have moved beyond this, developmental theories of childhood (including socialization theories) are not uncommon in the Western context (see Giddens, 1997).

This chapter will show that some of the most profound changes in our theorizing about children have been closely connected to international and national shifts in our thinking about children's rights and childhood. You will read about a paradigmatic shift, in discourse and theorizing, towards increased attention to children's rights. Within sociology this shift was marked by a move away from biological explanations and more rigid "ages and stages"–based developmental and socialization approaches towards more sociocultural approaches and approaches that see children as real people now, "being" and "doing," rather than as a category of people being acted upon or "becoming" (Qvortrup et al., 2009; Qvortrup, 2004, 1994; Lee, 2001, 1998). As a result, children, like women before them, are increasingly being seen as competent social agents, worthy of being theorized about in their own right. This way of theorizing about childhood has been most widely embraced by academics, who have labelled their approach the "new sociology of childhood." This approach and some of its criticisms will be presented later in the chapter.

This chapter shows that, like feminism, which developed into feminisms (e.g., liberal, Marxist, radical, and socialist, with internal critiques from post-colonial, post-structural), new social theories of childhood, particularly those that embrace social justice and human rights perspectives, contain their own internal criticisms and variations.

Theorizing the Pre- and Non-sociological Child: The Familiar "Nature–Nurture" Debate

On the Side of Nature

In the 1700s and 1800s, Europe saw the emergence of the Age of Enlightenment, which was marked by the questioning of religious authority and the rise of science. With this came an increasing emphasis on understanding the laws of nature and, subsequently, attempts at understanding how the social world works. A prominent thinker at the time was Charles Darwin (1809–1882), who developed the theory of natural selection, in which he sought to account for the rise of certain kinds of species and, more generally, why animals look and behave the way they do. His theory noted that the blueprint for behaviour and appearance lies in genes, that genes vary randomly, that some traits and characteristics are better suited to certain environments, and that over time certain kinds of traits come to be seen as normal in that species (Darwin, 1994 [1859]). While Darwin wrote more on diverse non-human species than on human behaviour, a number of thinkers, who came to be known as Social Darwinists, went to great lengths to apply Darwin's theory to understanding and explaining human behaviour. Social Darwinists, also called social biologists or biological determinists by some, have worked to explain human behaviour by looking to the biological and genetic makeup of individuals to understand why they do the things they do.

This body of thinking falls squarely on the nature side of the nature–nurture continuum, and has expressly argued that children are born with a set of prescribed characteristics that result in specific personality traits. Within psychology, this thinking has been supported and maintained from evolutionary psychology and evolutionary developmental perspectives. The general ideas behind evolutionary psychology are that psychological characteristics, like biological characteristics, have evolved over a long period and should be seen as adaptations to the social and ecological circumstances that characterize human existence (Ploeger et al., 2008). One of the main tenets of evolutionary psychology is that the human mind comprises a collection of psychological adaptations, which arose through the process of natural selection (ibid.).[1] An example of this school of thought is a work by Michael Ghiglieri (2000), who titles a chapter "Born to be Bad?" in which he explains that girls and boys are "hardwired" differently, with the result that they engage in different types of behaviours from one another. Scientists like Steven Pinker (2002), in their attempts to debunk the nurture side of the nature–nurture debate, have argued that parenting has negligible effects on the upbringing of children. Overall, those who argue that behaviour is rooted in biology and genes, also tend to assume that "normal" children—regardless of the culture or historical time period in which they lived—develop the same way and along the same trajectory, as biology is much slower to change than culture.

Twins studies have often been used to try to prove the importance of genetic influences on behavioural differences. Most studies compare identical twins (monozygotic twins, genetically identical) with fraternal twins (dizygotic twins, 50 per cent genetically identical) to look for similarities and differences. Researchers typically try to measure genetic similarity, taking into account shared environmental influences (the home environment) and non-shared influences (different classrooms, different groups of friends, etc.). Through various measures, some found that, among other things, academic achievement of twins was substantially influenced by genetics (Segal, 2012; Walker et al., 2004). Similarly, research on twins by Eley et al. (2003) suggests that genetic effects are substantial and more significant than environmental effects. Interestingly, however, Edelbrock et al. (1995) found significant genetic influence on competence in school and on areas of problem behaviour, but significant shared environmental influence was detected on a number of other factors, including quality of social relationships, performance in school, anxiety or depression, and delinquent behaviour—suggesting some traits were the result of both nature and a shared environment.

Psychoanalytic Viewpoints

While we cannot call Sigmund Freud (1856–1939) a biological determinist, his work is nonetheless strongly influenced by biological assumptions. This is seen in his assumption that "normal" children (across time and space) move through a series of relatively fixed stages of psychosocial development in their development of personality (see Table 2.1). He argued that children were born with a fixed set of innate drives—the id—driven by the pleasure principle (which seeks to maximize pleasure and minimize pain), which eventually need to be curbed. Having said this, he also recognized the importance of interactions with others (for example, with mothers and fathers in relation to the Oedipal complex). According to Freud, normal development progresses as children move through fixed stages in fairly consistent ways, with boys and girls developing along the same trajectory until the phallic stage (Freud, 2003, 1971). In doing this, Freud assumed the existence of a universal, naturally developing, unconscious child.

Table 2.1 Developmental Stages

Sigmund Freud's Stages of Psychosocial Development in Childhood

Id → ego → superego
repress biological drives → internalize social norms

Age, Years	Birth–1.5	1.5–3	3–5	5–6	6–Puberty
Stage	Oral	Anal	Phallic	Latency	Genital

Erik Erikson's Stages of Psychosocial Crisis

Age, Years	Birth–1	1–3	3–6	6–12	12–20	20–40	40–65	"Old Age"
Crisis/Stage	Trust vs Mistrust	Autonomy vs Shame/Doubt	Initiative vs Guilt	Industry vs Inferiority	Identity vs Confusion	Intimacy vs Isolation	Generativity vs Stagnation	Ego integrity vs Despair

Jean Piaget's Stages of Cognitive Development

Age, Years	Birth–2	2–6	7–11	12–Adulthood
Stage	Sensorimotor	Preoperational	Concrete Operational	Formal Operational

George H. Mead's Development of the Self

I (subjective/spontaneous) → Me (objective/social)

Age	Infancy	Early Childhood	Childhood	Late Childhood
Stage	Imitation	Play	Game	Generalized other

Since Freud, a fairly large number of theorists of childhood have created their own stage-based developmental approaches. For example, following in Freud's psychoanalytic footsteps, Erik Erikson (1902–1994) theorized stages of development that emphasized the sociocultural, rather than sexual, determinants of personality. Similarly, Jean Piaget's (1896–1980) psychoanalytic background and education (he studied under Carl Jung) led him to focus on the reasoning processes of children; he observed his own children and concluded that cognitive development proceeds in four genetically determined stages that follow the same sequential order (see Table 2.1). Erikson, Piaget, and a number of others, each recognizing to varying degrees the combined roles of biology and environment (society), helped to develop branches of child studies that moved away from strictly biological explanations to more constructivist (in psychology) and constructionist (in sociology) explanations. Nonetheless, for the most part, stage-based developmental approaches in general—and psychoanalytic approaches in particular—tend to see difference and developmental divergence from the fixed sequential stages as problematic or pathological (Turmel, 2008; LeVine, 2003). Before we explore this criticism in more detail, let us see how the constructionist/constructivist and the "nurture" side of the nature–nurture debate developed.

From Behaviourism to Symbolic Interactionism and Constructivist/ Constructionist Approaches

On the nurture (cultural/social determinist) side of the nature–nurture continuum, we find psychologists and behaviourists like John Watson (1878–1958) and B.F. Skinner (1904–1990). Both Watson and Skinner believed that human development should be understood according to observations of overt (visible) behaviour rather than according to speculations on unconscious and innate motivations (genetic or otherwise) that are unobservable. They also both believed that the building blocks of human development are the learned associations between external stimuli and observable responses. Watson, for example, argued that children are infinitely malleable (mouldable) and that development is a continuous process that involves behavioural change shaped by a person's unique environment (which differs from person to person).

One of Watson's most famous and most quoted statements captures this sentiment best:

> Give me a dozen healthy infants, well formed, and my own specified world to bring them up in and I'll guarantee to take any one at random and train him to become any type of specialist I might select—doctor, lawyer, artist, merchant, chief, and yes, even beggar-man and thief, regardless of his talents, penchants, tendencies, abilities, vocations, and race of his ancestors. There is no such thing as an inheritance of capacity, talent, temperament, mental constitution, and behavioural characteristics. (1925: 82)

Watson argued that a child's environment and the people who surround him or her are largely responsible for what he or she becomes. B.F. Skinner (1953), labelled a radical behaviourist, added that in response to this external "hand-ling" (stimuli) from others, both animals and humans learn to repeat acts or behaviours that lead to favourable outcomes and suppress those that pro-duce unfavourable outcomes. While agreeing with Skinner's emphasis on the external, some, like Albert Bandura (1925–), have been critical of Skinner's radical behaviourism for viewing humans too mechanistically, as beings who thoughtlessly respond to positive and negative stimuli, and not recognizing humans as beings who process information cognitively (see Grusec, 1992).

Like Skinner, Charles Horton Cooley (1864–1929), someone closely linked to symbolic interactionism (which stresses the importance of human symbolic communication and interaction in human and social develop-ment), has also been linked to the nurture side of the nature–nurture debate. He, too, was criticized for having a too highly deterministic and rigid view of human/social development. Cooley is most famous for his notion of the "looking-glass self" in personality development.

According to Cooley, one's self-concept emerges and is maintained through this looking-glass self, which is developed via a three-part process. First, we imagine what we appear to be like to another person; then, we imagine how that person judges us; finally, we feel pride or mortification based on what we *think* others think of us (Cooley, 1956). In other words, according to Cooley, our self-image is constructed according to what we assume others think of us—like with a mirror or looking glass, we see our-selves reflected back, then feel pride or shame depending on how we think others will judge us. He was criticized by some, such as George Herbert Mead (1863–1931), one of his contemporaries, for theorizing an oversocial-ized sense of self, far more dependent on perceptions of what others think of us than most people actually are.

George Herbert Mead argued that while the self is inherently social, it is made up of two parts, the "I"—the biological basis of our existence, which is sensual, impulsive, and physiological; and the "me"—the learned and acquired social component made up of all that we learn (values and norms) and come to know through our interaction with others (Mead, 1962). He explained that children move through distinct stages (see Table 2.1) through which they eventually come to learn the general rules and regulations—modes of conduct—that members of the society use and expect.

In looking at this nature–nurture debate, we find little consensus and considerable diversity in theorizing about personality development. Each of these approaches has obvious strengths and weaknesses. But one thing that many of these approaches have in common is that they appear to exclude children as a main focus of study. They are interested in the self, personal-ity, and human behaviour and motivations—adults in the making—but not necessarily in children as thoughtful and sentient persons, worthy of study in their own right. Childhood, for the most part, has been studied as a series of future-oriented, transitional stages of development towards adulthood, and primarily as a way to better understand adult personalities and pathologies (see Wyness, 2006). But as Oswell (2013) demonstrated, childhood is mediated by sociohistorical conditions that need to be taken into account.

Adding Children to the Theoretical Focus . . . But Not Yet Fully There

Increased emphasis on children themselves and on their social environments is found in the work of theorists like Albert Bandura (1925–), Lev Vygotsky (1896–1934), and Urie Bronfenbrenner (1917–2005). Upon briefly reviewing their work, we will see that while "adding" children to their theorizing, they nonetheless continue *not* to treat children as social actors. Instead, for the most part, children are discussed as being acted upon in their interaction with others and by their social environments.

Albert Bandura developed what is known as the *social learning theory* (or *social cognitive theory*) in childhood studies. Bandura, not unlike Skinner, emphasized the importance of children observing and modelling the behaviours, attitudes, and reactions of others around them (Grusec, 1992). In one of his more famous works, Bandura (1977: 22) explained that most human behaviour is learned observationally through modelling: "from observing others one forms an idea of how new behaviours are performed, and on later occasions this coded information serves as a guide for action." Social learning theory explains human behaviour in terms of ongoing reciprocal interaction between children operating cognitively under their environmental influences—a sort of combination of Cooley's looking-glass self (mental self-processing) and Skinner's operant conditioning (response to external stimulus and controls).

Urie Bronfenbrenner, a developmentalist, has also paid particular attention to the environmental context in which child development takes place. He focuses on how a person's biologically influenced characteristics interact with a set of environmental spheres and forces that shape behaviour and development, making his a bioecological theory. He explained that human development occurs within a set of overlapping ecological systems that operate together to influence what a person becomes as he or she develops (Bronfenbrenner and Morris, 1998; Bronfenbrenner, 1995). Bronfrenbrenner's model is often depicted as a set of circles, or spheres, one inside the other, with the innermost environmental layer—or smallest sphere—being the *microsystem,* which includes activities and actions in the person's immediate surroundings, such as the home, school, and peers, which shape behaviour. This sphere is encircled by the *mesosystem* or the connections and interrelationships between and among microsystems, such as the connection between a positive and supportive home environment and strong performance in school; the *exosystem,* which comprises the social systems that children are not directly experiencing but may influence their development, like a parent's work environment; and the *macrosystem,* which includes the cultural, subcultural, and social class context in which all other systems are embedded. This model attempts to capture the complexity and dynamic nature of human development, perhaps in an overly mechanistic way. That said, the model continues to be used extensively to this day (see Paat, 2013, on immigrant children and their families in the United States).

Less mechanistically, Lev Vygotsky's theoretical framework involves the recognition that social interaction plays a fundamental role in the development of cognition. Vygotsky examined the relationship between culturally specific practices and child development—as a result, his work has been labelled *sociocultural theory.* In it, Vygotsky focuses on how culture (values, beliefs, customs, etc., of a social group) is transmitted through social interaction—or co-operative dialogues—between children or learners and more knowledgeable members of society. Through these co-operative dialogues with mature members, children acquire culturally adaptive competencies. Once this happens at the social level, children then internalize knowledge at the personal level, allowing them later to engage in "inner speech" and higher mental functions (the child's ability to master himself or herself). Vygotsky thus explains consciousness as the product of socialization (Packer, 2008; Vygotsky, 1998 [1931], 1967 [1933]). Again, like with Bronfenbrenner's work, a Vygotskian perspective continues to be applied to a variety of areas of study, including an analysis by Kim (2013) of technology-mediated collaborative learning among Korean immigrant children at a school in Montreal.

Socialization Theories

Most theories presented to this point represent some of the varying ways in which psychologists have theorized about children and childhood, but sociologists have not been completely silent on the matter. Sociologists have been somewhat more interested in understanding how we learn to become "functioning" members of a society. As a result, a great deal of sociological work in this area has focused on **socialization.** Talcott Parsons (1966), for example, has written about socialization—or the internalization of the culture of the society into which a child is born. More recently, socialization has been described as the developmental learning process through which children learn how to enter into and participate in their social worlds (Danby and Farrell, 2004: 36). As a result, different cultures teach children different sets of expectations and conventions, which are perceived to be vital not only to the child but to the society as a whole. It is believed that without this intergenerational transmission of culture the society would be unable to reproduce itself. So, socialization is said to involve social integration through the child's internalization of norms.

Socialization has been defined as a complex and dynamic *lifelong* social experience by which individuals develop their human potential and learn the patterns of their culture (Handel et al., 2007). While stressing its "lifelong" nature, sociologists have distinguished between **primary socialization**, which takes place in childhood, and **secondary socialization** that takes place later in life, which is said to involve a "recalibration" of roles and identity based on changing expectations as the individual moves through the life course (as parents, workers, in retirement, etc.). As a result, socialization theory has at times been connected to *social role theory,* a more "functionalist" variant of the theory of socialization (Elkin, 1960).[2]

Children learn from what they are told directly, but also from what they see and hear. Therefore, socialization can be direct or indirect, intentional and unintentional, or accidental. Indirect learning often is treated as unidirectional but, in fact, it is reciprocal (two-way) in nature. It also takes place within a number of very diverse contexts.

Agents or **agencies of socialization** are the social institutions and individuals within them that most affect children's development. Because socialization occurs in many settings, agencies have commonly included the family, school, peer group, and the media. These will be discussed in more detail in some of the coming chapters of this book. One of the strengths of this approach is that it recognizes that each of these agencies will be configured differently in different cultures, and the nature and scope of the socialization that takes place within them are also variable across cultures (and subcultures), genders, social class, and over time.

As a result, a considerable amount of solid social research and writing continues to focus on childhood socialization. Robert LeVine (2003), for example, was trained in psychoanalysis, yet always opposed mainstream positions in developmental psychology and psychoanalysis in favour of more culturally rich and diverse explanations like socialization and enculturation. LeVine argues that not all children need or ought to develop along the same (ages and stages) developmental trajectory; there can be nonpathological development of the self that does not follow the same fixed set of stages, because of the wide variety of cultural forms that place different types of expectations on children. He uses recent ethnographic evidence to show this.

Despite the recognition of the variation that socialization can take— along cultural, social class, gender, and racial lines, for example—socialization is for the most part perceived still as largely imposed on children by authority figures or other. The children themselves, however, are rarely seen as important for decision-making within institutions of socialization (Bühler-Niederberger, 2010b). And while some have written about socialization as a "two-way street," children are treated and studied, for the most part, as passive recipients. As a consequence, socialization theory has been criticized for being "adult-centric" in its neglect of children as social actors. It has also been criticized for being "ahistorical in the generalization of a specific, socially constructed arrangement of childhood" and for ignoring "inequalities and particular interests implicated in this arrangement" (Bühler-Niederberger, 2010a: 160).

Recent Critiques of (Social and Psychological) Developmental Theories

Although the developmental approach, within both psychology and sociology, continues to be a dominant theoretical approach in childhood studies, it is not without its critics (Bühler-Niederberger, 2010a; 2010b). For example, Danby and Farrell (2004) have argued that developmental theories frame the child as an incomplete adult, as a becoming adult or adult-in-the-making (see Qvortrup, 2004, 1994; Lee, 2001, 1998). Developmental approaches posit children as underdeveloped and as lacking power and knowledge (Danby and Farrell, 2004: 36; Wyness, 2006). Childhood is conceptualized and treated as the deficit—the "not something" or the "not yet"—of adulthood, and children are valued for the adults they will become (Wyness, 2013). As a result, developmental theories often fail to see children as capable of being social agents or doers in their social worlds, and assume either biology or adults "do" things to and for children, who are seen to act as passive recipients (Bühler-Niederberger, 2010a). As noted above, this approach also tends to normalize certain ways of being, and problematizes or pathologizes others, which often leads to the creation of value-laden and stigmatizing categories such as that of "the at-risk child." This has led some to conclude, "instead of the century of the child, we got the century of the child professionals" (Stafseng 1993: 77). Lee (2001: 38) writes that prominent *sociological* views of development, namely socialization theories, highlight children's lack of mental "content" (cultural values and conventions), while *psychological* variants highlight children's inability to undertake mental processes that amount to rationality. In doing this, developmental approaches again tend not to focus on the "here and now" of childhood. Different and more sophisticated theorizing was necessary. As a result, a number of thinkers have argued for a different, more child-oriented approach, which also coincides with the rising awareness of children's rights.

Changing Times, Changing Theories? International and National Initiatives towards Children's Rights

Identity-centred critiques of traditional ways of knowing that were part and parcel of new social movements in the 1960s, 1970s, and 1980s displaced the dominant developmental and deviance-based approaches. This opened up a space for the inclusion of a plurality of voices previously silenced in social research and policy, and helped usher in a more rights-based study of children and childhood.

Some have noted that, historically, children's rights and the child liberation movement in the West was born of mid-twentieth-century resistance to hegemonic racial, ethnic, gender, and economic oppression (Danby and Farrell, 2004). Later, children's rights increasingly became the subject of legal theory, philosophy, political science, and social sciences until children's rights became enshrined in global human rights declarations such as the United Nations (UN) Convention on the Rights of the Child (CRC) (ibid.). In fact, a number of academics studying children have identified a paradigmatic shift in the 1980s and early 1990s that resulted in children and childhood becoming a new locus of concern (for example, see James et al., 1998). This shift has coincided with increased attention placed on children's rights and autonomy.

Box 2.1   UN Convention on the Rights of the Child (1989)—A Brief Overview

---

Four key commitments/principles:

1. best interests of child
2. survival and development
3. participation
4. non-discrimination

Preamble:

- Child requires special care and protection
- Stresses importance of parents (family), legal protection of children, and respect for cultural diversity

Articles:

1.	Definition of child: below 18 (unless nation says otherwise)
2.	Applies to all children and protected from all discrimination
3.	Best interests of the child; state to provide care if parents cannot
4.	State will undertake all appropriate measures to implement these rights
5.	State's duty to respect parental (family) rights
6.	State responsible for child's inherent right to life and development
7 and 8.	Right to name and nationality: state to protect child's identity
9.	Live with parent(s) unless not in child's best interests and maintain contact
10.	Right to leave/enter countries to reunify parents and children
11.	Prevent kidnapping of children abroad by parent or third party
12.	Child's right to an opinion and to be taken into account
13.	Child's right to freedom of expression
14.	Child's right to freedom of thought, conscience, and religion
15.	Child's right to freedom of association

In 1989, the UN General Assembly adopted the Convention on the Rights of the Child (CRC). The CRC includes a universally agreed upon set of standards and obligations that is expected to be respected by the governments who have signed the agreement. The CRC is founded on the principles of respect for the dignity and worth of each child, regardless of race, colour, gender, language, religion, opinions, origins, wealth, birth status, or ability, and the principles are expected to apply to every child everywhere. Its four main pillars or key commitments are (1) the best interests of the child; (2) survival and development; (3) children's participation; and (4) non-discrimination (see Box 2.1). In ratifying this agreement governments and organizations are obliged not to infringe on the parallel rights of others and

16.	Child's right to protection of privacy
17.	Access to appropriate information/mass media
18.	Both parents (guardians) have responsibility towards a child; working parents have access to child care services
19.	Protection from abuse, violence, and neglect
20.	Protection of children without families
21.	Adoptions to be carried out with best interests of child in mind
22.	Refugee children granted special protection
23.	Right of disabled children to special care for self-reliance
24.	Right to best health possible: preventative and primary care
25.	Periodic review of children placed in care
26.	Right of children to benefit from social security
27.	Right to adequate standard of living for proper development
28 and 29.	Right to education (primary); opportunities to develop personality and talents
30.	Right of minority and indigenous children to their culture
31.	Right to leisure and play
32.	Protection from economic exploitation and child labour
33.	Protection from drugs (and involvement in their production)
34.	Protection from sexual exploitation
35.	Prevention of sale and trafficking of children
36.	Protection from other forms of exploitation
37.	Prohibit torture, cruel treatment, capital punishment, life imprisonment, unlawful deprivation of liberty
38.	No child under 15 to take part in armed conflict
39.	Rehabilitative care for child victims of conflict, torture, neglect
40.	Special judicial proceedings when children commit crime
41.	Respect for national standards that are higher than CRC
42.	Obligation to make CRC widely known and translated into reality
43.	Set up a UN committee to see to enforcement of CRC
44.	States will keep track of their progress and report back to UN
45–54.	Articles 45 to 54 are administrative, relating to ratification, amendments, etc.

to help to improve conditions for children everywhere (UNICEF, 1990a). That said, notable authors like Mayall (2000) have pointed out that the CRC is itself contextualized in dominant Western concepts.

In 1990, at the World Summit for Children, world leaders made a joint commitment and issued an urgent, universal appeal to give every child a better future. This was the largest gathering of world leaders in history. Led by 71 heads of state and 88 other senior officials, mostly at the ministerial level, the World Summit adopted a Declaration on the Survival, Protection and Development of Children and a developed a plan of action for implementing the Declaration in the 1990s.

In 2002, the UN again called on world leaders to join in a global movement aimed at building "a world fit for children." This "new world" would be founded on a commitment to uphold certain principles and objectives, including a commitment to put children first; eradicate poverty; leave no child behind; care for every child; educate every child; protect children from harm and exploitation; protect children from war; combat HIV/AIDS; listen to children and ensure their participation; and protect the Earth for children. At the international level, the 1990s was a decade of great promises to and for children and children's rights—at least on paper.

In response to these international initiatives, Canada signed the CRC on 28 May 1990 and ratified it on 13 December 1991. It also created its own document, *A Canada Fit for Children*, which was expected to act as Canada's national plan of action in response to the international agreement, *A World Fit for Children*. It claims to lay out a road map to guide Canada's collective efforts for and with children. It calls for strategies that are child-centred, multisectoral, forward-looking, and collaborative. It also signals emerging issues and identifies ways to promote and to protect children's rights, including greater public awareness of the CRC. The document contains a declaration of Canada's commitment to children, highlighting Canadian governments' promise for children, and a plan of action that reflects a consensus on goals, strategies, and opportunities for action on key priorities within four central themes: supporting families and strengthening communities; promoting healthy lives; protection from harm; and promoting education and learning.

In the spring and summer of 1999, Canada's federal, provincial, and territorial governments held a public dialogue with Canadians. Participants in the dialogue were asked to consider a vision, values, and goals for Canada's children as proposed by the *National Children's Agenda*. They also discussed how to gather and share information about children's well-being and how to measure their progress. Participants expressed strong support for the vision, values, and goals set out by the *National Children's Agenda*. At the national level, the 1990s were shaping up to be the decade of and for children in Canada. But this, too, was mostly on paper.

In April 2007, the Standing Senate Committee on Human Rights released a comprehensive report with respect to the rights of children in Canada. This report, *Children: The Silenced Citizens,* clearly indicates that Canada's attempts at improving children's rights and fulfilling its international obligations were completely inadequate, a view echoed by various authors in *A Question of Commitment: Children's Rights in Canada* (Howe and Covell, 2007). The Senate Committee found that the large gap between "rhetoric and reality" leaves Canadian children vulnerable, with no representation at the level of the federal government to work on their behalf, and consequently called for the implementation of a Children's Commissioner (Andreychuk and Fraser, 2007). The report also put forth a long list of recommendations on a number of issues, including corporal punishment, bullying, sexual exploitation, child protection, youth justice, adoption, poverty, and health (ibid.). The underlying message was clear: Canada must fully incorporate the CRC into its policies, planning, and programs, and put into practice the other commitments made at both national and international levels.[3] Canada is no closer to this today than when the Senate Committee identified the problems.

Nonetheless, international movements and initiatives have helped to transform some of the thinking on and around children and childhood. A growing number of thinkers are questioning and challenging the notion of the adult as "the being" who "does" and the child as "the becoming" who "can't yet do." That is, the CRC, from which most of these other commitments emerged, came some 40 years after the UN General Assembly adopted the Universal Declaration of Human Rights in 1948. Noting this, Nick Lee (2001) asks, Why a special convention for children? Are they not "human" after all? Writing on this, Qvortrup (1994) claims that adults are seen as human *beings,* while children are treated as human *becomings*—unstable, incomplete, incapable of independent thought. Qvortrup (2004: 267) observes that "it is the fate of children to be waiting. They are waiting to become adults; to mature; to become competent; to get capabilities; to acquire rights; to become useful; to have a say in societal matters; to share resources." Prominent thinkers like Qvortrup and Corsaro (Qvortrup et al., 2009) also noted that demographic (shrinking family size), legal, and socio-economic shifts as well as globalization, have made children more visible, more valued as participants in the social world and less seen as problems to be rectified through policy. This type of awareness and critique has contributed to the development of a new sociology of childhood.

New Sociologies of Childhood

What has come to be called the "new sociology of childhood" has been in existence for more than two decades and has been especially prominent in the United Kingdom, Australia, Germany, and Scandinavia. It arose symbiotically with the rise of the global children's rights agenda, discussed above. So this theoretical understanding of children was created with the growth and expansion of the discourse of children's rights. Proponents of global children's rights movements and of the new sociology of childhood are seemingly committed to the view that children are more competent and autonomous than they appear or are allowed to be. They seek to overturn adult paternalism that refuses to recognize children's capabilities and rights. The goal of these theorists and of new theorizing is to provide a better understanding of childhood that recognizes the capacity of children for autonomy, competent decision-making, and their role as social agents—this would in turn better inform policy and research (James et al., 1998). The new sociology of childhood focuses on an appreciation of what children are in the present, rather than what they will eventually become (Corsaro, 1997, 2015).

This new sociology of childhood emphasizes the *agential* (i.e., children as active "doers" in and of their social worlds) in children's lives and activities. Bühler-Niederberger (2010a) noted that the concept of the child as a social actor implies a change in our thinking from future-oriented to present; the focus is no longer on children's preparation for adult life, but rather their ongoing interactions in everyday worlds. There was a sense among proponents of the new sociology of childhood that we must write children into the script and that being an apprentice is only part of the story of childhood (Mayall, 2000: 243).

Accepting the child as a social actor underlines children's competence and knowledge (Bühler-Niederberger, 2010a). Children do not just passively adapt to and learn from the culture surrounding them, as assumed in developmental and socialization theories, but actively participate in the cultural routines offered to them in and by their social environments (Corsaro, 1997, 2015). Children's own accounts show us that they are moral agents, who carry out important social activities that make and remake their relationships and daily lives. As such, children are seen and treated as active reproducers of meaning (King, 2007; Mayall, 2000, 2002), and are understood to be able to appropriate and reinterpret their situations and environments and so themselves contribute to cultural reproduction and change (Corsaro, 1997, 2015).

This new approach seeks to highlight both the agency of children and their social, political, and economic status in contemporary societies (James et al., 1998), combining both macro/structure and micro/agency approaches. This means that children are seen and understood through their talk and interaction as participating actively in the construction of their own social situation (agency), but children and childhood are also understood as being constituted in relation to the adult world (structures) in which they live

(Danby and Farrell, 2004; James et al., 1998). Through this theorizing, then, there is a new focus on the way that childhood has been constituted and reconstituted through the dynamic interplay of adult structures and children's agency (Wyness, 2006; 2013).

One of the earliest manifestations of this new sociology of childhood has itself been criticized as not moving far enough away from traditional theorizing on children. In a review essay of three books connected to the new sociology of childhood, Leena Alanen (2000) explains that James et al. (1998), while cleverly working to critically frame past social theories of childhood, themselves fall short in their own theorizing. Alanen (2000) argues that when James et al. identify and name four sociological childhood discourses (the tribal child, which treats children as exotic; the social structural child, which treats children as a structurally necessary stratum of society; the minority group child, which treats children as an oppressed group; and the socially constructed child), and declare the social structural/minority group construct to be superior, they, like those they criticize, continue to think in terms of *categories* of children—rigid and fixed ways of thinking. As an alternative, Alanen (2000) suggests *relational approaches* to thinking about children, noting that by framing our understanding this way and recognizing the many layers, intersections, and types of relationships children engage in, we take into account agency (individual actions), structure (enduring relations), and process (dynamic/changing contexts). Wyness (2013) also challenges us to reconsider the importance of adults (bring adults back into the discussion) when it comes to children's participatory roles in relationships. Wyness (2013) reminds us of the importance of intergenerational dialogue in a range of political and global themes that highlight both the participatory roles of children and their interdependence on adults.

Similarly, Mayall (2002) has pushed theorizing about children and childhood towards the incorporation of standpoint theory—the idea that children share a common, subordinated domain, and that their experiences vary according to their position within the existing stratified social and power hierarchies. Mayall suggests that we should recognize childhood as a social status and children as a minority social group, adding that childhoods are lived in specific ways in the interests of an adult-oriented society, but that individual children need to be listened to and understood, as their experiences expose fault lines in social norms for childhood.

These new lines of thinking and theorizing have had a significant impact on the ways children and childhood are understood and studied, at least in some parts of the world. In Canada, while some have moved in this direction (discussed in more detail below), sociologists, for the most part, have remained fixed on traditional developmental approaches. The good news is that considerable room exists for growth and improvement in this area of study.

New Approaches to the Study of Childhood in Canada

Ironically, as Canada signs on to international initiatives and begins, at least on paper, to develop initiatives to benefit children, Canadian sociology has moved away from childhood as a central area of focus. Indeed, there seems to have been a more active Canadian "sociology of childhood" until the 1980s. Most of what has been written in this area, particularly from a Canadian perspective, has used predominantly psychological and/or developmental approaches, as you will see from a considerable literature cited throughout this book.

Interestingly, as Canadian sociology shifts towards a much more critical and profound understanding of race/racialization, class, gender, sexuality, health and aging, environmentalism, and their intersections—all from an adultist perspective—it has rarely ventured into understanding how the traditional "isms"—sexism, racism, classism, ablism, etc.—relate to and may be amplified for children in this country. A handful of Canadian scholars, however, have made significant efforts in this direction. Much of the progress has taken place in interdisciplinary work across the country.

Howe and Covell (2011, 2010, 2009, 2007), for example, have written extensively on children's rights and have assembled the writing of a number of activists, academics, and proponents of children's rights to first assess then demonstrate that the Canadian state is falling far short of fulfilling its international obligations when it comes to implementing programs and policies that promote, advance, or protect children's rights in this country. Similarly, Jane Jenson (2004) has written extensively on the importance of adopting and fully implementing an "investing-in-children" policy paradigm at both the local/community and national levels. Meg Luxton (2002) has written on the importance of the social inclusion of children in the Canadian context, as have Stasiulis (2002), Moosa-Mitha (2005), and Mahon (2005) when writing about their difference-centred and more inclusive conceptualizations of children as citizens worthy of study, understanding, and attention in their own right.

Rebecca Raby (2012), chair of child and youth studies at Brock University, has used post-structural and critical theories to examine shifting constructions of childhood. Her work also theorizes young people's resistance and rights. Important work is also emerging out of the University of Lethbridge's Institute for Child and Youth Studies (I-CYS), a multidisciplinary research institute committed to examining what children (and youth) mean and do as social, demographic, artistic, legal, and existential categories.

At the other end of the country, in Newfoundland, sociologist, Karen Stanbridge (2007: 178) has explored how children were used and framed by opposing sides of the Newfoundland Confederation debate in 1948. Her work shows that while Newfoundland was considering joining Confederation, during the weeks between referendums, both the pro- and anti-Confederation sides used images of and appeals to children's corporeal, spiritual, and civic health to manipulate adult masses into supporting their political needs and ends. In doing this, she reveals a great deal about our society's views and treatment of children, showing that the framing of children in political contexts and propaganda has been used to reinforce the view that childhood in Canada is seen as a stage of becoming "flush with potential, yet fraught with danger unless properly managed" (ibid., 196). Here, Stanbridge, like Howe and Covell, Stasiulis, Moosa-Mitha, and Jenson, is attempting to inform Canadians of past and more recent practices that continue to marginalize and objectify children in this country. In doing this, they are also breaking new ground in theorizing about children and childhood(s) in Canada. It is clear, however, that there is still a great deal of room for improvement when it comes to developing a new sociology of childhood in Canada.

Summary

This chapter has traced important aspects of the history of social theorizing on and about children. We have seen that, for the most part, children continue to be marginalized, and remain far from the focus of attention in theories that profess to help explain child development. We have seen that it is clearly not enough to argue that children and childhood are immensely important to understand and study because "good genes" or "good developmental paths" or "good socialization" results in the creation of "good" or "normal" or "nonpathological" adults and societies. The new theories of childhood that have emerged alongside international initiatives aimed at improving children's rights remind us that children are worthy of research and theorizing in their own right.

No doubt, children cannot and should not be seen as mini-adults, nor can we ignore the fact that they are socially developing—but they can be recognized as people, social agents, doers, and as a disempowered group worthy of sociological attention. In doing this, we will begin to recognize the importance of understanding the subjective and collective experiences of children in the present. It will also help us recognize the dynamic nature of social relations and social structures, and how these affect the children who live in and through them. We need to recognize childhood as an important and permanent structure in society, which both adults and children help to shape and reshape, across (sub)cultures and time. At the same time we need to listen to children as they express what it is like to stand in their shoes and live in their worlds.

In 1988, Leena Alanen closed her article by reminding sociologists that they "need not—and should not—content themselves with the notion that children belong primarily to the province of psychology, education and pediatrics" (1988: 64). While there have been some Canadian sociologists who have not contented themselves with what other disciplines tell us about children, many others within sociology need a bit of reminding, or so it seems. As we come to see how children fare in the institutional locales that make up their social world, it will become obvious that more and better child-focused research could and should inform our understanding of Canadian children and childhoods.

Questions for Critical Thought

1. Do you have any brothers or sisters? Are they like you? In what ways are they like you? Not like you? What do you think accounts for the similarities and differences? Use some of the theories discussed in the chapter to explain your answer.

2. What would you say are your five best personality traits? Your five worst? Where do you think they came from? Compare and contrast two different or opposing theories presented in this chapter that seem to explain where these traits may have come from. Which do you think provides a better explanation? Why?

3. Canada has signed or adopted a number of international agreements that commit us to recognizing and implementing children's rights in a number of settings, circumstances, and institutions. Do you think Canada has successfully implemented its commitments? Where do we have evidence that these commitments have been implemented? Where do we still need to make changes and improvements? What further actions would you recommend?

4. Do we need a uniquely Canadian sociology of childhood? Why? Why not? What do you think it should look like?

Suggested Readings

Andreychuk, Raynell (Chair), and Joan Fraser (Deputy Chair). 2007. *Children: The Silenced Citizens: Effective Implementation of Canada's International Obligations with Respect to the Rights of Children. Final Report of the Standing Senate Committee on Human Rights.* Ottawa: Senate Committees Directorate. At: www.parl.gc.ca/39/1/parlbus/ commbus/senate/com-e/huma-e/rep-e/rep10apr07-e.htm; www.fncfcs.com/docs/Children_ TheSilentCitizens_April2007.pdf. The Senate Committee on Human Rights, formed in 2004, found in two earlier interim reports that Canada was not meeting its international obligations in relation to the rights and freedoms of children. This 2007 report focuses on the shortcomings of the Canadian government and contains a long list of recommendations for what Canada must do to remedy the situation.

Corsaro, William. 2015. *The Sociology of Childhood,* 4th edn. Los Angeles: Sage. This is the most recent edition of a classic textbook by Corsaro in which he maps the sociological study—outlining theories and research—of childhood. It includes sections on children and families in historical and cultural contexts, and includes important chapters on peers and peer culture.

Howe, R. Brian, and Katherine Covell, eds. 2007. *A Question of Commitment: Children's Rights in Canada.* Waterloo, ON: Wilfrid Laurier University Press. In this assessment of the extent to which Canada has fulfilled its commitments as outlined in the UN Convention on the Rights of the Child, the editors contend that Canada has wavered in its commitment and is ambivalent, politically and socially, about the principle of children's rights. The book includes chapters by specialists, experts, and activists in particular fields of children's rights, such as early childhood education and care, Aboriginal children, and refugee children and child asylum-seekers.

Mayall, Berry. 2002. *Towards a Sociology for Children: Thinking from Children's Lives.* Buckingham, UK: Open University Press. Mayall approaches childhood the way early feminists approached the study of women's lives: by working to include children in research, in the study and understanding of social life, in the construction of knowledge, etc. Mayall begins with the assumption that the underdog (children, like women before them) provides essential evidence of the working of the existing social order. The book treats childhood as a social position that requires attention and further consideration.

Qvortrup, Jens, Corsaro, A. William, and Michael-Sebastien Honig, eds. 2009. *The Palgrave Handbook of Childhood Studies.* Basingstoke: Palgrave Macmillan. This book contains important contributions by some of the top international scholars in the area, including Allison James, Leena Alanen, Berry Mayall, and the editors of the collection.

Websites

Government of Canada—A Canada Fit for Children
www.hrsdc.gc.ca/en/cs/sp/sdc/socpol/publications/2002-002483/canadafite.pdf
Canada's national plan of action calls for strategies that are child-centred, multisectoral, forward-looking, and collaborative. It also signals emerging issues and identifies ways to promote and protect children's rights, including greater public awareness of the UN Convention on the Rights of the Child. Four central themes are examined: supporting families and strengthening communities; promoting healthy lives; protection from harm; and promoting education and learning.

Government of Canada—National Children's Agenda
www.socialunion.ca/nca/June21-2000/english/index_e.html
In the spring and summer of 1999, Canada's federal, provincial, and territorial governments held a public dialogue during which participants were asked to consider a vision, values, and goals for Canada's children as proposed by the National Children's Agenda. They also discussed how to gather and share information about children's well-being, and how to measure their progress. Participants expressed strong support for the National Children's Agenda and suggested improvements. These are reflected in the amended vision statements included with the report available on this website.

International Sociology Association—Research Committee on the Sociology of Childhood
www.isa-sociology.org/rc53.htm
This website gives you access to information on RC53, the International Sociology Association's Committee on the Sociology of Childhood. The aim of RC53 is to contribute to the development of sociological and interdisciplinary childhood research and theorizing.

Library of Congress—Children's Rights: Canada
www.loc.gov/law/help/child-rights/canada.php

> This website contains an overview of Canada's record, on paper, of its treatment of children through its laws and policies. Keep in mind that this is from the point of view of US-based legal experts.

UNICEF—UN Convention on the Rights of the Child
www.unicef.org/crc/files/Rights_overview.pdf

> This link provides access to a summary of the UN Convention on the Rights of the Child. More details on this and other UN reports on children's rights can be found at other UNICEF sites: www.unicef.org/crc/>; <www.unicef.org/worldfitforchildren/files/A-RES-S27-2E.pdf; www.unicef.org/progressforchildren/2007n6/files/Progress_for_Children_-_No._6.pdf; www.unicef.org/wsc.

United Nations Human Rights—Committee on the Rights of the Child
www.ohchr.org/EN/HRBodies/CRC/Pages/CRCIndex.aspx

> The Committee on the Rights of the Child is the body of independent experts who monitor the implementation of the Convention on the Rights of the Child. It also monitors implementation of the Optional Protocols on involvement of children in armed conflict and on sale of children, child prostitution, and child pornography. In December 2011, the UN General Assembly approved a third Optional Protocol, which allows children to submit complaints regarding violations of their rights under the Convention.

3 Doing Research on and with Children

Learning Objectives

◎ To reflect on how we know what we know about children.

◎ To think critically about how adult-centred research on children is different from child-centred research with and by children.

◎ To learn about the research process and the many questions that arise and decisions that are made *before* starting research.

◎ To explore a range of methodologies available to researchers in the data-collection process.

◎ To see what kinds of ethical issues need to be considered when doing any research, but especially when doing research that involves children.

◎ To discover the expanding array of research on children, by children.

Introduction

I have been teaching a required second-year, introductory research methods course for a number of years, and each first day of class I walk into the room before a sea of students and the majority of faces share one expression. If a comic-strip balloon were used to express what they are thinking, one collective balloon would be enough to capture the thoughts of most in the room: "I don't want to be here. I'll never do research!" I'm not sure I convince all of my students by the end of the term, but at least some realize that doing research can be fun and rewarding, and more importantly, that understanding other people's research can be very valuable.

The reality is that most of my students will *not* end up in jobs that require them to conduct "academic" research; however, some will be asked by their employers to help them apply for grants to secure funding; to become involved in fundraising or awareness-raising campaigns; or to figure out ways to identify, understand, and better serve the needs of their customers, students, patrons, or clients—the families, parents, and children they work for. Understanding the research process will assist them (and you, I hope) with all of these. Beyond this, and more immediately, understanding research helps to demystify it.

So many of us "trust the experts" unquestioningly because numbers confound us. But not all research involves numbers and not all numbers are valid and informative. Because of our (often irrational) fear of numbers, and of research in general, many of us resign ourselves to accepting "the truth" as computed by "the scientists." Understanding the research process allows you to identify and understand the steps that were taken by researchers to arrive at certain kinds of conclusions. It shows you that researchers had other options, but chose a particular approach over many others available to them. For many reasons, by studying *this,* they have chosen not to study *that.* By including *these* people in the study, they have chosen not to include *those,* etc. Understanding research methods allows you to see that when certain methodological choices are made, they are made for a number of scientific *and* ideological reasons (to understand or prove a particular point and/or support a certain set of assumptions). Understanding rather than fearing research will allow you to critically assess other people's work.

You may now find yourself asking, "Why should I care?" The answer is both simple and complex. As students, (future) workers, (future) parents, and citizens, you should know that policy decisions often are made based on research findings. For example, some research findings help determine how much public money, if any, should go towards health care, child care, welfare, warfare, leisure, infrastructure, education, amateur sports, coun-selling services, prisons, public broadcasting, housing, playgrounds, etc. Research also helps determine who should be served, supported, funded, heard, ignored, or studied further.

In this chapter you will see that engaging in research involves mak-ing many decisions long before you begin data collection. You will see that researchers have many options available to them, and that their choice of topic, the questions they ask, the method of data collection (and then analy-sis) they choose, and the research participants and partners they involve are chosen consciously and due to specific reasons or restrictions. All research, and particularly that involving human subjects, should include formal and informal ethical evaluation. We will explore some of the guide-lines set out by state and other agencies, which are important to consider when research involves children. A great deal of literature on the ethics of research with children has been about risks that children should not be exposed to through participation in research. We will see that some research about children casts adults in the role of "expert," with children as pas-sive subjects. On the other hand, recent work in the area has focused on a general interest in empowering children through their inclusion in research (Edwards and Alldred, 1999; Mason and Danby, 2011). This chapter will try to show that while it is important that we have high-quality and reliable research *about* children, it is also important to have equally solid research *with* and *by* children.

From Adult Perspectives (Research *about* Children) to Children's Voice (Research *with* and *by* Children)

So much of what we know about children today comes from adults, either reflecting upon their own experiences as children[1] or reporting on the experiences of children for whom they have responsibility—as parents, guardians, teachers, or other "experts." This is not to say that this research is not valuable, insightful, or important. Many adults have contributed a great deal to our understanding of children and childhood by sharing their attitudes and experiences from when they were young, or as adults, on behalf of children. Having said this, we are increasingly involving children themselves, as subjects, contributors, and participants—rather than objects—of the research process (Mason and Danby, 2011; Tay-Lim and Lim, 2013). Some in this camp have gone as far as to argue that adult "proxies," who often include parents and teachers, are unlikely to be able accurately to represent children's views and understanding of their worlds, no matter how well-intended or informed they may be (Mahon et al., 1996).

Nonetheless, adults have appointed themselves the understanders, interpreters, and translators of children (Morrow and Richards, 1996). As a result, until recently, much of the research on children is conducted from the point of view of adult researchers and adult study participants on children's behalf. This has happened, in part, because in our culture we view children as innocent, naive, "special," and incapable. Orellana (2001) noted that the exclusion of children from the research process actually comes down to our belief that children are simply adults in the making (not-yet adults; not-yet actualized; undeveloped; see also Grover, 2004).[2] On the other hand, adult researchers and adult study participants are treated as "experts" and as the people most knowledgeable about children's lives, almost to the outright exclusion of children from research about them.

Some have noted that children have not participated in research because of the obvious power differences between adult researchers and children and for fear that children will be intimidated or coerced in their diminished social position. Children's participation in research can be daunting, as power differences between the "expert" or researcher and the child can and do reflect well-established power and cultural differences between children and adults (Christensen, 2004). But by excluding them from the research process are we not simply reinforcing their powerlessness? Children have been given little room to manoeuvre in adult worlds, and they are clearly not seen as experts on their own worlds and lives.

Increasingly, researchers are making commitments to listening to children and to seeing them as reliable informants of their own experiences—as co-constructors of meaning and understanding (Tay-Lim and Lim, 2013; Mason and Danby, 2011). Malcolm Hill (2006), for example, conducted research on children's attitudes towards study participation, an extremely underresearched area, and found that although they are normally passive when it comes to choice of research method used, they negotiate differing degrees of engagement when it comes to time control, comfort with the research medium, and privacy. In other words, children were not vocal about which research technique researchers should use when studying them, but they were considerably more vocal in how research should unfold, how long data collection should take, how involved they should be, and how their privacy can and should be protected vis-à-vis other children, teachers, etc. Hill (2006) found that children's views on research are affected profoundly by notions of inclusiveness and fairness.

Pia Haudrup Christensen (2004: 165) noted that "the recognition of children's social agency has significantly changed children's position within the human and social sciences and led to a weakening of taken-for-granted assumptions found in more conventional approaches to child research." This means that as we come to take children's views and experiences into account, we are significantly altering our traditional understanding of children and childhood. To do this, Christenson suggested researchers enter into children's "cultures of communication," but at the same time not treat children as different from adults. Others, in contrast, have argued that we *should* treat children's competencies as different, but "different" should not translate to "weaker than" adults (Morrow and Richards, 1996). In sum, Punch (2002) reminds us that the way researchers perceive children influences their choice of methods. Let us examine some of these choices.

The Research Process

All research involves a great deal of thinking, planning, and choosing: who and what to study and where, when, and how to study them. Often, however, one's discipline, theoretical orientation, and broader epistemology (i.e., stance on what should pass as acceptable knowledge) help shape some of these decisions. That is, if one believes that getting the "big picture" or having a *macro* approach is most important, he or she is not likely to sit and talk to a select group of individuals, have a one-on-one discussion, or observe a group of children interacting on a school playground, which are examples of close-up research or a *micro* approach. Psychologists, for example, are more likely than sociologists to use experiments and clinical trials. And, if you are wont to believe that only "scientists" or "experts" create knowledge, you will not ask children what they believe is important to study, how best to do that, and how to involve them. In contrast, proponents of participatory action research (PAR) critique this view, questioning the possibility of objective social sciences and calling for a more inclusive research process that engages people, including children, actively in all stages of knowledge generation (Gray and Donnelly, 2013; Teram et al., 2005).

Qualitative and Quantitative Approaches

In the social sciences we often divide research into qualitative and quantitative approaches. **Quantitative research** involves the numerical representation and manipulation of observations for the purpose of describing and explaining social phenomena. Put simply, when we think of quantity, we think of the *amount* of something, which involves numbers, measuring, counting, and mathematical computations. The statistical analysis of survey data (and secondary data analysis), discussed above, is one of the most common examples of quantitative analysis. You will find numerous examples of quantitative research and analysis throughout this book, with analysis of the National Longitudinal Survey of Children and Youth (NLSCY; discussed below) as one of the most commonly cited.

Qualitative research involves nonnumerical examination and interpretation of observations for the purpose of discovering underlying meaning, patterns, and relationships. This type of research is a little more complicated, as "quality" often has us thinking about the what, how, when, or where of things, and can involve trying to look for and understand meaning, metaphors, and symbols. Qualitative research is especially important when doing research with children as it "provides an opportunity to tap into the richness of children's thoughts and feelings about themselves, their environments and the world in which we all live" (Mishna et al., 2004). It allows researchers to interact directly with children—observing them or allowing them to answer questions in their own words. In contrast, quantitative methods such as survey questionnaires are problematic when working directly with children, because most require a level of literacy not acquired by younger children. Most surveys, therefore, are completed by adults on behalf of children. Mishna et al. explain that qualitative research with children helps us discover unexpected differences in perceptions between adults and children.

Qualitative research includes a range of techniques, which are used alone or in combination. These include participant observation or ethnographic research, qualitative interviews, and focus groups. Participant observation and ethnographic research (studying people as they go about their daily lives) have been used extensively by anthropologists, social workers, and sociologists, who aim to understand and describe a culture or way of life by entering its natural setting. Ethnographic research places researchers in the midst of whatever they are studying and involves their taking part, to greater and lesser degrees, in close social interaction with informants over extended periods of time. The long-term character of this approach helps provide important insights (Christensen, 2004).

Researchers engaging in this type of research can become completely immersed in the subculture, at times blending in, undetected, and participating almost fully in group activities. On the other hand, researchers can choose to take a semi-participatory role, in which their research objectives are not hidden from the people being studied and their participation in group activities is moderate. Lastly, and further removed, the researcher can choose to be a detached observer, examining exchanges within the group "from a distance," without participating. Nancy Mandell (1988) noted that some researchers have argued that our hierarchical structure of age and adult ethnocentrism precludes adult researchers from taking a complete participant role when working with children because we simply can't "blend in." Mandell, however, advocates for complete involvement of adults by their taking the "least-adult role." She explains that by casting aside assumptions about adult superiority based on age and cognitive maturity, adults can gain access into children's worlds. To do this, adults must engage in joint action with the children, build rapport, learn children's access rituals, follow children's ways, and understand children's language (ibid.).

Research takes many forms and involves a number of possible methods, used exclusively or in combination. But even before determining methods, researchers need to think about the purpose of their research. That is, are you trying to break new ground in an underresearched area by doing *exploratory research*? Are you wanting to understand *why* something is happening, by doing *explanatory research*? Are you aiming to describe situations or events through *descriptive research*? Or are you seeking, through *evaluative research*, to assess whether a policy or program, once implemented or introduced, is actually effective?

Let us look at one example of exploratory research. Marjorie Faulstich Orellana (2001) noted that many studies that have looked at Mexican and Central American immigrant children have, for the most part, treated them as a problem or have focused on their future—how they *will be* educated, acculturated, and assimilated into the host/new society—rather than on their present. Orellana (2001) sought to shed light on the contributions these children made, on a daily basis, to their families, classrooms, and schools and how children themselves support, sustain, and sometimes change these institutions. By focusing less on where children are going and more on how they are getting there (living, contributing, and learning) Orellana's (2001) research broke new ground and illuminated parts of children's lives previously unexplored. Similarly, Monica Valencia, a Master's student whose research I supervised, found interesting insight though her exploratory research with immigrant children.

Anyone doing research can begin with a theory or hypothesis and aim to test its value and application in a particular setting. This is called *deductive research*. Others begin the research process by noticing something

<table>
<tr><td>

**Box
3.1**

</td><td>

Ryerson Researcher Finds Drawings Open a Window to an
Immigrant Child's World

</td></tr>
</table>

Young immigrant children often can't articulate—or aren't even asked—about their feelings and experiences in moving to a new country. But, as a Ryerson University researcher discovered, pictures they draw can speak volumes about the sadness, fears and anxieties that come with being a newcomer to Canada.

Many academic studies have looked at struggles immigrant children experience, such as the cultural clash, family conflict, ethnic identity crises, or difficulties in adjusting to school. It turns out, these issues seem to matter more to researchers and adults than the kids themselves.

Monica Valencia [author of the study "Yo Cuento: Latin American Immigrant Children Tell their Stories" (Yo cuento means "I narrate/I matter")] found a different way to gain access to the inner world of immigrant children: She gave them crayons and paper and asked them to make pictures about what was most significant to them about their migration to Canada.

To her surprise, the 10 children in the study — aged nine to 11, from five Latin American countries, and all in Canada for less than five years at the time — touched on four recurring themes: sadness over the separation from grandparents, anxiety over constant uprooting (even after arrival in Canada), frustration over learning a new language, and appreciation for peers who helped them make the transition.

Research participant Christian. . . who depicted his separation from his grandmother, said that when his family moved from Ecuador to Toronto in 2006, when he was four, no one had explained to him what immigrating to another country really meant.

[. . .]

"I felt like I just got a huge punch in my stomach. I felt horrible being separated from my family. Other kids (here) greeted me with 'Hello' but I had no clue how to speak English. It was extremely frustrating and I felt so useless."

[. . .]

Valencia said her child-centred approach, using loosely structured drawing, writing and oral storytelling sessions, gave children various ways to explore sensitive topics they find hard to articulate in words.

"We underestimate the maturity and sophistication of children. A lot of researchers pick their own topics of importance and impose the agenda on children through surveys and structured interviews," said Valencia, who was uprooted from her native Colombia at age 11.

"The adults are more interested in immigrant children's academic achievements and their acquisition of the language. These kids' internal issues don't get much attention."

Source: "Ryerson researcher finds drawings open a window to an immigrant child's world", by Nicholas Keung, March 4, 2014. Reprinted with permission – Torstar Syndication Services.

happening, with no theory in mind, and then trying to assess what is actually happening and why. This is called *inductive research,* which is often linked to *grounded theory* or the ongoing building of theory and understanding from qualitative observations—from the ground up. Grounded theory and participatory action research, mentioned above, are distinct approaches within qualitative inquiry.

The Time Dimension

As part of the planning process, researchers must also think about the *time dimension* of their research. In other words, a research project can focus on and collect information at a single point in time, which means the researcher is choosing to do a *cross-sectional* study. An example of this is Valencia's (Box 3.1) research on the stories contained within immigrant children's drawings. Had she instead spent one day a week for a few months observing and talking to the children about their drawings she would have been doing a *longitudinal study,* observing children at two or more points in time.

Longitudinal research is interesting and important when studying children and childhood, particularly if we are interested in understanding the changing nature of children's experiences with the passage of time and in changing social, cultural, or economic circumstances. An example of a longitudinal study (currently inactive, as data is no longer being collected) is cited throughout this book: the NLSCY.

As the name implies, the NLSCY was a long-term study of Canadian children from across the 10 provinces that followed their development and well-being from birth through early adulthood (Statistics Canada, 2010). Statistics Canada and Human Resources and Social Development Canada (HRSDC) began the study in 1994 and ended with Cycle 8 in 2009, with the purpose of understanding the factors that influence children's social, emotional, and behavioural development and to monitor the impact of these factors over time. The study contains a series of instruments and measures, including cognitive tests: the revised vocabulary test (PPVT-R), the Who Am I? self-assessment test, the Number Knowledge Test, a mathematics test, a problem-solving exercise and literacy and numeracy assessments; surveys of parents or guardians; and a questionnaire completed by older children. These extensive tests and measures recurred in cycles, every two years. By Cycle 8, the last time data was collected, the sample comprised 35,795 children and youths aged 0–7 and 14–25 years (ibid.).

The huge amount of data collected in this study has been made available (following strict security measures) for use by all levels of government, universities, and policy-making organizations. Therefore, as noted above, many of the studies you will read about in this book involve *secondary analysis* or the statistical reanalysis of NLSCY data collected by other people and for other purposes.

Unit of Analysis

When someone decides to engage in research, he or she must also choose the *unit of analysis*—who or what he or she will study. The choices are many and can include *individuals* (adults or children who are asked to share their own individual experiences and attitudes), *social groups* (households, families, classrooms, or ethnic groups, in which, typically, someone speaks on *behalf* of the whole group), or *social artifacts* (things or objects that make up part of the social world, for example, ads, jokes, clothes, etc.). In research on or about children, in which the unit of analysis is the *individual,* it is often not the child himself or herself who is directly involved in the research, but rather a parent or guardian, sometimes referred to as the "person most knowledge-able" (PMK), who participates on behalf of the child. For example, in the "child questionnaire" of the NLSCY, the PMK is asked a long series of questions about the child's education, health and medical conditions, developmental milestones, temperament, literacy, communication skills, activities, behaviour, sleep habits, motor and social development, relationships, etc.[3]

While this can provide valuable information, it is clearly different from having children themselves respond. Research has found that children as young as ages three and four can and have provided important insights, through interviews, into their daily lives and health experiences (Farrell et al., 2002; Irwin and Johnson, 2005).

Some interesting research on and about children has been done using *social artifacts*. For example, content analyses have been done—some of which appear in the media chapter in this book—of commercials, ads, toys, clothes, websites, television programs, movies, and books aimed at, created for, or targeting children. Research (like Valencia's in Box 3.1) has shifted focus somewhat, intentionally analyzing things created *by* children—their stories, jokes, drawings, crafts, etc. Danby et al. (2011) highlight the value of using concrete materials during the interview process. Similarly, Shaw et al. (2011) at the National Children's Bureau Research Centre (in the United Kingdom) note that physical props can be useful when explaining fairly abstract ideas such as the goals of the research and how the project is funded, or to facilitate discussion on issues more generally. Danby et al. (2011) described a study conducted by a novice interviewer. They explained that midway through an interview with a five-year-old girl, the interviewer invited her to participate in the sticker task. The child was given a set of stickers and asked to use the stickers to represent herself, her friends, and her twin. The child placed the stickers in specific locations on the page before her. The proximity of the stickers representing her twin and her friends to the sticker representing herself indicated the closeness of her relationships, as she perceived them (Danby et al., 2011). Allowing children to use familiar props, like dolls, stickers, blocks, etc. gives them the opportunity to use the objects to reconstruct, role play, or re-enact aspects of their lives and tell us their stories, regardless of their ability to express themselves verbally. In the case of the sticker task, concrete materials—stickers—shifted the focus away from the child's verbal responses and abilities towards the physical activities being played out. This helped the child concretize the concept of friendship and intimacy. As this example illustrates, it is not uncommon, and in fact it is preferable, to use a range of activities and tools when including children in research. It is also important to remain flexible in how tools are used (Teachman and Gibson, 2013; see Box 3.2).

As seen in the examples above, qualitative interviews are often part of this combined approach and are used extensively when doing ethnographic or field research, or as a stand-alone method in social research. Qualitative interviews allow the researcher to pursue topics in depth, and give the study participants the freedom to answer in their own words and help direct the flow of conversation. With research on or with adults, many studies involving qualitative interviews attempt to match the interviewer with characteristics of the interview participants. For example, in order to help build comfort,

Box 3.2   A Toolkit of Customizable Interview Techniques

Teachman and Gibson (2013) interviewed six pairs of study participants. Each pair consisted of a child with cerebral palsy, 7–18 years of age, and one of his or her parents. All the children used some type of walking therapy or walking aid (e.g., walker, wheelchair) for some of their mobility needs. Teachman and Gibson describe their innovative customizable data collection toolkit:

> Initially we anticipated the need to develop an interview guide based on normative developmental assumptions about participants' cognitive and language skills; however, based on newer critical approaches to research with children (Christensen, 2004), we decided to develop methods that we could readily individualize. . . . Based on a number of novel or emerging interview methods and techniques, we then prepared a toolkit of materials to support a dynamic, individualized interview process. These methods included (a) warm-up activities, (b) role play with puppets, (c) vignettes about an imaginary child who has cerebral palsy, (d) cartoon captioning, (e) photographs depicting children's geographies, and (f) sentence starters. Selection and presentation of these interview methods (along with more traditional interviewing question-and-answer discussion) varied according to each participant's self-representation, demonstrated abilities, preferences, and comfort during the interview. We did not use all methods with every child. We aimed to optimize the existing skill, confidence, comfort, and experience of the interviewer through use of the toolkit to elicit the highest quality data. . . .

identification, and rapport, interviewers are matched by gender, by ethnic or racial origin, or by other social characteristics relevant to the study. This approach poses a particular challenge when working with children (Mahon et al., 1996). As we see above, researchers have turned to the creation and adoption of more varied and imaginative research methods when children are involved.

Like Teachman and Gibson (2013) in Box 3.2 above, Lewis (2004) outlines a number of approaches researchers can use when interviewing children, but also reminds us that having these options should not lead to the over-formalization of the process of hearing children's voices. She reminds researchers to permit children to respond with "I don't know" and requests for clarification, particularly because children often assume adults already have the answers. She suggests using statements rather than questions. Statements with which the child can agree or disagree seem to trigger fuller responses from children. If using questions, she notes that open and moderately focused questions seem to generate better, more complete responses

The interviewer card game in our study involved choosing from a deck of question cards, then playing the role of interviewer by asking the question printed on the card. Two identical sets of three cards were prepared: one set for the participant and an identical set for the interviewer. The child was given the opportunity to go first by selecting one of his or her cards, and then reading the question to the interviewer, who would answer the question. The questions were as follows: Can you tell me a little bit about yourself? What is your best talent? If you could have any super power, which super power would you choose? Even though the questions did not relate to our research focus (concerning the value of walking and walking therapies), some of the children's responses provided rich insights into ways they viewed themselves, their bodies, their mobility options, and their assistive devices, as in this excerpt from an interview with a 13-year-old girl:

Interviewer (I): If you could have any super power, what would you choose?

Child (C): Make my wheelchair have wings and fly.

I: That sounds like a lot of fun. Where would you go?

C: Around the world.

I: What color would it be?

C: Pink.

Source: Teachman, Gail and Barbara Gibson. 2013. 'Children and Youth With Disabilities: Innovative Methods for Single Qualitative Interviews', Qualitative Health Research, 23, 2: 266–7.

from children (avoid yes or no questions; avoid successive prompts; avoid repeating questions). She also reminds researchers to consider the reasonable limits to a child's competence and capability (as we all have them); to allow for "collective voices," rather than only individual voices; and to show children that they are being listened to through follow-up actions and responses to study findings.

Irwin and Johnson (2005) similarly provide a number of important insights when interviewing young children, including advice on building rapport (reducing "stranger danger"); being patient; incorporating play strategies; interviewing in spaces that allow for movement because children's daily spaces involve activity; and allowing for responses that do not have a sequential beginning, middle, and end. That said, Irwin and Johnson explain that a researcher must still be prepared to "go with the flow" and adapt to changing circumstances, events, and personalities. Being innovative seems especially important when working with children (Shaw et al., 2011). For example, MacNaughton (2001) used anti-bias persona dolls (dolls of various races, sexes, shapes, sizes, etc.) to draw out immigrant children's voices and to help explain their silences. Similarly, Ackroyd and Pilkington (1999) used drama education to understand children's ethnic identity construction in multicultural settings. But before *any* of this can happen, researchers need to consider a range of ethical issues, which some argue are particularly pertinent and unique because the research involves children.

Ethics in Research, Especially Including Children

Ethics refers to a set of moral principles and codes of conduct. All research that involves human subjects is expected to follow specific guidelines set out to protect them from exploitation in research. In September 1998, three large national research funding agencies/councils—the Canadian Institutes of Health Research (CIHR), the Natural Sciences and Engineering Research Council (NSERC), and the Social Sciences and Humanities Research Council (SSHRC)—launched the *Tri-Council Policy Statement: Ethical Conduct for Research Involving Humans* (TCPS). The TCPS was established to ensure that the research these organizations fund (and hopefully all other research) complies with their policy involving human subjects. It codifies a common ethical framework that, first and foremost, ensures free and informed consent and privacy and confidentiality of research participants. It mandates the creation and outlines the composition of Research Ethics Boards that review individual ethical protocols, and provides a detailed account of its guiding ethical principles.

Unlike the TCPS, which set out to outline special precautions when involving children in research, the new TCPS 2 (2010) has placed more attention on *not* excluding children from research (see Box 3.3). Although the issue of obtaining informed, adult consent still dominates the discussion of including children in research, there is considerably less emphasis on children's vulnerability as persons. This is a vast improvement over the first TCPS, which declared that "the notion of harm applied to children should be understood differently from harm in adults," as "harm induced in children may have longer-term consequences to their growth and development."

Children's Vulnerability—Same or Different from Adults'?

Numerous researchers in recent years have made serious commitments to include children in the research process. However, there is lack of consensus about how best to protect the interests of children as participants in the research process. As a result, there seems to be a split among researchers as to how to frame ethical issues when children are involved. Some believe

---

Box 3.3   Excerpt from *Tri-Council Policy Statement 2*

Article 4.4: Children shall not be inappropriately excluded from research solely on the basis of their age or developmental stage. The inclusion of children in research is subject to Article 4.6.

Article 4.6: Subject to applicable legal requirements, individuals who lack capacity to consent to participate in research shall not be inappropriately excluded from research. Where a researcher seeks to involve individuals in research who do not have capacity to consent for themselves, the researcher shall, in addition to fulfilling the conditions in Articles 3.9 and 3.10, satisfy the [Research Ethics Board] that:

   (a) the research question can be addressed only with participants within the identified group; and
   (b) the research does not expose the participants to more than minimal risk without the prospect of direct benefits for them; or
   (c) where the research entails only minimal risk, it should at least have the prospect of providing benefits to participants or to a group that is the focus of the research and to which the participants belong.

Application: Children and individuals with cognitive impairments or intellectual disabilities may lack capacity to consent to participate in particular research initiatives. As a result, they have, historically, experienced both over-inclusion as populations of convenience for some research and unjustified exclusion from other research. Yet the advancement of knowledge about their social, psychological, and health experiences and needs may depend on their appropriate participation in research. Their inclusion in research requires special considerations. . . .

Source: Tri-Council Policy Statement: Ethical Conduct for Research Involving Humans 2014. The Canadian Institutes of Health Research, the Natural Sciences and Engineering Research Council of Canada, and the Social Sciences and Humanities Research Council of Canada, 2014.

that children are and should be treated as a "vulnerable group" that requires unique ethical considerations—particularly because of power differences between adults and children, but also because of differences in the cognitive abilities and resources among children (e.g., their lack of knowledge on how to withdraw from research, the different ways they communicate, and their different understanding of the world around them) and the extra dimension of risk when children are involved (Mishna et al., 2004; Thomas and O'Kane, 1998). Thomas and O'Kane note that although most ethical issues that arise when working with children are also present in research involving adults, there are important differences nonetheless. Punch (2002) points out that research with children is potentially different because of adult perceptions of children, children's marginalized position in adult society, and because some view, treat, or understand children as inherently different from adults.

Others believe and have argued that children do not require special or different sets of ethical guidelines (Christensen, 2004), because in granting them special treatment and protection we reinforce the view that children are incompetent and, therefore, especially vulnerable (Mahon et al., 1996). Danby and Farrell (2004) concurred, explaining that adult-centred research may actually be perpetuating stereotypical, normative views of children as ignorant, capricious, and untrustworthy. They added that the adultist (involving a "principle of care") version of childhood assumes that adults know best, that adults make decisions over and for children, and that children accept these decisions (Danby and Farrell, 2004: 42). Some have added that this "overprotective" stance towards children inevitably reduces their ability and right to participate in research (Morrow and Richards, 1996).

Children's Competence

When researchers begin conceptualizing research with children, they expect or encounter colleagues with questions about children's ability to know and understand social phenomena. Many are especially questioned about children's ability to understand notions like "consent," "confidentiality," and the "voluntary nature of research." Some researchers reassure us that children are concerned and aware of the importance of privacy in research (Hill, 2006; Christensen, 2004). Christensen, for example, reminds us that children are aware of the possible "exploitation" of information and importance of confidentiality because this is already part of their world. So much of what children do and how they do it is performed through the engagement of telling and keeping secrets, revealing secrets to other children, and/or telling adults (Christensen, 2004). While their understanding may vary greatly depending on their individual experiences, even very young children are increasingly aware of who they should and should not speak to, who to trust and confide in, and what to report to adults. In many cases, these are not foreign concepts to them. Danby and Farrell (2004) challenge us to overcome some of our stereotypical and normative assumptions that children are incompetent and that adults know best and always work in and for the best interests of the child. On the other hand, some have raised the point that when working with children, full confidentiality may never be fully guaranteed because the researcher would have the duty to pass on information to appropriate professionals, such as in cases that may include abuse (Mason and Danby, 2011; Shaw et al., 2011).

Clearly, considerable complexity and diversity exist in the views of researchers when it comes to ethical issues surrounding children's participation in research; nonetheless, there is growing consensus to respect children's interest and willingness to participate in research after parents or guardians have provided consent. That is, many researchers agree that after parents or guardians consent to have the child participate in research, the child himself or herself should be given clear information, then the choice to refuse to participate through a dissenting process—respecting children's rights (Mishna et al., 2004). To add to this, Thomas and O'Kane (1998) suggest that methodological soundness may improve ethics in research. They argue that the reliability, validity, and ethical acceptability of research with children can be improved by using approaches that give children control over the research process and methods that reflect children's ways of seeing and relating to the world. We would do well to recognize that children are similar to adults, but possess different competencies. This also challenges us to develop a wide range of innovative research tools and techniques using pictures, diaries, sentence completion, creative drawing and writing techniques, and workshops (Mason and Danby, 2011; Shaw et al., 2011; Teachman and Gibson, 2013). These more child-centred methods force the researcher to explore, to reflect upon, and to understand children's social location, as they, at the same time, critically assess their own assumptions about themselves as researchers and about children. In doing this, we may find that there is a great deal to learn about children and from them.

Research by Children

In projects around the world, children and young people have been involved in developing research agendas, as interviewers and peer researchers, and in analysis and dissemination. For example, a study of play spaces in the United Kingdom involved 32 primary schoolchildren from two schools in Leeds as researchers (Burke, 2005). The child researchers were given disposable cameras over a one-week period and were asked to record and reflect upon (through the creation of a photo diary and photo elicitation) their preferred places and spaces for play. The data generated in the study by the children aimed to influence policy and planning surrounding play strategies and spaces at the local and national levels.

Some research by children has been done on what many of us would consider very serious issues affecting the lives of children. For example, street children ages 11–16 years, in Hanoi, Vietnam, helped identify research questions and ethical rules as they became researchers and participants in a pilot study on physical and emotional punishment. Following extensive training, particularly on self-protection, the 20 children who volunteered to be child researchers were asked to complete observation sheets, recording the type of punishment they witnessed, by whom, where, and why (Enkhtor, 2007).

Similarly, child researchers and child participants from low-income and socially marginalized groups were involved in a study aimed at understanding the transport, mobility, and access issues of children in parts of India (Lolichen, 2007). The study sought to determine and map out the kinds of loads children carry (for work, family, and school), the modes of transport they used, the weight of the loads, the distance loads were carried, and the difficulties children faced along the way. Child researchers and child respondents, supported by adults, used participatory rapid appraisal (PRA), which included a transect walk, to map the space, relations, physical barriers, and other obstacles that children encountered daily in their neighbourhoods. The study also involved interviews, flash cards, traffic count, and focus groups with children as researchers and participants.[4] Not only did children learn about the research process and about some of the challenges experienced daily by children, but lower-caste children also were empowered by becoming engaged in decision-making and governance. Such a study reminds us that doing research can empower children to participate actively in their own education and to make original contributions to knowledge.

Closer to home, we have a concrete example of the social activism of Craig Kielburger, who, at the age of 12, read a newspaper article on the slave labour of children, did more research, and came to help thousands of children around the world (Box 3.4). Children like Kielburger remind us to challenge the implicit definition of research as "academic," "empirical," and "sociological." They remind us to extend our understanding to include all aspects of what research entails—everything from brainstorming with peers to living through challenging circumstances and wanting to know why and what can be done about it. Including the voice of children in studies organized and directed by adult academics is an important step forward, but this is not the same as recognizing and acting upon one's own sociological imagination, as many children have done and will continue to do.

Recent research is looking at how children can and should be included in data analysis, which is a stage of research from which children have been even more widely excluded (Coad and Evans, 2008; Shaw et al., 2011). Coad and Evans explain that children should be involved in data analysis, which includes coding, interpreting, and categorizing data, selecting quotes, and

Box 3.4   Free the Children. Craig Kielburger: Children's Rights Crusader

How it all started . . .

Free The Children's mission is to create a world where all young people are free to achieve their fullest potential as agents of change. And we couldn't have a better blueprint for success: the organization was founded by Craig Kielburger in 1995 when he gathered 11 school friends to begin fighting child labour. He was 12.

A morning to remember.
That morning, Craig flipped through the Toronto Star in search of the comics, he was struck by a story. A raw, but courageous story of a boy his age named Iqbal.

Iqbal Masih was born in South Asia and sold into slavery at the age of four. In his short life, he had spent six years chained to a carpet-weaving loom. Iqbal captured the world's attention by speaking out for children's rights.

A dream is sparked.
Eventually, Iqbal's wide media coverage caught the attention of those who wished to silence him. At 12, Iqbal lost his life defending the rights of children.

What Craig learned from Iqbal's story was that the bravest voice can live in the smallest body.

Craig had to do something.

A movement begins.
Craig gathered together a small group of his Grade 7 classmates from his Thornhill, Ontario, school and Free The Children was born.

Free the children from poverty. Free the children from exploitation. Free the children from the notion that they are powerless to effect change.

Those are the messages that sparked Craig's passion, and continue to fuel the mission of the organization today. Every day the movement grows and every day more young people are free to achieve their fullest potential.

A network of young people grows into a movement.
Today, Free The Children is an international charity and educational partner, with more than 2.3 million youth involved in our innovative education and development programs. Since its inception, Free The Children has worked in more than 45 countries. Free The Children currently works in eight developing countries with its Adopt A Village program.

Source: Free the Children (2015).

verifying adult researchers' analysis. This, they argue, if done with the right measure of support and training, results in a shift in the balance of power towards children, as it addresses issues of adult accountability to children.

Summary

In this chapter we see that the way researchers conceptualize and think about children has a profound impact on the way we study them. In turn, the way we study them has a profound impact on our understanding of children and childhood, as the way we see them affects the ways we *listen* to them. Treating children as weak, incapable, incompetent, and vulnerable perpetuates the treatment of children as objects in research and invisible and inconsequential in everyday life. Until we change this, we are likely to continue to undervalue children's competencies and voice—in turn, undermining children's rights.

Doing research with children is challenging because it requires that the researcher ensures that the practices employed in the research process reflect children's experiences, interests, values, and everyday routines (Christensen, 2004). The researcher must also think about how children routinely express and represent these interests and values in their everyday life (ibid.). In doing this planning and thinking, researchers learn more about themselves, about children, and about the research process.

Punch (2002) reminds us that good research with children involves, among other things, knowing the participants, not imposing the researcher's own perceptions and views, building trust and rapport, using clear and accessible language, considering innovative methods, and creating a comfortable research context. In looking over this list, are these also not equally valuable and necessary for doing research with adults? By looking closely and critically at research done with and on children, there seems to be a great deal to learn about doing research involving all human subjects.

Questions for Critical Thought

1. What do you believe is the most important and pressing issue affecting children in Canada today? How would you go about studying this issue? Where would you begin? What kind of research would you engage in? Who would you include as collaborators in the study? Why? Who do you expect would fund this research?

2. From this book's bibliography, select and locate one research article. What kind of study is it? What research method was used? What is the unit of analysis? What were the key findings? What were the major shortcomings of the study? If you were part of this research team, what would you recommend be done differently?

3. You decide that you want to conduct a study of children's attitudes towards school. How would you go about doing this research? What ethical issues do you need to consider?

4.   You have been asked to redevelop or create a new set of guidelines on ethical considerations and issues arising when doing research involving children. Outline the process you would use to do this. Who would you consult? How would you go about making decisions about what to include in the guidelines? How would your guidelines look? What would you include or exclude?

Suggested Readings

Greig, Anne, Jayne Taylor, and Tommy MacKay. 2007. *Doing Research with Children*. London: Sage. This book is divided into three sections. The first includes the main theories and approaches in doing research with children; the second outlines different frameworks and techniques for conducting both qualitative and quantitative research with children; the third explores the unique nature of children as research subjects. It discusses special ethical issues raised in research with children.

Leadbeater, Bonnie, Elizabeth Banister, Cecilia Benoit, Mikael Jansson, Anne Marshall, and Ted Riecken, eds. 2006. *Ethical Issues in Community-Based Research with Children and Youth*. Toronto: University of Toronto Press. Many researchers shy away from doing research that includes children because of strict ethical guidelines and procedures involved in research with "vulnerable" populations. This collection brings together the work of over two dozen researchers in 15 papers that discuss some of the unique challenges and issues arising from working in this area.

Mason, Jan, and Susan Danby. 2011. "Children as Experts in their Lives: Child Inclusive Research," *Child Indicators Research* 4, 2: 185–9. This is the introductory article in a special issue of a journal that focuses on the major paradigm shift in child research from a focus on the child as object to a focus on the child as subject and actor in research. Articles in this special issue note the importance of including children's own perspectives and subjective perceptions in research.

Shaw, Catherine, Louca-Mai Brady, and Ciara Davey. 2011. *Guidelines for Research with Children and Young People*. London: National Children's Bureau Research Centre. At: www.nfer.ac.uk/nfer/schools/developing-young-researchers/ncbguidelines.pdf. These guidelines have been produced by the National Children's Bureau (NCB) Research Centre in the United Kingdom for researchers who are contemplating involving children and young people in their research. They set out NCB Research Centre's general approach to research with children and young people, and provide practical guidance for researchers, illustrated throughout with examples from recent work at the NCB's Research Centre.

Websites

Ethical Research Involving Children
childethics.com/
The international Ethical Research Involving Children (ERIC) project aims to assist researchers and the research community to understand, plan, and conduct ethical research involving children and young people in any geographical, social, cultural, or methodological context. The ERIC approach views children as persons in their own right: worthy and capable of recognition, respect, and a voice in research.

Free the Children

www.freethechildren.com

> Free the Children is the world's largest network of children helping children through educa-
> tion, with more than one million youth involved in innovative education and development
> programs in 45 countries. It was founded in 1995 by international child rights activist
> Craig Kielburger, the second youngest Canadian to receive the Order of Canada, who also
> has been nominated for the Nobel Peace Prize. The organization has received the World's
> Children's Prize for the Rights of the Child (also known as the Children's Nobel Prize) and the
> Human Rights Award from the World Association of Non-governmental Organizations.
> This website provides information on a number of their projects, activities, and initiatives
> around the world.

National Longitudinal Survey of Children and Youth (NLSCY)

www.statcan.ca/cgi-bin/imdb/p2SV.pl?Function=getSurvey&SDDS=4450&lang=en&db=I
MDB&dbg=f&adm=8&dis=2

> The NLSCY is a long-term study of Canadian children that follows their development and
> well-being from birth to early adulthood. The study is designed to collect information
> about factors influencing a child's social, emotional, and behavioural development and to
> monitor the effect of these factors on the child's development over time. This website con-
> tains a description of the study, target population, sampling technique, questionnaire, etc.

New South Wales Commission for Children and Young People

www.kids.nsw.gov.au/kids

> The commission is an independent organization that works with others (universities,
> communities, other organizations) to make New South Wales (NSW) a better place for
> children. It reports directly to the NSW Parliament, and the Committee on Children and
> Young People oversees their work. They conduct research into issues affecting children
> (children at work, child deaths, poverty, parental employment, child-carers, etc.). The site
> provides access to some of their research and discusses ethical issues of doing research
> with and for children.

Panel on Research Ethics

www.pre.ethics.gc.ca/eng/policy-politique/initiatives/tcps2-eptc2/Default/

> This Government of Canada website gives you access to the *Tri-Council Policy Statement
> 2—Ethical Conduct for Research Involving Humans* (www.pre.ethics.gc.ca/pdf/eng/tcps2/
> TCPS_2_FINAL_Web.pdf). It also provides information on the Interagency Advisory
> Panel on Research Ethics, a body of experts established in November 2001 by three
> Canadian research agencies—the Canadian Institute of Health Research (CIHR), the
> Natural Sciences and Engineering Research Council (NSERC), and the Social Sciences
> and Humanities Research Council (SSHRC)—to support the development and evolution
> of their research ethics policy.

UNICEF

www.unicef.org/index.php

> The United Nations Children's Fund (UNICEF) aims to help build a world in which the rights
> of every child are realized. Its creation stems from the belief that nurturing and caring
> for children are cornerstones of human progress. UNICEF works with international bodies
> to overcome the obstacles that poverty, violence, disease, and discrimination place in
> a child's path. The website contains access to guidelines on doing ethical research with
> children (www.unicef.org/evaluation/files/TechNote1_Ethics.pdf) and on children as
> researchers in the community (www.unicef.org/teachers/researchers/problem_id.htm).

4   Parent(s) and Child(ren)

Learning Objectives

◎   To learn about the exchange of values, beliefs, and behaviours that occurs between parents and children.

◎   To explore some of the longer-term trends within and among families.

◎   To assess some of the recent trends in families with young children.

◎   To learn about the role parents play in the construction of a gender identity.

◎   To explore some cross-cultural variations in child-rearing practices.

◎   To examine research on social class differences in expectations placed on children.

◎   To consider recent research on child-rearing in same-sex families.

◎   To recognize that "raising" children is shaped by a multitude of intrafamilal and extrafamilial factors.

Introduction

Childhood is one of the most highly regulated parts of our lives. From birth, we need others to survive and to grow, but throughout childhood, others govern almost every aspect of our lives. The most obvious "others," for most children, are parents. The behaviours and attitudes of parents are, in turn, shaped by the society in which we live. In fact, some have argued that parenting is highly politicized (Edwards and Gillies, 2013). Something as seemingly personal as naming one's child is directly and indirectly affected by the society in which we live. Imagine choosing to name your son "Matilda" or "Gertrude"; the names seem inappropriate along gender lines, of course, but they also sound archaic, and "of another time." While the idea of naming your son Matilda, or Satan, for that matter, seems ridiculous, it leads us into a long list of topics related to ideas around what are deemed to be appropriate child naming and rearing practices, the role of parents, families, and culture in shaping those ideas and the wide range of influences, constraints, and limitations placed upon parents by the societies in which we live. In this chapter, we will see that parents are shaped by culture, and other social forces, and at the same time reproduce that culture through some of the expectations they place on their children.[1]

We will begin with a critical discussion of the notion of *socialization* and the *bidirectional* transmission of values, beliefs, and behaviours that occurs between parents and children. You will then read about some of the longer-term trends that have shaped, altered, and influenced Canadian families in the past. We will briefly assess how expectations around parenting have changed and what that has meant to Canada's children. Next, we will look at some recent trends and patterns among and within Canadian families with young children. We will explore why and how intergenerational transmission of values and beliefs occurs, specifically looking at the example of parents' roles in the construction of a gender identity. Variation is considerable in the ways this happens and why, so we will explore some cross-cultural variations in child-rearing and look at social class differences in expectations placed on children. Child-rearing and parenting are also shaped by family type (structure/form) and society's response to that type, which we will look at towards the end of the chapter. The chapter's goal is to demonstrate that a considerable amount of work takes place within families, but that the nature and type of exchanges between parents and children are shaped by both intrafamilial and extrafamilial factors.

Socialization—Unidirectional and Bidirectional Transmission

We seldom think about how profoundly Locke's notion of the child as tabula rasa has affected the way we think about child-rearing. For a very long time, behaviourists and developmentalists have written about children as almost infinitely malleable and the socialization process as *unidirectional,* or one-way, i.e., from parents to children. Increasingly, social scientists are noting that socialization is a reciprocal affair or a two-way process. Researchers like Kerry Daly (2004: 5) explain that it would be a mistake to think of socialization in terms of a simple linear transmission model, in which culture shapes parents and parents in turn shape children. Others remind us that an infant is a social organism who is socialized by others but who also socializes them (Fitzgerald et al., 1999). Similarly, Burton et al. (2005) write about the *simultaneity* of parenting and child behaviour (in which parents and children both are "players") when it comes to parenting style and child outcomes.

From the outset, despite our preconceived notions about children and childhood, infants force parents to rethink who they are and how they do things. For example, a classic piece by Anne-Marie Ambert (1997) notes that despite what parents expected their infants to be like, each baby requires different types of care that shape parents' perceptions of and experiences surrounding the "easiness" of their baby. Ambert (1997) explained that "easy" babies make parents feel adequate, happy, rewarded, and successful as parents, whereas more "challenging," demanding, or less healthy babies often make them feel inadequate, stressed, and ineffective. While this is occurring, parents' own lives and larger social environments shape their attitudes and practices when it comes to child rearing. These factors include *intrafamilial* factors—the age at which they have their child, the nature of their relationship, the number and age of other children they have, the types of social support they receive from family and friends, etc.—and *extrafamilial* factors—the neighbourhood in which they live, their work experiences, and their social class, background, and culture, to name a few. Some have explained that the ecological context in which parents live provides assets and hurdles that affect parenting (Bronfenbrenner, 1977; Bronfenbrenner and Ceci, 1994). In this intricate web, children also socialize parents.

Studies of immigrant children, who act as language brokers for their parents (Guan et al., 2014; Wong and Tseng, 2008; see also Chapter 8) or of Canadian parents—digital immigrants—and their children—digital natives—(Bittman et al., 2011; Prensky, 2001; Steeves, 2005; see also Chapter 6) help uncover this bidirectionality. Immigrant children sometimes possess knowledge of the English or French language and of Canadian culture that their parents do not possess and so share that knowledge with their parents, as do children of the Internet generation share information of the digital world with their parents. This bidirectional exchange is increasingly a part of our understanding of parenting and child-rearing, but it was not always so in the past. Shifts in notions of parenting have become evident since World War II.

How the Changing Nature of Work and Families Impacts Parenting

The post-war period, especially the 1950s, was an anomalous time for Canadian families. After the war and the return of Canadian soldiers, marriage rates soared, especially among younger women. For those aged 15 to 19, the marriage rate more than doubled, climbing from 30 marriages per 1,000 in 1937 to 62 marriages per 1,000 in 1954 (Prentice et al., 1988). The average age of brides at first marriage fell from 25.4 in 1941 (during the war) to 22 years by 1961. They married younger and had children at younger ages. The sharpest increase in birth rates occurred among younger women—women under 25. One result of having children at a younger age was that women tended to have more. What resulted was a **baby boom**—a demographic bulge of births occurring in this post-war period.

Changes in fertility rates during this period contributed to the redefinition of motherhood, childhood, and child-rearing. This also eventually triggered a shift towards the idea that children are treasured emotional investments, emotional anchors for modern couples, and proof of the couple's permanency and commitment (Kehily, 2010). Before this, particularly in rural Canada and during early industrialization, a significant number of women (and children) were in the labour force or working the land beside adult men. Older children were expected to care for younger children. Being a woman did not exclusively mean being a mother. Families could not afford to have mothers be child-minders first and foremost. Although women could not own property or vote, they nonetheless, in rural societies, worked the land; and later, with industrialization, worked in factories, as did their husbands. Women as well as men contributed to the household as producers.

With the coming of the baby boom, womanhood was redefined and more closely equated with "motherhood," at least in the short term. This shift coincided with the return of Canadian men/soldiers to jobs previously held by women during World War II; once women were returned to the home, middle-class notions of motherhood evolved. Being part of the middle class at that time often meant that one (male) income was enough to raise a family, creating a new class of stay-at-home moms. Mothers could, and some felt they should, devote more time and attention to child-rearing and other activities that enhanced the home. This situation flourished to the point that pressure was placed on working-class mothers, who were viewed as "neglectful" of their families, even though they needed to work to support them.

With these changes there emerged images of the **traditional nuclear family** as a Canadian ideal (while not always the reality), with the husband in the labour force and mother in the home caring for their growing family. This thinking about family roles was reflected in the ever-expanding number of sometimes contradictory magazine articles on parenting or mothering, and the rise in popularity of child psychologists and child care experts. Many of these emphasized the importance of developing emotional bonds between mother (not father) and child. With increased attention on proper parenting, mothers' anxiety grew about their ability as parents.

The British psychologist, Dr John Bowlby, who coined the concept "maternal deprivation," was especially popular at the time. Bowlby (1958) argued that irreparable damage is done to young children when they are separated from their mothers for prolonged periods of time. He counselled mothers not to leave children under age three in the care of others except in emergency situations—even a holiday visit with granny is best kept short, he advised. He stressed that infants and toddlers needed the continuous care of their mothers.

Women received conflicting advice when it came to feeding: follow a strict time schedule, like their mothers had, or feed when the baby demanded it? Breastfeed or bottle-feed? The debates raged and women were bombarded with conflicting views. Women increasingly came to distrust the traditions in which they were raised and to rely on books about how to parent. The Canadian government issued a free publication entitled

The Canadian Mother and Child (Couture, 1940). More than two million copies were distributed to new and expectant mothers before its first revision, but eighth edition, in 1949.

The very popular Dr Benjamin Spock's *Baby and Child Care,* first published in 1946, sold more than 50 million copies by the time of the author's death in 1998, at age 94. Dr Spock contradicted and challenged some of his contemporaries. He encouraged understanding and flexibility on the part of parents in regard to raising children, and stressed the importance of listening to children and appreciating their individual differences. He was criticized by some of his peers as being overly permissive, and was even blamed by some for having helped form the generation of young Americans that protested against the Vietnam War and launched the youth counterculture movement of the 1960s. Spock himself became an important anti-nuclear and peace activist in his later years. This was also a time when ideas about "free range" parenting (Edwards and Gillies, 2013)—more laissez-faire parenting—emerged to challenge the overprotective intensity promoted by those like Bowlby.

Starting in the 1960s and 1970s, mothers' increasing labour force participation rates raised fears of the effects of maternal deprivation on children (Daly, 2004). Nonetheless, women's labour force participation rate continued to rise, in many instances because the male-breadwinner/female-homemaker model did not allow for the standard of living people had come to expect. In fact, one of the most profound shifts in our thinking about parenting in recent history was triggered by the rapidly growing number of women, especially mothers of young children, in the labour force—resulting in a big increase in the number of dual-earner couples and the rise of **intensive mothering**, which will be discussed below in more detail. In 1976, for example, about 42 per cent of all women over the age of 15 worked for pay, making up 37 per cent of the labour force that year (Statistics Canada, 2000). Only 27.6 per cent of women with children under the age of three and 31.5 per cent with children under age six were in the labour force (Ferrao, 2010). By 2009, almost 7 in 10 married women with a child under age six (66.6 per cent), and about 8 in 10 with a child between the ages of 6 and 15, were in the labour force (Ferrao, 2010) (see Table 4.1).

We are also currently experiencing a baby boom of sorts, partially attributed to higher fertility levels among women in their thirties (Milan, 2013). That said, although older women are having children, Canadian women in general are having fewer children throughout their lives than in the past, resulting in more one-child families. In 2011, the total fertility rate in Canada was 1.61 children per woman, down from 1.68 in 2008 and 1.67 in 2009 (Milan, 2013). While Canadian families are typically smaller, we are increasingly recognizing and counting a larger number of family forms. For the first time, the 2001 Canadian census recognized and

Table 4.1 Employment rate of women with children by age of youngest child, 1976 to 2009

Year	Employment rate (%)					
			Youngest child			Women under 55
	< 3 y	3–5 y	< 6 y	6–15 y	< 16 y	w/ no child at home
1976	27.6	36.8	31.4	46.4	39.1	60.9
1981	39.3	46.7	42.1	56.2	49.3	66.0
1986	49.4	54.5	51.4	61.9	56.7	69.3
1991	54.4	60.1	56.5	69.0	62.8	72.6
1996	57.8	60.5	58.9	69.8	64.5	72.4
2001	61.3	67.0	63.7	75.3	70.1	76.8
2002	61.9	68.1	64.5	77.0	71.4	77.9
2003	62.7	68.5	65.1	76.7	71.6	79.0
2004	64.5	69.4	66.6	77.0	72.4	79.3
2005	64.7	70.6	67.2	77.4	72.8	78.7
2006	64.3	69.4	66.4	78.2	72.9	79.9
2007	65.1	72.6	68.1	79.4	74.3	80.9
2008	64.6	70.3	66.8	80.0	73.8	81.2
2009	64.4	69.7	66.5	78.5	72.9	80.4

Source: Ferrao (2010: 9).

counted same-sex *common-law* couples as families, with some 34,200 same-sex common-law couples (0.5 per cent of all couples) defining themselves as families. Of these, 19,000 were male same-sex couples, of which 3 per cent (570) had children; of 15,200 female same-sex couples, 15 per cent (2,280) had children (Statistics Canada, 2002). The same Census found married or common-law couples with children aged 24 and under living at home represented in only 44 per cent of all families in Canada, down from 49 per cent in 1991 and 55 per cent in 1981 (Statistics Canada, 2001). There were also an increasing proportion of couples who choose to live in common-law relationships (increasing from 5.6 per cent in 1991 to 14 per cent in 2001); and 1,311,190 families headed by a lone parent, representing 16 per cent of families in Canada (Statistics Canada, 2002).

The 2006 Census showed greater diversity, because, as of 2005, for the first time same-sex couples could legally marry. Again, the Census found fewer married-couple families (68.6 per cent, down from 70.5 per cent in 2001); more common-law families (15.5 per cent, up from 13.8 per cent in 2001); more lone-parent families (15.9 per cent, up from 15.7 per cent in 2001); and more same-sex families (0.6 per cent) (Milan et al., 2007).

The 2011 Census revealed even more variation. That Census counted 9,389,700 families, up 5.5 per cent from 8,896,840 in 2006 (Statistics Canada, 2012). The proportion of married couple families was still the largest (67.0 per cent), but the overall proportion of married couple families in relation to other types of families has again decreased (from 68.9 per cent in

2006), as, among other things, for the first time, the 2011 Census counted stepfamilies. In 2011, 7.4 per cent of couples with children were *simple stepfamilies* (in which all children were the children of only one of the spouses or partners); 5.2 per cent of couples with children were *complex stepfamilies* (comprising at least one child of both parents as well as one child of one parent only). In total, 10 per cent of children under the age of 14 lived in stepfamilies (see Figure 4.1). Since the 2006 Census, the number of common-law couples (now accounting for 16.7 per cent of all families) rose by 13.9 per cent, surpassing the number of lone-parent families (now accounting for 16.3 per cent of all families); lone-parent families increased by 8.0 per cent (male lone-parent families increased by 16.2 per cent, compared with a 6 per cent increase among female lone-parent families). The number of same-sex married couples nearly tripled between 2006 and 2011, and the number of same-sex common-law couples rose 15.0 per cent. The 2011 Census counted 64,575 same-sex couple families (21,015 were same-sex married couples and 43,560 were same-sex common-law couples). Interestingly, 4.8 per cent of children under the age of 14 lived in households that contained at least one grandparent. Of these children, 0.5 per cent lived in *skip-generation* families, which included grandparents but not parents (Statistics Canada, 2012).

What do these changes mean for young children? Young children residing in Canada today are much more likely than ever before to be raised by mothers who are older (Statistics Canada, 2007b), more educated, and working for pay (Healthy Child Manitoba, 2003). For some children this

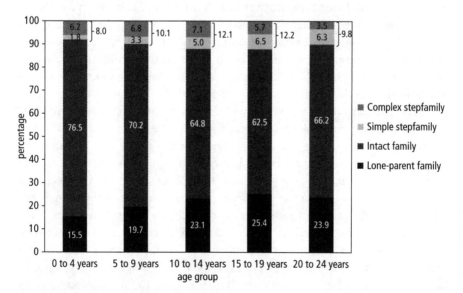

Figure 4.1 Distribution (in percentage) of Children Living in Selected Family Structures by Age Group, Canada, 2011
Source: Bohnert et al. (2014).

has meant more economic stability, resulting from living in two-career or two-earner families (but child poverty rates remain high; see Chapter 10). This is in sharp contrast to the popular view that contemporary family life is characterized by a decline in values of duty and responsibility, undermining good parenting (Edwards and Gillies, 2013). Edwards and Gillies note the claim that parenting standards have dropped are not supported by the recent trends in parenting practices. Contrary to popular belief, shrinking family size has meant that children are more likely to be surrounded by adults. In fact, children are more likely to spend *more* time with their parents than in the past (Quirke, 2007; Daly, 2004; Healthy Child Manitoba, 2003). The expectation of intensive, science-led, and attentive parenting, which accompanied the rise of smaller families, were less common in the 1960s when children were most often surrounded by other children (Edwards and Gillies, 2013). Some, like Duschinsky (2013: 79) have noted that as industrial capitalism renders our social bonds more fragile, parents' hopes increasingly become invested in the lives and happiness of their children, which in itself adds new pressures on parents and children. Edwards and Gillies (2013) noted that expectations that parents should actively cultivate cognitive and emotional skills in their children reflect uniquely contemporary preoccupations. Margaret Nelson (2010) similarly noted that we are seeing "parenting out of control" and the rise of anxious parenting, as well-intentioned parents—helicopter parents—find themselves going to extremes to remove all obstacles from their child's "path to greatness." This has also come to be known as **intensive parenting**, or to be more precise, **intensive mothering**. A number of scholars have identified central themes of intensive mothering, which include but are not limited to the notions that caring for children is primarily the responsibility of the mother, parenting should be child-centred, that children are sacred, and that mothers should intellectually stimulate children to ensure appropriate brain development (Schiffrin et al., 2014). Parents, but especially mothers, are expected to devote their time and energy to enriching their child, and cultivating the child's needs so that she or he can reach her or his full potential. Given the near universal use of the Internet and cell phones, mothers are expected to be informed and monitor their children at all times. According to Romagnoli and Wall (2014), while widely accepted as the "proper" way to raise children, intensive mothering is consistent with neoliberal notions of individual responsibility and risk management, and is based on middle-class ideals. It has also been found to have negative mental health consequences for mothers, reducing mothers' level of life satisfaction (Rizzo et al., 2013). At the same time, the latest trend in popular culture is blaming individual mothers for being too intense, suggesting that they relax and stop being "smother mothers." Connected to this the *family adaptation model* of parenting seems to prevail, in which parents are

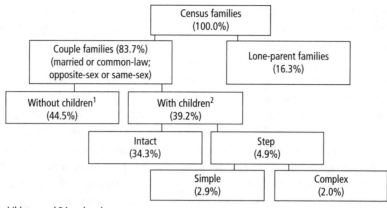

Figure 4.2 Overview of Census Families
Source: Statistics Canada (2012: 18).

1. Without children aged 24 and under.
2. With children aged 24 and under.

expected to navigate the pressures of paid and unpaid work as well as multiple and complex schedules that include an adequate amount of family time (Daly, 2004). With more mothers working for pay, more expectations have been placed on their partners to get involved in parenting, to compensate for mothers' absences. This has been labelled the *compensation model* when it comes to parenting (ibid.).

Redefinition of Fatherhood

Fatherhood has received far less attention than motherhood (Fitzgerald et al., 1999), yet historical analyses suggest a number of periods of influence that have shaped our modern views of the father's role in child development (Lamb, 1987). Although fatherhood has been slow to change, mostly due to lack of exposure to appropriate paternal role models (Daly, 1993; also see Duindam and Spruijt, 2002), there have been paradigmatic shifts in the role over time. Lamb (1987), for example, notes that in colonial times the father was seen as the disciplinarian, moral teacher, and head of the household. With industrialization, the father was absent more often from the home and seen as the provider or breadwinner. In the post-war period, fatherhood also entailed more disposable income and relatively greater leisure, creating opportunities for a larger role in child-rearing—but he still was not expected to be the primary caregiver or nurturer (ibid.).

Increasingly, we see literature arguing that men are taking on more responsibility for children's daily lives (Marshall, 2006), embracing the role of the "new father" (McGill, 2014), and that some can and do "mother" (Doucet, 2006). In fact, Doucet found a small but increasing number of men for whom providing care for their children was a significant part of their daily lives. Similarly, Marshall (2006) reports that the proportion of stay-at-home fathers increased from 4 per cent in 1986 to 11 per cent in 2005, in some cases resulting from their unemployment (or underemployment) and in others a consequence of their affluence. Increasingly, fathers are expected to be both providers and nurturers. Using two waves of the Child Development Supplement to the Panel Study of Income Dynamics (N = 1,139), McGill (2014) examined the relationship between employment and father involvement. Results suggest work hours are *not* strongly related to father involvement. Despite generally long work hours, "new fathers" appear to secure time with their children by cutting back on, or incorporating their children into, their own leisure time (McGill, 2014). Similarly, Daly, Ashbourne, and Brown's (2013) study of 215 geographically dispersed Canadian fathers (which included new fathers, young fathers, immigrant fathers, gay fathers, fathers of children with special needs, indigenous fathers, and separated and divorced fathers) found that fathers undergo a reorientation of values and behaviour in response to the influence of their children. This reorientation included redefined priorities, an altered sense of purpose, a different awareness of what it means to be a man, changed relationships, a rebalancing of the importance of self and other, and a rescheduling of their everyday lives.

Contrary to popular belief, mothers and fathers are spending *more* time with their children in direct care than in the past (Quirke, 2006; Sayer et al., 2004; Daly, 2004; Arendell, 2001). In 2010, parents reported spending 2 hours and 31 minutes a day on child care as their primary activity, up 21 minutes from 1998 (Béchard, 2011). When measuring time spent caring for children while performing another activity, such as cooking or cleaning, parents spent 4 hours and 52 minutes a day caring for children under the age of four. Regardless of the child's age, women spent more time on care than men did—6 hours 33 minutes per day (while performing other activities) compared with 3 hours 7 minutes per day (Béchard, 2011). But the time parents spend with their children is more goal-oriented, structured, and saturated with activity (Daly, 2004), undoubtedly connected to the rising popularity of intensive parenting. For many, parenting has come to involve finding and negotiating programs, registering children, paying fees, volunteering for fundraising, attending practices, driving children to games, classes, or recitals, speaking with teachers and coaches, monitoring practice, and praising them for their efforts (Berhau and Lareau, 2001, in Daly 2004; Nelson, 2001). Daly notes that as they bow to pressures on their time, parents seem to be aiming to raise more independent and "efficient" children— all the while preparing and positioning them for success. Modern parenting magazines have added to this pressure.

Parenting Magazines Today

Parenting "manuals" are certainly not new. Widely read Western child-rearing manuals of the nineteenth century uniformly stressed the importance of obedience (Stearns, 2014). While the message has changed, parenting magazines of today are not much different from parenting manuals of the past in their goal of telling parents how best to raise their children. Published advice about parenting is abundantly available through a variety of formats, such as the Internet (including self-published "mommy blogs"), magazines, advice columns, and books. Information is available on a wide range of topics, from breastfeeding, infant care, and healthy physical development (Frerichs et al., 2006) to divorce and stepfamilies (Lagoni and Cook, 1985), and even to advice about terrorism (Dolev and Zeedyk, 2006). Analyses of parenting advice and magazines have found the emergence of a globalized series of messages that reflect Western cultural assumptions as far away as China. Hoffman and Zhao (2007) compared American and Chinese parenting magazines and found that, despite some differences in parenting advice on early childhood and child care, a number of recurring and converging themes existed across the two cultures, including the role and importance of scientific experts and expertise, individualism, and the importance of self-expression.

Furedi (2001) noted that parenting magazines and other media reinforce the idea that the modern family is in crisis. This in turn has had a destabilizing impact on parents, leading them to question their abilities as parents while simultaneously creating a sense of fear and paranoia, reinforcing the notion that today childhood is in crisis (also see Kehily 2010 and Nelson 2010). This paranoia is then reflected in parents' approach to child safety and fear of risk. Parents' fear for their children's safety may be out of proportion to the risks posed; however, it does not stop them from playing an overactive role in all aspects of child-rearing to the point at which households appear to function as autonomous entities with little connection to the neighbourhood or even to the extended family.

An analysis of Canadian parenting magazines published between 1959 and 2003 found a significant shift in emphasis from engaging in "fun" activities with children and fending off the "I'm bored syndrome," to an increased focus on schooling (choosing schools and programs, encouraging reading, etc.) and on children's cognitive development (Quirke, 2006). This is no doubt consistent with the shift towards intensive parenting, but more accurately intensive mothering, as the parenting ideal.

Analyses have found that parenting magazines, despite their inclusive titles, still are written primarily for mothers and often include and reinforce traditional gender stereotypes and myths (Spees and Zimmerman, 2002; see Chen 2013 for a critique of the notion of "mommy blogs"). For example, when analyzing messages about breastfeeding and formula-feeding in popular American magazines, Frerichs et al. (2006) found that stories provided individualized advice that placed much of the responsibility on the mother, while diminishing the role of the partner and of society in general. That is, although breastfeeding is clearly a gender-specific activity, parenting magazines were found to cover more individual-level advice to mothers on what they should do and how they should do it, rather than on the broader health-related, emotional, and economic benefits of breastfeeding (ibid.). They very seldom mentioned a partner or other support systems, and rarely covered broader social and environmental issues connected to breastfeeding (ibid.). It seems clear that despite the increased attention placed on the changing role of fathers (the new nurturant father, men mothering, etc.), much of the popular literature on parenting and child-rearing remains gendered and stereotypical, targeting white, middle-class mothers (Prusank and Duran, 2014).

Parenting and Child Gender Socialization and Identity

Though every society responds to the genetic differences between males and females somewhat differently, all seem to call attention to difference. Different and, at times, unequal treatment of men and women is learned early in life. In childhood, we all learn to behave in patterned, culturally prescribed ways. What is deemed properly masculine and feminine is communicated to us through **gender socialization** via family, peers, media, and other institutions around us. It begins at birth and continues throughout our lives, and children quickly form a wide constellation of gender conceptions and stereotypes—**gender schema** or organized knowledge structures—from the cues around them. In fact, children are "wonderfully skilled" "gender detectives" who actively search out cues about gender starting in their toddler and preschool years (Martin and Ruble, 2004: 67; Kane, 2006). Between the ages of five and seven, their gender knowledge is consolidated and peaks into a rigid "either–or" scheme, which relaxes somewhat as they get a little older (Martin and Ruble, 2004). Even those who argue that gender differences in infancy are biologically based recognize that the socialization process and gender-differentiated expectations and experiences amplify early differences to produce profound gender differences during childhood (Pellegrini et al., 2007; Campbell and Eaton, 1999). But when does it start and how does it happen?

Some of the first gendered experiences and expectations happen in our parental homes. If you ask parents today if they treat or raise their sons and daughters differently, many are likely to say "no," claiming to openly reject common gender stereotypes (Freeman, 2007; Kane, 2006). However, studies show that from a very young age girls and boys are handled and spoken to differently (Morrongiello and Hogg, 2004); are differently rewarded or punished for their attention-seeking behaviours (Fagot, 1986); are exposed to different types of toys, clothing, and room décor (Kane, 2006); and are granted different amounts of freedom and responsibility (Ross and Taylor, 1989; Nelson and Robinson, 2002). Kane (2006) found that fathers engage in more differentiated treatment of sons and daughters than do mothers, and for fathers and mothers, boundary enforcement and maintenance of traditionally gendered roles and behaviour are more evident in the treatment of sons than of daughters. Similarly, comparing reactions of mothers and fathers to the risk-taking behaviour of two-year-old sons and daughters, Morrongiello et al. (2010) found few differences between mothers' and fathers' reactions, but reactions varied for sons versus daughters. They found that parent reactions to risk-taking by sons focused on discipline while reactions to the same behaviours by daughters focused on safety; mothers reacted to sons with anger and to daughters with disappointment and surprise. They also found that parents attributed risk-taking to personality for sons and to situation for daughters, and believed that daughters could be taught to comply with safety rules more than sons. Consistent with other research, and despite popular views that gender doesn't matter, results suggest that parents continue to socialize boys and girls differently regarding risk-taking.

These findings were not unlike those in a classic study by John and Sandra Condry (1976), who assessed the effects of labelling on people's behaviour towards newborn infants. Research subjects (adult men and women), after watching an infant, were asked to rate the infant's emotional responses to four different arousing stimuli. Half the subjects were told the infant was a boy and half that it was a girl. Subjects reported seeing different emotions and different levels of emotional arousal depending on the sex attributed to the infant. The same infant's behaviour was interpreted differently depending on what sex the baby was *believed* to be. Furthermore, the subjects—whether male or female—who were highly experienced with infants saw a greater difference between the two groups due to the sex label than inexperienced subjects (Condry and Condry, 1976). The researchers concluded that we judge babies differently depending on their *perceived* sex. We bring gendered expectations to our meeting with the baby and see only what is consistent with these expectations. As a result, we are likely to interact with baby boys and girls differently, based on our expectations and perceptions.

Kane (2006) found that while both mothers and fathers across a variety of social locations—from different racial and class backgrounds—often celebrated what they perceived to be gender nonconformity of their young daughters (playing with trucks and not dolls, for example), heterosexual fathers were more likely to be motivated by hegemonic masculinity and to be less tolerant of some of their sons' nonconformity in this regard.

Children learn gender roles from what parents *say* (intended roles and expectations) and from what they *do* (often unintended). Many studies show that gendered expectations placed on children are more pronounced in families with more gender-typed parenting roles (Lindsey and Caladera, 2006; Tenenbaum and Leaper, 2002; Cunningham, 2001). Not surprisingly, where parents held more traditional roles, we see more differential treatment (Cunningham, 2001). Having said this, we should be reminded that these attitudes and practices, products of the culture in which we live, like culture itself, do change and fluctuate—resulting in considerable variation across families and family types.

Cross-Cultural Diversity in Parenting

As we will see in more detail in Chapter 8, some cultures have different or "non-Western" ideas about how children should be raised while others do not, and these often are reflected in differences in child-rearing ideologies and practices. Studies of parenting in different parts of the world reveal some variations in parenting styles. It was found that Western parents focused more on individualism and independence; for example, children in Western Europe and North America were encouraged to exercise autonomy and maturity earlier in life (Rose et al., 2003). Asian parents were more likely to emphasize traditional Confucian values and collectivist traits, were more directive, and stressed academic achievement (Jose et al., 2000; Helwig et al., 2014). South Asian parents maintained a high level of control over their children and focus was placed on selflessness, social duties, and familial obligations (Rose et al., 2003). A study comparing Canadian mothers in southern Ontario and Chinese mothers in Beijing found that Chinese mothers had higher scores on overall involvement and connectedness in mother–child interactions compared to Canadian mothers (Liu et al., 2005; Liu and Guo, 2010). Consistent with other studies, recent research found Chinese mothers were less **authoritative parenting** and more **authoritarian parenting** (more on this below) than Canadian mothers (Liu and Guo, 2010).

While some studies have uncovered differences across cultures when it comes to parenting styles, others have found similarities instead, and have attributed some differences to social class and socioeconomic status. For example, Emmen et al. (2012) compared beliefs about motherhood among Dutch, Moroccan, and Turkish mothers living in the Netherlands. In their study, 75 mothers with at least one child between the ages of six months and six years described their views about the ideal "sensitive" mother, which were found to be highly similar within and across cultural groups. However, they also found that family income mediated the relationship between ethnic background and sensitivity beliefs, such that mothers from lower-income families had lower sensitivity-belief scores. In other words, their findings suggest that socioeconomic status affects the value that mothers placed on the importance of sensitivity when it comes to mothering.

For many minority and immigrant parents, maintaining their ethno-cultural heritage was a central part of child-rearing and parenting (Brown et al., 2007; Aycan and Kanungo, 1998). We will explore this in more detail in Chapter 8.

Social Class and Parenting

Researchers have argued that some of the variation in parental expectations surrounding childhood socialization is the result of social class differences in parenting styles. For example, in a classic study, Melvin Kohn (1977) found that working-class parents, due to the nature of their work lives and experiences, tended to stress conformity, neatness, obedience, and orderliness in their children. In contrast, middle-class parents placed more emphasis on their children's independence, self-reliance, and autonomy. They were also seen as more permissive in their parenting, while working-class parents were more likely to stress stricter discipline. More recent research has found similar differences across social classes that also were believed to be affected by the nature of parents' work (Lareau, 2000) and the **cultural capital** or symbolic capital—the social know-how of socially approved or valued practices, social status, and prestige—with which parents equip their children (Bourdieu and Passeron, 1977).

Annette Lareau compared parenting styles of middle- and working-class American parents with children 7 to 10 years of age. She found that middle-class children spent more time engaging in adult-organized activities that stressed public performance and skills development. In contrast, working-class children spent more time on informal play, visiting kin, and "hanging out" (Lareau, 2000). Lareau (2003) argues that middle-class parents used a *concerted cultivation model* of parenting, while working-class parents adopted a *natural growth model* (also see Yi-Ping and Chin-Chun, 2014; Cheadle and Amato, 2011).

Lareau explains that the concerted cultivation model of middle-class parenting involves the deliberate cultivation of the children's talents in order to optimize their position in school, sports, etc., and ultimately in their careers. She found family life was organized around the child's school and extra-curricular activities, and that the many extracurricular activities were chosen for their educational value and took precedence over "kin time." Parents encouraged their child's verbal fluency via conversation with adults, while sibling relations were more acrimonious. In contrast, the natural growth model of working-class parents is less concerted and less focused on optimizing children's talents. Instead, this model concentrated on the accomplishment of natural growth, in that parents provide care and safeguards for their children with less emphasis on external organized activities (Lareau, 2003). Lareau found the working-class model was characterized by a greater separation of child and adult spheres, and there was more free-flowing time for kids to create their own activities at their own pace. Parents stressed stricter discipline, more physical punishment, and expected more obedience and respect. Children developed verbal fluency from their peers, but they also had more frequent and closer contact with kin of all generations, and sibling relations tended to be close and cordial. Researchers like Val Gillies (2005), however, warn us not to pass judgment or jump to conclusions about the universality of "successful" middle-class parents and "inadequate" working-class parents.[2] Similarly Holloway and Pimlott-Wilson's (2014) analysis and critique of parenting classes suggest that parenting classes are part of a professionalization of parenting that has sought to impose middle-class mores on working-class parents. They argue that there is a distinct class bias inherent in the wider professionalization of parenting, which reflects both opportunities and challenges to families of different class backgrounds.

In many cases, middle-class parents were not only granting a certain economic capital to their children, but cultural capital as well, to allow their children to successfully navigate modern, Western capitalist economies and societies (Lareau, 2000, 2003). This was especially true of middle-class parents' dealings with the school system. Thus, Weininger and Lareau (2003) find that while not all middle-class parents are equally assertive, they tend to talk more, wield educational authority discourse more effectively, and more overtly challenge the authority of teachers than do working-class parents. As a result, middle-class parents are able to manipulate the educational system to a greater extent in advocating on behalf of their children to gain more individualized academic attention for them. In sum, middle-class parents not only had the economic resources (for tutors, computers, study space, trips, etc.) that advantaged their children, but had the social status, authority, and knowledge of the dominant discourse or cultural capital, as well. Some have argued that parents' income, however, in and of itself, does not have a significant impact on child outcomes, but that parenting styles, in contrast, do (Dooley and Stewart, 2005).

Parenting Styles and Child Outcomes

A recent study found that child outcomes, such as a child's adjustment, grades, and behaviour, are positively associated with support and negatively associated with harsh punishment, and this did not vary significantly by families' race, class, level of education, or structure (Amato and Fowler, 2002). Their results suggest that early parental monitoring and support, and not the parents' race, ethnicity, education, income level, etc., may help to prevent children from developing potentially troubling or dangerous behaviours later on. Similarly, a study by Pratt et al. (2001) found a positive relationship between mothers' **authoritative parenting** style[3] (involving high levels of acceptance and responsiveness and high levels of control over children) and more positive, optimistic views of adolescent behaviour (also see Chen, 2014; Watabe and Hibbard, 2014). Mothers' positive views in turn helped them embrace some autonomy-fostering practices used with adolescents. In other words, the more responsive and engaged they were as parents, the more positive they felt about their children, which in turn helped them to adopt more positive parenting practices—a kind of reciprocal or ripple effect. The impact of fathers' attitudes and behaviour was found to be less consistent (Pratt et al., 2001).

Another study found that mothers whose parenting style was labelled as authoritative by their own and their children's assessment also showed greater endorsement of children's nurturance rights (the idea that children should be cared for and protected by parents) compared with mothers who were **authoritarian** (low levels of acceptance and responsiveness and high levels of control) or **uninvolved** (low on responsiveness and low on expectations or control) (Day et al., 2006). Positive parenting attitudes, at least in mothers, seem to lead to positive outcomes in children, particularly in their views towards their mothers and in their behaviours.

A Canadian study of close to 3,000 children (ages 2–11) from 96 different Canadian neighbourhoods found that children had high levels of physical aggression and lower prosocial behaviour in families where more **punitive parenting** (highly disciplinary parenting) was used (Romano et al., 2005). Similar results were found in a Statistics Canada study by Eleanor Thomas (2004). Punitive parenting is also more likely to lead to abuse (see Chapter 12). However, it should be noted that change is possible and the children of parents whose parenting practices changed from punitive to non-punitive eight years later scored just as low in aggressive behaviour as children living in an environment where parenting was not punitive when children were younger (Statistics Canada, 2005a).

Let us keep in mind that often much of the literature on parenting and child outcomes focuses on the values, views, and behaviour of individual parents; however (to return to a point raised earlier in the chapter), much of what parents think and do results from their own experiences and the changing social context in which they live. As a result, when parents raise children, they tend to reflect and reproduce, or consciously attempt to counter, larger and changing social values and norms.

Same-Sex Parenting and Socialization

Since the 1980s there has been growing attention placed on same-sex parents—either in efforts to show how "normal" they can be or to closely monitor and "test" their parenting abilities. Some of the earlier studies of same-sex parenting and lesbian mothers in particular have found that the non-supportive social milieu in which they exist is one of the major factors distinguishing lesbian families from other families (Nelson, 1996), and despite legal changes in the definition of families, little seems to have changed on this front (Short, 2007; Suter et al., 2008). Some people have concerns regarding the children of same-sex parents. Ambert (2006) and others have explained that these concerns are often linked to the unsubstantiated fears that children will grow up to be psychologically maladjusted, that they will be molested by their parents or parent's partners, and that they will become homosexual themselves. None of these concerns have been supported by the research (ibid.).

In fact, a recent UK study comparing 41 gay father families, 40 lesbian mother families, and 49 heterosexual parent families with an adopted child three to nine years of age, through standardized interview and observational and questionnaire measures of parental well-being, quality of parent-child relationships, child adjustment, and child sex-typed behaviour found more positive parental well-being and parenting in gay father families compared with heterosexual parent families (Golombok et al., 2014). The study found that child externalizing problems (acting out, for example) were actually greater among children in heterosexual families; however, it was family process variables and particularly parenting stress, rather than family type that were found to be predictive of child externalizing problems (Golombok et al., 2014).

Studies have also shown that there are no significant differences between children raised by gay or lesbian parents and children raised by heterosexual parents on measures of intelligence, school performance, peer relations, personality characteristics, social development, emotional adjustment, or behaviour problems (Wainright et al., 2004; Tasker, 2001; Bigner, 1999; Patterson, 1996; Flaks et al., 1995; Green et al., 1986). There are no significant differences in the likelihood of their children becoming gay or lesbian (Patterson, 2006; Wainright et al., 2004; Golombok et al., 2003; Patterson, 1996; Bailey et al., 1995; Green et al., 1986). Often, because of stigma and intolerance, same-sex couples who have children create a network of "chosen" family for social and emotional support (Short, 2007; Ambert, 2006). Yet, studies have found no significant differences in family stability, parenting skills and abilities, and the value they place on children (Short, 2007; Bos et al., 2004; Golombok et al., 2003; Siegenthaler and Bigner, 2000; Bigner, 1999; Flaks et al., 1995; Bigner and Jacobson, 1989a, 1989b). In fact, some go a long way to "do family" through creating and supporting family rituals and positive identity (Suter et al., 2008).

Social attitudes seem to be changing and possibly improving when it comes to acceptance of LGBTQ families; however, Taylor (2009) warns that we should be cautious of the framing of contemporary "normative gayness" as middle class, which inevitably marginalizes the experiences of working-class LGBTQ families with children. Taylor explores the difference that class makes in accessing, claiming, and gaining a respectable "homonormative status" when parenting. Taylor's work also helps us to move beyond simplified or decontextualized academic literature that compares children of LGBTQ parents to those of heterosexual families, as not moving beyond such work runs the risk of glossing over other types of potential exclusions, nuances, and sets of lived experiences of children and their families (see Epstein, 2009).

Summary

The roles of parents—motherhood, fatherhood—and child-rearing itself have been transformed by the changing nature of work, family structures, and size. As women, as a group, have been pulled out of and back into the labour force, ideas about mothering and motherhood have changed. With women's increasing involvement in the labour force, men's fathering roles were and continue to be transformed as well. But with these changes, we see changes in our ideas about parenting—in terms of how it should happen, the forms it takes, and the role children themselves play in the process. We have noted both consistency and change in gender socialization; variations and similarities occurring across cultures; and differences and similarities between working-class and middle-class families and between heterosexual and same-sex families. Primarily, children learn a great deal about who they are and are expected to become, starting at a very early age, through their parents. But parents are shaped by their children, too, and by the larger social context or environment that they inhabit. In the chapters to come, we will see the role that other individuals, social groups, institutions, and organizations play, sometimes complementing and other times at odds with what takes place in the home.

Questions for Critical Thought

1. Do you think there is less pressure today than in the past on children to conform to traditional gender stereotypes? Is this true for both girls and boys equally? What do you think accounts for continuity or change on this matter over time?

2. Did you experience intensive parenting when you were growing up? How do you think its presence or absence has affected your life? What do you think intensive parenting will do to and for children growing up today?

3. How much control do you think parents really have over determining how their children will "turn out"? What other people, institutions, or things play a role in shaping both parenting practices and child outcomes?

4. You become a parent (congratulations!). How much say or autonomy will you give your two-year-old child when it comes to making decisions about everyday things (clothes, activities, food, etc.)? What about your four-year-old? Your seven-year-old? Your 10-year-old? Reflecting back on the UN Convention on the Rights of the Child, when is the right time to start allowing children to make choices on their own? Is this important to you as a parent? Why or why not?

Suggested Readings

Doucet, Andrea. 2006. *Do Men Mother?* Toronto: University of Toronto Press. This award-winning book uses interviews and focus groups with 118 fathers to question and challenge the enduring gendered structuring of our society and to criticize a body of literature grounded in white, middle-class families' experiences around parenting and family relations.

Faircloth, Charlotte, Diane Hoffman, and Linda Layne, eds. 2013. *Parenting in Global Perspective: Negotiating Ideologies of Kinship, Self and Politics.* New York: Routledge. This collection includes an introduction outlining changing parenting roles and responsibilities between the 1960s and 2013. It has chapters on parenthood in a time of ecological crisis (in Scotland), on "supernannies" in the United Kingdom, on parenting and power inequalities of undocumented migrants in the southern United States, on refugee parents, on breastfeeding and attachment in London and Paris, on Ethiopian adoptive children, on resistance to intensive mothering in Spain, and on mothering and postpartum depression in Brazil (among others).

Spock, Benjamin. 2004 [1946]. *Baby and Child Care,* 8th edn. New York: Pocket Books. For several generations, parents across the world have relied on the advice of Dr Benjamin Spock. By the time of his death, in 1998, the book had sold tens of millions of copies in close to 40 different languages. While controversial and highly debated, this book, many times revised, contains advice on breastfeeding, the physical care of children, raising nonviolent children (socialization), and most recently, same-sex parenting.

Taylor, Yvette. 2009. *Lesbian and Gay Parenting: Securing Social and Educational Capital.* New York: Palgrave Macmillan. This book explores the intersections between class and sexuality in gays' and lesbians' experiences with parenting. Among other things, it investigates initial routes into parenting, household divisions of labour, schooling choice, and community supports.

Websites

Canadian Association of Family Resource Programs (FRP Canada)
www.frp.ca/
FRP Canada promotes the well-being of families by providing national leadership, consultation, and resources to those who care for children and support families. They have launched a website for parents, ParentsMatter.ca, and provide access to "Making Choices: Parenting Program Inventory." The site also contains links to parent resource

sheets on a range of topics, with some resources available in multilingual formats. It also includes a long list of links to other parenting websites across Canada and in other parts of the world.

Family Service Association of Toronto (FSA)
www.fsatoronto.com/
The FSA in Toronto has as its mandate to promote the well-being of vulnerable and disadvantaged children, newcomers, individuals, and families, and helps people with a variety of life challenges, assisting families and individuals through counselling, community development, advocacy, and public education programs. The FSA website provides access to policies, laws, resources, fact sheets, research reports, social services, etc.

Family Services Ontario
www.familyserviceontario.org/
Family Service Ontario offers help to residents in nearly all communities across the province. It provides access to a wide range of services and programs on a range of issues including relationship counselling, financial management, mental health and addictions, domestic violence and abuse, support for LGBTQ families, etc.

Growing Healthy Canadians
www.growinghealthykids.com/
Growing Healthy Canadians: A Guide for Positive Child Development was created to promote and illustrate the idea that the healthy development of children and youth is a shared responsibility. This guide offers a unique perspective on how best to promote the well-being of young people.

LGBTQ Parenting Connection
www.lgbtqparentingconnection.ca/home.cfm
The LGBTQ Parenting Network promotes the rights and well-being of lesbian, gay, bisexual, trans, and queer parents and prospective parents, as well as their families and children through education, research, outreach, and community organizing.

Public Health Agency of Canada—Parenting Resources and Support
www.phac-aspc.gc.ca/hp-ps/dca-dea/parent/support/index-eng.php
This site provides information for parents regarding different health concerns and issues for different stages of life and development. It provides resources to parents on a wide range of topics including father involvement, family—community supports, spanking, etc.

5 Schooling and Peer Groups

Learning Objectives

◎ To learn about the structure and state of Canada's elementary school systems.

◎ To briefly survey the history of Canada's public education.

◎ To review competing theories of education.

◎ To think about similarities, differences, and overlaps among competing theories.

◎ To critically assess the notion of meritocracy and the idea of the "level playing field."

◎ To assess the role and importance of peers in children's learning and development.

◎ To consider what the future of Canada's elementary school systems might be like.

Introduction

Canada has one of the most highly educated populations in the world, particularly since the 1990s (Organisation for Economic Co-operation and Development [OECD], 2013). On the down side, public funding for all levels of education in Canada accounted for 76 per cent of total funding to education in 2009, considerably lower than the 84 per cent average among OECD countries. Canada also had one of the least generously publicly funded post-secondary education systems among OECD nations, making it one of the countries with the highest post-secondary tuition (OECD, 2013). Canada ranks significantly worse—18 out of 38—when access to primary education is considered (OECD, 2013). In this chapter we will review what is happening to and in Canada's public elementary education system(s). While all of Canada's children are expected to attend some type of formal schooling, we will consider how Canada's children fare.

Table 5.1 Access to Education

Indicator	Canada	OECD Average
Enrolment rates	2010	2011
3-year-olds (ECE)	1%	67%
4-year-olds (ECE and primary school)	48%	84%
5–14-year-olds (all levels)[a]	99%	99%

[a]Canada ranks 18 of 38 in primary school enrolment among OECD and G20 countries.

Source: OECD (2013: 3).

In this chapter we will briefly look at how elementary school education is organized in Canada, noting that many of the current structures reflect historical trends and features. As a result, the development of public education in Canada's past will be examined. From there we will consider some competing theories about the role and importance of education in shaping the lives and identities of Canada's children. Once in school, children are influenced not only by these formal structures and hierarchies, but also by enduring and highly influential relationships with peers who often shape or mediate the way in which school is experienced. We will see what Canadian research tells us about the effect of peers on children. The chapter concludes with some speculation on what the future may hold for Canada's elementary schools and students.

The Current State of Affairs

In the 2011–12 school year, there were just over five million students enrolled in elementary and secondary public school programs in Canada, down 0.4 per cent compared with the year before. Between 2007–8 and 2011–12, the number of young Canadians enrolled in an elementary or secondary public school decreased year over year (Statistics Canada, 2013a). Only Manitoba, Saskatchewan, Alberta, and Nunavut registered gains in enrolment, while all other provinces experienced significant drops year over year. Because school attendance is compulsory up until the age of 16 years in most parts of the country, and up until the age of 18 in New Brunswick and Ontario (unless they graduate before then), these changes simply reflect demographic trends, including declining birth rates, immigration, and internal migrations (Statistics Canada, 2007c). For the last few decades, immigration to major Canadian cities like Toronto, Vancouver, and Montreal have kept enrolments growing in their respective provinces; however, economic downturns in those provinces coupled with booming economies in the Prairies have affected school enrolment trends. Today, internal migrations, most often for economic reasons, have resulted in the transfer of families with school-aged children from provinces such as Newfoundland and Labrador to Alberta (Blouin and Courchesne, 2007).

While student enrolment rates decreased slightly overall, the number of educators employed in public education registered a slight increase. In 2009–10, there were 337,600 educators in Canada, up 0.5 per cent from the previous year. As a result, the national student-to-educator ratio continued its decade-long decline, reaching 14.0 students per educator (Statistics Canada, 2011). Only one year later, in 2010–11, the number and percentage of educators dropped in about half the provinces, reducing the number of educators by 0.2 per cent across the country (Statistics Canada, 2013b). Despite this, the student-to-educator ratio for Canada dropped again to 13.8 (Statistics Canada, 2013b).

The total expenditure of public elementary and secondary school in Canada in 2010–11 was $59.1 billion, up from the $49.9 billion in 2006–7. This amounted to $12,557 per student annually, up from $10,321 in 2006–7 (Statistics Canada, 2013b). With respect to all these figures, we should keep in mind that considerable variation occurs across provinces and territories, in part due to economic and social circumstances within and across provinces, but also because education is under provincial jurisdiction, and decisions affecting education, including funding, generally occur at the provincial level.

Canada's 10 provinces and three territories (13 jurisdictions) have responsibility for their own educational system and policies. Preschool programs and kindergartens are operated by local educational authorities to provide one or two years of pre–Grade 1 education, and each province and territory has a ministry or department of education responsible for elementary and secondary education (Statistics Canada, 1996a). Public education[1] is provided "free" to all children who are citizens or permanent residents until about the age of 18, and school attendance is compulsory, although the age range of mandatory attendance varies from jurisdiction to jurisdiction. Children with special needs are accommodated in various fashions—in separate programs or in integrated classrooms—depending on the jurisdiction. The transition between elementary and secondary school also varies by jurisdiction, as school boards break up the elementary–secondary school continuum differently: kindergarten to Grade 8, then Grades 9 to 12, or kindergarten to Grade 6, then Grades 7 to 9 (junior high), and finally Grades 10 to 12; in Quebec, secondary school ends at Grade 11 (ibid.). But no matter how the present grades are divided, Randall Collins (2006) reminds us that this age-graded schooling system is a recent invention, as in the past, schools had pupils ranging in age from 10 to older than 20, all reciting the same lesson. In fact, he explains that our current age consciousness was developed in large part because of the construction of age-graded schools (Collins, 2006). Today, in Canada, many of these age-graded variations are the result of negotiations and power-sharing agreements between the federal and provincial governments, which took place around the time of Confederation in 1867.

Historical Overview of Public Education in Canada

When we speak of the history of public education in Canada, we must remind ourselves that we are really talking about *histories*. We will touch upon only some of these histories, but each province and territory has had its unique struggles, cast of characters, and developmental trajectories, some with regional variations and characteristics,[2] urban–rural diversity, religious and other cultural clashes and compromises,[3] and unique economic and social challenges.[4] There have also been other variations, some along cultural lines, including the "special" treatment of Aboriginal children and the experiences of French Canadians within and outside Quebec. As a result, the histories of public education in Canada are complex, political, and sometimes highly problematic.

One of the most common historical accounts of the introduction of public education in what became Canada (then Upper Canada/Canada West) dates back to the early nineteenth century and the work of John Strachan and Egerton Ryerson. The Scottish Anglican Bishop, John Strachan, for example, was involved in the establishment of "common" schools in what is now Ontario (then Upper Canada). Working-class common schools, which emphasized learning by rote and appropriate behaviour—punctuality, neatness, obedience, Christian precepts, etc.—were set up in contrast to the already established "grammar schools" for the upper classes, which emphasized "the classics" (Latin and Greek language and literature), English language and literature, and maths and natural science.

In 1846, as chief superintendent of education in Upper Canada, Egerton Ryerson sought to reduce the Anglican influence on schooling through the introduction of secular, tax-supported, "free" public education for the masses, regulated by a centralized department of education. The Common Schools Act of 1865 provided free, nonsectarian public education, which authorized the appointment of school masters, a superintendent, and a board of education to establish school districts, appoint teachers, set curricula, prescribe textbooks, etc. But by then, separate schools for Protestants and Catholics had also been officially sanctioned since 1839 under the Durham Report. Ryerson brought separate and common/public schools together, under state control, which then became incorporated as such into the Constitution Act of 1867, also known as the British North America (BNA) Act, when Canada became a country.

Section 93 of the BNA Act, Canada's founding constitutional document, made education the sole responsibility of the provinces and established guarantees to public education in the religion of one's choice, which was Protestant or Catholic at the time. We did not then, nor do we now, have a federal department of education. In 1867, the four provinces that made up Canada (Ontario, Quebec, Nova Scotia, and New Brunswick) each had their own distinct elementary and secondary school systems for Protestants and Catholics, paid for through local property taxes. As other provinces joined Confederation, they adopted much the same approach, except Manitoba, which in 1890 revoked the right to have publicly funded separate schools (which was especially displeasing to the province's large French Catholic minority).

French Catholic education has had a somewhat different, complex, and unique history (for developments in western Quebec, see Bouvier, 2002).

For example, a relatively large number of French Catholic schools were run by nuns and priests from the earliest settlements in New France, where there were schools for girls even before there was one for boys (Dumont et al., 1987). With the French defeat by the English in 1759, the French retained the right to their religion and language. For nearly two centuries, the Roman Catholic Church maintained strict control over education, among many other aspects of Québécois society (McRoberts, 1988). The 1960s and the Quiet Revolution ushered in a period of dramatic change in Quebec, marked by increased secularization, the restriction of Catholic domination of public and private life, and an increased demand for and importance being placed on French-language higher education. This period also was marked by heightened nationalist sentiment among Quebecers, with French-language education and use a central bone of contention (Stevenson, 2006).

Another turbulent area in Canadian history is linked to First Nations education. To this day, the education of Canada's First Nations stands separate from the education of other children and remains under federal jurisdiction and control, though in recent decades many Aboriginal bands have gained complete or partial control over education within their communities. Even before the federal government and bureaucracy controlled Aboriginal education, Aboriginal children were the target of "special" educational drives by European settlers and various religious orders, often aimed at assimilating and Christianizing Aboriginal populations (see Barman, 2003). Aboriginal children encountered very different circumstances, depending on the settler nation that conquered them, the religious order in the region, and the indigenous group itself. Nonetheless, the ultimate goal of the government was the same—forced assimilation. One of the vehicles eventually adopted in the 1800s was the residential school system.[5] Sadly, Egerton Ryerson's belief in the creation of a different and separate system of education for Aboriginal children influenced the establishment of what became the Indian Residential School system that has devastated First Nations peoples across Canada. While Ryerson did not implement or oversee Indian Residential Schools, his ideas were used to create their blueprint. Its brutal legacy remains to this day (Royal Commission on Aboriginal People, 1996; see also Chapter 9).

With the exception of Aboriginal peoples, who are still under federal jurisdiction for historical reasons, and because of economic, cultural, and other social differences, it was believed that each province would best be positioned to design and administer educational policy to suit the needs of their populations and economies. As a result, Canada has a fragmented and highly diverse set of educational practices, with decision-making remaining highly decentralized at the national level, but highly centralized within each province (Barakett and Cleghorn, 2008).

Theories on the Role and Impact of Education on Children

Throughout the 1950s and into the 1970s, structural functionalism emerged as a dominant school of thought in North American sociology and the sociology of education in particular (Taylor, 1994). Functionalists generally assume that society is like a living organism—a self-regulating and stable system of interrelated parts that work together for the proper functioning of the whole. A society's institutions, including the educational system, are in place to fulfill specific social needs and functions vital to social survival and equilibrium or to a stable social order. In Western societies, stable order includes democracy and **meritocracy** (the granting of opportunity and rewards based on skill and ability rather than status—i.e., *achievement* rather than *ascription*—and the school system is in place to foster these (Taylor, 1994). Schools also have *manifest* (intended, obvious) and *latent* (unintended, hidden) functions, including the transmission of knowledge and culture (norms and values), and the provision of opportunities for social mobility and social networking.

Talcott Parsons, like Davis and Moore (1945),[6] was a proponent of functionalism who outlined, directly and indirectly, the functions of education. For example, Parsons (1975) argued that education is an important agent of socialization that works to promote our achieved status—the idea that we are judged on merit and hard work. In other words, schools operate on and teach us about meritocratic principles or "earned difference" based on ability and effort and are places where everyone is granted equal opportunity to succeed on a level playing field. While ensuring that everyone has access to the same opportunities, the best students—the hardest working and most skilled—will emerge to perform the most important jobs, with the highest rewards, to the overall benefit of society. So for Parsons, schools instill the values of achievement and equality of opportunity (i.e., everyone has an equal chance to succeed). He also argued that schools perform the function of role allocation—preparing students for their future places in life—by matching inherent talents to the jobs for which the students are best suited. He, like other functionalist theorists of education, saw the assignment of different rewards to various positions in society as a necessary technique to motivate talented individuals to achieve high-status positions (Barakett and Cleghorn, 2008). This theoretical approach, while seeming logical from some standpoints, has met considerable criticism, as we will see below.

Conflict Theories of Education

During the 1970s a number of critiques of functionalist approaches emerged, particularly from conflict theorists who argued that society is not in a balanced or ordered state and certainly not a meritocracy. Conflict theorists have instead argued that societies are built on struggles for power, wealth, prestige, and control, and those in power also tend to control institutions like schools to promote their interests and goals.

Bowles and Gintis (1976), for example, tried to show that the fundamental structure of schools is not meritocratic, but a tool for shaping minds and bodies for capitalist purposes—to create obedient, docile workers or to generally fit into the capitalist economic niche in which they are expected and needed. Both the formal and hidden curriculum, they argued, aimed to reinforce the existing class structure, despite the fact that some individual teachers were highly committed to equality. But Holloway and Pimlott-Wilson (2014), like others, have noted that despite what happens at the individual level, neoliberal states are increasingly seeking to shape the development of future citizen-workers in new and expanded ways.

To challenge the notion of meritocracy, Bowles and Gintis showed that IQ scores had a very low correlation with earnings, but family background was a substantial determinant of income in adulthood, even for those who shared similar IQ scores. In other words, they showed that it is not how much one knows, but rather the family one comes from that helps determine one's place later in life. Education is simply a vehicle for maintaining a stratified system that only *appears* to provide equality of opportunity, success, and rewards. Pierre Bourdieu explained how this was possible.

Bourdieu argued that the language, texts, other resources, and practices (curriculum and pedagogy) used in schools reflect the interests, values, and tastes of the dominant power group (Bourdieu and Passeron, 1977). He added that children of the elite acquire most of the valued ideas and resources—**cultural capital**—long before entering and outside of the formal school system (as we saw in Chapter 4). If this is indeed so, schools do not function on meritocratic principles, with equality of opportunity, as there is no such thing as a level playing field from the onset. Elite and middle-class students enter school having already acquired an understanding of what is expected of them (middle-class values = cultural capital) and are then evaluated by middle-class standards—inevitably "succeeding" where working-class children are more likely to fail, or will need to work disproportionately harder.

Richard Rothstein (2004) studied American schools and found that, in early childhood, children of lower social classes exhibited more anti-social behaviour than did children from higher social classes. He went on to explain why, noting that middle-class children scored higher on ability tests because they knew how to predict and to provide the expected "right" answer rather than the truthful answer. Like Bourdieu, Rothstein found that middle-class children would know what was expected of them to have learned in their middle-class homes. Middle-class values are reinforced and rewarded at school and later rewarded in the workplace. In other words, parental economic resources, and parents' levels of education shaped child outcomes rather than the individual child's personal effort or ability.

Myth of the Level Playing Field in the Canadian (Public) Elementary School Context

Despite the fact that elementary school education is "free" (publicly funded) in Canada, children from families with low income continue to be at a disadvantage in a number of ways. A group of Grade 4 and 5 students from North Bay, Ontario, reported that poverty is "feeling ashamed when my dad can't get a job"; "pretending that you forgot your lunch"; "being afraid to tell your Mom you need gym shoes"; "not buying books at the book fair"; and "not getting to go on school trips" (Canadian Teachers' Federation, 2008: 2). The Canadian Teachers' Federation has found that many children from low-income families experienced reduced motivation to learn, delayed cognitive development, lower achievement, less participation in extracurricular activities, lower career aspirations, interrupted school attendance, an increased risk of illiteracy, and higher drop out rates. All of this has been confirmed by Statistics Canada's analysis of nine-year-old children's readiness to learn, which was found to be correlated with level of household income (Thomas, 2009; see Figure 5.1).

Thomas (2006; 2009) found that children in lower- and higher-income households differed in several measures of readiness to learn. She found that children from very low-income households tended to have lower achievement than children from more affluent homes on most measures, but many of these differences were not large enough to reach statistical significance (Thomas, 2009). Thomas found that a higher percentage of children from very low-income households repeated a grade compared with children from more affluent backgrounds. Thomas (2009) also reported that more children from very low-income households had parents who reported that their children were not doing well at school compared with parents of children from higher-income households. In her earlier analysis

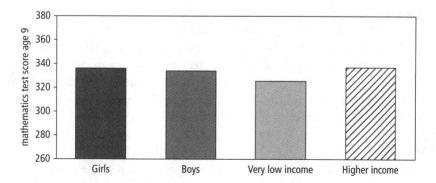

Figure 5.1 Mean Mathematics Test Score at Age 9 (Grade 3) for Girls and Boys from Lower-Income versus Higher-Income Families
Source: Thomas (2009: 13).

of five-year-olds, Thomas (2006) found that receptive vocabulary scores, communication skills, number knowledge, and copying and symbol use scores were affected by things like daily reading, positive parent-child interactions, participation in organized sports, lessons in physical activity, and lessons in the arts, all of which were affected by family socioeconomic status. In other words, it is not that parents in low-income families did not want their children to succeed, or did not understand that children need certain things to succeed, but rather they lacked the resources to assist them. Looking back to when these children were three years of age, Thomas (2006) found that the higher the income level, the higher the percentage of children who participated in one or more early childhood education activities. By the time a child entered elementary school, she or he was typically already advantaged or disadvantaged compared with other children because of the parents' socioeconomic status (see Tremblay et al.'s 2001 study of Grade 3 standardized test scores for similar results).

Differences in educational outcomes of children from diverse socioeconomic backgrounds have been well documented both in Canada and internationally (Brooks-Gunn and Duncan, 1997; Elliot, 2013; Kohen and Guèvremont, 2014; McEwen and Stewart, 2014; Thomas, 2006, 2009; Tremblay et al., 2001). It is abundantly clear that Canadian children are not stepping into the elementary school system on equal footing and, as a result, have lower success rates and rates of school completion, affecting their life chances into adulthood (Brooks-Gunn and Duncan, 1997).

The Canadian Teachers' Federation (2008, 2014), citing a number of sources, has argued for a multipronged approach to remedying the negative relationship between poverty and school outcomes, which includes school-based policies (inclusive curriculum, improved staffing, reduced class size, professional development, more school resource personnel, improved school budgets, and broader community connections to coordinate recreation and social service delivery) as well as broader social and economic policies (universal child care, investment in social housing, improved health care, increased minimum wages, labour market protection, and fairness). They explain that one set of reforms (school-based policies) without the other (broader social and economic policies) will be insufficient. Implementing such changes would go a long way towards levelling the playing field. We should also keep in mind, however, that other inequalities, based on (dis)ability,[7] race,[8] and gender contribute to an uneven playing field.

Gender and Education

According to Thomas (2009), gender differences in achievement are evident from kindergarten to university. Somewhat surprisingly, in Canada, and as in other jurisdictions, Grade 3 girls have been found to outperform boys in reading and writing in standardized tests and in school achievement, while in mathematics, differences are small or nonexistent (Thomas, 2009). Today, women outnumber men in undergraduate university enrolment, particularly in the social sciences and humanities, but this clearly was not the case even a few decades ago. If you look back a few centuries, it was not uncommon for scholars to argue that women were unfit for formal education,[9] citing biological reasons like women's wombs controlling their minds.[10] We may have come a long way, particularly after feminists of several generations have fought to have women gain access to formal education, but in the elementary school years, children's formal and casual encounters are still gendered and often separated by sex (Lesnick, 2005), to the point that it is almost "meaningful to speak of separate girls' and boys' worlds" (Thorne, 1990: 61). However, according to Thorne (1990, 1993), differences between girls and boys often are exaggerated, their similarities ignored, and the amount and nature of cross-gender play, even in reinforcing gender stereotypes and differences, are often unrecognized. And while Thorne (1993) reminds us to do otherwise, we typically resort to simple dichotomies and dualities, with teachers, organizational structures, and students themselves continuing to create different types of opportunities and barriers for boys and girls (see Sadker and Sadker, 1991; Lesnick, 2005).

Connell (2010: 611) notes that schools and school systems have embedded gender politics in their curricula, their organization, their routines, and their community relations, so that even when individual teachers do not use gender as a basis for sorting children into groups when organizing activities, children segregate themselves along gender lines in lunchrooms and playgrounds. For example, a study of barriers to recess physical activities involving focus groups with 111 fourth graders at 17 different schools found that there were both intergender and intragender differences in the perception of these barriers (Pawlowski, et al., 2014). While weather was discussed as a barrier by both girls and boys, conflicts with peers were perceived as a barrier by those boys who played ball games. Girls, on the other hand, said that they would like to have more secluded areas added to the school playground, even in large schoolyards where lack of space was not a barrier. In line with gender-stereotyped behaviour, girls requested more "hanging-out" facilities, while boys wanted activity-promoting facilities.

Recent research reminds us that masculinities and femininities come into being as people interact and relate, and are often much more complex than we anticipate rather than simply a series of dualisms (Connell, 2000; 2010). Connell (2010) reminds us that there is a powerful process of regulation happening through the use of such dualisms, which obliterates differences within categories and marginalizes other key issues including intersections of race, class, and gender.

Along the same lines, Swain (2005) argued that although there are two complementary gendered cultures sharing the one overall school world, these cultures are further nuanced by social class and race or ethnicity. Swain noted that the most common reaction at the elementary school level by boys about girls was one of detachment and disinterest, particularly in the private, elite elementary school under study. Swain found that children in the "upper-class" private school in the study had little interaction across genders, with few positive feelings for each other. In contrast, in the working-class school in the study, children engaged in more integrated play and more boys genuinely liked those girls who were most like themselves.[11] Despite differences along class lines, Swain (2005) found that many girls refused to be dominated by boys and some deliberately exercised power over them.

Like Swain, Gilbert and Gilbert (1998) refused to treat boys as a uniform demographic group despite popular press reporting of boys as such.[12] They, however, noted that while girls are often encouraged to resist traditional roles, boys rarely are encouraged to do the same, especially in school settings. They state that because schools are in place to reproduce rules, roles, routines, and relationships, "[g]ender is pervasively and powerfully implicated in this shaping" (ibid., 114). Gilbert and Gilbert examined school organization, management, and symbolism, finding all of these, for the most part, competitive, authoritarian, hierarchical, and gendered; they also found that specific school interventions often restrict the range of acceptable versions of masculinity from which boys can construct male identities. For example, the amount of attention schools pay to disciplining boys for aggressive behaviour—which may not actually work to curb boys' aggression—should be supplanted with opportunities that enable boys to select identities that make sense to them from among the many forms masculinity may take. Gilbert and Gilbert also note that schools consciously and unconsciously model hegemonic masculinity. This is likely contributing to why girls outperform boys in primary and secondary school settings. But Connell (2010: 612) notes that contemporary gender orders contain multiple structures that are frequently contradictory. This may help us understand why, despite the fact that girls outperform boys, Sherman and Zurbriggen (2014) found that girls still reported that boys could do significantly more occupations than they could, especially when they considered male-dominated careers. To combat such barriers and to move closer to gender justice for all children, clearly more can and should be done in the very earliest years of formal schooling, if not sooner.

Children with Disabilities Accessing the Educational System

Globally, the percentage of children under the age of 14 living with a disability has been estimated at about 5 per cent according to the World Health Organization (Kowalchuk and Crompton, 2009). In Canada, in 2006, the Participation and Activity Limitation Survey (PALS) identified about 125,000 children ages 5 to 14—or about 4 per cent of children in this age group, who lived with their parents, who had disabilities (Kowalchuk and Crompton, 2009). The types of disabilities these children had covered a wide range of physical and non-physical limitations, with the most common types being learning disabilities (71 per cent); chronic physical limitations, such as diabetes, asthma, or heart disease (62 per cent); speech conditions (46 per cent; and chronic non-physical limitations, such as autism or attention deficit disorder (42 per cent). Almost two-thirds (65 per cent) of children with disabilities in Canada were boys (Kowalchuk and Crompton, 2009). As we noted earlier in the chapter, educational policies vary widely across provinces, yet share a basic commitment to ensuring education for all students, including children with disabilities. Canadian public schools are legally required to ensure that all students receive free and appropriate education. Over the past several decades, there has been significant growth in the integrated school system within Canada, where, in previous generations, many children would have been educated in segregated settings or denied an education entirely. Nonetheless, each province and territory, school jurisdiction within any one province, and even individual schools within each jurisdiction often vary in their decisions about which children will receive special education and how these children will have their unique educational needs met (Kohen et al., 2008). Policy differences include differences in the criteria used to determine the services for which children are eligible, in the services provided to children with similar disabilities, and in the allocation of resources for providing these services (Kohen et al., 2008).

As a result, about half of parents who completed the PALS reported having experienced difficulty in obtaining special education for their child regardless of the type of disability or level of severity (Kohen et al., 2008; Kowalchuk and Crompton, 2009). The main reasons given by parents for unmet needs for special education were the lack of services and staff within schools. Related to this, the main reason given by parents for unmet needs for educational aids was that of a lack of funding in the school system.

Table 5.2 Disability Rates for Children Aged 5–14 Years, by Sex and Age Group, Canada, 2001 and 2006

Age, years	Child Disability Rates				Disability Rates among Boys				Disability Rates among Girls			
	2001		2006		2001		2006		2001		2006	
	N	%	N	%	N	%	N	%	N	%	N	%
5 to 14	154,720	4	173,180	4.6	97,180	4.9	110,440	5.7	57,540	3	62,740	3.4
5 to 9	70,370	3.7	73,880	4.2	45,050	4.6	47,870	5.3	25,320	2.7	26,000	3
10 to 14	84,350	4.2	99,300	4.9	52,130	5.1	62,570	6	32,220	3.3	36,730	3.7

Source: Statistics Canada (2008).

New Sociology of Childhood on Education

Schools have been criticized for more than their reinforcement of gender identities and roles and their inability to accommodate the diverse needs of children with disabilities. For example, according to Nick Lee (2001: 77), school remains for the most part an area of social life in which children are "understood and treated as sites of investment, as human becomings requiring special treatment." Lee adds that school is a machine for making "passive beings." He explains that, from the outset, classroom order is a key goal, with classrooms designed so that each child had a specific place to sit, their own chair and desk, etc. Teachers test all pupils to determine their rank and rate of progress, and this information is in turn used to establish standard expectations. Lee notes that the goal of education, for the most part, has been to turn a diverse mass of people into a homogeneous class of passive becomings—despite some new, more child-centred approaches that treat children as "active" becomings.

Similarly, focusing on the Canadian context, Wotherspoon (2009) and Stasiulis (2002) have noted that schooling at the elementary and secondary levels in this country tends to be a depoliticizing and disempowering experience for children and youth. Some theorists have suggested that a truly child-centred approach to education should give children a context in which to have more rich and diverse social experiences, and should engage and challenge them into more self-directed development and learning (Lee, 2001). Smith (2007) similarly notes that, especially in school settings, children have lacked voice and visibility, and children's rights discourse and theoretical orientations are beginning to highlight the importance of participation rights for children. Smith explains that children need to be encouraged and supported to become active participants and social actors in early childhood and primary school settings. She argues that these new participation rights and their new role as citizens will then act as part of the ongoing learning process for and towards active child citizens (see also Stasiulis, 2002).

The Importance of Peers

Despite the recent shift towards increased focus on learning and pre-academics in early child development, Missall and Hojnoski (2008) have strongly argued that children need both social and academic skills to make the transition successfully from preschool environments to formal schooling and to continue to adapt successfully in later years. They explain that regardless of the theoretical models, terminology used, or specific focus, social competence is important for successful development. Peer-related social skills, such as initiating interactions, negotiating, and maintaining interactions are especially important (Missall and Hojnoski, 2008).[13] The nature and types of peer-related experiences children have in school affect their development. Missall and Hojnoski cite studies showing that children with prosocial skills were more likely than others to engage in appropriate levels of classroom participation (independent and co-operative work) and to experience higher levels of school achievement. Similarly, but in reverse, Oh et al. (2008) found that friendlessness, friendship instability, and exclusion starting in elementary school were significant predictors of social withdrawal following the transition into middle school.

Buysse et al. (2008) noted that the ability to form meaningful relationships with others is a key determinant of quality of life. Peer acceptance and friendship in childhood are particularly interesting and important. They define *friendship* as a positive, reciprocal relationship between two children and define *peer acceptance* as an index of a child's social status among his or her peers (are they accepted, rejected, ignored). They explain that friendship is differentiated from other social relationships for children since friendship (1) is dyadic in nature (two-person shared activities); (2) means that each child must consider the other a friend; (3) is closely tied to mutual liking and attachment; (4) is voluntary (children can't choose their siblings, parents, teachers, etc. but can choose friends); (5) involves proximity and shared experiences; and (6) is characterized by enjoyment and positive affect (ibid.).[14] Children themselves, not surprisingly, have told researchers that friends and peer "relationships" of various types are an important part of the school experience (Dockett and Perry, 2005).

Heterosexuality in Elementary Schools

Some have argued that girls are more interested in bridging the gender worlds earlier than boys for both platonic and romantic relationships; boys, in contrast, seem to see cross-gender play as threatening. On the other hand, a growing number of studies on romantic relationships in elementary school tell of the reinforcement of dominant versions of heterosexual masculinities (Gådin, 2012; Swain, 2005). For example, Connolly (1998) found that boys were able to gain a significant level of status by having, or at least professing to have—as "going out" often meant going nowhere—a girlfriend. Renold (2000) similarly noted that among 10- and 11-year-old boys "having a girlfriend" heightened a boy's status. Likewise, in almost every case in Swain's (2005) study, boys wanted to do little more than to possess a girl, use her as a status symbol, or gain the ability to "claim" the relationship.[15] Having a girlfriend or being a boyfriend became a signifier of a boy's heterosexuality and his hegemonic masculinity (Renold, 2007). Homophobia, in contrast, has been used to police gender in schools, often through bullying tactics, starting at a relatively young age (bullying is discussed below).

Affect and Prejudice in Attitudes towards Peers

Elizabeth Nowicki (2008) conducted research on elementary schoolchildren's attitudes and prejudice towards peers of lower and higher academic ability from one's own or from a different racial group. Using different types of dolls and different sets of labels or descriptions (e.g., "learns new things easily") for each doll, she found that children generally favoured their own group and groups of children with higher ability, but social categorization and racial preference also varied by the child's gender and age. Younger children (average age 5.6 years), for example, showed more negative biases towards out-group target children, for example, favouring same-race children over different-race children. Particularly with younger children, race was more important than learning ability. Older children (average age 9.9 years) had more positive beliefs about children of higher ability than children of lower ability regardless of race. Consistent with other research, younger children's prejudice seemed based more on external attributes, such as race, while older children's prejudice seemed based on internal attributes (such as real or perceived learning ability). It was found that for the most part, younger boys, older boys, and older girls held consistently positive attitudes towards the target groups (of various learning abilities and races), but younger girls stood out as having more pronounced biases. Nowicki found that younger girls most wanted to interact with the same-race and higher-ability children and least wanted to interact with the different-race and lower-ability children. There appeared to be an additive effect, in the case of younger girls, as the two social categories, race and learning ability, intertwined (ibid.).[16]

Recent research investigating elementary school children's thoughts on why they believe their peers with intellectual or learning disabilities are sometimes socially excluded at school yielded interesting results. Nowicki et al. (2014) asked 49 children in Grades 5 and 6 who attended inclusive classrooms to provide their views on the matter and to sort their peers' responses into meaningful categories (concept mapping) (see Table 5.3). They identified the following four main themes in their own and their peers' responses as to why children with disabilities may be excluded: (1) the thoughts and actions of other children; (2) differences in learning ability and resource allocation; (3) affect, physical characteristics, and schooling; and (4) negative thoughts and behaviours (Nowicki et al., 2014).

Table 5.3 Children's Thoughts on Social Exclusion (Cluster Items and Bridging Values for Concept Map)

Cluster 1: The thoughts and actions of other children (0.20)

- They don't do well in school so people think these kids can't learn anything (0.00)
- Because those other people think kids with learning problems are very different (0.02)
- They don't know a lot (0.02)
- They aren't part of our community (0.07)
- They have brains that are all messed up (0.08)
- Because other kids think those kids are like dumb (0.09)
- Other kids are too cool to play with them (0.10)
- If they are blind other kids think they can't read (0.19)
- Other kids think that they're better than kids with learning difficulties because of the way they are born (0.23)
- Other kids don't think kids who have learning problems are cool enough to hang with them (0.23)
- Other kids think it's contagious and they could get it (0.24)
- Other kids just let their own friends in instead of new (0.25)
- People think kids with disabilities are not good enough (0.27)
- Other kids just ignore them (0.28)
- Because other kids think kids with disabilities can't play the games properly (0.30)
- "I'm better than you so I'm not going to hang out with you" (0.30)
- Other kids get a better mark on a test and that's why they start bullying (0.32)
- Other kids just don't like them (0.43)
- All the smart kids play together and they exclude the kids that aren't that smart (0.48)

Cluster 2: Differences in learning ability and resource allocation 0.39

- 'Cause they don't know how to learn very well (0.17)
- They don't have the same interest as other kids (0.21)
- They get to go and do easier work (0.31)
- They have hands that are disabled (0.32)
- Other kids are mad because the kids with special needs get attention and other kids don't (0.35)
- They are going to get upset easily and ruin the whole game (0.41)
- They are getting way more attention and the teacher is always helping (0.44)
- They aren't the same as most (0.52)
- Maybe other kids are jealous (0.54)
- They are kind of like gross sometimes (0.68)

Cluster 3: Differences in actions and physical characteristics (0.58)

- They have like difficulty pronouncing words (0.19)
- Because like how they look (0.28)
- They get excused from class (0.40)
- Because they are mean to everybody (0.48)
- They do different things (0.50)
- Because they have a special teacher (0.52)
- They might not understand what is going on at school (0.58)
- People don't want to pressure them to learn (0.59)
- They can't really hear (0.70)

Continued

Table 5.3 *Continued*

- Other kids don't want to get them frustrated (0.74)
- Kids with learning disabilities are kind of scared (0.93)
- Other kids don't want to get in trouble for it (1.00)

Cluster 4: Negative behaviours and thoughts (0.65)

- Other kids think kids with learning difficulties don't need help in special activities (0.38)
- Because other kids think kids with learning difficulties are weird or not nice (0.46)
- If they are mean and push (0.50)
- Maybe other people think kids with learning difficulties are stupid (0.52)
- Other kids are being mean (0.70)
- They feel like not smart (0.82)
- They might be made fun of (0.89)
- Because some people don't know what to do (0.94)

Source: Nowicki et al. (2014: 351).

In a similar study, Nowicki and Brown (2013) invited 36 children between the ages of 9 and 12 to share their ideas on how to socially include classmates with learning or intellectual disabilities at school. The children generated 80 strategies, which they categorized into major themes. These included focusing on the need for teachers to intervene in academic and social situations, incorporating child-to-child instructional strategies, being supportive, focusing on similarities between children with and without disabilities, and modelling appropriate behaviours (see also Lindsay et al., 2013, who elicited children's perceptions of the desirable components of two commonly used social inclusion programs in Ontario). Research involving children as participants shows that some exclusion is the result of children lacking knowledge and contact with children who are not like themselves (Lindsay et al., 2013). It also reveals that children can and do actively and effectively participate in creating knowledge, understanding, and solutions when it comes to social inclusion of their peers (Lindsay et al. 2013; Nowicki and Brown, 2013; Nowicki et al., 2014). That said, bullying and victimization persist.

Peer Victimization—Bullying

While aggressive and antisocial children tend to be rejected by peers (Van Lier et al., 2005), they nonetheless continue to have a strong influence on the experiences of their classmates. Researchers estimate that between 10 and 40 per cent of children are chronic victims of bullying; this number is believed to be even higher in the early grades (Leadbeater and Sukhawathanakul, 2011). Analyses of various prevention programs recommend that adults address the problem early and with developmentally appropriate approaches as research shows that the consequences of bullying can be devastating and long term (Leadbeater and Sukhawwathanakul, 2011; Lindsay et al., 2013; Nickerson et al., 2013; Nowicki and Brown, 2013). For example, Beran et al. (2008), using National Longitudinal Survey of Children and Youth (NLSCY) data, found that children who were bullied at school were more likely than others to obtain low levels of achievement, particularly if they showed low enjoyment of school and their parents provided little support. Similarly, Lamarche et al. (2007) note that peer victimization predicts an increase in children's (particularly boys') teacher-related reactive aggression. Beran (2008) found that those who are bullied at younger ages tended to be bullied later on. Those most often bullied by others tend to be members of marginalized groups— for example, boys with stereotypically feminine characteristics and behaviour (Robertson, 2008). Other attributes targeted by bullies were appearance, academic achievement, race, and gender (Aboud and Miller, 2007).

Name-calling is one of the most common forms of bullying among elementary school children, and peer intervention seemed to occur more in the lower grades than in the upper (Aboud and Miller, 2007). A study of children's decisions to disclose peer victimization found that powerlessness, victim self-blaming, fear of retaliation, fear of losing the relationship if the bully is a "friend," and expectations regarding the effectiveness of adult interventions were found to impede disclosure (Mishna and Alaggia, 2005). Children are telling us that adults can do more to confront peer victimization.

Questions about the Future

Peer groups are a good example of how children enter an existing culture or locale and individually and collectively reproduce it (Corsaro, 2005). While observing and listening to children's voices in peer-group contexts, adults can play a significant role in making both school and peer relations more meaningful, empowering, and positive experiences. At times, it does not take much to do this; at other times it is very complex, wide-ranging, and takes a great deal of work, as building more empowering and inclusive spaces involves standing up to powerful global forces.

New Media, Technology, Commercialism, and Thinking about Sustainable Education

Some of the increased spending in schools is the result of the growth of computers in the classroom—virtually all elementary schools had computers and were connected to the Internet by 2004. Some have argued that technology in the classroom can produce positive experiences for children. For example, a Norwegian study that included a survey and qualitative interviews with children ages 10 to 12 years found that new media technologies, such as instant messaging and e-mail, offer children new ways of communicating both positive and negative content to build and strengthen relationships with schoolmates and other friends (Kaare et al., 2007; see Chapter 6). But some have also noted, with alarm, a considerable rise in commercialism in Canadian schools, particularly with rising costs and reliance on private funding sources (Canadian Teachers' Federation, 2006).

In response, groups and initiatives have emerged to try to (re)construct a more inclusive and democratic social participation, starting in places like the classroom (see Cote et al., 2007). In creating a more child-focused classroom, we should pay close attention to environmental sustainability and inclusive, globally focused approaches to learning. Creative, inclusive, sustainable, and empowering solutions require a great deal of work, to be sure, but can also be exciting and rewarding for educators as well. There is no doubt, however, that the creation of a democratic and socially inclusive education must include planning and input from children themselves. We may be surprised by how much children can teach us.

Summary

In this chapter we saw that education in Canada should be understood as *educations*, as there is considerable variation across provinces and throughout Canadian history. We should also note that despite these differences, theories of education tell us that the role and effect of education on children is relatively homogeneous considering the main aim of education is to help create "functioning" members or society (functionalists); to maintain the power hierarchy, class divisions, and the status quo, which serves the dominant ideology (conflict approach); to maintain a patriarchal division of power between men and women (feminists); or to keep children inactive and powerless as citizens (children's rights perspective).

The chapter critically assessed and deconstructed the idea of education as a great equalizer and as a level playing field, showing that in Canada today, children who come from economically disadvantaged households find themselves more likely to struggle in school, compared with children from households with a higher socioeconomic status. We then looked at competing explanations for the role peers play in the classroom experiences and lives of children. The chapter concluded by raising the question of what truly child-focused education systems might look like given that our current systems have much room for improvement.

Questions for Critical Thought

1. While children from different income households have considerably different experiences and outcomes in Canadian schools, having more education, regardless of social class is preferable to having less. Discuss what this means and outline a series of arguments you would make to convince children from lower-income households to stay in school longer.

2. Girls and boys score differently in school, have different experiences, and face different challenges. What do you believe accounts for the differences? Should boys and girls be schooled apart? Why? Why not?

3. What would you say is the single most challenging issue to tackle when it comes to the Canadian educational system(s)? Why? What suggestions would you make to help improve things? What needs to be done? How? By whom?

4. You have been asked to create a learning space and environment for Grade 4 children that is child-focused, inclusive, sustainable, and empowering for everyone. How would you do this? What would it look like? What do you see as the biggest challenge to achieving your goals?

Suggested Readings

Janovicek, Nancy, and Joy Parr, eds. 2003. *Histories of Canadian Children and Youth.* Toronto: Oxford University Press. This edited collection contains a number of important and interesting pieces on the historical development of schooling in different regions of the country. For example, Jean Barman writes on Aboriginal education in Canada, and Robert McIntosh writes on Nova Scotia. Also of interest is Ian Davey's chapter on the rhythm of work and school in Canada's past.

Nowicki, Elizabeth, J. Brown, and M. Stepien. 2014. "Children's Thoughts on the Social Exclusion of Peers with Intellectual or Learning Disabilities," *Journal of Intellectual Disability Research* 58, 4: 346–57. Their study combines a number of important areas of research including the social exclusion of children with intellectual and learning disabilities, peer relations, bullying, and the importance of including children in research and policy-making.

Thomas, Eleanor. 2009. "Canadian Nine-Year-Olds at School," *Children and Youth Research Paper Series.* Ottawa: Statistics Canada. At: www.statcan.gc.ca/pub/89-599-m/89-599-m2009006-eng. This report describes the school experiences of nine-year-old Canadian children. It includes a comparison of children from families with very low income and those from higher income backgrounds, as well as a look at how girls compare with boys.

Websites

BullyingCanada
http://bullyingcanada.ca
>   BullyingCanada is a website created by youth across Canada for young people who seek to speak out about bullying and victimization. The site contains information about bullying, access to news stories, and a video library, among other resources.

Canadian Teachers' Federation
www.ctf-fce.ca/
>   For more than 80 years, the Canadian Teachers' Federation has advocated for a strong public education system in Canada and throughout the world. This site contains information on teaching in Canada, professional development, national and international initiatives, briefs, analysis and reports, and a number of other teaching-related publications.

OECD—Education at a Glance
www.oecd.org/edu/eag.htm
>   Education at a Glance is a source of information on the state of education around the world. It provides data on the structure, finances, and performance of education systems in more than 40 countries, including OECD members and G20 partners.

6 Children, the Mass Media, and Consumerism

Learning Objectives

◎ To look at the role of the mass media in the lives of children.

◎ To learn about recent trends in children's media consumption.

◎ To assess the impact of the mass media on children.

◎ To explore the ongoing debates surrounding violence in the media and the sexualization of girls.

◎ To understand why and how companies market to children.

◎ To look at the role children play as consumers.

◎ To uncover and better understand trends in children's access to the mass media.

Introduction

Until recently, television dominated children's media consumption. Today, television competes with computers, video games, cell phones, tablets, and other mobile, Internet-connected devices for children's time and attention. The result is that children are completely immersed in media experiences from a young age. Much has changed since the first edition of this book was published, as new ways of communicating have been rapidly expanding and are being taken up by even very young children. This has created new opportunities and new challenges (Livingstone, 2009).

Not long ago, one of our biggest concerns, as adults, was the amount of violence in children's television programming. For example, on 1 November 1994, the Canadian Broadcast Standards Council decided that the children's program *Mighty Morphin Power Rangers* violated the Canadian Association of Broadcasters' violence code. Global Communications Ltd, the broadcaster against which the complaint was filed, requested that the program's producers provide a modified, less violent version of the show to air in Canada. This interesting and controversial ruling left in its wake a series of questions and challenges, which linger to this day—as we will see below—with the rise of "new media" that has come to displace the old.

This chapter will allow us to explore a number of questions surrounding children and the mass media. We will begin by examining children's changing media consumption patterns, followed by a section on what various researchers have found to be the effect of television viewing and mass media consumption on children. This leads us to the ongoing debate about the impact of violent and sexual media content on children. We will also look at how and why children are seen and treated as consumers by looking at advertising and marketing to children. We will review newer and more recent trends, which have led some to wonder, and perhaps to worry, about the future of children and childhood in this country.

Background

The development of moving images or pictures dates from 1884, but television as we know it was not mass-produced and widely available until the 1950s. One of the first mass producers of television sets was the Radio Corporation of America (RCA). It may come as a surprise to many, that much of the advancement in this technology was fuelled by the company's work with the American military and national defence (Donne, 1997) and by rapidly growing advertising revenues (Rutherford, 1997). By the 1960s television became the chief medium of advertising and advertising revenue. From the outset, advertising has shaped both television programming and schedules (ibid.). In other words, the underlying purpose of mainstream television was and continues to be the sale of goods for profit—the commercials— and not the entertainment.

Unlike other media that may require reading, writing, and other more advanced skills, visual media like television are accessible to children of almost all ages. As early as the 1950s, to appeal to children, the 30-minute, once-a-week formatting of programs was established (Alexander, 1997). By the 1960s, Saturday morning cartoons—much cheaper to produce than live-action programs—became a lucrative time slot for many television networks. Because the audiences for children's shows change rapidly (children grow up) and because children don't seem to mind reruns, programs are shown several times in a year, reducing costs and maintaining profits; strong syndication markets for children's shows also keep profit high (ibid.). Because of this, children are seen as a special class of citizens and consumers when it comes to popular culture and the mass media.

How Hooked Are They?

Today, children are considered to be *digital natives*—people born and raised in the age of digital technology, and therefore familiar with computers and the Internet from an early age. As early as 2000, a study by Media Awareness Network (2001) found that 86 per cent of children in their Canadian sample used the Internet. By 2005, a follow-up study found that 94 per cent of children reported that they had Internet access at home, and by the time these children reached Grade 11, half of them had their own Internet-connected computers separate from their family computers (Media Awareness Network, 2005). In 2005, 45 per cent of children had access to a family cell phone; another 23 per cent had their own cell phones, and around half of these could use those phones to surf the Internet (44 per cent) and text message their friends (56 per cent) (Media Awareness Network, 2005). These numbers are only higher today, as access to the Internet outside of school reached 99 per cent (Steeves, 2014a; also see Statistics Canada, 2013j). Johnson et al. (2010) noted that trends clearly indicate continued increase in the number of children accessing the Internet, the amount of time they spend online, and the complexity of their online behaviour.

Over the past few years, an increasing use of social media has been noted for all age groups, including children, with children's digital media in particular becoming a hotbed of innovation (Kids' Media Network, 2013). That said, relatively little research has been done on Internet use by children during the preschool and middle-childhood periods. The first Quebec-wide survey of Internet use by children, conducted in 2011 by the Marie-Vincent Foundation (2011), found that three in four children 3 to 12 years of age go online and that one in two interacts with other people on the Internet, via social networks, chatting, or online gaming. The survey also revealed that 80 per cent of parents believed the Internet can be a dangerous source for the sexual exploitation of children. That said, nearly 50 per cent of parents said that they do *not* talk with their children about the possible dangers of surfing the Internet, even when it was found that 1 in 10 children had been in contact with someone they didn't know (Marie-Vincent Foundation, 2011).

An American study by Gutnick et al. (2011) found that while children have more access to all kinds of digital media, and are spending more of their day accessing it, television continues to exert a stronghold over younger children, who continue to spend more time with it than any other medium. Children appear to shift their media habits around the age of eight, when they increasingly turn to the Web over television (Gutnick et al., 2011).

The average hours per week of television viewing in Canada has not changed very much in recent years, hovering around 22 hours per week (Statistics Canada, 2005f); however what has changed is who is watching. Canadian research shows that children and teens are spending increasingly less time in front of the television, but this is being offset by the increasing number of hours that their grandparents are spending watching it (Statistics Canada, 2005f). As noted above, with new media battling for children's attention, the amount of time spent watching television has, for the most part, declined particularly for children over the age of eight.

Viewing times and media consumption were also found to vary along class and racial lines, particularly in the United States. For example, one American study found that lower-income, Hispanic, and African American children consume far more media than their middle-class and white counterparts (Gutnick et al., 2011; see also Berry, 2007; Roberts and Foehr, 2004; Alexander, 1997). One study found that children who lived in neighbourhoods that were perceived by their mothers as unsafe watched more television (Burdette and Whitaker, 2005).

Television versus Internet Use: Benefits and Risks

A number of researchers have attempted to compare the effects of television watching and Internet access on children. To start, the negative effects of television watching on children's cognitive development and educational achievement have been well documented, and are associated with displacement of cognitively more valuable activities, especially in infancy and early childhood (Bittman et al., 2012). Television has also been associated with disruption of concentration, reduced parental mediation or active co-viewing, and sleep disturbances (ibid.). Increased hours of viewing or excessive viewing have also been found to lead to overconsumption of inappropriate types of content (ibid.). In contrast, Bittman et al. (2012) found that having access to the Internet was positively related to recognizing words, while having a television in the child's bedroom was significantly associated with poorer vocabulary at age four. That said, their research found that among preschoolers, any dose of media, including television watching, was *safe*, provided that there was a stimulating home environment, sufficient family income, a good amount of cultural capital, and supportive parenting. This, they explain, implies that the children most at risk of delayed language acquisition are not affected by the media per se, but rather by their socioeconomic backgrounds and the level of parental involvement when it comes to media consumption (Bittman et al., 2012).

At the same time, other research suggests that the Internet provides children with more developmental advantages than disadvantages, even when controlling for family socioeconomic characteristics (Johnson, 2010). Even more concretely, Johnson's (2013) results suggest that Internet use during childhood is a complex behaviour that varies across children and contexts. Instant messaging and community-based Internet use in childhood, for example, were associated with decreased literacy skills, while some other applications used at home and at school were associated with increased literacy skills. In light of these complexities and competing results, it is not surprising that Johnson (2010) notes that there are at least two conflicting public anxieties surrounding children and the Internet: that children without Internet access are cognitively and socially disadvantaged compared with others and, on the flipside, that the Internet may harm children due to the potential exposure to inappropriate content. Whatever the case may be, Livingstone (2009) points out that many parents feel ill-equipped to assist children in their struggles with it, as many parents are not completely comfortable with the medium themselves.

Children, Media, Risk, and the State

According to a number of researchers, the risks that children face online manifest in numerous ways (Mascheroni et al., 2014; Cunningham et al., 2010; Livingstone, 2009). Livingstone (2009), for example, divides the risks into broad categories, including being exploited for commercial purposes and being exposed to sexual, radical, racist, or other disturbing content. These risks can involve children as recipients, participants, or actors.

The most obvious risks, which will be discussed in more detail below, are sexual risks, including exposure to pornographic or sexual content, situations in which children interact with strangers, or circumstances in which children produce and distribute their own pornographic content (Livingstone, 2009).

Mascheroni et al. (2014) asked children about their perceptions of risk. Using empirical material collected in the EU Kids Online III network in nine countries, they found, among other things, that when asked about risk, children distance themselves from their own positive experiences on the Internet, instead adopting the media's "moral panic" frames, particularly surrounding "stranger danger." Children used vivid vocabulary to describe the perceived risk evoked by sensationalist messages used in news coverage of crime stories. For example, Maltese 9- and 10-year-old girls mentioned the following:

> . . . he could take advantage of you before killing you. If you do not do what he says, he could touch your private body, hurt you, throw stones at you or smack you with a belt or stab you with a knife. (Mascheroni et al., 2014: 30)

The study found that children adhere to stereotypical representation of strangers as older men affected by mental disorders: "schizophrenic" or "crazy guys" who groom children online in order to later kidnap, rape, or even kill them (Mascheroni, Jorge, and Farrugia, 2014). While sensational-istic, these concerns are clearly shared by the adults in these children's lives.

In Canada, in 2011, the federal government passed Bill C-22 to require Internet service providers (ISPs) to report to authorities any content they host that is abusive of children and to co-operate with law enforcement investigations associated with these activities. As we will see in upcom-ing chapters, the duty to report child abuse and exploitation is a general duty for Canadians, embedded in provincial legislation. With this new law, the federal government has now included specific legal obligations for ISPs, given the proliferation of child abuse images online (Government of

Canada, 2014). On a positive note, these types of dangers are relatively small for most children.

In contrast, *cyberbullying* is a real and growing concern. Studies suggest that online harassment can have harmful consequences for children. Interviews and focus groups with children revealed that cyberbullying was perceived as the worst thing that could happen to them online (Mascheroni et al., 2014).

Cyberbullying has been defined as intentional, repetitive aggression involving power imbalance between the victim and perpetrators, which is carried out by means of electronic communication (ibid.). Children's own testimonies include a variety of experiences, including witnessing, experiencing, or being aware of hate speech; disrespect; fights; gossip; rude and nasty comments; and annoying, unwelcome, or sexual messages (Cunningham et al., 2010). Children are also concerned about data misuse, threats, blackmail, insults, trolling, racism, or religious harassment (Mascheroni et al., 2014). Children identified and spoke about the painful consequences of cyberbullying, including depression and suicide. Some of the more high-profile victims of cyberbullying in this country have been young women and girls—a problem closely connected to the more general problem of the sexualization of this population.

Gender, Sexuality, Sexualization, and the Media

Hawkes and Dune (2013) note that in the Anglophone West, narratives of the sexual child have been dominated by anxieties about the sexualization of girls and about "sexting." They explain that the Internet seems to breed panic around the idea of the sexual child, in that children, and especially girls, are assumed to be susceptible to the dynamics of corruptibility and loss of innocence (see Box 6.1) (Hawkes and Dune, 2013). Disney pop star Miley Cyrus, for example, has been the focus of considerable attention because of her sexually explicit dress, song lyrics, and dance moves. Although their stories are not new, Cyrus and others like her have fanned the flames and heightened concerns that girls are being pushed to self-sexualize at younger and younger ages due to the influence of the media (Lamb et al., 2013). But this debate is complex. To start, many recognize that often young female stars like Cyrus are packaged as a sexualized commodity by powerful people or corporate interests around them; on the other hand, some have argued that these displays reflect the stars' own agency (ibid.). Furthermore, the conversations and discourse surrounding these stars' performances reflect very diverse interpretations: that stars like Cyrus represent a culture that is morally corrupt and oversexualized; that they reflect a culture that is progressive (often used as a criticism of the competing discourse of conservatism); or, further still, that their displays of sexuality represent a form of empowerment (ibid.). Regardless of which of these positions we take, Lamb et al. (2013) note that we cannot lose sight of the fact that these displays represent objectification, they maintain and enhance an unequal status between men and women, and sexualization gets reduced to an argument about "too sexy too soon" rather than "too sexy for whom."

Graff et al. (2013) used content analysis to examine changes in the number of sexualizing characteristics (e.g., wearing low-cut shirts and high-heeled shoes) and childlike characteristics (e.g., wearing polka-dot print, Mary Jane–style shoes) present in depictions of girls over time in the magazines *Seventeen* (issues from 1971 to 2011) and *Girls' Life* (issues from 1994 to 2011). They found increases in the total number of sexualizing characteristics across time in both magazines. That said, Starr and Ferguson (2012) note that there are few empirical studies that have

---

Box 6.1   Preteen Girls Read "Tween" Pop Culture

Vares et al. (2011) report on a three-year study of how 71 "tween" girls in New Zealand make sense of the popular culture they encounter in their everyday lives. Interestingly, and not surprisingly, the girls themselves offer diverse, complex, and contradictory responses to popular representations of femininity and the "sexualization" of preteen girls. Most were not simply passive victims of a sexualized media. Vares et al. (2011) found that tweens were simultaneously "critical" of sexualized images yet "felt bad" about themselves in response to the same images—taking us beyond the passive–active binary. Tween girls were keen to position themselves as critical viewers who simply did not parrot celebrity behaviours. Some Grade 8 girls, in response to the interviewer raising the point that some believe that watching sexualized content is going to influence the tweens in some way, noted the following:

> Carla (8W2): No, I don't, I don't get that because . . . people say because like, those stars like Vanessa Hudgens and Miley Cyrus like, take pictures of themselves and then send them around, well, like, I'm not gonna do that just cos they did.
>
> Jessica (8W2): Yeah.
>
> Destiny (8W2): It's gross.
>
> Carla (8W2): Like, actually, it's just yuck.
>
> Samantha (8W2): It's just stupid.
>
> Destiny (8W2): We weren't brought up that way.
>
> Carla (8W2): Yeah, like I, I—my parents didn't bring me up like that at all, so like

explored this topic from the point of view of girls. Using paper dolls, Starr and Ferguson (2012) examined self-sexualization among 60 six- to nine-year-old girls living in the Midwestern United States. Simultaneously, using maternal reports, they also investigated potential risk factors, such as hours of media consumption and maternal self-objectification, and potential protective factors, such as maternal television mediation and maternal religiosity, to better understand these young girls' experiences with sexualization. Their findings supported social cognitive/social learning theory, as the girls overwhelmingly chose the sexualized doll over the non-sexualized doll as being more popular and to represent their ideal self. That said, they also found that maternal television mediation and maternal religiosity reduced those odds (Starr and Ferguson, 2012). The study found that it was not so much the amount of girls' media

---

Jessica (8W2): My parents would kill me.

Multiple: Yeah . . . .

Destiny (8W2): . . . My parents think that if I watch that kind of thing [Rihanna music video] that I'm going to turn out like her, and, just because like, the, the fashionable clothes she wears doesn't mean I wanna look half naked.

Multiple: Yeah. (Vares et al., 2011: 148–9)

Vares et al. (2011: 150) also point out that these media images do negatively affect girls' attitudes towards themselves:

Ilsa (7C3, v-log): Well this is my usual magazine *Girlfriend* . . . . This is that sort of stuff that makes me feel kinda sad actually [image of teenage girl in a "sexy" schoolgirl outfit: very short skirt, tight top and cleavage showing] making girls dress up like that. [An ad for Clean and Clear face wash with a photo of two girls faces with "perfect" skin.] That makes me feel I could probably look like that, of course, that's probably what it's supposed to make you feel. I don't like that that much because I doubt it works . . . are sorts of ordinary ads you'll find in your everyday magazines, *Dolly* and *Girlfriend,* about stars and people, hottest looks and stuff like that. But the thing is, most of the girls that I know have a skin problem called eczema and that's just like me—I've got eczema and it's really bad because seeing people's skin so perfect (images of celebrities like Lindsay Lohan and Kate Hudson) compared to mine makes me feel kinda sad, makes me feel like I wish that I had a better life.

Girls had a range of interpretative repertoires; they expressed fears about the harmful effects of media "sexualization," but also made sophisticated deconstructions of media products. Vares et al. (2011) remind us that the tweens' subjectivities were far more complex and fluid than our often simple binaries on the topic suggest.

Source: Excerpts from "Preteen girls read 'tween' popular culture: Diversity, complexity and contradiction" by Tiina Vares And Sue Jackson and Rosalind Gill. *International Journal of Media and Cultural Politics,* Volume 7, Issue 2, August 2011.

consumption that affected their self-sexualization, but rather maternal self-objectification and maternal religiosity that played a role (ibid.).

There is no doubt that a considerable amount of gender socialization takes place through the media. There is abundant evidence that in prime-time programming, as well as in children's programming, stereotypes persist. For example, Smith et al. (2010) did a content analysis of gender-related portrayals in 101 of the highest-grossing G-rated films released in the United States and Canada from 1990 to early 2005. Males outnumbered females by a ratio of 2.57 to 1, and this has not changed in 15 years. They also found that female characters were more likely than male characters to be young and traditionally depicted; in terms of personality traits, females were more likely to be smart, good, and beautiful compared with males (Smith et al., 2010). For boys, a main concern surrounding the media is their exposure to violent content. Erwin and Morton (2008) noted that before children even enter kindergarten they are exposed to over 4,000 hours of television; by the time they leave elementary school, children will have witnessed 8,000 murders and 100,000 acts of violence on television alone. That said, Gerbner and his colleagues have been quantitatively measuring (counting) the amount of violence on television since 1967 and found that the violence index over the years since they began their work remained fairly stable (Alexander, 1997). What is cause for concern these days is the rise in popularity of ultraviolent action games that are aimed at mature audiences but are being accessed by children, especially boys. Polman et al. (2008) conducted an experimental study of 57 children between the ages of 10 and 13. Some played a violent video game, some watched the same violent video game being played by someone else, and some played a nonviolent video game. Aggression levels were measured following the activities. They found that after actually playing the violent video game, boys behaved more aggressively compared with the boys simply watching the game being played; the girls' gaming conditions were not related to aggression (Polman et al., 2008). This study suggests that, specifically for boys, playing a violent video game would likely lead to more aggression than watching television violence (Polman et al., 2008). A Canadian study found that parents' and children's reports of child preferences for mature and violent video games were significantly related to children's perpetration of bullying and cyberbullying (Dittrick et al., 2013). On the other hand, some have argued that violent video game exposure was not found to be predictive of delinquency or bullying and may actually have a cathartic effect for some (Ferguson et al., 2014).

Why is this important? Studies done in the 1950s suggested that watching violent media had a cathartic effect, actually reducing viewers' aggressive behaviour (Zuckerman and Zuckerman, 1985). Catharsis theory maintains that viewing violence actually purges the individual of negative feelings and this decreases the likelihood of engaging in aggressive behaviour. Stimulation theories, in contrast, argue and predict the opposite.

Recent experimental studies on the impact of viewing violence have shown that the effect is quite complicated (Kirsh, 2006). Many have noted that television is not the only factor causing violent outbursts in children, and the precise impact of media violence is modified by age, sex, family practices, and the way the violence and its consequences are presented (Alexander, 1997; Ferguson et al., 2014; Polman et al., 2008). As early as the 1980s, some have argued that violent or aggressive behaviour in boys may actually have more to do with how much, in what way, and by whom they are supervised, rather than simply what they watch (Zuckerman and Zuckerman, 1985). Research revealed that prior aggression levels in children, as well as the context and general message of what was viewed, influenced the mimicking of violent behaviour.

Why is all this important? We've known for some time (as have advertisers, as we will see below) that the media has a major impact on children's (and, for that matter, adults') knowledge, attitudes, and behaviour (Zuckerman and Zuckerman, 1985). Research in the area suggests that children understand the images they see, and often seek to emulate characters on television. This means that the media plays a **prescriptive** role (suggesting how we should behave), and, as we have seen in Chapter 4, learning socially prescribed gender roles begins early in life. Children learn to draw upon their **gender schematic** knowledge (the activation of gender stereotypes) in many things that they do (Kee et al., 2005; Cherney, 2003; Durkin and Nugent, 1998; Bem, 1981). In addition to gender stereotyping, researchers such as Levin and Carlsson-Paige have found that people who are racialized are inadequately represented in positive roles and over-represented in negative ones. Levin and Carlsson-Page (2007: 435) warn that "because of children's cognitive stage of development, these messages have a great potential to negatively impact their developing sense of themselves and others," particularly because children of colour tend to consume more hours of media per day. Similarly, disability scholars have long called for better representations of people with disabilities in popular culture (Holton, 2013). The importance of better representation cannot be understated, particularly since there is evidence that children with disabilities easily get interested in television and computer games when they can identify with fantasy figures in the games; as a result, some children get motivated to try difficult motions or actions, thus stretching their capabilities (Wasterfors, 2011).

Counter stereotypical images have been useful in combatting stereotypical socialization (Durkin and Nugent, 1998; Calvert et al., 2007; Pohan and Mathison, 2007)—and a number of television programs have attempted to do this. At the same time, stereotyping does not occur through programming alone. It is also, and especially, evident in advertising that targets children of all ages.

Children as Consumers and the Role of Advertising

Today, children are immersed in a culture of consumption, to the point that almost every aspect of their lives is characterized by a buy-and-consume mentality. They are receiving an endless barrage of messages about their purchasing power and their need to consume. In fact, children are increasingly defined and viewed by their spending capacity. Girls are especially targeted under mounting pressure to emulate a feminine ideal. And this has had physical, emotional, and social outcomes that have been found to be detrimental to children. For example, we know that children who eat fast food have poor diet and health outcomes. At the same time, fast food is heavily marketed to children using child-directed marketing (CDM) (Ohri-Vachaspati et al., 2015).

By the time a child reaches the age of seven, she or he has watched an average of more than 20,000 commercials per year (Sutherland and Thompson, 2001). Studies show that most children understand that the role of commercials is to persuade them to buy products (Alexander, 1997). There are those who have argued that even if and when they don't understand them, young children (for example, those between the ages of two and five) still are influenced by the commercials they see (Sankaran et al., 1998). By the age of 12, children were even able to name commercials they believed to be untruthful (Sutherland and Thompson, 2001).

According to one estimate, Canadian children between the ages of 4 and 12 had an approximate spending power of $1.1 billion more than 10 years ago, and YTV (a Canadian children's channel) research predicted a steady increase in growth, particularly among **tween** spending, with tween (ages 9–14 years) spending increasing by $100 million each year in the last four years of the 1990s (Sutherland and Thompson, 2001). According to the 2008 YTV Kids and Tweens Report, within their households, kids influence 97 per cent of breakfast choices, 95 per cent of lunch choices, 98 per cent of where families go to eat casual meals, 95 per cent of their clothing purchase, 76 per cent of software purchases, 60 per cent of computer purchases, 98 per cent of family entertainment choices, and 94 per cent of family trips and excursions (Poulton, 2008).

These YTV Kid and Tween Reports have been issued since 1999, and while they cannot be considered "scientific studies," they provide an indication of the type and amount of spending and the influence children have on household spending. On top of their own spending, as we see above, they influence grocery purchases, where families go on vacation, and what kinds of cars the family will buy; they often accomplish these ends by a special kind of "nagging" that has come to be known as **kidfluence**—the power children have over parental, household, and adult purchases (Schor, 2004; Sutherland and Thompson, 2001). One American estimate had children ages 4 to 12 years of age *directly* influencing $330 billion in adult purchases more than 10 years ago, and "evoking" another $340 billion, with global estimates for tween influence topping $1 trillion in 2002 (Schor, 2004).

Other than "Wow," some of you may be thinking "So what? What's the big deal? Why should we care?" A number of social scientists have studied the effects of advertising on children and have found that beyond persuading children to request specific products (Connor, 2006; Otnes et al., 1994a), they also modify self-esteem (Hargreaves and Tiggermann, 2003); shape children's attitudes towards food, medicine, and their health, often contributing to obesity and poor health (Lewis and Hill, 1998; Zuckerman and Zuckerman, 1985); and shape attitudes towards alcohol and cigarette consumption (Collins et al., 2003), particularly among girls ("Study Finds Girls Overexposed to Alcohol Advertising," 2004). Advertisers also use, misuse, or overuse stereotypical images of girls and boys (Gannon, 2007; Pike and Jennings, 2005; Davis, 2002; Johnson and Young, 2002; Klinger et al., 2001; Larson, 2001) and members of diverse racial groups (Harrison, 2006) in order to sell their products. Beyond this, they have also been found to affect how children play (Kline, 1993), think about themselves and others (Pike and Jennings, 2005), and use language (Otnes et al., 1994b).

According to cultivation theory (Gerbner et al., 2002) and social learning theory (Bandura, 2002), recurrent messages get learned through observation. Gerbner et al., for example, suggest that those who spend "more time 'living' in the world of television are more likely to see the 'real world' in terms of the images, values, portrayals and ideologies that emerge through the lens of television" (Gerbner et al., 2002: 47). As relatively heavy viewers of television, children are especially vulnerable to holding views and values and engaging in behaviour they have seen on television (Bandura, 2002). Let us explore some of these issues in more detail using the example of food advertising.

Children's Health, Watching Television, and Food Commercials

According to recent research, the media can affect children's health and weight in at least two different ways: media activities may displace other activities that require more energy, such as playing sports, and so reduce children's total energy expenditure, and exposure to media may affect children's energy intake (Suziedelytea, 2015). Children's exposure to advertisements for fast food, soft drinks, sugary cereals, and "junk food" may lead to higher consumption of high-calorie foods. The problem is so widespread that the World Health Organization has recently recommended the worldwide reduction of food and beverage marketing directed at children (Potvin and Wanles, 2014). In Canada, prevalence rates for overweight or obese children ages 6 to 11 years increased from 13 to 26 per cent between 1978 and 2004 (Potvin and Wanles, 2014). Things seemed to be getting so bad that in 2010, the national and provincial ministers of health identified marketing to children as one of the three policy priorities to help curb childhood obesity in Canada (Potvin and Wanles, 2014).

In Canada advertising is, for the most part, self-regulated by industry. The Canadian Radio-Television and Telecommunications Commission (2014) has guidelines around children's advertising (any paid commercial message carried during children's programming and any commercial message that's directed to children). It basically notes that broadcasters must adhere to the Broadcast Code for Advertising to Children published by the Canadian Association of Broadcasters in co-operation with Advertising Standards Canada. Advertising Standards Canada (2014) has developed a Broadcast Code for Advertising to Children. The Children's Code reminds advertisers that children's advertising should respect and not abuse the power of the child's imagination, but only "guides" advertisers and agencies in preparing commercial messages that adequately recognize the special characteristics of the children's audience. In contrast, in Quebec, commercial advertising aimed at persons younger than 13 is generally prohibited.

What we currently have in place is the Canadian Children's Food and Beverage Advertising Initiative (CAI), initiated in April 2007 and implemented in December 2008 by 16 large food and beverage manufactures (including Cadbury Adams Canada, Coca-Cola Canada, Hershey Canada, Janes Family Foods, Mars Canada, McCain Foods Canada, PepsiCo Canada, and Unilever Canada). These companies pledged to not direct any advertising to children younger than 12 on multiple media platforms, including television, radio, print, and the Internet. Some of the larger fast food chains and processed food companies committed that 50 per cent of their advertising directed at children younger than 12 would consist of "healthier dietary choices" (Potvin and Wanles, 2014), but each company was left to independently define those "healthier dietary choices."

Potvin and Wanles (2014) recently conducted research to assess whether children's exposure to television food and beverage advertising has changed since the implementation of the self-regulatory CAI. They assessed the number of advertisements aired on 27 television stations (on children's specialty stations and on generalist stations) in Toronto and Vancouver for May 2006, 2009, and 2011. The average number of food and beverage spots seen by children ages 2 to 11 years was determined for the various time periods, and a percentage change was calculated. Potvin and Wanles (2014) found that on all stations, between 2006 and 2009, children's total average exposure to food and beverage advertising increased by 16.8 per cent in Toronto and 6.4 per cent in Vancouver. They found that significant increases were seen in spots advertising snacks and yogurt in both cities, and for fast food in Toronto (ibid.). Potvin and Wanles (2014) conclude that children's exposure to food and beverage advertising has actually increased since the implementation of the CAI, and that the current self-regulatory system is not working.

The reality is that Canadian developers of digital online content for kids also have few guidelines for ethics, monetization, and marketing. As a result, in the spring of 2012, the Kids Media Centre, made up of faculty and students at Centennial College in Toronto, embarked on a set of research projects aimed at better understanding developer challenges, practices, and attitudes around content creation in the ever-growing children's digital landscape. Their goal was to develop a framework for understanding and creating ethical and appropriate marketing practices when trying to reach young audiences. Among other things, they created a discussion paper, the Ethical Framework and Best Practices Report, that provides an overview of legal, regulatory, and child development considerations aimed at the creators of children's digital media (see http://kidsmediacentre.ca/downloads/ Ethical-Framework-Best-Practices-kmc.pdf). But the fact remains, neither governments nor industry are working very hard to make things better for children. That said, there have been positive developments, both older and newer, in television and the Internet.

All Is Not Lost—Educational Media and Media for Education

Some have found that children who spend a great deal of time watching television do poorly in school. On the other hand, those who spend a moderate amount of time watching television actually perform better than non-viewers (Alexander, 1997). This likely is linked to, and depends on, what children are watching, with whom, and how.

Some television programs actually help (some) children develop important skills that contribute to early educational success (Ennemoser and Schneider, 2007; Uchikoshi, 2005, 2006; Kendeou et al., 2005; Linebarger et al., 2004). Many programs have, in fact, been created for educational purposes—for the teaching of specific skills or for enhancing international understanding. In other words, some programs are intentionally designed to teach **prosocial behaviour**, or to teach and to model socially valued responses, such as sharing, co-operation, and understanding.

UNICEF, for example, has asked and acted upon the question, "Can television save lives?" UNICEF launched videos targeting children with the goal of distributing AIDS information to children across Africa (www.unicef.org/videoaudio/video_4915.html). Closer to home, when we mention educational television, we often think of programs like *Sesame Street* or *Mr Dressup*. In fact, educational television was said to have been "revolutionized" in 1969 with the creation of *Sesame Street*. Since then, this show has become one of the most popular children's programs worldwide. It also is one of the most-studied children's programs in the world.

Sesame Street grew out of the civil rights movement, in the spirit of social reform, with the aim of advancing Martin Luther King's idea of a beloved community, where he asked people of different nationalities to join hands and respect one another (Mandel, 2006). Recognizing the widening gap between low- and middle-income Americans, it was originally financed by the American federal government and nonprofit organizations with the aim of educating disadvantaged, urban preschoolers (Mandel, 2006; Fisch and Truglio, 2001). The promotion of the idea of "the beloved community"—a quest for social justice and for the levelling of differences between rich and poor and culturally diverse groups—has lasted onscreen for four decades (Mandel, 2006), reaching more than 120 million viewers, from more than 130 different countries (Cole et al., 2001). It has been especially successful because of its somewhat unique approach to the localizing of its content. That is, many countries are increasingly critical of the often highly aggressive American marketing strategies aimed at expanding US programs and markets internationally. Many nations fear their own loss of culture and the Americanization and commodification of childhood. Aware of these fears, *Sesame Street* and *Sesame Workshop* have taken a different approach to expanding their programs worldwide. They have incorporated a co-production process, with which local producers in countries around the world contribute to and negotiate the inclusion of nationally and culturally appropriate programming. This has come to be known as "glocalization" (Moran, 2006). For example, *Sesame Street*'s glocalization strategy in Spain involved the production of *Barrio Sésamo/Barri Sésam* (see Moran, 2006). In Israel, the West Bank, and Gaza, Israeli–Jewish, Israeli–Palestinian, and Palestinian preschoolers have access to *Sesame Street's Rechov Sumsum/Shara's Simsim*, which aims to promote respect and understanding across cultural lines in potential high-conflict zones and situations (Cole et al., 2003).

Interestingly, in Japan, *Sesame Street* was most popular in English, but flopped when it became localized in 2004 (Freedman, 2014). Freedman (2014) explained that Japan's public television broadcast *Sesame Street* from 1971 to 2004 to teach English to children. In 2004, *Sesame Street* was moved to a commercial TV network and was localized, yet the program was cancelled in 2007 because it stopped tapping into consumer desires for an idealized American childhood (Freedman, 2014). Ironically, when New York was removed from the screen and English was replaced with Japanese, *Sesame Street* could not compete with Japan's already extensive children's television market (Freedman, 2014).

Researchers analyzing Dutch episodes of *Sesame Street* broadcast between 1977 and 2003 found that over the 26-year period the formal pace of the program increased dramatically, from about four scenes per minute to about eight per minute, while the speech rate decreased from 175 words to 139 words per minute (Koolstra et al., 2004). For some, this calls into question the program's educational and developmentally appropriate qualities and its formerly unique approach that set it apart from its fast-paced, action-packed, commercial competition. Today, *Sesame Street,* like most other TV programs has a Web presence (www.sesamestreet.org), and a considerable amount of educational (and noneducational) content is now available online.

In Canada, news outlets in 1999 reported that the Ministry of Industry, John Manley, announced that Canada became the first nation in the world to connect its public schools and libraries to the Internet. He boasted that as of 30 March 1999, every Canadian public school, First Nations school, and public library that wanted to be connected by Industry Canada's SchoolNet partnership was brought online. More than 15 years later, it was not surprising to read that one study found that parents made choices about non-parental child care programs based on the technological components of a program. That is, the study by Rose et al. (2013) revealed that the child-focused technology variables that emerged as most influential to parents' decision-making were educational software usage, television usage, and Internet availability.

The Internet has also provided children with disabilities many opportunities to communicate, interact, and learn that would not have been available in the past. Lyttle (2014) notes that there is a wide selection of good mobile apps for children with special needs. She lists a number of collections that identify useful apps, including "Apps and Autism: Tools to Serve Children with Special Needs," "The Best iPad Apps for Special Needs Kids" (collected and published by *The Washington Post*), "Our Favorite Apps for Children Who Are Visually Impaired," and "Power Up! Apps for Kids with Special Needs and Learning Differences" (Lyttle, 2014).

There is no doubt that a wealth of information has been unearthed and widely shared on the Internet. It is our duty and challenge to try to assess, and to help children assess, what is most useful and what should be questioned or avoided.

Summary

In this chapter we saw that a considerable amount of children's free time, energy, and money is spent consuming traditional and newer forms of electronic and mass media. We also saw that children glean a great deal of positive and negative information from mass media of all types. What they see and hear on television and the Internet influences how children dress, what they eat, and the goods they choose or that they convince their parents to buy. The mass media teach children how to think about themselves as citizens, and as gendered and racialized beings.

As noted above, Canada-wide studies found that almost every Canadian child has access to Internet at home. Canadian children's use of the Internet begins at surprisingly young ages and has taken up an increasingly large part of their lives. There is ample evidence that today's children have integrated digital culture "seamlessly" into their lives (Montgomery, 2007). Parents, in contrast, seem to be experiencing a few new challenges and concerns. But children are not simply passive users or weak and vulnerable victims. Most are aware of news stories about online stalking and have household rules about chat rooms, providing personal information online, online pornography, and meeting online acquaintances face-to-face (Steeves, 2005).

That said, researchers have been and will inevitably continue to pay close attention to changes in children's digital media consumption, particularly around issues of child protection from online stalkers and other potential forms of abuse and misuse. On the other hand, new and better government and industry initiatives are needed to regulate what is being produced and more and better education on the part of parents, teachers, and children themselves is required.

Learning to successfully navigate and make informed choices about media consumption can provide children with important life lessons. To help young children on their way, it seems especially important that their parents, teachers, and role models become more aware, on their own account, of the role of the media in their everyday lives.

Questions for Critical Thought

1. You have been asked to prepare a fact sheet and guide for primary school teachers on children's use of the Internet and Internet safety. What would you include? What tips would you give teachers when it comes to addressing these issues with children in their classes? What activities might you include?

2. What were your favourite television programs when you were a child? Do you think these programs affected the way you thought about yourself? The products you consumed? How you viewed and treated others? How do you think your own experiences compared with trends presented in this chapter?

3. You have been hired to design a new educational program targeting preschoolers. What would it look like? How would it be delivered? What medium would you use? What kinds of characters would you include? How wide an audience would you aim for? How would you address concerns about inclusion of diversity in your program? Would it involve commercials? If not, how would you fund such a program? How would you "sell" your ideas and to whom?

4. Record three episodes of one children's program. Do an in-depth analysis of the program's use of stereotyping and diversity (gender, race, class, disability, etc.). How would you measure stereotyping and diversity? What would you count? Do an in-depth analysis of the amount and type of commercials aired throughout that program. What kinds of products are being pitched? What is the sex, age, race, class, body type, etc. of the children in the commercials? What are they actually doing? What are your overall findings? Do you have any recommendations on how to improve upon the trends that you have documented?

Suggested Readings

Kids Media Centre. 2013. *An Ethical Framework for Content Creators in the Children's Digital Space*. Toronto: Kids Media Centre (Centennial College and Ontario Media Development Corporation). At: http://kidsmediacentre.ca/downloads/Ethical-Framework-Best-Practices-kmc.pdf. This report presents an ethical framework for digital publishers and developers engaged in the marketing of child-targeted digital media content. It includes a synthesis of key legal policies and guidelines governing the creation of digital content for children in Canada and the United States. It focuses on three key areas: child privacy and safety, child development, and ethical marketing and monetization practices.

Kirsh, Steven. 2006. *Children, Adolescents and Media Violence: A Critical Look at the Research*. Thousand Oaks, CA: Sage. This book does a very good job of presenting a range of theories to help explain the effect of media violence on children and youth. It provides a critical overview of theory and research and also identifies age-related gaps in the literature.

Livingstone, Sonia M. 2009. *Children and the Internet: Great Expectations, Challenging Realities*. Cambridge: Polity. Livingstone endeavours to understand the gap between the optimism that suggests that the Internet has the capacity to allow children to be transformed by the current media culture and the real and perceived challenges and risks that are generated thorough online interactions. Among other things, she offers an overview of how the Internet affects the way that childhood is conceptualized.

Media Awareness Network. 2005. *Young Canadians in a Wired World—Phase II*. Ottawa: Media Smarts. http://mediasmarts.ca/sites/mediasmarts/files/pdfs/publication-report/full/YCWWII-trends-recomm.pdf. This is a follow-up report to the 2001 study, *Canada's Children in a Wired World: The Parents' View*, prepared for Industry Canada, Health Canada, and Human Resources Development Canada. It investigates patterns of Internet use in Canadian families and parental attitudes and perceptions about the nature, safety, and value of children's online activities.

Schor, Juliet. 2004. *Born to Buy*. New York: Scribner. Drawing on her own survey research and access to and analysis of the advertising industry, Schor assesses the size, scope, and effectiveness of marketing that targets children. She reveals interesting trends in the commercialization of childhood. While Canadian children do watch a great deal of American television, readers should be aware that this book is American, with American statistics and trends that do not always directly apply to Canadian society.

Steeves, Valerie. 2014. *Young Canadians in a Wired World, Phase III: Encountering Racist and Sexist Content Online*. Ottawa: Media Smarts. At: http://mediasmarts.ca/sites/mediasmarts/files/publication-report/full/ycwwiii_encountering_racist_sexist_content_online.pdf. This report summarizes the findings of a national survey conducted in 2013 of 5436 Canadian students in Grades 4 to 11. Students were asked about their experiences with racist and sexist content on the Internet. Among other things, the study found that more than one third of all students in Grades 7 to 11 reported seeing racist and sexist content at least once a day or once a week when they were online.

Websites

Cybertip
https://www.cybertip.ca/app/en/about

Cybertip is part of the Canadian Centre for Child Protection, a charitable organization dedicated to reducing child victimization on the Internet. Cybertip.ca was set up in 2002 as a "tip line" for reporting the online sexual exploitation of children.

Kids Media Centre
https://kidsmediacentre.ca/

This is a research centre and children's industry think tank at Centennial College's Centre for Creative Communications, involving a collaboration between Centenntial's Children's Entertainment Program and Early Childhood Education labs. It researches children's media experiences and provides tools to help kids' content producers develop meaningful entertainment.

Media Smart
https://mediasmarts.ca/

Media Smart is a Canadian nonprofit, charitable organization for digital and media literacy. Its belief is that children and youth have the critical thinking skills to engage with media as active and informed digital users. The organization promotes media and Internet education by producing online programs and resources for parents and teachers. The website also contains findings from their ongoing study series, *Young Canadians in a Wired World.*

Youth Media Alliance
https://www.ymamj.org/index_en.html

Youth Media Alliance seeks to improve the quality of media content created for children and youth. It conducts original research investigating the impact of screen-based media on young people, and lobbies governments to generate interest in all matters concerning screen-based content for young Canadians.

7 Early Childhood Education and Care in Canada

Learning Objectives

◎ To learn about some contemporary changes in the Canadian economy and their link to a growing need for nonparental child care.

◎ To explore the accessibility of licensed child care in this country.

◎ To get an overview of who is currently caring for Canada's children and learn about different types of care.

◎ To consider early childhood education and care policies in Canada.

◎ To learn about how Quebec's family policies and child care initiatives differ from those in the rest of Canada.

◎ To see how Canadian initiatives compare internationally.

◎ To examine ongoing debates surrounding child care in Canada.

◎ To look at the child care industry in Canada and the work lives of child care providers and workers.

Introduction

A Government of Canada report on the federal government's role in early childhood education and care (ECEC) opens with the following:

> The rising participation of women in paid work (1) has heightened demands for affordable, high-quality child care programs. At the same time, developments in neurobiology and the social sciences have highlighted the importance of the early childhood period in setting the stage for long-term emotional, behavioural, and intellectual well-being. (2) These factors have resulted in a greater focus on the need for early childhood programs that can:
>
> • prepare children to succeed at school;
> • improve the well-being of vulnerable children; and
> • enable the participation of parents in the labour force and in continuing education. (Cool, 2007: 1).

The report, updated in 2007, goes on to acknowledge that Canada does not have a national child care program, and more importantly, that Canada lags behind other Organisation for Economic Co-operation and

Development (OECD) nations with regard to early childhood development programs, both in terms of the proportion of gross domestic product (GDP) spent on public funding of ECEC and in terms of enrolment of children in preschool education (Cool, 2007). Things got worse, rather than better, after that point. In this chapter we will explore the current state of affairs when it comes to ECEC, child care policy, and the child care sector in this country. We will begin by looking at some recent shifts in the Canadian economy and their link to a growing need for nonparental child care. We will unpack and explore what has been happening to child care policy in this country over the past few decades. We will also investigate some of the recent changes that have taken place in Quebec over the past decade or so. We will see that Quebec is in fact closer to other developed nations when it comes to public support for child care, while the rest of Canada lags far behind. Part of the problem, some believe, has to do with the ongoing debate surrounding child care in Canada that seems to remain unresolved, including questions about whose responsibility is nonparental care in this country. The chapter ends with a closer look at the child care "industry" in Canada, and some of the conditions and challenges faced by early childhood educators today. After reading about the state of nonparental child care in this country and the treatment of caregivers and educators in the industry, we may be left wondering if the Canadian state is serious about supporting its children and families.

The Economic Need for Nonparental Care

Over the past few decades, Canada has been developing into what has been called a "post-industrial" society (Bell, 1973). In his writing, Daniel Bell (1973, 1976) explained that this meant a move towards an information society, where the main sources of innovation are derived increasingly from the production of ideas and not from the production of goods. He predicted a fundamental shift from a goods-producing economy to a **service economy** and the growth of professional and technical classes. Put simply, he predicted that we would see a shift from the bulk of workers holding blue-collar or "dirty" jobs, requiring less education, to their holding white-collar, "clean," and "smart" jobs, requiring higher levels of education. Instead of working with machines in manufacturing jobs (Gera and Mang, 1998), with **globalization**, many jobs are moving to other parts of the world where labour is cheaper, and a growing proportion of workers in Canada are expected to work with people, in service-sector jobs (Statistics Canada, 2004c). A recent labour force survey revealed that there were employment gains in professional, scientific, and technical services; in accommodation and food services; in public administration; and in agriculture; however, manufacturing was the lone industry to post a notable decline (Statistics

Canada, 2013d). But the news is not all positive in the decades-long restructuring of the Canadian economy that has been driven by global economic change (ibid.).

The share of employment accounted for by knowledge workers has increased in all regions of the country, and knowledge workers have become "a highly-prized commodity" (ibid.). However, also well documented is a bifurcation or split within the service sector, and a polarization of jobs and earnings (Hughes and Lowe, 2000; Lowe, 2000). That is, while some of the new jobs are highly skilled and knowledge-based, most new jobs being created in Canada's "new economy" are low-paid, low status, and part-time, often with nontraditional work hours, or what some have colloquially termed "McJobs" (Albanese, 2009). By 2011, some three-quarters of Canadians worked in the service sector of the economy, and of the 10 broad occupational categories in Canada, the sales and services category was the largest, with the retail sector alone employing 11.5 per cent of the country's paid workers (Statistics Canada, 2013d). Statistics Canada also noted that among the 500 occupations listed in the National Household Survey, the most common occupation for women was retail salesperson, accounting for 4.7 per cent of all employed women, followed by administrative assistant (4.0 per cent), registered nurse or psychiatric nurse (3.4 per cent), cashier (3.3 per cent), and elementary school or kindergarten teacher (2.9 per cent) (Statistics Canada, 2013d). Similarly for men, the most common occupation was retail salesperson, accounting for 3.3 per cent of all employed men, followed by transport truck driver (2.9 per cent), retail trade manager (2.5 per cent), carpenter (1.7 per cent) and janitor, caretaker, and building superintendent (1.7 per cent) (Statistics Canada, 2013d).

While unemployment rates have improved since the 2008 economic recession, they continue to fluctuate (employment growth slowed in 2013), not all parts of the country have "shared equally in the improvements" (Akyeampong, 2007: 5; Bernard and Usalcas, 2014; Statistics Canada, 2014b), the (relatively well-paid) manufacturing sector remains one of the weakest sectors of the economy (Statistics Canada, 2013d). Most of the economic gains have occurred in western Canada, while Ontario has been hard-hit by reduced activity in manufacturing, in the auto industry in particular (Akyeampong, 2007; Statistics Canada, 2014b). More Canadians are (involuntarily) working part-time—often multiple, part-time jobs—temporary (contract, seasonal, or casual) jobs, shift work, or are self-employed (LaRochelle-Côté and Uppal, 2011; Galarneau, 2010). As a result of these employment trends, family earnings instability and inequality have grown since the 1990s (Morissette and Ostrovsky, 2005). According to Statistics Canada, in 1980, the ratio of household debt to personal disposable income was 66 per cent; by 2011, that ratio surpassed 150 per cent, meaning that households owed more than $1.50 for every dollar of disposable income they had (Chawla and Uppal, 2012).

How does that affect child care? With widespread worker displacement (White, 2003), an increasing proportion of families find themselves relying on individuals holding multiple jobs or having multiple incomes per household. While women's growing labour force participation rates have something to do with their rising levels of education and women's greater desire for economic independence, families increasingly depend on women's incomes to make ends meet. This trend is not new. Women have been entering the labour force in large numbers since the end of World War II, but some things are different today. Fertility rates remain low (with a slight increase in recent years; Statistics Canada, 2007b), but the proportion of women with young children in the labour force has, for the most part, been increasing steadily. By 2009, almost 73 per cent of women with children under the age of 16 living at home were in the workforce, as were 66.5 per cent of mothers with children under the age of six (Ferrao, 2010; see Table 7.1). What is clear and different is that more women, especially women with young children, need and want to enter the labour force, yet not all can or do, at least not without assuming additional challenges related to finding nonparental care for their children.

For most families with young children, except perhaps some in Quebec (more on this below), child care remains one of the largest expenses when raising a child, and this has had an impact on the number of women who can and do enter the labour force, subsequently also affecting women's experiences when they try to balance paid work and family responsibilities.

Table 7.1 Employment Rate of Women with Children, by Age of Youngest Child, 1976 to 2009

	Employment rate (%)					
Year	Youngest child < 3 y	Youngest child 3–5 y	Youngest child < 6 y	Youngest child 6–15 y	Youngest child < 16 y	Women < 55 y, with no children at home
1976	27.6	36.8	31.4	46.4	39.1	60.9
1981	39.3	46.7	42.1	56.2	49.3	66.0
1986	49.4	54.5	51.4	61.9	56.7	69.3
1991	54.4	60.1	56.5	69.0	62.8	72.6
1996	57.8	60.5	58.9	69.8	64.5	72.4
2001	61.3	67.0	63.7	75.3	70.1	76.8
2002	61.9	68.1	64.5	77.0	71.4	77.9
2003	62.7	68.5	65.1	76.7	71.6	79.0
2004	64.5	69.4	66.6	77.0	72.4	79.3
2005	64.7	70.6	67.2	77.4	72.8	78.7
2006	64.3	69.4	66.4	78.2	72.9	79.9
2007	65.1	72.6	68.1	79.4	74.3	80.9
2008	64.6	70.3	66.8	80.0	73.8	81.2
2009	64.4	69.7	66.5	78.5	72.9	80.4

Source: Ferrao (2010: 9).

Over the past decade or so, for a growing proportion of mothers with young children, the average time spent on paid and unpaid work increased (Marshall, 2006). Furthermore, part-time and casual labourers, many of whom are women, are experiencing increased stress levels and other physical and emotional problems due to work conditions (Zeytinoglu et al., 2005) and the challenges associated with balancing paid and unpaid work (Dean, 2007; MacDonald et al., 2005). These problems coincide with the rise of **neoliberal governance**, which includes a move away from public funding of social support services. Accompanied by (re)**privatization**, or the downloading of more work onto families, these policies increase women's responsibility for the daily maintenance and care of family members, a situation known as **social reproduction** (Bezanson and Luxton, 2006: 3; Bezanson, 2006; Stinson, 2006; Gill and Bakker, 2003; Perrons, 2000). We have seen governments becoming less involved in the provision of social services precisely at a time when families in general, and women in particular, need it most. Women are expected to do more for their families (things previously done with public funds or tax dollars, such as fundraising for basic school supplies) at a time when they actually have less "free" time to do it. Furthermore, with cuts to public expenditure and privatization, "good jobs" for women are being replaced with insecure, low-waged employment (Stinson, 2006; Statistics Canada, 1998), with one of the "fastest growing industries in Canada" being low-waged jobs in areas like customer service call centres (Akyeampong, 2005: 5).

In sum, a growing proportion of women are entering the labour force, and increasingly relying on nonparental child care at a time when **welfare states**, like Canada, have been withdrawing from funding social services and when local economies are changing and being challenged by globalization and privatization (McDaniel, 2002). Quebec, in contrast, has been revamping policies to reflect the increased need and desire to assist families, and women in particular, with the mounting challenges associated with juggling paid and unpaid work (more on Quebec's polices will follow). For most families, in most provinces, the need for nonparental child care has increased, as have fees, while the number of government-regulated, **licensed/regulated child care spaces** has not kept pace with demand.

Broadly speaking, the term *early childhood education and care* in this country includes all care arrangements that provide education and care for children under the age of six (and at times up to the age of 12). This can actually include a wide array of care arrangements ranging from formal to informal care, live-in or not, permanent or temporary care, for fee or not, for-profit or not-for-profit, licensed or unlicensed (centre and home or family child care), etc. These can be located in a range of facilities, including private homes, schools, workplaces, places of religious worship, shopping malls, etc. Many parents, willingly and unwillingly, use multiple care arrangements at some point as their own and their children's needs and circumstances change.

Public support for child care for the purpose of enabling women to engage in paid work is not a new or recent phenomenon. In fact, during World War II (in 1942), to help women become more involved in war production, the federal government developed the Dominion–Provincial War-Time Agreement, which established a federal–provincial cost-sharing program to help set up provincially run child care centres for women with young children working in industries deemed essential for the war effort (Doherty et al., 2003). The Ontario and Quebec governments, the two most industrialized provinces in the country, established these special and temporary child care facilities, which were invariably closed down (or "unfunded"—some stayed open in Ontario) at the end of the war when men returned to re-enter the workforce. The expectation was that Canadian families would return to the single-earner model in which stay-at-home mothers cared for their children.

Although support has been growing over the past three decades for publicly funded child care, today, the care of young children so women can enter the labour force is treated as a private matter and the responsibility of individual families. Parents must pay for most of the cost of care, with the exception of a limited number of low-income parents who can demonstrate they are eligible for fee subsidies if and when spaces are available.

Need, Availability, and Cost of Care

Growing Need and Availability

Statistics Canada reported that the population of children four years of age and younger increased 11.0 per cent between 2006 and 2011, making this the highest growth rate for this age group since the 1956 to 1961 period during the baby boom (Statistics Canada, 2012c). Of these children, most lived in dual-earner, two-parent families and required some form of nonparental care. That said, Ferns and Friendly (2014) reported that in 2012, there were full- and part-time centre-based child care spaces for only 22.5 per cent of Canadian children under the age of six—an exceptionally small increase from the 21.8 per cent in 2010. Things were even worse for children under the age of 12: only 20.5 per cent of them have a regulated space, and even then, there is considerable variation across provinces (see Figure 7.1).

Over the past decade or so, coverage rates have been creeping up steadily; however, there is a sizeable gap between need and provision of spaces. Ferns and Friendly (2014) point out that between 2010 and 2012, the supply of regulated child care centre spaces for those ages five and under grew by only 0.7 per cent, even when family child care was included in the count, and spaces for those ages 12 and under grew by only 0.6 per cent. This is especially alarming, they note, given that even during the years of limited growth, after 2006 (more on this below), increases had never dropped

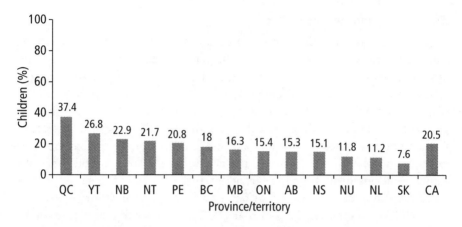

Figure 7.1 Percentage of Children 0–12 Years for Whom There Is a Regulated Child Care Space, by Province/Territory, 2012
Source: Ferns and Friendly (2014: 7).

below 1 per cent (Ferns and Friendly, 2014). Looking closely at the number of young children with mothers in the labour force, we see that about one million children under the age of five do not have a regulated space in a local child care centre should they need it (see Figure 7.2). Clearly, most of these children are cared for outside of regulated care facilities by relatives and nonrelatives. The vast majority of caregivers are women—most caring for children for pay (more on this below)—with the General Social Survey (2010) revealing that women spent an average of 50.1 hours per week on child care, more than double the average time (24.4 hours) spent by men (Milan et al., 2011).

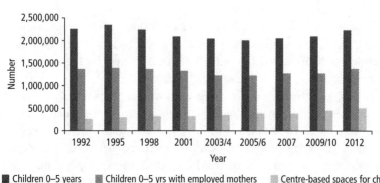

Figure 7.2 Percent of Children 0–5 Years of Age for Whom There Is a Regulated Centre-Based Child Care Space, by Province/Territory, 2012
Source: Ferns and Friendly (2014: 7).

Who Is Caring for Canada's Children?

Contrary to the belief that modern nuclear families are less dependent on extended family than they were in the past, recent research shows that grandparents are increasingly being relied on to play a more significant role in the care of their young grandchildren (Fergusson et al., 2008). In fact, with this rising trend, we have seen a growth in a body of literature on grandparenting and child care, with a significant portion of this literature focusing on the effects of this care on both children and grandparents. For example, despite popular views to the contrary, one study found that with some variations in family type, grandparent care was associated with elevated rates of hyperactivity and difficulty with peers at age four (Fergusson et al., 2008). Another study comparing different types of infant care found grandparent care scored slightly lower than other types of care, including that of child-minders, nurseries, or nannies, with regards to safety, health, and the ability to offer children learning activities (Leach et al., 2008). How caring for grandchildren affects grandparents is less clear. One study, for example, found that this near-parental caring role resulted in increased stress on grandparents (Lumpkin, 2008), while another study found no evidence to suggest that caring for grandchildren had a dramatic or widespread negative effect on grandparents' health (Hughes et al., 2007). Another still (involving 5,610 women and 4,760 men, ages 50 to 80 years), examining whether the provision of child care helps older adults maintain better cognitive functioning, found that intensively engaged grandparents have lower cognitive scores than all other grandparents; however, the authors show that this is attributable to background characteristics and not to child care per se (Arpino and Bordone, 2014). Despite negative or contradictory findings, it is clear that under the current circumstances, families are relying on the care and support of grandparents. Families are also relying on nonrelatives in unregulated care arrangements, some with but most without formal early childhood education (ECE) training.

According to findings from the National Longitudinal Survey of Children and Youth (NLSCY), the proportion of children in care (excluding children in regulated child care centres) with an ECE-trained caregiver increased nationally from 18 per cent in 1999 to 24 per cent in 2003 (Bushnik, 2006). That is, there is a growing number of private caregivers, working outside of regulated child care centres, with ECE training. Once this number was broken down, it was found that about 36 per cent of children cared for outside the home *by a nonrelative* in 2003 had a caregiver with ECE training (up from 26 per cent in 1999), while about 12 per cent of children cared for outside the home *by a relative* had a caregiver with ECE training in 2003 (up from 7 per cent in 1999) (ibid.). The proportion of children in care *at home* with an ECE-trained caregiver (relative or nonrelative) remained stable over time, at about three-quarters of nonrelatives and 90 per cent of relatives without ECE training (ibid.). Despite the positive shifts, in most cases, when children are cared for by relatives and nonrelatives outside of regulated child care centres, they are likely to be receiving *custodial care* (supervision) rather than *developmental care*. Receiving developmental care means receiving care that involves enhancing a child's development, which often widens the range of developmentally appropriate activities children are exposed to.[1] When researching whether training actually matters, Fukkink and Lont (2007), in reviewing studies published between 1980 and 2005, found that specialized training for caregivers has a significant positive effect on children. But developmental care often comes at a higher cost to parents, if and when it is available.

Cost of Regulated Child Care

Not only are regulated child care spaces with ECE-trained caregivers in short supply in this country but they are very costly as well. In 2011–12, provincial and territorial funding allocations to regulated child care totaled $4,016,815,891, with Quebec accounting for 60 per cent or $2,392,649,000 of this amount (Ferns and Friendly, 2014). Even then, according to an OECD report, the cost of centre-based child care is most expensive for working couples in English-speaking countries, including Canada, as well as in Portugal, and Switzerland (Immervoll and Barber, 2005). The study found that in these countries, the out-of-pocket expenses of couples with two young children can consume as much as 20 to 40 per cent of their entire family budget for the year. In Canada, child care expenses cost families between 27 and 42 per cent of their household income, making it among the most costly among OECD countries (ibid.).

According to Ferns and Friendly (2014), in 2012, the Canada-wide median monthly fee was $761 for infant care, $696 for toddler care, and $674 for preschool-aged care. The lowest fees—$152 per month ($7 per day) or $1,824 per year—for infants were paid by Quebecois parents while the highest fees—$1,152 a month or $12,516 per year, more than average university tuition—were paid by Ontario parents (Ferns and Friendly, 2014). These regional variations reflect differences in child policies across the country.

Child Care Policy in Canada

More than 40 years ago, Canada published the findings of the Royal Commission on the Status of Women (1970). The document forcefully declared the need for a universal, affordable child care program as a stepping stone towards women's equality. In the decades since, promises of a national child care strategy have come on and off political agendas with few concrete results. Even when the discourse around child care shifted to a more child-centred social investment strategy, demonstrating the contribution of quality child care to child development, children's rights, and even economic development (see Abner et al., 2013; Hübenthal and Ifland, 2011; Warner and Prentice, 2013), we have seen few improvements in child care policy in Canada.

Early childhood education and care is governed by provincial and territorial policies and regulations. We do not have a unified, national approach to ECE and care in Canada, and other supports to families with children are split between federal and provincial/territorial jurisdictions. As a result, there is considerable variation across the country when it comes to who cares for children, at what cost, and how. Each province and territory has its own set of legislated requirements for the operation of centres and home-based child care. Having said this, attempts have been made at the federal level to meet with the provinces and territories and come up with general agreement in the area.

Despite the lack of progress throughout the 1970s and 1980s, things appeared to be changing in the late 1990s, with the federal, provincial, and territorial governments' development of the *National Children's Agenda* (NCA) in 1997, followed by the Federal/Provincial/Territorial Early Childhood Development Agreement (ECD) in 2000 and the *Multilateral Framework on Early Learning and Child Care* of 2003 (Government of Canada, 2004). The NCA confirmed that children's well-being was a national priority while the ECD and the *Multilateral Framework* more concretely outlined commitments to enriching provincial early learning and care programs, based on principles of inclusion, affordability, accessibility, quality, and parental choice.

The *Multilateral Framework* was built upon earlier agreements reached between federal, provincial, and territorial governments on early childhood development, and was intended to guide new investments in regulated early learning and child care programs, particularly for children under age six. Its prime objective was to support the participation of parents in employment or training by improving access to affordable, quality early learning and child care (Government of Canada, 2004). Ministers responsible for social services agreed to the *Multilateral Framework* in 2003, and by 2005 the federal budget announced the development of a national Early Learning and Child Care Initiative. The 2005 budget committed $5 billion, to be spent nationally over the next five years, with $700 million paid into a third-party trust in the 2005 budget year. The provinces were given the flexibility to draw on these funds on a per capita basis as needed, up to the end of 2005–6, while a framework for quality programs and services across the country was being developed (Government of Canada and Government of Quebec, 2005; City of Toronto, 2005; Government of Canada, 2004).

These commitments were short-lived. In 2004–5, the federal Liberal Party was re-elected, only to be replaced by a Conservative minority government early in 2006. The Conservatives replaced funding commitments to the provinces with their own Universal Child Care Benefit (UCCB). This "universal benefit" gave families a $100 monthly payment for each child under six and professes to provide parents with "more choice in child care" (Government of Canada, 2006). Starting in 2015, the UCCB was increased to up to $1,920 per year for each child under the age of six (Government of Canada, 2015). Even with this increase, given the cost and limited availability of existing spaces, the promise of a national child care plan remains unfulfilled. What remains clear is the growing need for affordable child care, and it seems that only Quebec has a system seriously and systematically attempting to respond to this need.

Quebec

Today, Quebec, like other provinces, relies heavily on women's paid labour; however, it was not always so. In 1976, the labour force participation rate of women ages 25–44 in Quebec was well below the Canadian average (30 per cent compared with 36 per cent, nationally). It reached the Canadian average by 1999, and since 2000 has surpassed it by 4.2 per cent (76 per cent compared with 72 per cent nationally) (Roy, 2006). According to Roy and others, this has occurred in part since and because of the 1997 introduction of Quebec's child care program (Albanese, 2011).

The demand for affordable day care in Quebec dates back to the 1960s. The province financed its first child care pilot project in 1969 (Government of Quebec, 2003) and laid out the first policy on child care services in 1974. The Office des services de garde à l'enfance (OSGE) was founded in 1980 and since 1988 various public policy statements on child care services have been issued and assessments of parents' needs and preferences have been made, especially after 1993 (ibid.). In 1997, Quebec implemented $5-per-day child care for all four-year-olds using child care at least three days a week, regardless of a family's household income and employment status (Albanese, 2009; Government of Quebec, 2003; Tougas, 2001a, 2002; Bégin et al., 2002). By 2000, all children—regardless of age or financial need—had access to the program. Bill 145 set up a network of early childhood and child care agencies out of nonprofit child care centres and home-based care agencies, for children ages 0 to 12 (Albanese, 2006; 2011; Tougas, 2001a). Bill 145 also introduced full-time, full-day kindergarten for five-year-olds and for four-year-olds living in at-risk neighbourhoods. It expanded school child care at reduced fees ($5/day/child) for school-aged children in need of before- and after-school care (Japel et al., 2005), such that by 2005 there were 1,613 child care services in Quebec schools, with 81 per cent of public elementary schools offering them (Albanese, 2011; Commission on Elementary Education, 2006; Tougas, 2001b). In 2004, the cost increased to $7 per day; nonetheless, the province had 321,732 regulated child care spaces, accommodating 52 per cent of the province's children, compared with the 15–31 per cent accommodated in the rest of the country (Bushnik, 2006;

Albanese, 2011); this amount triples Quebec's 1992 level (Roy, 2006). Also, by 2004, close to 60 per cent of all spaces created in Canada were in Quebec, amounting to 43 per cent of all children registered in regulated child care (Roy, 2006; Albanese, 2011).

Some have suggested that Quebec, which over recent decades has seen the rise of separatist and nationalist parties in power, developed this program as part of a nationalist **pronatalist** strategy. Quebec had the highest birth rates in the country in the first half of the twentieth century, but in more recent years the Quebec rates have been the lowest. Some have argued that Quebec now seeks to boost birth rates, in fear that French language and culture are under threat by depopulation (see Albanese, 2011). However, Quebec also has had a recent history of progressive social programs, which emerged in the early 1960s as part of the Quiet Revolution and sought the socioeconomic advancement of Francophones through state intervention (Beland and Lecours, 2006; Albanese, 2011). Since the late 1990s, more emphasis has been placed on supporting working families. Even Canada's parental leave benefits and program, considered generous by some standards and ideologies, has been improved on and surpassed in Quebec's recent revamping.[2]

In these efforts, Quebec finds itself closer to a social democratic model in its policy intents and generosity (Baker, 2006; Krull, 2007; Albanese, 2011), like many other developed nations of the world, while the rest of Canada lags far behind.

International Comparisons

Canada has what has been called a "welfare state." This means that the state (government and civil service or bureaucracy) accepts some responsibility for the protection and promotion of the economic and social well-being of its citizens, through supports like unemployment insurance and access to basic health care and education. But not all welfare states are alike. In fact, scholars have looked at welfare states and have come up with subcategories or classifications to distinguish "more generous" states from "less generous" and more "laissez-faire" ones that involve less government involvement. Canada, like the United States, has been classified as a "liberal welfare state," which means that it is among the less generous, relying on the free market rather than extensive state support to families and social programs (Esping-Andersen, 1990). Within liberal welfare states, a shared basic assumption is that the state will "step in" if citizens are in dire need, often with targeted rather than universal social programs; otherwise, the state leaves social welfare decisions to individuals. Having children and using nonparental child care are seen as personal lifestyle choices and the responsibility of individual citizens and households ("you want them, you pay for them"). Of course, "more generous" or social democratic variants of welfare states do not follow this model or agree with these basic premises, which is obvious when we look at how Canada compares to other developed nations regarding ECEC.

The OECD, representing 30 of the most economically developed (and democratic) countries in the world, has been collecting comparative economic and social data for more than 40 years. In 2006, it published *Starting Strong II*, a report comparing ECEC across economically advanced nations (*Starting Strong III*, published in 2012, did not include Canada in its country policy profiles). The report notes a growing need for nonparental care across nations and, increasingly, such care is seen as a public good. It identifies some of the challenges encountered in ECEC policy-making and service coordination, compares availability and access to services, and provides a series of recommendations on how to improve quality of care and access to care. The 2012 report noted that regardless of which stage of policy development and implementation countries are at, research has suggested that there are five key factors or policy levers needed to be effective in developing quality in ECEC. These are as follows:

- Policy Lever 1: Setting out quality goals and regulations
- Policy Lever 2: Designing and implementing curriculum and standards
- Policy Lever 3: Improving qualifications, training, and working conditions
- Policy Lever 4: Engaging families and communities
- Policy Lever 5: Advancing data collection, research, and monitoring (OECD, 2012: 9)

Canada can stand to improve on all fronts, as what was especially striking in the 2006 report—even before the Conservative government's scrapping of past child care commitments and initiatives—was Canada's poor showing compared with other developed nations. In 2004, Canada had one of the highest female labour force participation rates in the world (76.6 per cent for women 24–34 years of age), after Portugal, Denmark, and Norway, while only 24 per cent of children under the age of six were in regulated care (OECD, 2006). Most striking was that of the 14 countries compared, Canada ranked lowest (below even the United States) in public expenditure on ECEC services as a percentage of GDP (ibid.) (Table 7.2). What this means was that while we are among one of the richest nations in the world, we were also the least "generous" when it came to public spending on ECEC. It also means that a larger proportion of the cost of care remains in the hands of individual families, as we saw above.

Table 7.2 Public Expenditure on ECEC Services (Children 0–6 Years), Selected OECD Countries

	Public Expenditure as % of GDP
Canada	0.25
Australia	0.4
Italy	0.43
Germany	0.45
Netherlands	0.45
United States	0.48
United Kingdom	0.5
Austria	0.55
Hungary	0.8
France	1
Finland	1.3
Norway	1.7
Sweden	1.7
Denmark	2

Source: OECD (2006), Starting Strong II: Early Childhood Education and Care, OECD Publishing, Paris. http://dx.doi.org/10.1787/9789264035461-en.

Immervoll and Barber (2005), authors of another OECD report on the cost of child care, also found Canada to be one of the least generous of states among those compared, resulting in one of the most expensive, inaccessible, and underdeveloped child care systems in the developed world.

Impact of Regulated Child Care on Children

Many factors, including lack of political will and jurisdictional wrangling, have contributed to a virtual paralysis in the establishment of child care programs and policies closer to those found in other developed nations. Often, proponents of the status quo have criticized the use of child care, let alone the expansion of services using public funds, noting that it is harmful to children. For example, condemning scholarly writing and using largely anecdotal arguments, Joseph Alderson (1997: 53) wrote that "the typical child in day care simply does not receive the same amount of individual attention, or the same degree of focused intensity, he would receive from a parent. . . . As for the people running the programs, caring for children is, for many of them, not a source of pride or prejudice; they just go through the motions. . . . In short, the best and most natural domicile for raising a child is the family." Similarly, Michael Meyers (1993: 486) argues against educating young children in child care settings as there are "health reasons to consider." He explains that "children undergo a certain amount of stress when learning," adding that "when a child is placed in a situation where they are required to learn certain topics in a certain time frame, the possibility for stress naturally increases" (see also Baker et al. 2005; Vermeer and van Ijzendoorn, 2006). On the other hand, there is a growing body of research supporting the value of high quality child care provided by trained early childhood educators, especially on children facing various disadvantages (Berry et al., 2014; Goelman et al., 2014; Campbell et al., 2014; Sheridan and Pramling Samuelsson, 2013).

Children themselves, when asked what they liked best about attending child care centres, usually described their play experiences—and research shows that play involves a great deal of learning (Ceglowski, 1997; Howard and McInnes, 2013). Recent studies confirm that children benefit from high quality child care. For example, the Early Years Study (commissioned by then Ontario Premier Mike Harris) by McCain and Mustard (1999) played a key role in demonstrating that ECEC produced important developmental outcomes for children. Similarly, Palacio-Quintin's (2000) meta-analysis of 200 studies on child care found that no authors reported a negative impact of child care on intellectual development, and all research done on children from disadvantaged economic backgrounds or with learning disabilities found that they seemed to develop better in regulated child care. Furthermore, Palacio-Quintin found that studies showed that full-time attendance did not negatively affect the mother–child relationship, and children with weaker attachment to their mothers actually benefited from strong teacher–child attachment (compensatory or protective role). Studies reported that children were more social and co-operative, and demonstrated more prosocial behaviour and superior social awareness.

Children with special needs and various disabilities have benefited from attending inclusive child care centres (Killoran et al., 2007; Wendelborg et al., 2013; Wiart et al., 2014). That said, child care spaces are limited for all children, let along those with disabilities. Wiart et al. (2014) administered surveys to centre-based and family/home child care agencies to determine the current state of inclusion of children with special needs in child care programs in one Canadian province, and to identify child care staff practices and program characteristics that support inclusion. Not surprising, all 318 centre-based child care programs and 25 family/home child care agencies (47 per cent response rate) reported positive attitudes towards the philosophy of inclusion, yet 36 per cent of the centres and 29 per cent of home child care agencies did not accept children with special needs when families contacted them. They also found that 36 per cent of centre-based programs and 40 per cent of home child care agencies were unaware of how to access specialized support services for the children in their programs. Fifty-four per cent of centre-based programs and 96 per cent of home-based child care agencies reported that they were not housed in accessible spaces (Wiart et al., 2014). As Crawford and her colleagues (2014) point out, more can and should be done to improve access and quality of care for children with disabilities (see Box 7.1).

Box
7.1

Quality of Care: Strategies for Inclusion in Play among Children
with Physical Disabilities in Child Care Centres

Sara Crawford and her colleagues (2014) at the School of Occupational Therapy at
the University of Western Ontario (London, Ontario) conducted a critical review of
existing research and literature on strategies that facilitate inclusion in play among
children with physical disabilities in child care centres. They identified and mapped
two main strategies: role of the adult facilitator and environmental factors. Each of
these had substrategies, which together underscored the importance of adopting
play inclusion strategies in the child care environment.

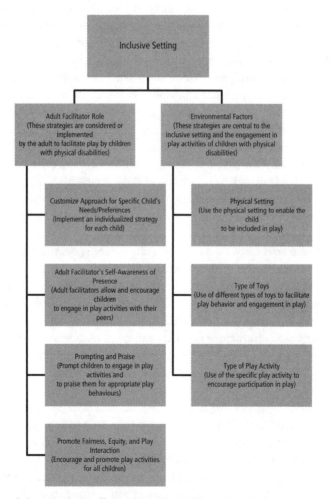

Source: Crawford, Sara K. Karen N. Stafford, Sarah M. Phillips, Kathleen J. Scott, & Patricia Tucker. 2014. 'Strategies
for Inclusion in Play among Children with Physical Disabilities in Childcare Centers: An Integrative Review', Physical
& Occupational Therapy in Pediatrics 34, 4, p. 415. Reprinted by permission of the publisher (Taylor & Francis Ltd,
http://www.tandfonline.com).

As noted above, quality of care is affected by many factors at a macro policy level (OECD, 2012), as these factors trickle down to the more micro level, affecting the size of the group of children being cared for, the density in the centre, teacher training, worker stability (low turnover rates), high-quality educational programs, good sanitary conditions, and good parent–centre relationships and communication. Much of this, however, remains outside the control of individual early childhood educators, given the nature of the work and the current working conditions in the profession.

Child Care Workers and the Child Care "Industry"

A recent OECD (2012) report noted that across countries and within them, we see a wide range of qualifications for staff working in the ECEC sector. They note that for the most part, among countries they investigated, there are more professional development opportunities for kindergarten and preschool staff compared with child care–centre staff, with only limited opportunities for home-based child care staff. The study also notes that improving working conditions will inevitably improve the quality of ECEC services (OECD, 2012). The report explains that the quality of ECEC can be improved with increased staff job satisfaction and retention and this can be achieved through better staff–child ratios and low group size; competitive wages and improved benefits; a reasonable schedule or workload; lower staff turnover; working in a good physical environment; and having a competent and supportive centre manager (OECD, 2012). Reading this, a number of questions come to mind. First, are these conditions not in place today? Second, if not, then why not? Finally, and perhaps most difficult to answer is, why do these problems or issues straddle national borders?

Work conditions for those working in the ECEC sector in Canada, like in many countries, have not been very favourable, however, things appear to be improving somewhat. In 2001, the minimum average salary for a schoolteacher with basic educational training and credentials in Canada ranged from $28,000 to $50,000, depending on the province or territory (Doherty et al., 2003). Staff with some training working in child care centres earned, on average, about half of that. In 2000, in Canada, child care workers received an average salary comparable to that of a parking lot attendant—$20,600—far below the $34,000 average income (Stafford, 2002; Tougas, 2002). In the United States, in 1998, there were more than two million people, mostly women, working at home-based child care or child care centres. Their median annual income was $10,500 for in-home care and $17,310 for in-centre care, with neither receiving much in terms of benefits. These represented the lowest-paid jobs in the occupational listing of the American Bureau of Labor Statistics and had a 50 per cent turnover rate (Dinerman, 2001).

Unionization is rare in child care; in 1998, less than 14 per cent of centres across Canada reported having unionized workers (Doherty et al., 2003). Only Quebec has pay levels set by a central bargaining process that involves the provincial government. For those in other provinces or territories, wages and salaries are set by boards of directors or by the owners of individual centres (ibid.).

More recently, results of a Canada-wide study of wages, work conditions, and practices in child care centres, published in *You Bet We Still Care!* (Flanagan, Beach, Varmuza, 2013), revealed that there have been significant changes in Canada's ECEC sector since the previous (1998) *You Bet I Care!* study was released. Participants in the more recent study identified significant program and policy changes that have affected work conditions. These include the following:

- introduction of provincial/territorial (PT) policy and funding initiatives that influence human resources, including wage subsidies, educational support, bursaries and incentives, and revised policies regarding recognition of post-secondary early childhood credentials;
- increasing involvement and oversight of ECEC programs from ministries of education;
- introduction of early childhood curriculum frameworks;
- increased support for human resources from national bodies such as the Child Care Human Resources Sector Council and from national/provincial/territorial early childhood organizations; and
- changing relationships between child care centres and school-based kindergarten programs. (Flanagan et al., 2013: 1)

Flanagan, Beach, and Varmuza's (2013) comprehensive study of the sector found that on average, program staff who responded to their national survey had worked in the sector for 12 years (or a median of 10 years), one quarter had worked for five years or less, while another quarter had worked for 18 years or more. Almost 90 per cent reported holding post-secondary ECE-related credentials, with 74.4 per cent reporting having completed this at a community college and 11 per cent at a university (Flanagan, Beach, and Varmuza's, 2013). Almost 60 per cent had completed a two-year ECE diploma, up from 48 per cent who responded to the 1998 survey.

The study also found, for the most part, real improvements in hourly wages compared with the 1998 study. Flanagan et al. (2013) found a median hourly wage of $16.50 for program staff and $22.00 for a program director, representing an annual salary of $30,146 and $40,194, respectively, for those employed full-time. This was a significant improvement from the 1998 average hourly wage of $11.48 for a program staff and $16.49 for directors. As a result of these improvements, the report also noted that program staff earned 69 per cent of the average hourly wage for all employees in all sectors in Canada ($23.92) and program directors earned 92 per cent of that. Clearly, there is still room for improvement.

The profession remains highly feminized, with women representing 98.3 per cent of teaching staff and 96.4 per cent of directors (Doherty et al., 2000). Such work remains undervalued because many continue to believe that the work involved in caring for children is natural, inevitable, and easy for women (Albanese, 2007). In addition to providing developmentally appropriate care for groups of children, full-time staff often are expected to engage in active planning and preparation, interaction with parents, meal and snack preparation and cleanup, general maintenance of space, supervision of practicum students, staff supervision, meeting with people other than parents, administration, etc. (Albanese, 2006; Doherty et al., 2000). Jean-Jacques Rousseau (1974 [1762]: 5) wrote that "the earliest education is most important"—comforting words, indeed. However, he completed that sentence with "and it undoubtedly is women's work." While it is true that most of the teachers of our earliest childhood were women and for children today, they continue to be women, we should not assume that this work is natural, inevitable, or easy. For as long as we do, such work will remain overlooked, undervalued, and underpaid. Caring for other people's children, particularly in groups, is difficult work requiring a wide array of skills. Until we recognize the value of this social role and its contribution to children, families, and the nation, Canada is likely to remain at the bottom of the heap, compared with other developed nations.

Summary

In this chapter we saw that over the past few decades a need has grown for nonparental child care because an increasing number of women with young children wish to or are obliged to enter the labour force. We also saw that while there is a growing need for nonparental child care, the number of licensed child care spaces remains inadequate for a number of reasons, including cost and inaccessibility, across most of the country. Children often are cared for by untrained adults; although they may have the children's best interests in mind, they may not have the training to provide adequate and informed care within a range of intellectually stimulating activities and environments. Most parents are forced to leave their children in the care of people who can provide only custodial care because of a lack of options available to them; this is clearly the result of policy decisions made at the federal and provincial levels.

We saw that while there seemed to be progress in the development of a national approach to child care funding since the late 1990s, progress stalled after 2006. Quebec, in contrast, has continued to forge ahead, implementing a range of programs aimed at helping families with young children to manage the difficult task of balancing paid work and family responsibilities. Quebec's child care programs are much closer to the social policy initiatives of other developed nations, while the rest of Canada lags behind in comparison. In fact, while other countries have recognized the need for and social benefits of ECEC, we continue to debate whether it harms Canada's children or whose responsibility it is to fund it. These are important questions to ask, yet having a parent—most often a mother—stay home to raise children is not a viable option for a large and growing number of Canadians and Canada's well-being as a nation depends on the well-being of its children. The better question may actually be, how do we create accessible options of high quality and opportunities that mutually benefit parents and children, while at the same time recognizing the difficulty, value, and skills involved in doing this well?

Questions for Critical Thought

1. What do you believe are the most important factors in determining "quality" care? What do you believe we need to do to achieve this? Who should pay for it? How?

2. What do you think accounts for our current government's approach to child care? Do you agree with the approach? What recommendations would you give to our federal government?

3. Do you believe that the state should be more involved in the creation, financial support, and maintenance of more licensed child care spaces? Why? Why not? If yes, which level of government should be given the responsibility? Why? How would you get others to agree with you?

4. Write an op-ed piece outlining your stance on the state of ECEC in Canada today. What should change, if anything? What should stay the same? Include five or six distinct points that you believe will convince others to support your views.

Suggested Readings

Cleveland, Gordon, and Michael Krashinsky, eds. 2001. *Our Children's Future: Childcare Policy in Canada*. Toronto: University of Toronto Press. This collection of papers from some of Canada's leading researchers on child care and family policy includes discussions of "quality," lessons from Quebec, delivery models of child care services, universal child care, child care workers, etc.

Ferns, Caroline, and Martha Friendly. 2014. *The State of Early Childhood Education and Care in Canada 2012*. Toronto: movingchildcareforward.ca. At: http://childcarecanada.org/sites/default/files/StateofECEC2012.pdf. This report provides a snapshot of Canadian ECEC in 2012, using data collected by Childcare Resource and Research Unit. It includes an overview of the demographic context in which policy shifts in Canadian ECEC are taking place. It also includes detailed information on child care spaces, public funding, parent fees, ownership or auspice, Aboriginal child care, and human resources.

Flanagan, K., J. Beach, and P. Varmuza. (2013). *You Bet We Still Care! A Survey of Centre-Based Early Childhood Education and Care in Canada. Highlights Report.* Ottawa: Child Care Human Resources Sector Council. At: www.wstcoast.org/pdf/YouBetSurveyReport_ Final.pdf. Building on past Canadian research, including *Caring for a Living* (1991) and *You Bet I Care!* (1998), *You Bet We Still Care!* (2012) presents a detailed picture of human resources for the ECEC sector in Canada.

OECD. 2011. *Doing Better for Families.* Paris: OECD. www.oecd.org/els/soc/doingbetterforfam- ilies.htm. This book looks at how family policy is developing in various countries around the world. It compares different ways in which governments support families and seeks to answer numerous questions: Is spending on family benefits going up, and how does it vary by the age of the child? What are the effects of parental leave schemes on female labour supply, and on child well-being? Are child care costs a barrier to parental employ- ment and how can flexible workplace options help?

Prentice, Susan, ed. 2001. *Changing Child Care: Five Decades of Child Care Advocacy and Policy in Canada.* Halifax: Fernwood. *Changing Child Care* brings together essays on past and more current issues affecting child care in this country. It provides a good overview of federal and provincial child care policy development and advocacy from World War II to 2000.

Websites

Childcare Resource and Research Unit
www.childcarecanada.org/index.shtml
> The Childcare Resource and Research Unit provides an impressive and wide-ranging collection of policy documents and national and international research reports. It has regularly updated sections such as "What's New Online" and "Childcare in the News," which contain links to political speeches and national and international news stories on child care.

Department of Indian and Northern Affairs—Early Childhood Development
www.ainc-inac.gc.ca/ps/ecde/index_e.html
> This Department of Indian and Northern Affairs website provides information, fact sheets, and documents on Canadian government initiatives for Aboriginal children. Among other things, it has links to fact sheets on Aboriginal Head Start programs, reserve child care programs, etc.

Finding Quality Child Care
http://findingqualitychildcare.ca/
> This site provides resources for Canadian parents in understanding and accessing high- quality child care. This site and an accompanying video were developed by the Childcare Resource and Research Unit and the Canadian Union of Postal Workers.

Organisation for Economic Co-operation and Development (OECD)
www.oecd.org/edu/school/startingstrongiiiaqualitytoolboxforecec.htm
> This OECD site provides access to an online version of *Starting Strong III,* with compara- tive data on ECEC.

8 Newcomer Children in Canada

Learning Objectives

◎ To learn about Canadian immigration policies and the role they play in shaping the experiences of newcomer children and families.

◎ To learn how many children have come to Canada in recent years, from where, and under what circumstances.

◎ To explore some of the challenges faced by newcomer children within both their new and their original cultures.

◎ To learn about newcomer children's adaptation into their new country.

◎ To understand how the lives of newcomer children compare to those of other Canadian children.

◎ To learn about refugee children and see how their lives compare with those of immigrant and Canadian-born children.

Introduction

I came to Canada when I was five-and-a-half. While I did not have to struggle with many of the "adult" challenges associated with settlement, being an immigrant child was not without its trials. Apparently, I was a chatterbox as a child, in my mother tongue, and I loved school *before* I came here. Once in Canada, I was tongue-tied; my school lunches looked and smelled different from other children's (Toronto, back then, was not as diverse as it is today); my clothes were different; my shoes were leather, not canvas . . . I felt that I didn't belong and was ready to drop out of school at the age of six. But of course, my parents and the state wouldn't allow it.

I picked up English quickly and soon found myself translating for my parents at the local grocery store, bank, and government offices. It's very unlikely that Canadian-born eight-year-olds know and can translate the word "mortgage" into another language, but for many newcomer children it's not unusual. Among other things, this chapter will highlight some of the experiences and challenges faced by newcomer children as they adapt to a new country.

This chapter begins with a brief historical sketch of Canadian immigration policy, with emphasis on the importance placed on country of origin in determining who was allowed to enter Canada, under what circumstances, and with whom. This is followed by an overview of recent immigration numbers and trends. We then look at research findings on how the lives of newcomer children compare with those of other Canadian children. You will read about some of the challenges associated with the juggling of expectations placed on newcomer children by both their new and "old" culture or society, their experiences within the educational system, and their overall health and well-being. You will also learn about the impact of refugee status on children. The chapter concludes with recommendations on what we as a society can do to assist children from racially and ethnically diverse backgrounds.

Changing Immigration Policy—A Brief Historical Overview

When we think of Canadian immigration and immigration policy, children often do not come to mind first. But immigration has a great deal to do with children because one of the aims of immigration in this country, from the beginning, has been to help populate the nation, and later, to help offset declining fertility rates.

When Canada as a nation came into existence in 1867, John A. Macdonald and his Conservative government dreamed of a country (which initially comprised only Nova Scotia, New Brunswick, and portions of present-day Ontario and Quebec), extending from the Atlantic to the Pacific Oceans. But there was a long way to go before this could be realized. One problem was that in the late nineteenth century, while birth rates were high and exceeded death rates, more people were leaving Canada, mostly for the United States, than entering it, resulting in a population loss (McKie, 2000). Therefore, one of the early goals of immigration policy was to help populate the country, especially the West, before our neighbours to the south could lay claim to it. The goal was to attract farmers, agricultural labourers, and female domestics from Great Britain, the United States, and Northern Europe (Knowles, 1992). The government had its unofficial list of preferred immigrants and an even longer list of those considered "undesirable" (Albanese, 2009).

The Canadian government employed a number of initiatives to recruit and maintain a select group of fit, permanent settlers to the West. For example, to attract Mennonites, an Anabaptist sect committed to a simple life and pacifism, the government offered freedom from military service and from swearing the oath of allegiance, freedom of religion, and travel assistance of $30 per adult to "Mennonite families of good character" (Albanese, 2009: 50). This was in sharp contrast to the treatment of equally necessary labourers deemed "undesirable" for permanent settlement: Chinese, Southern European, and South Asian migrant workers. When migrants were needed as sources of cheap labour, the government did all it could to create transitional "bachelor" communities. Women, wives, and children were discouraged from migrating with the hope that permanent communities would not be established. In other words, when migrants were deemed acceptable, entire families were recruited and encouraged to settle; when they were deemed undesirable, men were encouraged to migrate alone and temporarily, so as not to settle, have children, and a future in Canada (Albanese, 2009). For example, to deter mass migration, and especially the entry of Chinese women and children, in 1886 the Canadian government levied a head tax of $50 per Chinese migrant, later raised to $100, then $500 by 1903. Many left behind wives and children, with the hope of returning to China after earning money in Canada. Between 1904 and 1923 the $500 head tax levied on all (and only) Chinese immigrants effectively limited Chinese family life in Canada.

Looking through the first hundred years of Canadian immigration history (1867–1967), we see that immigrant children and children of immigrants were desired if they were deemed to be of the "right stock" (country of origin) and were prohibited through discriminatory practices if they were believed to be from "undesirable" **ethnic** (those who share ancestral origins, customs, beliefs) and **racial/racialized** (a classification of people into categories based on real or imagined physical characteristics) groups. It was only in the 1960s that the government abolished almost all restrictions to immigration based on ethnicity and race. The new emphasis was on the economic needs of the country, and for the economy to flourish, a growing population was necessary.

Changes to the Immigration Act of 1967 removed race restrictions for entry to Canada and introduced a merit point system. "Independent" (economic) immigrants were granted entry to Canada based on the number of points accorded for various qualifications they possessed—including education, job skills, knowledge of English or French, etc.—and *not* the colour of their skin or country of origin. The removal of national origin restrictions resulted in a shift in the number of immigrants from places other than Europe and the United States. As a result, there was a significant change in the composition of Canada's population, including a rise in the number of **visible minority** or *racialized* immigrants—peoples classified as non-Caucasian in race or non-white in colour. Furthermore, because of these shifts in our immigration policies and the introduction of the points system in particular (which literally scores the value of immigrants of a particular age and educational level), the majority of immigrants arriving today—about half—are between the ages of 25 and 44, and of childbearing years (Citizenship and Immigration Canada [CIC], 2014b). Many of these individuals come to Canada with young children.

Recent Immigration Numbers and Trends

In 2011, just over 7.2 million people living in Canada—or 22 per cent of the population—were first generation, born outside of Canada, representing some 200 countries (Dobson et al., 2013). Close to half of these immigrants came after 1985. For example, in 2001, about 1.8 million people in Canada were immigrants who had arrived in the previous 10 years; of these, about 310,000 or 17 per cent were children ages 5 to 16 years (McMullen, 2004). In 2013 alone, more than 16,000 children under the age of five and another 17,368 ages five to nine accompanied their parents to Canada (CIC, 2014c; see Table 8.1).

In 2013, some 48,300 children under the age of 15 entered as permanent residents, down from the highest number in 10 years of 57,591 in 2005 (CIC, 2014c). The vast majority of these arrived with their parents as "economic immigrant," via the points system (CIC, 2014c). Some arrived as refugees, a category of newcomer defined and regulated by the Immigration and Refugee Protection Act of 2002, which replaced the Immigration Act of 1976).[1] The largest proportion of all who arrived in 2013 came from Asia and the Pacific region. The largest proportion of refugees in 2013 arrived from Africa and the Middle East (CIC, 2014d). The majority of newcomers to Canada in 2013 settled in the largest cities in Ontario (40 per cent of all immigrants, with 35.1 per cent of all immigrants to Canada settling in Toronto alone), Quebec (20.1 per cent), Alberta (14.1 per cent), and British Columbia (14.0 per cent) (CIC, 2014e). This influx of newcomers has had a major impact on the composition—the look, sound, and needs—of schools and communities in the major urban centres where newcomers settled.

As in the rest of the population, the vast majority of children 14 years of age and younger arriving to Canada lived with their relatives (CIC, 2007h). Recent immigrants of all ages were more likely than other Canadians to live with relatives, in extended families. Newcomer children were more likely than other Canadian children to live in extended families, with their grandparents in particular.

However, most newcomer children, like other Canadian children, lived in nuclear families, but family sizes tended to be larger for immigrant families

Table 8.1 Permanent Residents of Canada Younger than 15 Years of Age, 2004–2013, by Age

	2004	2005	2006	2007	2008	2009	2010	2011	2012	2013
0–4 y	16,742	18,326	16,405	15,924	16,317	15,987	20,177	17,774	17,514	16,167
5–9 y	17,620	20,204	17,569	16,196	17,065	17,413	21,196	18,375	18,391	17,368
10–14 y	16,545	19,061	17,345	16,159	16,910	16,894	19,291	16,720	16,234	14,824
0–14 y (total)	50,909	57,591	51,320	48,279	50,292	50,294	60,664	52,869	52,139	48,359

Source: CIC (2014c).

(Bélanger, 2006). Children in recent immigrant households were more likely to live with parents who were legally married rather than those who were living as common-law partners. Newcomer children were also less likely than other Canadian children to live in lone-parent families, but were more likely than others to live in overcrowded housing (CIC, 2007i).

While the economic contribution of immigrants is well established (Palameta, 2004), immigrant parents are less likely than other Canadians to work full-time, year-round. As a result of these and other employment trends, very recent immigrants have wages and salaries that are about 74 per cent of the Canadian average, up from 65 per cent in 1995. The average recent immigrant, however, receives a lower amount in government transfer payments than his or her Canadian-born counterpart (ibid.), meaning that a larger proportion of immigrant income comes from wages and salaries, and less from employment insurance, social assistance, tax credits, child benefits, etc. As a result of all this, recently arriving newcomer children are much more likely than earlier immigrants or Canadian-born individuals to live in families with incomes below the **median family income** (income that falls in the "middle" of the income range or spectrum in a society). It is also important to note that a large proportion of recent immigrants are racialized, and that a high number of racialized Canadians are living in poverty. Recent reports reveal that those from racialized groups made up 54 per cent of all immigrants in Canada, yet comprised 71 per cent of all immigrants living in poverty (National Council of Welfare, 2013). Furthermore, 90 per cent of racialized persons living in poverty are first-generation immigrants (ibid.). The factors behind these rates include an overrepresentation of racialized groups in low-paying jobs, labour market failure to recognize international work experience and credentials, and racial discrimination in employment (Campaign, 2000, 2007a). In contrast, children of immigrants who came to Canada before 1981 and who had below-average earnings in the first generation were found to have surpassed their parents in the second generation, and were more educated and earned more on average than Canadians of similar age whose parents were born in Canada (Statistics Canada, 2005c).

Understanding the statistics, rates, and trends that generally characterize the lives of newcomer children will help you to understand those you work with, study with, and live among. Knowledge of the similarities and differences in the immigrant experience compared with those who are second-generation Canadians or from families of longer residence may prevent your making incorrect assumptions about who newcomer children are, what their lives are like, and where they come from. Becoming sensitive to the variety of experiences you will encounter as a social practitioner and worker will allow you to be more creative and respectful. A small gesture can go a long way in helping a newcomer child feel more comfortable. For example, as one 11-year-old boy reported, "it felt great when Mrs Brown asked me to talk about Nurouz [the Persian new year] in class. I was happy. I told them what my parents taught me. I felt happy to talk about my country, my traditions, and where I come from to the kids in class. Because, you know, they don't really know" (Sadeghi, 2008).[2] Here, a simple gesture on the part of an understanding teacher turned an often difficult and potentially traumatic experience—moving to a new country, not speaking the language, and starting a new school—into a positive and proud moment.

Understanding Immigrant Children's Experiences

A focus-group study with newcomer parents, service providers, and community leaders, looking at newcomer engagement in early childhood development services and supports (for newborns to six-year-olds) in the Peel Region, just outside Toronto, revealed some important insights into the lives of newcomer parents and their children (Joyette, 2014). The study was specifically trying to understand which newcomer parents were accessing early childhood development services and what factors were contributing to a previous research finding that there is a reduction in use of services the longer the family has been in Canada. The insights revealed in the study reach beyond the original research questions. The study found that newcomer parents of young children were highly motivated during the first six months after their arrival, but became disillusioned as stressors mounted once they were here (Joyette, 2014). Their use of services dropped for a number of reasons, including, on a mundane level, parents' (mostly mothers') reliance on use of public transit (with strollers, etc.)—which added significant effort and expense—to access services (Joyette, 2014). More significantly, for some, cultural practices of the immigrant's country of origin inhibited participation; for example, in situations in which it was customary for a male relative to accompany a woman, his finding employment left her unable to attend. Prohibitive costs of programs and limited knowledge of English were also barriers (Joyette, 2014). As a result, many newcomer mothers in particular felt isolated, and overwhelmed, as many lacked traditional family supports. Parents were concerned about their children losing culture, language, and values; some felt judged and pressured to conform to Canadian norms; some felt stigmatized when accessing publically funded services or low-cost programs (Joyetter, 2014). Some parents did not understand the value of play-based learning and believed more attention should be paid to academic achievement, even in programs and services for very young children. Lastly, some simply felt unaware of the availability of programs and supports (Joyette, 2014). Taken together, these findings provided insights into the lives and challenges faced by newcomer parents. They also have implications for how children themselves experience settlement.

For example, Colbert (2010), in *Welcoming Newcomer Children: The Settlement of Young Immigrants and Refugees,* reminds us of the importance of understanding the settlement experience from the unique perspective of the child. Colbert challenges us to consider the distinctive settlement needs of young children. But this was not always the case in the past.

Before the 1990s, a traditional approach to research on immigrant offspring stressed an optimistic scenario, embedded in linear or straight-line theory (Boyd, 2000). This "straight-line" approach argued that with the passage of time, and with each succeeding generation, the descendants of immigrants would become like other Canadians. Recent models challenge this view, and some identify different possible outcomes for newcomer children, including (1) **assimilation**, or the "blending in," with economic success; (2) continued emphasis on ethnic identity resulting in integration into **ethnic enclaves**, often with involvement in ethnically owned or controlled businesses; or (3) the assumption of underclass identities and integration into marginal labour markets (Boyd, 2000). Even more recently, results from studies like the National Longitudinal Survey of Children and Youth (NLSCY) reveal that, on average, children of immigrants generally do at least as well in school as the children of Canadian-born parents. Despite successes, challenges persist, as we will see below.

Settlement, Adaptation, and Other Challenges

Settlement is a complex process and a time of uncertainly for everyone involved, including children. Some have argued that every child's needs throughout the process are distinct, even when compared with those of their siblings and adult family members (Colbert, 2010). When children enter a new country, they can expect to experience changes and disruptions which require a great deal of **adaptation** or adjustment to fit into a new culture (see Chapter 3, Box 3.1). The integration of newcomer children into the host society depends on their parents' social and economic status and well-being, the age at which they immigrated, their knowledge of English or French, the type of support they receive in school, and a host of other factors.

Parents and Parenting

Every culture has ideas about how children should be socialized, and this is reflected in differences in child-rearing ideologies and practices. It is commonly believed that when immigrants move to a new country they are faced with different, sometimes conflicting ideas on the matter. Closer analysis reveals that similarities exist across cultures, and there is also change over time *within* cultures (Ochocka and Janzen, 2008). Shimoni et al. (2003) conducted a pilot study of immigrant fathers of preschool children from diverse ethnic groups (Yugoslavians, South Americans, South Asians, and Hong Kong Chinese and mainland Chinese) to determine what factors shaped their perceptions, values, goals, and hopes around fatherhood. When asked about values and beliefs that guide their fathering, all respondents mentioned honesty, integrity, and respect for others. All wanted their children to grow up educated and financially secure, and with positive family relations. Most spoke of opportunities that Canada would provide, which their children would not have received in their country of origin. Differences were found in response to questions about the importance of preserving ethnic culture and traditions and the importance of religion (ibid.). Very similar results were found by Ochocka and Janzen (2008) in their study involving 50 focus groups with newcomer parents in Ontario.

While various studies have compared parenting styles of newcomer parents, especially mothers, to those of Canadian-born parents (see Liu et al., 2005), Ochocka and Jenzen (2008) remind us that focusing on culture alone is too simplistic when trying to understand immigrant parenting. They instead encourage us to consider a wide range of ecological contextual factors. To start, parenting in a new country can be difficult given that although parents' lives have been profoundly disrupted, they often attempt to provide a stable environment for their families (Ochocka and Jenzen, 2008). Ochocka and Jenzen encourage us to consider the impact of parental social support networks, socioeconomic status, and economic hardships endured by parents, which would inevitably affect parenting. Parenting practices, as is the case with Canadian-born parents, also depend on the maturity of the parents; the number, age, gender, and personalities of their children; as well as the families' cultural and religious backgrounds (ibid.). Furthermore, we should consider how long parents have lived here, how much contact they have had with other members of Canadian society, and parents' own world views that help them interpret the world around them (ibid.). As a result, Ochocka and Jenzen (2008) developed a framework for better understanding newcomer parents and parenting.

This broader framework begins by identifying parents' *orientations,* or the beliefs and values that form parents' expectations for their children's behaviours and hopes for their children's futures; their *parenting styles* (how they relate and interact with their children); the host *country context* (which may be similar or different from their own); *parenting modifications* (the changes parents make to their parenting orientation and styles as a result of living within the new host country context); their *parenting contributions* (the ways in which immigrants contribute to an understanding and practice of parenting within their new host country); and the *parenting supports* needed for immigrant parents (to help them process any parenting modifications and encourage mutual exchange and understanding between themselves and others in their new country). In other words, Ochocka and

Jenzen (2008) challenge us to think about newcomer parenting in more complex and nuanced ways than we have in the past. Only then can we begin to understand the intricacies in the lives of newcomer children.

Despite parents' best efforts, some children experience role strain as they are called upon to be both dependents and *cultural brokers* for their parents (Chung, 2013; Hua and Costigan, 2012; Ali and Kilbride, 2004). At times, as children attained proficiency in English (or French), they became cultural and language interpreters for their parents, or cultural brokers, resulting, to a certain extent, in dependency role reversals. Parents can then became reliant on children for support in the new society (Ali and Kilbride, 2004). This can be difficult for both generations, as parents fear the destabilization of their authority and children may experience embarrassment and fear discrimination over their parents' lack of knowledge (Momirov and Kilbride, 2005).

Racism and Discrimination

The experiences of newcomer and other visible minority children are at times plagued by *racism* (individual and institutionalized attitudes and behaviour linked to the belief in the superiority of one's own race to the detriment of others) and other forms of discrimination at both the institutional and individual levels, denying them a sense of belonging and driving them into social isolation and alienation (Van Ngo and Schleifer, 2007). For example, children as young as three or four have been found to favour individuals with whom they share group membership, and have negative evaluations of individuals belonging to groups they consider to be dissimilar (Nowicki, 2008; Nesdale et al., 2005, 2007).

Children who attract negative attitudes because of their "racial" difference from the majority often face significant stumbling blocks in school (Nowicki, 2008). At the institutional level, when children do not see their race, language, or culture reflected in the classroom, they do not feel part of the group (Cohen, 2008). They come to internalize the dominant discourse and perceive themselves as inadequate and inferior (Quaicoe, 2007). In response to this, Cohen (2008) reminds us that family practices differ considerably, so each child's enculturation is unique. Acknowledging this combination of circumstances has implications for teachers and others working with racially and culturally diverse children; they need to adjust their practices to help create safer, more accessible and inclusive spaces. By doing this, they will not only improve the experiences of newcomers and other minority children but enrich their own and Canadian-born children's experiences as well. One 11-year-old child reminds us of this when she says, "Canada, to me, is about multiculturalism . . . is learning about all these different cultures, their languages, their worlds, all these people who come to Canada from different parts of the world, and we live here, together. I would have never had this chance to know all these different cultures" (Sadeghi, 2008).

Despite changes, discrimination persists and children feel it. Oxman-Martinez and Choi (2014), for example, analyzed data from the New Canadian Children and Youth Study (NCCYS), a national longitudinal survey of 515 foreign-born immigrant children (ages 11–13) from three ethnic groups (mainland China, Hong Kong, and the Philippines) living in Montreal and Toronto. Their study of the influence of an inclusive school environment, social and psychological isolation, and perceived discrimination by peers and teachers on the psychosocial and academic adjustment of immigrant children revealed that being exposed to more inclusive school environments had a significant effect on social competence and academic performance of immigrant children. Their study showed that after controlling for the children's sociodemographic background variables, teachers' discriminatory attitudes and psychological isolation contribute to immigrant children's low self-esteem, social competence, and academic performance. Not surprisingly, peer discrimination was also negatively associated with self-esteem and social competence. Inclusive school environment, social and psychological isolation, and discrimination were found to be critical factors affecting the developmental outcomes of immigrant children, and these in turn affected children's future prospects.

Language Retention and Education

A great deal of **acculturation** for newcomer children takes place in school. Because of the importance of schooling in this process, some cultural variations in attitudes towards parenting have resulted in tension between parents and educators (Joyette, 2014; Anisef and Kilbride, 2001). A key area of concern is first- and second-language acquisition and retention.

Many children arriving in Canada do not speak one of the two official languages and require English as a Second Language/French as a Second Language (ESL/FSL) training in their Canadian schools. Because immigration is regulated at the federal level and education falls under provincial jurisdiction, language-training programs vary from province to province and some suffer from lack of resources.

Lack of knowledge of English (or French) impacts skills development in school, especially depending on the child's age at arrival (Corak, 2011). Interestingly, a now classic study using NLSCY data from 1994 to 1998 found that children of immigrant parents start school with less developed skills in reading, writing, and mathematics (particularly if their mother tongue is neither English nor French) than do their classmates with Canadian-born parents, but overcome this disadvantage and in some cases even exceed the performance of children of Canadian-born parents before the end of elementary school (Statistics Canada, 2001; Worswich, 2001). Children from immigrant families whose mother tongue was neither English nor French (allophone) "caught up to" (or surpassed) their peers by age 10 or 11, and those with English or French mother tongues did so by age nine. Similar results were found through the analysis of data from the 2000 Program for International Student Assessment study. This analysis shows that the average performances of newcomer children converge with those of Canadian-born peers after the immigrant student has lived in Canada for about 14 years (McMullen, 2004).

Studies show that loss of the first language occurs rather quickly following immigration for most children. Turcotte (2006) notes that use of ancestral language shows a marked decline, especially once children leave their parental home, despite evidence that knowledge of additional languages is a significant asset later in life. Not all immigrants are equally likely to pass on their mother tongues to the next generation. Turcotte also found that parents with the highest levels of education and those with the highest incomes are least likely to pass on their mother tongue, whereas those who partnered with someone of the same mother tongue or who reside in Quebec are more likely to pass on their mother tongue.

The loss of the first language has some potentially negative effects on **assimilation** or the loss of distinctiveness through the absorption into the dominant culture and language. According to a classic study by Bernhard et al. (1996), newcomer children may come to believe that their home language has little or no value and is not necessary for accomplishing goals in Canadian society. Pacini-Ketchabaw and Armstrong de Almeida (2006) found that discourses in school policies and among teaching professionals privilege English and monolinguals over minority languages and bilinguals, thus promoting the quick learning of English at the expense and threat of loss of the first language. When children learn English quickly parents may become less able to communicate with their children and, thus, are limited in their ability to transmit values, advice, and responsibilities (Bernhard et al., 1996). Pacini-Ketchabaw et al. (2001) believe that parents and children would benefit if educators had a greater understanding of bilingual issues, and Bernhard et al. (1996) suggest that teacher-education institutions promote the enrolment of linguistically diverse teacher trainees.

Health and Emotional Status

As noted above, newcomer children often learn a new language rapidly and some become high achievers in school, but many also struggle, experience discrimination, witness difficulties at home, fall behind in school, and experience developmental challenges related to their resettlement experiences. Because of the major life disruptions associated with migration, some newcomer children develop mental health problems requiring specialized care. That said, few studies on immigrant family health have explored the impact of immigration and settlement experiences on children's overall health (Simich et al., 2009).

According to Ahmed (2005: 5), "health is the most desirable outcome among all of the child development outcomes as it is linked with all other outcomes." As a result, it is important to look at and understand the health outcomes of newcomer children. A study by Simich and her colleagues (2009) revealed that newcomer children's health was correlated with several factors, including parents' level of education, neighbourhood safety, and with key factors in family functioning (including whether family members support each other in a crisis; whether family members feel accepted for who they are; and whether family members confide in each other). Not surprising, Beiser et al. (2014) found that parents' depression and poor mental health, intrafamilial conflict, and resettlement stress each affected children's psychological well-being.

A classic study by Beiser et al. (2002) on poverty and mental health among newcomer children in Canada compared the mental health of three subgroups: newcomer children (children born in a foreign country to non-Canadian parents who are now in Canada), Canadian-born children of immigrant parents, and non-immigrant children living in poverty. They found that new immigrant families were much more likely than Canadian families to be poor. On the other hand, they enjoyed a mental health advantage—they fared better—than non-immigrant children on a number of mental heath measures. They also found that immigrant girls had even fewer emotional problems than immigrant boys. In contrast, non-immigrant girls living in poverty tended to have more emotional problems than non-immigrant boys in the same situation. Furthermore, Asian immigrant children had a mental health advantage over European or white immigrant children. Beiser et al. speculated that while new immigrants are more likely to be underemployed, unemployed, and living in poverty, they may be optimistic that these difficulties will eventually be overcome, thereby helping to protect immigrant families from breakdown and dysfunction. In this respect, the shared goal of the family may tend to promote unity, and the act of immigration, in most instances, is likely based on hope for the future, even, and perhaps especially, for refugees.

Similarly, Ma's (2002) analysis of NLSCY data revealed that newcomer children fared better behaviourally and emotionally than non-newcomer children. However, urban characteristics such as socioeconomic conditions, social climate, and the availability of social services had much stronger effects on newcomer children compared with other children, and were found to account for behavioural and emotional problems in newcomer children. The social environment was found to be more important for newcomer children's emotional health, while demographic characteristics, such as gender, age, family structure, family socioeconomic status, and family size, were the most significant factors among non-newcomer children (ibid.).

Ahmed (2005) compared the health outcomes of newcomer children to native-born Canadians, but also compared three different immigrant subgroups (American, Asian, and European) and found that health outcomes for children in immigrant families were similar to those in native-born families. Variations, however, existed across immigrant groups. In contrast to Beiser et al. (2002), Ahmed (2005) found that Asian immigrants had health outcomes slightly below the native-born group, while American and European immigrant children fared better than the native-born. Ahmed optimistically observes that statistical evidence suggests the health status of children in immigrant families would improve in relation to the length of time of residency of immigrant parents if it was low initially. We should be careful, however, not to overestimate the resiliency of newcomer children, and not assume that children will simply "bounce back" following seemingly invisible emotional challenges or distress surrounding processes like racialization, for example. An eight-year-old refugee girl eloquently explained it this way: "Back home, I used to be blondish and the tallest girl in my class; since I came to Canada, I am the shortest and I turned dark" (Fantino and Colak, 2001: 591).

When newcomer families do access the health care system, research shows that some face numerous challenges. These challenges include language obstacles, discrimination, fear of Western medicine, and lack of knowledge of health care services (Lindsay et al., 2012). Research indicates that newcomer patients from minority backgrounds who have limited English proficiency are often misdiagnosed and incorrectly treated

---

Box 8.1

Challenges and Recommendations for Health Care and Community Service Providers Working with Immigrant Families Raising a Child with a Disability

Lindsay and her colleagues (2012) used qualitative interviews and focus groups with health care and community services providers to help us develop a better understanding of the experiences of service providers working with immigrant families raising a child with a physical disability. They found that health care providers encounter challenges when providing care to immigrant families raising a child with a disability, which include the following: (1) lack of training in providing culturally sensitive care; (2) language and communication issues; (3) discrepancies in conceptualizations of disability between health care providers and immigrant parents; (4) building rapport; and (5) helping parents to advocate for themselves and their children (Lindsay et al., 2012). While clinicians themselves recommended that service providers receive more and better training on providing culturally sensitive care, they also shed light on some of the more nuanced challenges, including some related to gender and caregiving. For example, some clinicians (ibid.). As a result, many, including care providers, have called for improved training in culturally sensitive care (see Box 8.1).

Parents and Children Migrating Apart: Recent Trends

Refugee Children

When we think of immigration, we tend to imagine that whole families migrate together as intact units, but sometimes they don't. For example, since the 1990s there has been growing attention placed on the increasing numbers of unaccompanied or separated children seeking asylum in the West (Human Rights Watch, 2009; Ali et al., 2003; Sadoway, 2001).

The laws affecting refugees are different from immigration laws. Refugees are generally defined by international regulations, in bodies like the United Nations High Commission for Refugees (UNHCR). The UNHCR defines *refugees* as children and adults who reside outside their country and cannot return due to well-founded fear of persecution because of their race, religion, nationality, political opinion, or membership in a certain group. Half of the world's 22.3 million refugees and displaced peoples are children. Every day, nearly 5,000 children become refugees. Canada, since World War II, has resettled 800,000 refugees. Between 2004 and 2013, there were between 5,857 and 8,386 newcomer children arriving in Canada as refugees each year (CIC, 2014c). Most came from non-European countries—conflict zones in Africa, the Middle East, and the Pacific region—and they, like other arrivals, settled in major cities in Ontario, Quebec, British Columbia, and

described gender-related challenges when providing care to immigrant families. A clinician describes her experience:

> It's a bit of a conundrum because often times in certain cultures the male is the head of the household. He's the one who's doing a lot of the talking and advocating. But the female [has] almost 100% responsibility for the kid. And so it creates this situation where the communication and the questioning happens with one family member but that's not the family member who's primarily responsible for the child.... Even if there's an interpreter there, there's often, you know, a dominant person and it's often the male. So the mom does get left out and the information doesn't get transmitted to her even when there is an interpreter (Focus group #1, Hospital Social Worker). (Lindsay et al., 2012: 2012; also see Jennings et al., 2014, who argue that immigrant mothers with disabled children are doubly marginalized.)

Lindsay and her colleagues recommend that service providers share more information with families about the resources and services available to them. At the same time, they suggest that it is important to build better partnerships with parents to ascertain parents' and children's culturally specific needs and priorities.

Source: Lindsay et al. (2012).

Alberta. Some of these arrived alone (Human Rights Watch, 2009; Ali et al., 2003; Ingleby and Watters, 2002) as "unaccompanied children," who are under the age of 18, separated from both parents, and "not being cared for by an adult who, by law or custom, is responsible to do so" (UNHCR, 1994: 21).

Refugee children, whether migrating with or without adults, must deal with the disruption that comes with migration, dependency reversal at home, and challenges associated with identity development while bridging generational and cultural gaps (Fantino and Colak, 2001). In addition, they face challenges associated with having experienced tragedy and trauma, including war, persecution, dangerous escapes, refugee camps, witnessing violence, killing, and atrocities against family members, as well as in some cases having served as child soldiers. Not only have they lost everything familiar to them, but they are denied the possibility of returning to their home countries (Beiser et al., 1999). Once in Canada, they can face a number of challenges surrounding settlement, including lack of understanding about their plight, marginalization at school (Ali et al., 2003), limited access to health care and other services (Evans et al., 2014), and the assumption that children are resilient and will "mend" (Fantino and Colak, 2001). Most of us cannot begin to imagine some of the conditions refugees have fled, let alone what it may be like for a child, especially one left alone; but, if properly equipped, schools can and have provided excellent contexts for carrying out preventative and therapeutic activities and support (Rousseau et al., 2005; Ingleby and Watters, 2002).

Transnational Families

Aside from refugees, in many other instances nuclear families are forced to live separately across national borders for personal, economic, and political reasons. These have been referred to as multilocal or *transnational families,* and have resulted in exceptional experiences for parents and children (Kim et al., 2014). Transnational families face unique parenting challenges before and after parents reunite with their children. Bernhard et al. (2006), for example, found that when families make the decision to separate, they assume they will be reunited quickly. As parents work to establish themselves in Canada, their children, back home, are often cared for by grandparents or other guardians. In some cases, grandparents and others provide less guidance and discipline than would have traditionally been given by a parent, and these guardians generally lack parental authority. In other cases, the caregivers exercise some control, but are inclined to spoil and indulge the children. When they are reunited, especially after unexpectedly long separations, the parents and children may have drifted apart. Some children become resentful of having been left behind (Bernard et al., 2006) some rebel against the heightened levels of discipline and control parents, especially mothers, try to re-establish (ibid.), and still others struggle to fit in once they are in Canada.

Teachers and administrators who work with children experiencing some of the negative effects of their domestic situations often cannot or do not investigate the root causes of problems (Bernard et al., 2006). For example, Bernhard et al. found that service providers were usually not aware of the range of problems experienced by some of these families, especially mothers. The shame and stigma some felt after leaving children behind often caused them to keep to themselves and stay "off the radar" of social services.

Satellite Children and Astronaut Families

On the other end of the socioeconomic spectrum are "astronaut families," often involving older newcomer children. In Asian astronaut families, for example, one or both parents spend much of their time (often for economic reasons) in Hong Kong or Taiwan, leaving their children to complete their education in Canada (Chiang, 2008; Irving et al., 1998). "Satellite" children are sons and daughters of ethnically Chinese immigrants to North America who have returned to their country of origin after immigration. Many are from affluent families, so the single most important barrier to adjustment is language, rather than socioeconomic and employment status (ibid.). However, other challenges they face include changes in family structure, parental absences, youth identity construction, and their visible minority status.

Summary

In this chapter we saw that Canada, both past and present, is indeed a land of immigrants. On the other hand, despite its self-proclaimed, long-standing humanitarian tradition, many arriving in Canada have had their share of government-induced and -supported hardships. Newcomer children and children of immigrants arriving today face challenges not faced by many of their Canadian-born peers. At the same time, most newcomer children fare quite well in terms of educational and health outcomes, despite the obstacles they face. We saw that while we may assume that all children and especially newcomer children live with their parents, some, including unaccompanied refugee children, children in transnational families, and satellite children, do not—at least temporarily.

Newcomers continue to help build the future of Canada. Therefore, it is extremely important that we understand the distinctive settlement needs and experiences of newcomer children—especially from the point of view of children themselves. We have a great deal yet to learn about them, but more importantly, we have much to learn from them. Imagine how the learning experience could be transformed for everyone in a classroom, if newcomer children could openly share their cultures and experiences with others. Learning about some of their triumphs and challenges is but a first step.

Questions for Critical Thought

1. How are the lives of newcomer children similar to and different from those of other Canadian children? What do you think accounts for similarities and differences within and across groups?

2. What are some of the unique challenges experienced by newcomer children? What, if anything, should be done to assist them in their adaptation? Who should be responsible for this?

3. You are to design a workshop for elementary schoolteachers and early childhood educators working with culturally diverse children. Who or what would you include in the workshop? What would a child-focused approach to education and care of culturally diverse Canadians look like?

Suggested Readings

Ali, Mehrunnisa, Svetlana Taraban, and Jagjeet Kaur Gill. 2003. "Unaccompanied/Separated Children Seeking Refugee Status in Ontario: A Review of Documented Policies and Practices." Toronto: Joint Centre of Excellence for Research on Immigration and Settlement, Working Paper Series. This paper is available on the Metropolis Project website (discussed below). It provides an overview of the literature on the issue of unaccompanied or separated children seeking asylum in Western countries. The paper provides information that can help students, researchers, and policy-makers better understand some of the challenges faced by these children.

Beiser, M., A. Goodwill, P. Albanese, K. McShane, and M. Nowakowski. 2014. "Predictors of Immigrant Children's Mental Health in Canada: Selection, Settlement Contingencies, Culture, or All of the Above?" *Social Psychiatry and Psychiatric Epidemiology* 49, 5: 743–56.

Colbert, Judith. 2010. *Welcoming Newcomer Children: The Settlement of Young Immigrants and Refugees.* Toronto: Fairmeadow. This book is an easy-to-read and practical resource for teachers and other professionals interested in supporting young newcomer children from birth through to age eight. It draws on international research in diverse fields, examines values and beliefs from a non-Western point of view, and questions accepted practices, priorities, and standards.

Pacini-Ketchabaw, Veronica, and Ana-Elisa Armstrong de Almeida. 2006. "Language Discourses and Ideologies as the Heart of Early Childhood Education," *International Journal of Bilingual Education and Bilingualism* 9, 3: 310–41. This article presents findings from a study of parents' views of their children's language development and the practices of early childhood educators living in a mid-sized Canadian city. It critically discusses the discourses that shape views of young children's bilingual development.

Websites

Caring for Kids New to Canada
www.kidsnewtocanada.ca/beyond/resources
> This website helps health professionals provide quality care to immigrant and refugee children, youth, and families. It was developed by the Canadian Paediatric Society with experts in newcomer health.

Caring for Newcomer Children
http://cmascanada.ca/caring-for-newcomer-children/
> Caring for Newcomer Children, funded through Citizenship and Immigration Canada, was founded in 2000 to monitor and support programs that provide on-site child care for the children of newcomer parents enrolled in Language Instruction for Newcomers to Canada ESL courses. They have expanded to create and offer training and resources for child care professionals who wish to better serve immigrant families. The website includes videotaped workshops, quick-tip videos, and lecture series that can enhance your knowledge of caring for newcomer children from experts in the field.

CERIS—Centre of Excellence for Research on Immigration and Settlement
http://ceris.ca/
> CERIS was established in 1996 as one of the regional centres of excellence under the national Metropolis project. It is a partnership of Toronto's three universities (Ryerson University, University of Toronto, and York University), and three major community organizations (Ontario Council of Agencies Serving Immigrants, Social Planning Toronto, and United Way Toronto) with representation from all levels of government. CERIS created and houses a significant body of knowledge created by and for researchers, policy-makers, and practitioners in migration and settlement.

Citizenship and Immigration Canada
www.cic.gc.ca
> Immigration has gone under different departmental names within the federal government since Confederation. Citizenship and Immigration Canada was established in 1994 to "link immigration services with citizenship registration; promote the unique ideals all Canadians share; and help build a stronger Canada." The website contains facts and figures, research reports, regulations, advice to newcomers, etc.

9 Aboriginal Children

Learning Objectives

◎ To map the history and experiences of Aboriginal children and their families in Canada.

◎ To assess the impact of colonialism on the lives of Canada's First Nations families.

◎ To identify some of the similarities and differences between the lives of Aboriginal children and those of other Canadian children.

◎ To consider the valuable insight gained by learning more about and from Aboriginal children.

◎ To review some of the suggested ways of improving the well-being of Aboriginal children in this country.

Introduction

Canada has been called a land of immigrants. This is not an entirely accurate label if you consider the history of Canada before colonization. Before Europeans stepped foot in North America, there were more than 500 distinct indigenous peoples straddling what came to be the Canada–US border. Each had its own culture, economic structure, and system of governance. As European settler societies spread across the continent, colonial (and later, Canadian) governments negotiated treaties with groups of Aboriginal peoples to appropriate lands from Aboriginal control and clear the way for more settlement. After initial contact with Europeans, the experiences of diverse indigenous groups varied depending on the country of origin of the colonizer and the nature of the economic and social relationships with the settlers and their (overseas) governments. The tragic reality is that almost all of these indigenous groups have suffered at the hands of a settler population (Morrison et al., 2014). Some like Jaccoud and Brassard (2003) make the point that Aboriginal marginality begins in early childhood. We will see that this seems to be as true today as it was 150 years ago.

Morrison et al. (2014), among many others, have noted that for much of Canada's pre-Confederation history, colonialist ideologies of racial and cultural supremacy among the European colonizers have contributed to a complex and ambivalent relationship with Aboriginal peoples. These relationships have been rooted in patronizing subordination, and in some more extreme cases, have resulted in outright **genocide**—the deliberate intent or act of killing a particular ethnic or cultural group or nation. Some have argued that from Confederation onward, Aboriginal peoples have been the most disadvantaged group in our otherwise affluent country (Waldram et al., 2006: 3). Let us consider why this is so.

In 1876, not long after Canada became a nation (in 1867), it created the **Indian Act**, which formalized First Nations' dependency on the Canadian state and regulated almost every aspect of social and economic life of whom it governed (more on this below). Through aggressive assimilation, federal policies led to population loss, displacement, and massive social disruptions among many Aboriginal peoples (Morrison et al., 2014). Over time, indigenous groups were forced onto small parcels of land—reserves—and were deprived of their rights to their traditional lands, resources, culture, and governance.

Despite changes, some of Canada's colonial practices continue to this day, and have had a detrimental impact on the well-being of First Nations children, their families, and communities (Assembly of First Nations, 2010). As a result, Aboriginal children's life experiences often vary within and across Aboriginal groups and when compared with those of other Canadian children (Findlay et al., 2014). In this chapter we will review some of the past and ongoing effects of colonization on the lives of Aboriginal children and their families. It will outline some of the causes and consequences of the often distinct experiences of Aboriginal children. While inevitably focusing on some of the negative outcomes of colonization, the chapter also aims to move beyond a deficit model—which focuses on the individual or group as the root of the problem—of understanding Aboriginal children's experiences by highlighting the valuable insight that is gained by learning about and from Aboriginal children in this country.

Colonization and the Indian Act

Five hundred years of colonization of the Americas has resulted in the decimation of Aboriginal institutions and social organizations—especially families (Royal Commission on Aboriginal Peoples, 1996a). The last 150 years were particularly affected by the *institutional racism* embodied in Canadian policies that governed the lives of Aboriginal peoples (see Green, 2006). According to Green (2006) institutional racism is diffused throughout the culture of the state (and private institutions) and is imbedded in the practices of those in positions of power.

Colonization is an economic process, but it also involves the implementation of social policies aimed at manipulating Aboriginal communities for the benefit of colonial goals. As noted above, colonial goals, including resource extraction and the settlement of European migrants, were served by the implementation of the Indian Act—federal legislation that regulated almost every aspect of Aboriginal life. Among many other things, the Indian Act defined who could call themselves "Indian" (a contested term for numerous reasons). According to the Indian Act, *Indian* refers to a person who is entitled (according to the state) to be registered as an Aboriginal person (Justice Canada, 2014). An Indian Register actually exists—a formal list of names of individuals recognized by the state as Status Indians or registered Indians. But before we delve deeper into the Indian Act, let us consider some of these terms and definitions.

Understanding Terminology

Most researchers, academics, and policy-makers acknowledge that there are many ways of defining the Aboriginal population, depending on who is doing the defining and for what purpose the term is being used. As we will see below, the Census of Canada provides data that are based on various terms and definitions: Aboriginal ancestry, Aboriginal identity, registered Indian, and band membership, to name a few (Newhouse and Peters, 2003b). *Aboriginal ancestry* refers to individuals who report at least one relative with Aboriginal origin on the "ethnic origin" question of the survey. *Aboriginal identity* refers to those who self-identify with at least one Aboriginal group. You will also see the terms *Indian, Métis,* and *Inuit* used in the Census. This is because Canada's First Nations, as defined by the Constitution Act, 1982, comprise **Indian** (Status/registered or non-Status), **Inuit** (Aboriginal people whose homeland is Arctic Canada), and **Métis** (those of mixed Aboriginal and European ancestry) peoples of Canada.

It is important to note that each of these three distinct groups continue to be made up of a large number of First Nations communities with their own unique heritages, languages, and cultures (for example, the Anishinabe, who are said to linguistically include the Abenaki, Algonquin, Arapaho, Blackfoot, Cheyenne, Chippewa, Cree, Delaware, Fox, Gros Ventre, Illini, Innu or Inuit, Kickapoo, Mahican/Mohegan, Maliseet, Menominee, Miami, Mississauga, Montagnais, Munsee, Nakawe, Nanticoke, Nipissing, Noquet, Odawah/Ottawa, Ojibwa/Ojibway/Ojibwe, Passamaquoddy, Penobscot, Potawatomi, Saulteau, Sauk, and the Shawnee; or the Iroquois/Six Nations, who include the Mohawk, Onondaga, Oneida, Cayuga, Seneca, and Tuscarora). But a *Status Indian* or *registered Indian* is a specific legal identity, formally recognized by the Indian Act—regardless of how individuals self-identified. Despite the many communities listed above to which a person could belong, if individuals did not fall under the specific terms laid out by the Act, they were not granted official status.

This may seem irrelevant at first, but this formal status regulates who is entitled to what, where one can live, with whom, and how. For example, until 1985, if a Status Indian woman married a non-Status man (a member of a

First Nations community not recognized by the Indian Act) or a non-Indian man, she lost her Indian status, as did her children. In other words, the state regulated whom Status Indian women could marry and what rights, privileges, and obligations they and their children were entitled to upon marriage. This was a doubly discriminatory stipulation, as the same did not apply to Status Indian men. Only after legal challenges in the 1980s was this part of the Indian Act changed.

The Indian Act has disenfranchised First Nations communities. Among many other things, because of stipulations within the Indian Act, Canada's natural resources wealth has flowed unfairly from Aboriginal lands to non-Aboriginal coffers, leaving many Aboriginal communities impoverished (Bland, 2013). Understandably, this has been another long-standing grievance among First Nations communities.

While there have been changes to the Indian Act, particularly after court challenges and protests, the Act effectively makes Aboriginal populations wards of the state. From the beginning, there was little debate that the overall goal of the Indian Act was to assimilate Canada's First Nations. One of the central instruments for accomplishing that goal, throughout most of the twentieth century, was the Indian Residential School system (Menzies, 1999; also see Assembly of First Nations, 2007b; de Leeuw, 2009; Government of Canada, 2014).

Residential Schools

By the Government of Canada's own recent accounts, the Indian Residential School system was extremely problematic (see Box 9.1), and represents an especially brutal part of Canadian social policy.

As noted in the Canadian government's own documents on residential schools, children were removed from their communities and families, often forcibly, to institutions aimed at "civilizing them" into European ways. The schools served as vehicles for marginalizing generations of Aboriginal young people (Bombay et al., 2013; Menzies, 1999; Timpson, 1995). Many were places of extreme emotional, physical, and sexual abuse (Royal Commission on Aboriginal Peoples, 1996a).

Not only were families torn apart by the initial removal of the children, they were further affected by their return, when as young adults they were expected to recommence "normal" family life, now among kin they had been taught to be ashamed of. As one former student of a residential school explained, "many of us raised our children the way we were raised at the schools. We disciplined our children with physical force, and we called them stupid, dumb, and lazy. We showed little or no emotion, and we found it hard to say we love them" (Timpson, 1995: 535). As a result, when

---

Box 9.1

Residential Schools

For more than 100 years, Aboriginal children in Canada were sent to special schools, called Indian Residential Schools. These schools were built and run by the Government of Canada and the Catholic, Anglican, Methodist, United, and Presbyterian churches. Over 150,000 First Nation, Métis, and Inuit children attended these schools between 1857 and 1996.

Life at residential school was hard for many children. Students were forced to speak English or French, and were punished if they spoke their own native languages. Often these children were taken from their families and placed in schools far away from their communities, sometimes for many years at a time. Many children were not given enough clothing or food. A lot of the schools were crowded and dirty. Some children died of disease. Others tried to run away.

Indian Residential Schools tried to make Aboriginal children talk, dress, think, and act like non-Aboriginal Canadians. At the time, the government and churches believed that this was the right thing to do. Today, we know it was not.

The last Indian Residential School was closed in 1996. On June 11, 2008, the Prime Minister of Canada apologized to all Aboriginal children who were sent to these schools for the many bad things that happened to many of them. Several of the churches that were a part of this system have also said they are sorry. Many former students have shared stories of their time at Indian Residential Schools to help all Canadians understand what happened and to help themselves heal and forgive.

Source: Kids' Stop: People and History. Aboriginal Affairs and Northern Development Canada. 2013. https://www.aadnc-aandc.gc.ca/eng/1302870688751/1302870910265.

---

many of these young adults formed their own families, usually in economically and socially depressed communities, they themselves experienced the removal of their own children through cross-cultural foster placement and adoption.

While it was not specifically a government policy, a spinoff of the Indian Residential School system was what came to be known as the "Sixties Scoop" (Johnson, 1983; Menzie and van de Sande, 2003). The term was coined by Patrick Johnston (1983), the author of *Native Children and the Child Welfare System*. The "Sixties Scoop" refers to the large-scale removal of Aboriginal children from their families, often without parental consent, into the child welfare system. In the mid-1960s, child welfare authorities entered First Nations reserves and communities and "scooped" children, often newborns, out of communities and families and into state care—in most cases, into middle-class, European–Canadian families.

The Indian Residential School system is often seen as a past transgression (ending in 1996); however, it continues to have lasting repercussions, affecting the lives of Aboriginal peoples today (Bombay et al., 2013). The trauma experienced in the Indian Residential School system in Canada has not ceased; having a familial history of residential school attendance has been linked to contemporary family stressors that continue to affect individuals, families, and entire communities (Bombay et al., 2014). Bombay et al. (2014) suggest that Indian Residential School attendance across generations appears to have cumulative effects, supporting the notion that Indian Residential Schools have contributed to historical trauma whose effects are still felt. Research demonstrating the intergenerational effects of these schools provides support for the enduring negative consequences of these experiences and their contribution to the ongoing disparities between First Nations peoples' and other Canadians' well-being (Bombay et al., 2014).

Aboriginal Children and Their Families Today

New data from the National Household Survey (NHS) show that 1,400,690 people reported an Aboriginal identity in 2011, representing 4.3 per cent of the total Canadian population (Statistics Canada, 2013e; 2014c; see Table 9.1).

Table 9.1   Aboriginal Population Estimates for Canada from the 2011 National Household Survey (NHS)

Concept	2011 NHS estimate[a]
Aboriginal identity[b]	1,400,690
Aboriginal group	1,374,215
Registered or treaty Indian status	697,510
Membership in a First Nation or Indian band	675,490
Aboriginal ancestry[c]	1,836,035

This table displays the results of the population estimates for Canada from the 2011 National Household Survey (NHS), using the different definitions of the Aboriginal population (see Statistics Canada, 2014c, for a description of each concept or way to identify as part of the Aboriginal population).

[a]Random rounding and percentage distributions: To ensure the confidentiality of responses collected for the 2011 NHS while maintaining the quality of the results, a random rounding process is used to alter the values reported in individual cells. As a result, when these data are summed or grouped, the total value may not match the sum of the individual values, since the total and subtotals are independently rounded. Similarly, percentage distributions, which are calculated on rounded data, may not necessarily add up to 100 per cent. Due to random rounding, estimates and percentages may vary slightly between different 2011 NHS products, such as the analytical documents and various data tables.

[b]Aboriginal identity refers to whether the person reported being an Aboriginal person, that is, First Nations (North American Indian), Métis or Inuk (Inuit), and/or being a registered or Status Indian (that is, registered under the Indian Act of Canada) and/or being a member of a First Nation or Indian band.

[c]Aboriginal ancestry includes at least one response in Question 17 [of the survey] to an origin that can be classified in one of First Nations (North American Indian), Métis, or Inuit ancestry, either with or without also reporting a non-Aboriginal ancestry.

Source: Statistics Canada, (2014c).

The Aboriginal population is a growing population. That is, the Aboriginal population, as measured by the NHS, increased by 232,385 people, or 20.1 per cent, between 2006 and 2011, compared with 5.2 per cent of the non-Aboriginal population in Canada (Statistics Canada, 2013e).

Of the people reporting an Aboriginal identity in 2011, 851,560, or 60.8 per cent, identified as First Nations (2.6 per cent of the Canadian population); 451,795 or 32.3 per cent identified as Métis (1.4 per cent of the Canadian population); and 59,445 or 4.2 per cent, identified as Inuit (0.2 per cent of the Canadian population) (Statistics Canada, 2013e). Of the 637,660 First Nations people who reported being Status Indians, nearly half (49.3 per cent) lived on an Indian reserve or Indian settlement. In 1951, the Census of Canada showed that 6.7 per cent of the Aboriginal population lived in cities. By 2001, that proportion had increased to 49 per cent (Newhouse and Peters, 2003). This proportion and the distribution of Aboriginal peoples, in general, varied across the country.

Ontario had the largest number of Aboriginal people, with 301,425 Aboriginal people living there, representing 21.5 per cent of the total Aboriginal population. That said, nearly 6 in 10, or 57.6 per cent of Aboriginal people lived in one of the four western provinces (16.6 per cent lived in British Columbia; 15.8 per cent in Alberta; 14.0 per cent in Manitoba, and 11.3 per cent in Saskatchewan in 2011; Statistics Canada, 2013a). Aboriginal people made up large shares of the population of the three territories—86.3 per cent of the Nunavut population was Aboriginal, as was 51.9 per cent of the Northwest Territories' population and 23.1 per cent of the Yukon's (Statistics Canada, 2013a).

The Aboriginal population is younger than the non-Aboriginal population because of higher fertility rates and a shorter life expectancy. First Nations and Inuit populations tend to have significantly higher fertility rates than non-Aboriginal populations, while Métis have a slightly higher fertility rate than the non-Aboriginal population (Statistics Canada, 2013e). Aboriginal children under the age of 15 made up 28.0 per cent of the total Aboriginal population, or 7.0 per cent of all children in Canada (Statistics Canada, 2013e). It is estimated that by 2017, about 42 per cent of the Aboriginal population in the Prairies will be under the age of 30, more than twice the number of persons younger than 30 in the non-Aboriginal population (Bland, 2013).

Aboriginal children under the age of 15 lived in varied arrangements. Like in the case of other children, most lived with either one or both of their parents, yet in 2011 only half (49.6 per cent) were living in a family with both their parents (either biological or adoptive), compared with three-quarters (76.0 per cent) of non-Aboriginal children. Just over one-third (34.4 per cent) lived in a single-parent family compared with

17.4 per cent of non-Aboriginal children (Statistics Canada, 2013e). We will discuss this in more detail below, but it is important to note that nearly half (48.1 per cent) of all children under the age of 15 in foster care were Aboriginal. Nearly 4 per cent of Aboriginal children were foster children compared with 0.3 per cent of non-Aboriginal children in Canada (Statistics Canada, 2013a).

Prejudice and discrimination at the institutional and interpersonal levels have had a profoundly negative impact on the health, cultures, and languages of Aboriginal peoples (Morrison et al., 2014). This marginalization and racism have resulted in a number of social problems for and within families (Green, 2006). For example, while there have been some improvements, past research shows that on-reserve registered Indians were more than twice as likely as other Canadians to have less than Grade 9 education; employment rates are 60 per cent lower; and average incomes are half the national average (Armstrong, 2000; also see Assembly of First Nations, 2007a). While conditions have been improving in recent years, Aboriginal peoples in Canada are much more likely than other Canadians to live in substandard, overcrowded housing arrangements (see Table 9.2).

Overcrowding on its own is not necessarily a problem; however, crowding has been linked to a number of negative health outcomes, including increased risk of transmitting infectious diseases, severe lower respiratory tract infections, and higher rates of injuries, mental health problems, and family tensions (Green and de Leeuw, 2012; Eni, 2009; UNICEF, 2009).

Table 9.2 Percentage of First Nations and Non-Aboriginal Populations Living in Crowded Dwellings, Canada, 1996 and 2006[a]

Population	Percentage living in crowded dwellings[b]	
	1996	2006
Total First Nations population	20	15
On-reserve	33	26
Off-reserve	10	7
Urban	8	6
Rural	17	10
Total non-Aboriginal population	3	3
Urban	3	3
Rural	2	1

[a]Data have been adjusted to account for incompletely enumerated reserves in 1996 and 2006.

[b]Crowding is defined as more than one person per room. Not counted as rooms are bathrooms, halls, vestibules, and rooms used solely for business purposes.

Source: Statistics Canada (2009a: Table 21).

Aboriginal Children's Health and Well-Being

By national and international accounts, Aboriginal children fall well below national health averages for Canadian children (Green and de Leeuw, 2012; Eni, 2009; UNICEF, 2009). In Canada, Aboriginal children experience higher rates of infant mortality, sudden infant death syndrome, tuberculosis, asthma and bronchitis, childhood obesity and diabetes, and experience lower rates of immunization compared with Aboriginal children (Eni, 2009).

Although infant mortality rates have been decreasing, from 27 (1979) to 8 (1999) per 1,000 live births across Canada, infant mortality rates on reserves are three to seven times higher than the national average (Eni, 2009). Eni (2009) explains that the leading cause of infant mortality in First Nations populations is sudden infant death syndrome, which is linked to maternal smoking, climatic circumstances, and socioeconomic factors, including substandard housing. Many First Nations children also have limited access to affordable, healthy, and nutritious food—or are considered to be "food insecure."

Food security refers to a condition in which all people—at all times— have access (physical and economic) to sufficient, safe, and nutritious food to meet their dietary needs for a healthy life (Egeland et al., 2010). Aboriginal peoples, living on- and off-reserve, have been found to face high rates of food *insecurity*. Research shows that among those living off-reserve, about one-fifth of households are food insecure—a rate three times that of non-Aboriginal households (Spence, 2008). Those living on-reserve and in remote communities are much worse off, as they face the challenges of high price, low quality, and limited availability of nutritious foods (see Table 9.3). In 2004, food insecurity rates ranged from 40 to 83 per cent in isolated Aboriginal communities, and almost 70 per cent of adults in Nunavut were food insecure in 2008 (Spence, 2008).

Egeland et al. (2010) investigated the prevalence of food insecurity among Inuit households with preschool children. Between 2007 and 2008, they conducted a survey of the health status of 388 randomly selected Inuit children between the ages of three and five across 16 Nunavut communities. They found that 69.9 per cent of Inuit preschoolers resided in households rated as food insecure—25.1 per cent were rated as severely food insecure. Of these 25 per cent who were severely food insecure, 75.8 per cent of children skipped meals and 90.4 per cent went hungry (60.1 per cent often did not eat for a whole day). Members of households rated as moderately food insecure reported experiencing times in the year before the survey was conducted when they worried food would run out (85.1 per cent), when they fed their children less expensive food (95.1 per cent), and when their children did not eat enough because there was no money for food (64.3 per cent)

Table 9.3 Price of Selected Food Items in Remote Northern Reserve Communities in Ontario Compared with National Average, April 2008

	Remote Reserve Average ($)	National Average ($)
Orange Juice (1 L)	3.82	3.67
Wieners (450 g)	4.55	2.71
Apple Juice (1.36 L)	2.77	1.83
Corn Flakes (675 g)	8.17	3.94
Peanut butter (500 g)	3.82	2.55
Oranges (1 kg)	5.27	2.17
Potatoes (4.54 kg)	11.29	3.97
Bananas (1 kg)	4.11	1.43
Flour (2.5 kg)	9.38	4.69
Eggs (1 dz)	3.34	2.56
Apples (1 kg)	6.79	2.95
Baby food (128 ml)	1.26	0.59
Bread (675 g)	3.70	2.43
Chicken (1 kg)	9.91	5.76
Ground beef (1 kg)	8.29	6.10
Milk (1 L)	2.90	1.96

Source: Spence (2008: 11).

(Egeland et al., 2010). At the same time, as a result of the high cost of fresh food in some remote communities, obesity in Aboriginal children is more than double the national average (Pigford et al., 2012).

As exemplified above, life on many reserves is characterized by poverty and the consequences of poverty (Bland, 2013). How do we begin to make sense of this?

Aboriginal children are born into a colonial legacy that results in low socioeconomic status, intergenerational trauma associated with residential schooling, loss of language and culture, and high levels of discrimination. These colonial legacies are considered to be social determinants of health (Green and de Leeuw, 2012). In other words, Aboriginal peoples' distinct sociopolitical, historical, and geographical contexts are important factors to consider when trying to understand the health of Aboriginal children. At the same time, some First Nations children continue to suffer at the hands of the Canadian state as a result of the jurisdictional complexities that confound the lives of Aboriginal people. Let us consider the case of Jordan River Anderson.

Jordan's Principle

Jordan River Anderson of the Norway House Cree Nation in Manitoba was born in 1999 with a rare neuromuscular disorder that required hospitalization from birth (Aboriginal and Northern Affairs Canada, 2013; Blackstock, 2009). Jordan was loved by his family (his mother, Virginia, stayed with him in Winnipeg; his father, Ernest, returned to northern Manitoba to look after the couple's other children; the Norway House Cree Nation leaders and community members raised funds to ensure that Jordan's medical transportation needs could be met once he was discharged from hospital; Blackstock, 2009). He remained in a Winnipeg hospital for the first two years of his life while his medical condition stabilized. Shortly after Jordan's second birthday, his doctors agreed that he was ready to go home. Jordan never made it (Blackstock, 2009).

The provincial and federal governments could not agree on who was financially responsible for Jordan's care, as "Indians" are governed by the federal government and health care is under provincial jurisdiction (Aboriginal and Northern Affairs Canada, 2013; Blackstock, 2009). Provincial and federal bureaucrats argued over every item related to his at-home care while he was forced to stay in hospital—at twice the cost of care if he were allowed to go home (Blackstock, 2009). The two levels of government were disputing over paying for services that are routinely available to other children in Canada.

As the two levels of government disputed—for three years—Jordan's condition deteriorated and he passed away in hospital before a resolution was reached. He was five years old and hadn't spent a day in his family's home.

In December 2007, the House of Commons unanimously supported a Private Member's motion (M-296) stating that "the government should immediately adopt a child first principle, based on Jordan's Principle, to resolve jurisdictional disputes involving the care of First Nations children" (Aboriginal and Northern Affairs Canada, 2013). Jordan's Principle is expected to be implemented in cases involving a jurisdictional dispute between a provincial and federal government. In these cases, a First Nations child living on reserve will continue to receive care while and until there is a resolution (Aboriginal and Northern Affairs Canada, 2013).

In a country as seemingly "developed" as Canada, it should go without saying that its children, and especially its Aboriginal children, are safe and cared for. But this is clearly not the case. Green (2006) explains that the systematic racism embedded in our political cultures stem from colonial relationships that grant preferential entry into social, political, and economic institutions to those who find themselves part of the dominant culture in ways that are not afforded to Aboriginal populations. Many young Aboriginal people continue to be disadvantaged by historical circumstances, government policies, and mismanagement (Bland, 2013). As a result, many continue to struggle.

In 1996, the Canadian state released the report of a Royal Commission on Aboriginal Peoples. It reported that breakdown in traditional families is a key factor in the social problems they are grappling with today. These families have had their culture devalued and ridiculed for generations, while enduring family disruptions propagated by assimilationist and abusive government policies. To this day, Aboriginal children are overrepresented in the child welfare system (Fallon et al., 2013; Blackstock et al., 2006; Trocmé et al., 2004)—a child welfare system that has devalued traditional indigenous systems of child protection by judging standards of care by dominant Canadian norms and through the use of non-Native foster homes (Timpson, 1995). Fallon et al. (2013) note that research stemming from the *Canadian Incidence Study on Reported Child Abuse and Neglect* (CIS) suggests that specific case characteristics, such as child maltreatment type, child functioning, and harm levels, do not account for the significant overrepresentation of Aboriginal children in out-of-home placements. Instead, poverty, poor housing, and substance misuse have been demonstrably related to all decision points in the overrepresentation of Aboriginal children in the child welfare system (also see Trocmé et al., 2004, 2005). These factors, when coupled with inequitable resources for First Nations children residing on reserves, have resulted in the overrepresentation of Aboriginal children in the Canadian child welfare system (Auditor General of Canada, 2008, 2011; Standing Committee on Public Accounts, 2009). Blackstock et al. (2006) recommend that the child welfare system itself be seen as an agent of colonialism. To help overcome this colonial legacy and reconnect children to their communities, many have suggested increased attention to providing more child-focused, indigenous education.

Education

As a result of being at higher risk for living in poor socioeconomic conditions, Findlay et al. (2014), citing recent research, have noted that Aboriginal children are more likely to experience language problems and have poorer school outcomes than other children in Canada. Findley et al. (2014) examined the developmental milestones for Inuit, Métis, and off-reserve First Nations children in Canada, based on developmental data collected from the 2006 Aboriginal Children's Survey. They found considerable variation in children's developmental milestones. Interestingly, they found that across all three Aboriginal groups, gross motor and self-help skills were found to be achieved *earlier* than among other Canadian children, whereas language skills were achieved slightly later compared with other children (Findley et al., 2014). They argued that chronic health conditions contributed to later achievement of developmental outcomes, but they also highlighted the importance of establishing culturally specific norms and standards in measuring developmental milestones rather than relying on those derived from general populations. They called for early and culturally appropriate intervention in assisting Aboriginal children (Findley et al., 2014).

While most services delivered to Aboriginal people continue to be offered by mainstream organizations (see Denison et al., 2014), there have been some improvements in the delivery of services to Aboriginal children in their early years. In fact, for obvious reasons, education has been a focus of special attention in recent decades. Ball (2004) suggests child-focused education in First Nations communities, developed by and with First Nations community members, with some thought and programming aimed at reviving First Nations languages and traditional teaching practices. This is now happening in some Aboriginal communities. The creation of more child-focused and inclusive learning environments would no doubt benefit all children in Canada, regardless of their cultural background.

Aboriginal Head Start

Many have noted that given past injustices committed against Aboriginal children in and through the Canadian educational system(s), there is an urgent need to bridge indigenous family and community cultural and linguistic experiences and provide educational services that are more responsive to the specific needs of Aboriginal children. Towards this goal, in 1995, the Government of Canada established Aboriginal Head Start to help enhance child development and school readiness of First Nations, Inuit, and Métis children living in urban centres and large northern communities (Health Canada, 2011; Public Health Agency of Canada, 2013). An expansion of the Aboriginal Head Start program for First Nations communities was announced in October 1998. This expansion was a result of commitments made to Aboriginal peoples in the 1997 Speech from the Throne, in response to recommendations found in *Gathering Strength: Canada's Aboriginal Action Plan* (Health Canada, 2011). The goal of Aboriginal Head Start is to provide funding for a more focused, culturally appropriate approach to early learning for Aboriginal children. The Aboriginal Head Start On Reserve (AHSOR) program funds activities that support the early learning and development of young children living in First Nations communities. The goal is to support early child development strategies—in education, health promotion, culture and language, nutrition, social support, and parental and family involvement—that are designed and controlled by the communities themselves. To do this, the Government of Canada provides about $59 million per year to support close to 10,000 children dispersed throughout some 300 Aboriginal Head Start programs on reserves in First Nations communities across Canada.

The AHSOR initiative is part of a network of programs that attempts to address early learning and healthy development for First Nations children living on and off reserve (see Health Canada, 2011). Other programs include the Human Resources and Skills Development Canada's (HRSDC) First Nations and Inuit Child Care Initiative (FNICCI) and a range of Indian and

Northern Affairs Canada (INAC)–funded child care programs in Alberta and Ontario. There is also an Aboriginal Head Start in Urban and Northern Communities program, which is a Public Health Agency of Canada–funded early childhood development program for First Nations, Inuit, and Métis children and their families living in urban and northern communities.

Given past experiences, it is not surprising that some Aboriginal families have approached mainstream early learning programs with caution (Hare, 2012). Some parents have had limited involvement in their children's education because of the historical legacy of schooling for Aboriginal peoples in this country. One caregiver who was assessing an Aboriginal Head Start program in Hare's research shared the following: "I know lots of parents, they just kind of get shy . . . or they might have had a bad experience with school so it's hard to make sure that they get that friendly atmosphere. And people experienced residential schools and just weren't comfortable in the school setting" (2012: 400).

Research by Piquemal (2005) has shown that because of past experiences, Aboriginal children too have struggled to share their experiences in the classroom (see Box 9.2). Piquemal explored ways in which two Aboriginal students, Oliver and Johanna, have taken an ethical stance related to the level of privacy that they feel applies to the exposure of their cultural experiences in the classroom context. She demonstrated how Oliver and Johanna choose to protect their cultural experiences from the formal school setting, showing how the two children chose to express their Aboriginality relationally and informally rather than explicitly to their classmates. Piquemal (2005) further explains that because private knowledge—spiritual knowledge, sacred stories, and personal stories—has been misappropriated by researchers, even Aboriginal children are reserved and cautious about sharing it.

Aboriginal Head Start programs, as well as other programs aimed at increasing First Nations control of First Nations education (Assembly of First Nations, 2010) have worked hard to demonstrate the value of locally controlled and designed education strategies aimed at providing Aboriginal children with a positive sense of themselves and a desire for lifelong learning. Programs emphasizing the value of indigenous knowledge systems seem to be especially important.

Indigenous knowledge systems involve learning processes that are social, intergenerational, oral (narrative), and experiential (Hare, 2012; Canadian Council of Learning, 2009). Furthermore, in indigenous knowledge systems, knowledge is often perceived to be contained within cultural practices. Songs, dances, and symbolic representations are valued as repositories of indigenous history and beliefs (Hare, 2012). Indigenous knowledge also emphasizes the importance of the relationship between the individual and the natural world (ibid.). Furthermore, traditional learning highlights the role of parents and extended family, elders, and spiritual leaders.

Box 9.2   Sharing a Piece of Oliver's Story

It was nine a.m., and the students were writing in their journals. Every day, they were given this special time to tell a story about an experience or to express their personal thoughts on different themes. That day, the theme was "About me." Luisa, the teacher, wrote sentences on the board as a way to help the students organize their thoughts. One of these sentences was "I remember the time when . . . ." I thought that this theme was a good one, as it invited students to think of an experience and to relate it as a story.

Oliver, a Grade 3–4 student, was sitting at his desk, and had been writing and erasing words a number of times. . . . Oliver briefly looked at me and then focused on his writing again. He erased some words again. . . . He looked at me again and smiled with uncertainty.

"I think I know what I want to write but I'm not sure . . . ."

Oliver started relating a story. His story was a very personal one that involved what anthropologists would call traditional cultural accounts. These cultural accounts were not the focus of his story, but its background; in other words, the event described incidentally occurred at a cultural gathering, but this cultural gathering was not the main subject of Oliver's story. At the end of his story, he looked at me and seemed to wait for my reaction. I simply said: "That's a very good story. Why don't you write about that?"

He smiled at me and said,

"OK." He looked down at his paper, paused, looked at me again and asked, "But is it going to be put up on the wall?"

I told him that I didn't know, and that he would have to ask Luisa.

Oliver said: "Well, then I don't want to write about that."

Source: Cultural loyalty: Aboriginal students take an ethical stance, Nathalie Piquemal. *Reflective Practice* Vol. 6, No. 4, November 2005, pp. 523–538. Reprinted by permission of the publisher (Taylor & Francis Ltd, http://www.tandfonline.com).

Korteweg et al. (2010) have noted that indigenous children's literature has a great deal to offer *all* educators, indigenous and non-indigenous alike. Not only does indigenous children's literature offer varied narrative codes and visual devices, but, through its arts-based representations, can push educators' conventional understandings of the environment. Korteweg et al. (2010) argue that these picture books create openings for dialogue about teachers' and students' environmental formations and can positively challenge and expand their ways of being and relating to the land and its people. In other words, indigenous authors are not only reclaiming their stories, land, and cultural ways of knowing, but also serve to expand world-view narratives that counter colonial discourses and approaches (ibid.). This change is imperative because the status quo has been devastating.

Tracy Whattam (2003), writing about her experiences and struggles in school, highlights the need for change. Box 9.3 presents some of her story.

Box 9.3   A Short Piece of Tracy Whattam's Story

I attended Tecumseh Elementary from kindergarten to Grade 7. I think I was lucky to have stayed in one school for the entire time. I loved school and fortunately I was good at it, considering my situation. I absolutely loved the teachers and learning. Socially it was torture. I longed to belong to the most popular group of kids, but I never felt like I fit in. Most of the time I felt different, apart from, excluded. I was an "Indian," or "breed," and I was smart. Most of the kids didn't like that so they never hesitated to ridicule me, maligning what I said or did. Of course it wasn't always like this: I did have some reprieves. But too often I ended up being with kids who were getting into trouble or with kids that I didn't respect, so I treated them the way I had been treated. A vicious cycle had been set up, and I wasn't skilled enough to pull myself out of it. . . .

Well, I left elementary school and looked forward to Grade 8 with, I think, all the regular excitement and apprehensions. Then another tragedy happened in my family, and I was sent to live with my best friend's family up on Boatbluff Light Station in northern British Columbia. I studied by correspondence for a year and I loved it because of the flexible scheduling. I loved living on the lighthouse. My backyard was the Pacific Ocean and a huge island we could explore at any time. I felt innocent and safe; I felt as though I could let my guard down, I could breathe.

For a year, killer whales, porpoises, eagles, dogs, wolves, deer, bears, the people of Klemtu and the family I stayed with were my closest friends. But I missed my family desperately, so despite my situation and beautiful environment, I was using substances to get high and numb my feelings. When they told me they were moving off the light station, I cried. I wanted to stay as much as they wanted to get back to civilization. Well, I moved home to Vancouver, and for the next three years I was in and out of the house. The problems I'd left home for hadn't been resolved in the time I'd been gone: our feelings had just been pushed aside. Sadly, the abuse continued in different forms. I failed Grade 8 twice. I was getting drunk and stoned, and there was no turning back. . . They had tried their best to raise me differently, to change what had happened in our family before, but it was too late. . .

[With determination and support, Tracy turned things around.]

I was hired by the principal and Jenna Dupuis (the former First Nations district coordinator) because there were a number of First Nations kids in this school who

Continued

were skipping, coming late, and having behavioral problems, and the administration didn't know what to do with them. The students and the staff weren't coping well. Sound familiar? I told them I would come to work if I could teach life skills in the school. I believed at the time that anybody could benefit from knowing these skills. . . It's ironic. Ironic because I didn't learn these skills at home. I didn't learn them at home because mom didn't learn them in residential schools. So how could she know how to teach them? You learn these skills in healthy families. I learned them from some dynamic non-Aboriginal women and men. It seems we've come full circle. . . I'm giving back through the public school system—to the Aboriginal community—part of what was taken from us through the residential school system.

Source: Whattam (2003: 437–8, 442).

Hopeful about the future, Wilfred Brass, Saulteaux Elder from Key Reserve in Saskatchewan, in February 1998 shared the following:

> You know, you young people, you have that daylight in your minds. Us, they put curtains around our minds, they tried to keep us in the dark, they wanted to keep us stupid, make us their slaves. But you young people, you have that daylight in your minds . . . we're gonna be ok. (Whattam, 2003: 435)

But change is slow in coming and continues to be hard won.

Idle No More, Self-Government, and the Future of Aboriginal Children

Many have argued that Aboriginal children would be better served by a new constitutional framework to govern First Nations–Canada relations (Bland, 2013). It has been regularly argued that First Nations communities need to be allowed to act in their own interests and in the interest of future generations through various forms of self-government (Bland, 2013). But until a new framework and approach is achieved, drawing attention to and battling for change has been left in the hands of individuals and communities. While there have been many protests and awareness-raising campaigns, one of the more recent and familiar is the Idle No More movement, which has quickly become one of the largest Aboriginal mass movements in Canadian history.

Idle No More began as a series of teach-ins throughout Saskatchewan aimed at protesting against parliamentary bills that were believed to erode Indigenous sovereignty and environmental protections (see www.idlenomore. ca). This sparked rallies and protests across Canada and beyond, drawing considerable international attention to a range of Aboriginal concerns. The National Day of Action on 10 December has inspired thousands to action, as a form of resistance against colonialism.

Idle No More quickly became an important centre of media attention. It also brought together a number of non-indigenous allies looking to work with indigenous populations against government policies that negatively affect our collective rights, our current social safety nets, and environmental protections.

Some have attributed the 2012–13 Idle No More movement to the actions of young Aboriginal people who have articulately, creatively, and angrily come together to raise awareness of and fight injustice against First Nations communities (Bland, 2013). The movement aims to ensure full indigenous participation in Canada's wealth and resources and to improve the quality of life of the next generation.

Summary

Aboriginal children growing up in this country have experienced considerable injustice, primarily at the hands of the Canadian state. Part of the problem that remains is that although Aboriginal children have been the victims of larger structural problems linked to assimilationist policies and socioeconomic deprivation, until recently solutions have been sought (to correct and protect) at the individual level, rather than at community or broader national levels. This chapter presented some of the legacy of Canada's colonial history and its effect on Aboriginal children and their families. It identified a number of differences between the lives of Aboriginal children and those of other Canadian children, but also attempted to show the importance of listening to and understanding the unique and valuable insights of Aboriginal children themselves. While we have seen some improvements in the conditions that undermine the well-being of Aboriginal children in Canada, there are many battles left to fight when it comes to the injustices experienced by Aboriginal children and their families. Giving greater autonomy to future generations is a logical first step towards improvement.

Questions for Critical Thought

1. How do the lives of Aboriginal children differ from those of other Canadian children? How are they similar or different from the lives of other Canadian children? What accounts for the similarities and differences?

2. Should anything be done to make Aboriginal children's lives more similar to other Canadian children's lives? Is assimilation into Canadian society the answer? Is there a way to protect Aboriginal cultures but do away with inequalities? What could or should be done? Who should do it?

3. Indian Residential Schools are a thing of the past, but their legacy continues. What can and should be done, if anything, to address ongoing challenges that have resulted from the Indian Residential School system?

4. Where do you see the future of Aboriginal children and families heading if nothing is done to address past and ongoing injustices?

5. Is Aboriginal self-government the best way to improve the lives of Aboriginal children in this country? If yes, how do we move closer to it? If no, what is the answer?

Suggested Readings

Assembly of First Nations. 2010. *First Nations Control of First Nations Education.* Ottawa: Assembly of First Nations. At: www.afn.ca/uploads/files/education/3._2010_july_afn_first_nations_control_of_first_nations_education_final_eng.pdf. This document updates the basic principles outlined in the Indian Control of Indian Education (ICIE) 1972 policy. This new document was developed to assist governments and First Nations communities in building education policies, programs, and services aimed to ensure the future prosperity of First Nations peoples. It provides strategic recommendations that may enable the development and implementation of education for First Nations learners at all stages of life.

Statistics Canada. 2013e. *Aboriginal Peoples in Canada: First Nations People, Métis and Inuit. National Household Survey 2011.* Ottawa: Statistics Canada. At: www12.statcan.gc.ca/nhs-enm/2011/as-sa/99-011-x/99-011-x2011001-eng.pdf. This paper is a summary of relevant information on Aboriginal populations in Canada drawn from findings of the most recent National Household Survey. Among other things, it provides an overview of the changes in the number of Aboriginal peoples in Canada.

UNICEF Canada. 2009. *Canadian Supplement to The State of the World's Children. Aboriginal Children's Health: Leaving No Child Behind.* Toronto: UNICEF Canada. www.unicef.ca/sites/default/files/imce_uploads/DISCOVER/OUR%20WORK/ADVOCACY/DOMESTIC/POLICY%20ADVOCACY/DOCS/Leaving%20no%20child%20behind%2009.pdf. This collection of articles is a supplement to the UNICEF's *The State of the World's Children 2009.* It presents an overview of the status of First Nations, Inuit, and Métis children's health in their rural, remote, or urban communities. It highlights jurisdictional hurdles facing these children and offers actions for addressing the health inequalities of First Nations, Inuit, and Métis children in this country.

Websites

Aboriginal Affairs and Northern Development Canada—Kids' Stop
www.aadnc-aandc.gc.ca/eng/1315444613519/1315444663239
Part of Aboriginal Affairs and Northern Development Canada's website, Kids' Stop is a website for kids that contains information about Aboriginal history, culture, languages, games, and stories. It also contains classroom resources for teachers.

Aboriginal Affairs and Northern Development Canada—Statement of Apology
www.aadnc-aandc.gc.ca/eng/1100100015644/1100100015649
Also part of Aboriginal Affairs and Northern Development Canada, this site contains the formal apology by the Prime Minister of Canada for the treatment of Aboriginal Peoples in the Indian Residential School system.

Aboriginal Head Start in Urban and Northern Communities (AHSUNC)
www.phac-aspc.gc.ca/hp-ps/dca-dea/prog-ini/ahsunc-papacun/index-eng.php

Aboriginal Head Start on Reserve
www.phac-aspc.gc.ca/hp-ps/dca-dea/prog-ini/ahsunc-papacun/index-eng.php
These two websites provide detailed information about Aboriginal Head Start (established in 1995). One of its goals is to develop programs that maintain high standards of child care and preschool education in each province and territory, but also celebrate diverse Aboriginal communities and their cultures across Canada. For more on the program's principles and guidelines also see www.phac-aspc.gc.ca/hp-ps/dca-dea/publications/ahsuni-papairun/index-eng.php.

Assembly of First Nations
www.afn.ca/
The Assembly of First Nations (AFN) is the national organization representing First Nations (i.e., registered Indian bands) in Canada. The AFN website contains a great deal of information and links to First Nations Child and Family Services, a residential schools update, an Action Plan on First Nations Child Welfare, etc. It also includes links to media, policy issues, publications, and upcoming events.

Health Canada—First Nations and Inuit Health
www.hc-sc.gc.ca/fniah-spnia/index-eng.php
This website contains information on Aboriginal family health, Aboriginal Head Start, and information on community-based health promotion. It also provides a link to lists of drinking water advisories in First Nations communities—a sad reality for many Aboriginal communities in this country.

Idle No More
www.idlenomore.ca/
This website provides information on the history and actions of the social movement known as Idle No More. But more importantly, it seeks to provide information on the historical and contemporary context of colonialism and the complex construction of ongoing oppression.

Inuit Health Matters
inuithealthmatters.aboutkidshealth.ca/en/pages/default.aspx
Inuit Health Matters was developed to help tackle some of the challenges that surround pregnancy and birth in Nunavut. These challenges include high-risk pregnancies and poor health outcomes connected with the loss of culture and traditions in these northern communities. This initiative aims to improve the health and well-being of new families among Canada's Inuit populations while recognizing the importance of traditional Inuit culture.

10   Child Poverty in Canada

Learning Objectives

◎   To critically explore the notion that Canada is the envy of the world.

◎   To note the 1989 Parliamentary commitment to abolish child poverty by the year 2000.

◎   To learn how poverty is measured in this country.

◎   To understand current rates and trends pertaining to child poverty.

◎   To better understand who is most vulnerable to poverty in Canada.

◎   To find out more about the impact of poverty on children.

◎   To investigate why child poverty exists and persists in Canada today.

◎   To assess how Canada compares internationally on measures of child poverty.

◎   To consider some of the differences across countries.

Introduction: Canada, the Envy of the World?

In November 2000, national news headlines read "Canada #1 in UN Survey—Again" (CBC News, 2000). The Canadian Broadcasting Corporation, like other news outlets, proudly boasted that for the seventh year in a row Canada ranked at the top of the United Nations (UN) Human Development Index (HDI), part of the annual UN *Human Development Report*. Starting in 1990, the HDI ranked 174 countries, measuring the basic conditions of people's lives, including life expectancy (Canada's is high at 79.1 years), adult literacy rates (99 per cent in Canada), and standard of living (US $23,582 gross domestic product [GDP] per capita in the year 2000). Using these types of measures, Canada sat at the top of the HDI. The less publicly celebrated part of the report is that the HDI is only a "partial" measure of human development, and the UN warns that Canada falls behind in areas like human rights and poverty. It is also important to note that by 2013, Canada dropped to number 8, on account of other nations improving their standings (United Nations Development Programme [UNDP], 2014).

That same month and year that Canada ranked first place, Campaign 2000 issued its first *Report Card* on child poverty in Canada. In sharp contrast to the UN's *Human Development Report,* this group reported that child poverty rates "grew to a record high" in precisely the years Canada was celebrating its top position on the HDI (Campaign 2000, 2000). At that point, one in five children lived in poverty—an increase of 402,000 since 1989 (ibid.). In this chapter we will begin by looking at the importance of the year 1989 to child poverty. We will then learn about the various ways that poverty is measured in this country and around the world. Then, we will look at just how many of Canada's children live in poverty, exploring trends over time, across provinces, and among various groups in this country. We will learn which of Canada's children are most vulnerable and why, and read about the impact of poverty on child development and outcomes. The chapter will consider Canada in international perspective so that we can more accurately assess whether Canada is truly the "envy of the word" and "the best place to live."

1989—A Special Year for Child Poverty in Canada?

In 1989, the child poverty rate in Canada was about what it is today, about 14 per cent (see Figure 10.1). For some, this may be viewed as a positive indication reflecting economic stability over the past 20 years. One could not be further from the truth. In 1989, Canada was viewed as a "social policy laggard" (Freiler and Cerny, 1998), meaning that, compared with the rest of the world, in providing social and economic benefits to Canadian families—particularly those with young children—Canada fell far behind other countries. Shamed into attention, on 24 November 1989 the Canadian House of Commons unanimously passed an all-party resolution seeking to achieve the goal of eliminating poverty among Canadian children by the year 2000. All parties seemed to have agreed that having 12 to 14 per cent

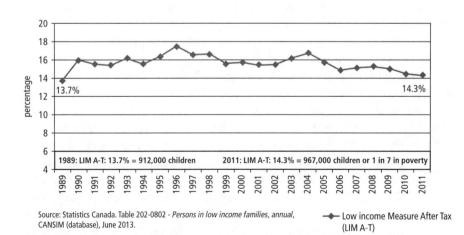

Source: Statistics Canada. Table 202-0802 - *Persons in low income families, annual,* CANSIM (database), June 2013.

◆ Low income Measure After Tax (LIM A-T)

Figure 10.1 Poverty Rates for Children in Low-Income Families in Canada, 1989–2011
Sources: With permission from Campaign 2000: end child and family poverty in Canada: http://www.campaign2000.ca

(depending on the measure) of Canada's children living in poverty was not acceptable and could be improved on.

The next year, in 1990, at the World Summit for Children, Canada reaffirmed its commitment by agreeing to the principle of "first call for children"—that the basic needs of children would be a priority in the allocation of resources (UNICEF, 1990b). One year later, in 1991, Canada ratified the UN Convention on the Rights of the Child. In doing this, it agreed to implement measures—to the "maximum extent" of its resources—to fulfill, among others, article 27: "The right of every child to a standard of living adequate for the child's physical, mental, spiritual, moral and social development." On paper, Canada seemed fully committed to tackling the issue of child poverty, with public pledges made at home and abroad. Indeed, the federal government began implementing changes to child benefits to begin to address some of these issues.

Since the 1989 commitment, the federal government revamped the child benefits system so that by 1993, the three key, more *universal* (reaching or intending to reach all families with children) federal child benefits—the family allowance, the refundable child tax credit, and the non-refundable child tax credit—were replaced by the *income-tested* Child Tax Benefit based on how much a family earns (McEwen and Stewart, 2014; Battle, 2007). This initiative increased benefits for working-poor families with children, maintained benefits for low-income families, reduced benefits for middle-income earners, and eliminated benefits for high-income families (ibid.). Despite this, throughout the early 1990s, child poverty rates skyrocketed. In 1995, there were about 1,472,000 children, or 21 per cent of all children, living in low-income families (Statistics Canada, 1996b). This was an *increase* of 538,000 children, or 58 per cent, since 1989, the year the House of Commons stated its commitment to eliminate child poverty by the year 2000 (Freiler and Cerny, 1998). In 1989, one child in seven was poor. Today, we are at the same ratio: one in seven (Campaign 2000, 2014).

In 1998 the federal, provincial, and territorial governments enacted more profound changes by introducing the National Child Benefit (NCB).[1] This restructured and attempted to coordinate disparate child benefits at the two levels of government through the income-tested Canada Child Tax Benefit (CCTB) and the NCB Supplement (see Figure 10.1). The goals were to help prevent and reduce child poverty, promote parental attachment to the labour force, and reduce overlap and duplication by harmonizing programs through a simplified administration (Government of Canada, 2007). The federal–provincial/territorial agreement was implemented based on the understanding that as Ottawa increased payments under the CCTB (to working and non-working poor families), the provinces and territories could reduce social assistance–related child benefits, freeing up provincial and territorial funds for reinvestment into other programs and services for low-income families with children (Battle, 2007). This meant that all low-income families with children, whether working or non-working, would receive more federal funding, while families on social assistance would still benefit from provincially funded social "welfare" programs. This resulted in only "modest reductions" in the number of children living in poverty (ibid., 32), particularly among those living in families considered to make up the "working poor"—but our child poverty rates remain high by comparison with other Organisation for Economic Co-operation and Development (OECD) countries (more on this below), using a number of different measures.

Measuring and Defining Poverty

Since the 1970s, Statistics Canada has been publishing low-income rates based on a measure called the low income cut-off (LICO). In Canada, this has become one of the most common approaches to measuring low income (Phipps and Curtis, 2000), but no commonly agreed-on measure of poverty currently exists across "developed" nations or within Canada itself (MacKinnon, 2013). In fact, Statistics Canada has maintained that the LICO neither can nor should be used as a poverty line (Mendelson, 2005). Nonetheless, many have interpreted this measure as such, particularly since Statistics Canada itself has noted that the LICO helps identify those who are substantially worse off than the average (Webber, 1998).

Low Income Cut-Offs

Low income cut-offs have been used for a number of decades as a way of measuring whether a family has to spend too large a proportion of its income on basic food, clothing, and shelter, compared with other Canadian families (making this a relative measure; see below). It was developed using 1959 Family Expenditure Survey data—a survey of household spending. The original calculations found that an average household spent about 50 per cent of its pre-tax income on basic food, shelter, and clothing. It was then decided that if a family spent 70 per cent of its pre-tax income on these essentials—20 per cent more than the average family—the family was considered to be in straitened circumstances (Webber, 1998). This threshold—what the average household spent, plus 20 per cent—was converted to a set of LICOs that vary by family and community size (ibid.; MacKinnon, 2013; see Table 10.1). Since this measure was introduced, average household spending on food, shelter, and clothing declined from 50 per cent of before-tax income to about 35 per cent before tax or 44 per cent after tax, resulting in major changes in LICO calculations since 1969 and regular annual updates based on the Consumer Price Index (Webber, 1998). Today, LICOs are calculated using either or both after-tax and pre-tax income, and a family is typically considered to be living in straitened circumstances if it spends approximately 55 per cent (the average

Table 10.1 Low Income Cut-Offs, After Tax, by Community and Family Size, 2011[a]

Family Unit (No. of Persons)	Rural Areas	Urban Areas			
		Under 30,000	30,000– 99,999	100,000– 499,999	500,000 and Over
1	12,629	14,454	16,124	16, 328	19,307
2	15,371	17,592	19,625	19,872	23,498
3	19,141	21,905	24,437	24,745	29,260
4	23,879	27, 329	30,487	30,871	36,504
5	27,192	31,120	34,717	35,154	41,567
6	30,156	34,513	38, 502	38,986	46, 099
7 or more	33,121	37,906	42,286	42,819	50,631

[a]1992 LICOs base.

Source: Adapted from Statistics Canada (2013f: Table 202-0801).

of 35 per cent plus 20 per cent) in the before-tax calculation of LICO or 44 per cent plus 20 per cent in the after-tax calculation (Statistics Canada, 2013g), or more, on basic food, clothing, and shelter. Again, this is standardized and calculated on family and on community size. For example, in 2011, a family of four, living in an urban area with 500,000 or more inhabitants, is considered to be "straitened" if it has an after-tax household income of $36,504.

The Low Income Measure

In the late 1980s, another measure, called the low income measure (LIM), was introduced for certain types of analyses (Webber, 1998). The LIM is set at 50 per cent of the median income,[2] which is calculated based on family size but not differentiated by community size, like the LICO. (It is actually much less complicated than it sounds.) The median income in Canada in any given year represents the middle score or value if all incomes in the country were ranked from highest to lowest. So, imagine lining up all incomes for every household in Canada, from highest to lowest, and finding the household income that divides that line in half. The LIM would consider a family to be in straitened circumstances (i.e., poor) if it has a household income of less than half the median (middle) Canadian income. For example, the median after-tax household income for Canadian families of four was about $79,720 in 2011 (Statistics Canada, 2013g). A family of four would be considered poor using the LIM if it had an after-tax household income of $39,860 less ($79,720 divided by two), regardless of where it lived (community size; Statistics Canada 2013g).

This measure has been used extensively in international comparisons done by organizations like the OECD, which documents and compares policies and practices among the most "developed" and economically "advanced" nations of the world. Both LICOs and the LIM are considered to be *relative measures*—measures that compare incomes and deduce that some are considerably lower in relation to others.

Many other measures currently are being used to determine low income, most of which remain relative.[3] In noting this, some have argued that in Canada we do not have "real" or *absolute poverty*, that is, a lack for some people of the basic necessities of life, but rather only *relative poverty*—implying that some Canadian children and families only "feel" poor compared with others. Another commonly used measure, the market basket measure (MBM) focuses more on the ability of a family to pay for the basic necessities in life. The MBM is based on the cost of a specific basket of goods and services representing a basic, modest standard of living. It includes the costs of food, clothing, shelter, footwear, transportation, and other expenses for a family of two adults (ages 25–49) and two children (Statistics Canada, 2013g). This measure accounts for geographic differences acknowledging different costs for rural areas in the different provinces.

Canadian children in Grades 4 and 5 living in North Bay, Ontario, remind us that no matter how we measure poverty, "real" or "relative" poverty for them means the following: "feeling ashamed when my dad can't get a job"; "pretending that you forgot your lunch"; "being afraid to tell your Mom you need gym shoes"; "not buying books at the book fair"; and "not getting to go on school trips" (Canadian Teachers' Federation, 2008: 2). To help contextualize this, let us consider another measure or concept known as *depth of poverty*.

Depth of poverty, or the *low-income gap*, is the amount of income a low-income household would need to reach the low-income threshold, or how much it falls short of the relevant LICO (Statistics Canada, 2007g; World

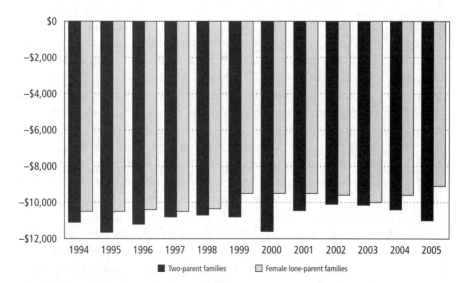

Figure 10.2 Depth of Poverty in Canada,[a] 1994–2005
[a]Using before-tax income.
Source: Statistics Canada (2008b).

Bank, 2011). The World Bank notes that this measure captures the consumption "shortfall' relative to the poverty line across a whole population. For example, a family with an income of $15,000, when a LICO is $20,000, would have a low-income gap of $5,000. It is a measure of *how poor* Canada's poor really are. The World Bank also notes that the poverty gap has been used as a measure of the minimum amount of resources necessary to eradicate poverty, or the amount that one would have to transfer to the poor in order to be lifted out of poverty. In 2009, Canada's poor families struggled to survive on incomes that averaged $8,000 *below* the LICOs (Campaign 2000, 2011). In other words, on average, low-income-gap families were so poor that they needed about $8,000 to *reach* the unofficial poverty lines.

By many accounts, including recent Statistics Canada calculations, the poor are getting poorer and the gap between the lowest- and highest-income families has widened (Campaign 2000, 2013). According to Campaign 2000 (2013), the average income of the wealthiest families with children increased dramatically to $271,224, while the average income of the lowest income families remained the same, at $23,024. They also note that inequality worsened significantly over the past decade, given that over the last two decades, Canada had the fourth largest increase in income inequality among advanced industrialized countries (Campaign 2000, 2013). By the government's own accounts, the majority of income for people in the lowest two income deciles came from government transfers (55.1 per cent in the second decile and 67.5 per cent in the lowest decile; Statistics Canada, 2013h).

Child Poverty—Rates and Trends

Since 1991, more than 120 organizations and groups from across Canada have joined forces with the goal of building awareness, educating the public, and shaping public policy on child poverty. This group has called itself Campaign 2000. Its name reflects its goal of building Canadian awareness and support for the 1989 all-party House of Commons resolution to end child poverty in Canada by the year 2000. To help do this, since 2000, this organization has used official Canadian statistics and resources, in the form of annual "report cards," to document and measure the (lack of) progress towards the goal of eliminating child poverty. Copies of these report cards are widely available, very readable and reliable (citing Statistics Canada data and studies), and provide a good source of information on child poverty rates and trends in Canada today.

In 2013, Canada had a child poverty rate of about 14 per cent—the same rate we had in 1989 (Campaign 2000, 2013). Using after-tax income as a measure, as noted above, one in seven children in Canada, or a total of 967,000 children, lived in poverty in 2013. Increasingly, many of the children living in poverty lived in households where at least one adult or parent worked full-time, full-year (ibid.). Child poverty rates also varied across the country. Some of the increase in provinces previously considered "have" provinces, like Ontario, may be the result of the numerous job losses in the once-prosperous manufacturing sector; high poverty rates in some provinces reflect their higher than average Aboriginal populations.

Who Is Most Vulnerable?

The risk of poverty is not the same for all children. In fact, some groups in Canada are considerably more likely than others to live in poverty. Campaign 2000 (2013) explains that the only reliable source to understand poverty in selected demographic groups, including racialized, Aboriginal, immigrant, and disability communities over time (until 2006), had been the long-form census, but in 2010 it was cancelled by the Conservative government. That said, by a number of different measures and estimates, the most vulnerable group, with the highest rate of child poverty, was found to be indigenous communities with some 40 per cent of children living in poverty, followed by 33 per cent of immigrant and refugee children (Campaign 2000, 2013). Racialized children and children with disabilities are also more vulnerable compared with other children (Spies et al., 2014; see Box 10.1). Finally,

---

Box 10.1   Childhood Disability in the Context of Poverty

A discussion paper prepared by Theresa M. Petrenchik (2008) from CanChild Centre for Childhood Disability Research at McMaster University in Hamilton, Ontario, for the Ontario Ministry of Children and Youth Services, noted the following:

> Children living in poverty are at greater risk for a disability or developmental delay, and caring for a child with disability increases the odds of a family living in poverty. Though reliable prevalence data for childhood disability in low-income families is currently unavailable, an estimated 30 per cent of Canadian children and youth with disabilities live in poverty. The strain of living poor, including material deprivation and social exclusion, coupled with the high costs of caring for a child with a disability creates chronic and unnecessary hardship in families.
>
> Childhood disability in the context of poverty means children and families must cope not only with the disability itself, but with the added burdens of poverty-related health disparities, social disadvantage, inadequate health-related services, and the extra direct costs (time, money, and resources) associated with a child's disability. A child with a disability living in poverty is also more likely to live in problem housing and to experience routine hunger than other children.

Source: Petrenchik (2008: 3).

despite some improvements over time, children living in female-headed, single-parent families remain among the most economically vulnerable.

There is no question that children are poor because their parents are poor. But contrary to popular belief, many of these children live in families where at least one parent is employed, although many of these parents earn only minimum wage or close to that. Many children living in poverty live in households in which two parents are employed, yet their low earnings and job insecurity make it difficult for them to break the cycle of poverty (Sharma, 2012). This has had negative repercussions for children living in these families.

Incomes and Outcomes: Impact of Poverty on Children

Ample evidence shows that as family incomes fall, risks of poor developmental outcomes in children's health, learning, and socialization increase (Burton et al., 2014; Chen, 2014; da Fonseca, 2014; Singh and Ghandour, 2012; Fauth et al., 2007; Robson-Haddow, 2004; Ross and Roberts, 1999). Statistical analyses reveal that higher income (regardless of the measure of income employed) is almost always associated with better outcomes for children (Phipps and Lethbridge, 2006). Also, the relationship between incomes and outcomes is most significant among younger children, such that increases in income for those at very low income levels are especially important for Canada's youngest (ibid.). But before considering results from statistical analyses, let us simply ponder what low income means in the lives of young children.

Healthy development includes access to basic nutrition and safe neighbourhoods (Campaign 2000, 2013; Kerr, 2004; Jones et al., 2002). Furthermore, lower income contributes to limited access to adequate housing, and inadequate housing means overcrowding, strained living conditions, residential instability, and poorer and less safe neighbourhoods (Anderson et al., 2014; McCartney et al., 2007). In addition, poor parents are less able to purchase products and services that assist children in their learning, and often cannot afford recreational activities that promote physical, social, emotional, and intellectual development; the alternative becomes more television watching (Berry, 2007; Burdette and Whitaker, 2005; Kerr, 2004). Therefore, the developmental risks associated with economic disadvantage have been well documented.

Despite some variations, studies show that child poverty negatively impacts physical (mortality, morbidity, accidents, and abuse), behavioural, emotional, and cognitive outcomes (Statistics Canada 2009b). The *Canadian Medical Association Journal,* for example, has noted that while there was a decline in the rate of unintentional injuries among Canadian children living in urban areas between 1971 and 1998, poor children were still twice as likely as children in affluent homes to die of an unintended injury (Stanwick, 2006). Income also has been found to have particularly strong associations with cognitive outcomes (as measured by Peabody Picture Vocabulary Test scores, and math and reading scores) and behavioural outcomes (Phipps and Lethbridge, 2006).

Early childhood poverty subsequently affected years of schooling such that poor children were less likely to graduate from high school compared with children who did not experience poverty or who experienced it later in childhood (Statistics Canada, 2009b; Brooks-Gunn and Duncan, 1997). Williamson and Salkie (2005) found that both before and after almost Canada-wide welfare reforms introduced mandatory welfare-to-work initiatives, preschool children in working poor families had higher school readiness scores than their peers whose families received social assistance. But preschool children in both working and non-working poor families had *lower* scores on the Peabody Picture Vocabulary Test–Revised (or PPVT–R, a measure of school readiness) than children in non-poor families (ibid.). Similarly, an analysis of National Longitudinal Survey of Children and Youth (NLSCY) data found that household income was a significant predictor for many measures of five-year-old children's readiness to learn at school (Verdon, 2007; Thomas, 2006).

Family income was associated with maternal emotional distress, parenting practices, and family stress, all of which affected parents' ability to cognitively stimulate children. Unsurprisingly, children from more affluent families had more access and exposure to activities in the home environment, including daily reading, participation in organized sports, and lessons in physical activities and arts, which predicted and positively affected greater readiness to learn (Verdon, 2007; Thomas, 2006).

Physical health scores have also had consistently positive associations with family incomes (Burton et al., 2014; Chen, 2014; da Fonseca, 2014; Singh and Ghandour, 2012; Phipps and Lethbridge, 2006). Although the great majority of children born in developed nations enjoy unprecedented levels of health, the wealthiest nations in the world are not necessarily the healthiest (UNICEF, 2013). The problem lies in the amount of poverty amid prosperity (income inequality) and the lack of social programs aimed at combatting it. Some have found the link between family income inequality and poor physical health to be so consistent that they have argued it is effectively a natural law: greater income equality within a society (i.e., less of a gap between the wealthy and the poor) results in better health outcomes for the entire society (UNICEF, 2013; Wilkinson, 2005; see also Chung and Muntaner, 2006).

Put simply, poor parents, because of limited resources, often have a difficult time supplying their children with the best food and adequate clothing and housing, resulting in exposure to harmful environmental conditions and increased stress. Children themselves are keenly aware of this. For example, children in New Zealand offered advice to governments on how they can help. Some noted the following:

> [The Government] should bring food or give [parents] a basic fund and then a little bit more money [a bonus] but not for cigarettes. If they don't spend it on food and they spend it on cigarettes, then they shouldn't get the little bit more [the bonus]. Then perhaps you might get people managing their money sensibly. If the famil[ies] are going to spend money on drugs, then the Government should bring you [children] food. The Government should monitor extra money for benefits and reward families who spend it sensibly. For people on benefits, keep prices, like for food and milk and uniforms[,] down. (Te One et al., 2014: 1060)

UNICEF (2013) compared what children had to say about their own lives. A recent report provides an overview of children's subjective well-being across 29 developed countries. Specifically, UNICEF (2013) mapped the proportion of children ages 11, 13, and 15 in each of the 29 countries who reported a high level of life satisfaction on a scale of 0 to 10. Canadian children, in particular, stood out as some of the least satisfied with their lives (See Figure 10.3). Policy-makers need to take note, as Canadian children's self-assessment of their well-being provides us with an important guide to critical factors that shape their lives. Clearly so much more can and should be done to improve their outcomes.

Children living in low-income families are not "destined" to live deprived lives. Jones et al. (2002) noted that the effects of long-term poverty on children are mediated and moderated by neighbourhood resources or social capital. They found that the local norms of some neighbourhoods, and particularly those with more social supports, can positively modify the effects of long-term poverty. Similarly, poor children who live in families with constructive and supportive relationships also have an advantage (Kerr, 2004). In fact, numerous studies show that children in low-income families benefit from parental supports in the form of high-quality child care (Campaign 2000, 2013; Esping-Andersen, 2007; McCartney et al., 2007; Prentice, 2007), anti-poverty programs (Gassman-Pines and Yoshikawa, 2006), and a host of other national- and neighbourhood-based initiatives (Bradshaw, 2002). But the problem is complex; explanations for why poverty exists and persists are varied and many, and so require a wide range of initiatives.

Explanations for Rates of Child Poverty

Children themselves may be contributing to family poverty because they are a drain on family resources. However, research shows that in some countries,

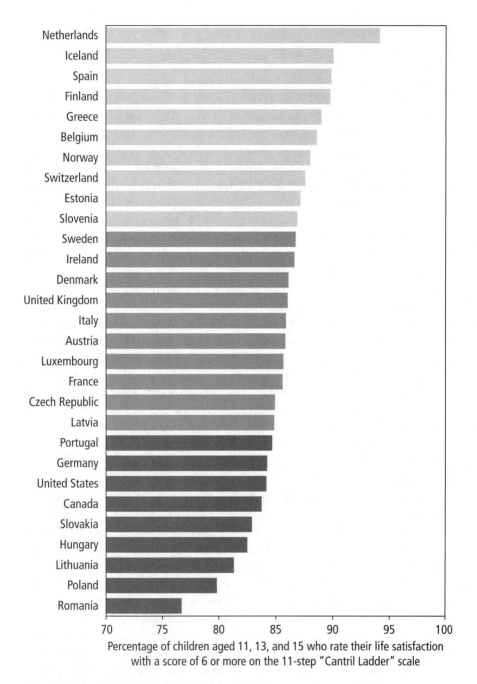

Percentage of children aged 11, 13, and 15 who rate their life satisfaction
with a score of 6 or more on the 11-step "Cantril Ladder" scale

Figure 10.3 The Children's Life Satisfaction League Table
Source: UNICEF Office of Research (2013). 'Child Well-being in Rich Countries: A comparative overview', Innocenti Report Card
2011. UNICEF Office of Research, Florence.

with more family-friendly social policies, disposable income falls only moderately when families have children. Using data from seven Western, industrialized countries, Sigle-Rushton and Waldfogel (2007) compared gaps in gross and disposable family income between families with and without children. They found that differences in earnings and labour market participation of women were major drivers in the gap in gross and disposable income. Taxes and government transfers also narrowed the differences, but only slightly.

This means that poverty rates have a great deal to do with parents' and especially mothers' access to the labour force, the wages they receive, and government policies aimed at assisting families towards getting and holding decent-paying, stable employment (Sharma, 2012; see Wiegers, 2002, on women and poverty). As noted above, many of this country's poor children are increasingly likely to be living in families where one or both parents are working, but they do not earn enough to make ends meet. This has a great deal to do with the changing nature of Canada's economy.

Numerous sources, including Statistics Canada, have documented the rise of precarious (insecure, temporary, part-time) employment characterized by poor job quality, low wages, and no health or pension benefits (also see Sharma, 2012). *Losing Ground: The Persistent Growth in Poverty in Canada's Largest City,* a report on poverty in Canada's largest and nominally wealthiest city—Toronto—noted that between 2002 and 2006, Canada lost nearly 250,000 jobs in the manufacturing sector, which meant the loss of high-wage, permanent jobs with low education requirements (MacDonnell, 2007). The report adds that, by 2002, an estimated 37 per cent of the Canadian workforce was employed in temporary, low-waged, precarious, "non-standard" jobs, which minimize labour costs to employers, as temporary work wages are on average 16 per cent lower than permanent work wages.

Furthermore, recent immigrants to Canada, who gravitate to Canada's largest cities, especially Toronto, parachute into this precarious labour market, with very high housing costs and a high cost of living. This has forced many—recent arrivals and others—to become multiple job holders in an attempt to make ends meet, which in turn contributes to family instability and increased child poverty rates. It is also important to note that in recent years there have been substantial cuts to social assistance benefits and shrinkage in Employment Insurance (EI) coverage (Battle, 2007).

In sum, children are poor for a large number of reasons, but principally due to their caregivers' relationship to the Canadian labour force and because of the high cost of housing and living (Campaign 2000, 2013; Sharma, 2012). Some are poor because their parents earn low wages or work at non-standard jobs; others have parents whose education limits them or whose educational credentials are not recognized in Canada, leaving them to face high levels of unemployment or underemployment (Sharma, 2012). Other children have experienced their parents' marital breakup (sometimes because of income instability and stress) or live in lone-parent households; still others have become poorer through government cutbacks in social spending (ibid.; MacDonnell, 2007; MacDonnell et al., 2004; Freiler and Cerny, 1998).

How Do We Compare Internationally and Why?

Other industrialized societies have been exposed to similar global economic pressures and shifts, but with remarkably different results when it comes to child poverty. In fact, international comparisons reveal that there does not appear to be a strong relationship between a country's per capita GDP and overall child well-being. For example, in international comparisons of child well-being, UNICEF (2013) revealed that the Czech Republic ranked higher than Portugal, the United Kingdom, and Canada. As we will explore in more detail below, high rates of child poverty have a great deal to do with income distribution, and the social policies that do and do not address this. Before this, let's review Canada's standing compared to other industrialized nations.

UNICEF's (2013) report *Child Well-Being in Rich Countries,* which benchmarks health and well-being among the world's richest countries, clearly shows that Canada's children are not adequately supported by the state. Using a range of measures of well-being, overall, Canada sits in the middle of the pack: seventeenth of the 29 countries compared (UNICEF, 2013). The numbers are even worse on a number of individual measures. For example, Canada ranked twenty-seventh out of 29 in childhood obesity, twenty-second in infant mortality, and twenty-first in child poverty rates (UNICEF, 2013; see Figure 10.4). As we saw in the previous chapter and as noted in various national and international reports, Aboriginal children fared even worse, with health outcomes far lower than Canadian averages.

International comparisons and reports like these reveal that while labour market conditions and social change played key roles in high child poverty rates, higher government spending on and better dispensation of family and social benefits clearly are associated with lower child poverty rates. These types of international reports note that in all countries, poverty levels are determined by a combination of three forces: social trends, labour market conditions, and government policies.

UNICEF's report cards on child poverty and well-being show that while all the nations studied make efforts to reduce levels of poverty through cash and other benefits to the unemployed and those living on low incomes, countries with the world's lowest rates of poverty, such as Denmark, Finland, and Norway, did a considerably better job in regard to government intervention. The greater the proportion of GDP devoted to family allowances, disability and sickness benefits, formal childcare provisions, unemployment

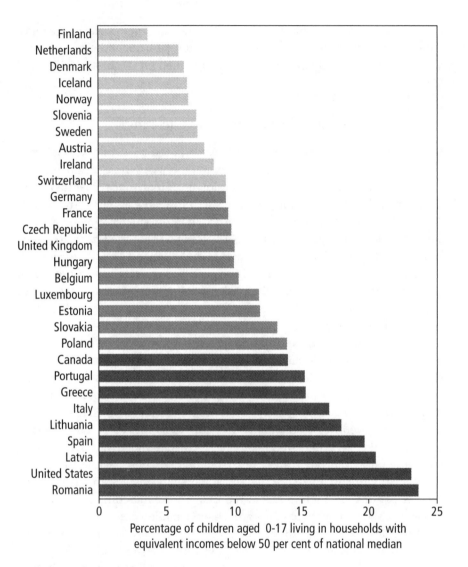

Figure 10.4 Relative Child Poverty Rates
Source: UNICEF Office of Research (2013). 'Child Well-being in Rich Countries: A comparative overview', Innocenti Report Card 2011. UNICEF Office of Research, Florence.

insurance, employment promotion, and other forms of social assistance, the lower the risk of growing up in poverty (UNICEF, 2013). On top of *how much* was spent, it was also important to factor in how government support was *distributed*. For example, in France the tax and benefits system does not favour any particular age group, while in the United Kingdom the system favours children. Despite this, the child poverty rate in the United Kingdom is double that of France. The UNICEF (2013) report explains that when benefits are universally provided—provided to all, rather than aimed at low-income families—though seemingly more expensive, they actually work best. Highly targeted social expenditures focus resources on those who need it most, but may mean that recipients have little incentive to move from welfare to work (ibid.).

Canada, like the United Kingdom, has made considerable efforts to reduce poverty; however, our initiatives appear to be a tattered patchwork of policies and programs compared with some European nations with low rates of child poverty. Compared with Western European countries with low child poverty rates, even among lone female parents, Canadian policies (like those of the United Kingdom and the United States) basically reflect a focus on individual responsibility as a principal cause of poverty, and this approach to the understanding and treatment of families does not recognize society's shared responsibility for children (Freiler and Cerny, 1998). Such a view basically assumes that having children is an individual lifestyle choice and the responsibility of those who choose to have them. The state will step in to assist families, but only after they find themselves in dire need. In contrast, Western European nations with low poverty rates embrace a social responsibility (social democratic) framework that assumes that children are essential to the society and as such are the responsibility both of parents *and* of the state (ibid.). They have more unified social and family programs and policies that express society's shared responsibility for children, provide an adequate income floor for families with children, reduce gender inequalities, expand family time options for parents, and ensure an adequate and consistent living standard for all children and families (ibid.).

The National Council of Welfare (2007)—an organization now unfunded and dismantled by the Conservative government—assessed anti-poverty strategies in other countries and found that the European Union (EU) framework contained objectives that Canada could learn from and emulate. One of the most obvious was an EU framework that promoted social cohesion, equality between men and women, interaction among policies, and transparency, good governance, and the monitoring of policy. Especially effective was the EU framework that did not isolate the problem of poverty but instead viewed it as connected to larger economic, social, and political issues (ibid.).

In Canada, we do not have to look very far for initiatives that resemble these more unified social democratic/social responsibility policy models, like those already in use in parts of Europe. For the last 20 years or so, Quebec has been unfolding components of a family policy unparalleled in North America, aimed at reconciling work and family, promoting gender equity, and reducing family poverty (Roy and Bernier, 2007). At the 1996 Summit on the Economy and Employment, the province's Premier announced a significant shift in family policies. The 1997 White Paper argued for policy coherence and integration across domains (across social assistance, early childhood education, and employment). Its goals were to ensure fairness by offering universal support to families, providing more assistance to low-income families, facilitating the balancing of work with parenting, and fostering child development and equal opportunity (Albanese, 2011; Jenson, 2001; Paquet, n.d.). In 1997, as a cornerstone of the new family policy, Quebec introduced $5/day child care for four-year-olds using child care at least three days a week, regardless of a family's income and employment status (Albanese, 2011; Government of Quebec, 2003). It has been argued by many that high-quality, affordable child care is one route out of poverty (Esping-Andersen, 2007; McCartney et al., 2007; Prentice, 2007).

Quebec also developed a unified anti-poverty strategy that was initiated by a broadly based citizens' movement (Torjman, 2010; National Council of Welfare, 2007; Noël, 2002). The collective, made up of 30 provincial organizations and 15 regional groups, was formed in 1998 to hold public consultations and propose social reform. This initiative resulted in the unanimous adoption by the provincial legislature in 2002 of Bill 112, the Act to Combat Poverty and Social Exclusion, a plan aimed at cutting poverty in half by 2012 (Government of Quebec, 2004). While they have not succeeded to reach that goal, Quebec continues to be seen as a leader on this front with seven provinces introducing poverty reduction strategies or plans. Campaign 2000's *Report Card 2012—Children of the Recession* has also documented some of Quebec's successes towards that yet unfulfilled goal. For example, the report card noted that from 2004–10, Quebec's Government Action Plan to Combat Poverty and Social Exclusion brought together a slate of measures valued at $4.5 billion, and from 2004 to 2007, the number of children under the age of 18 living in poverty decreased from 8.3 per cent in 2004 to 7.3 per cent by 2007. Campaign 2000 (2012) noted that these improvements reflect investments in employment supports for low-income earners, an increase in the minimum wage, and increasing a refundable tax credit for child assistance to enhance the disposable income of low- and medium-income families. In 2010, the Quebec government announced a second Action Plan for Solidarity and Social Inclusion, committing another $7 billion into 2015 (Campaign 2000, 2012).

Quebec demonstrates to the rest of Canadians that combatting child poverty is not impossible or out of reach. This also highlights the importance of creating a unified national strategy that recognizes poverty as linked to larger economic, social, and political issues. More specifically, fighting poverty would require the creation of a better, more integrated system of income supports and services aimed at helping a larger number of Canadians and families.

Child benefits for low-income families have increased substantially in value since the late 1990s, but a number of policy analysts have suggested increases and improvements to the current system (for details, see Battle, 2008). At the same time, more needs to be done to build strong neighbourhoods, help new-comers to fulfill their potential, make housing more affordable, provide liv-able incomes, create employment and retraining opportunities, and increase investments in infrastructure (MacDonnell et al., 2004). Attention also needs to be placed on improving women's access to and position in the labour force (Sharma, 2012; Wiegers, 2002), which would inevitably require the creation of a universal, nation-wide, accessible, affordable child-care program (UNDP, 2014; Albanese, 2011; McCartney et al., 2007; Prentice, 2007; Penn, 2004). Indeed, *universalism* has been identified as the answer to a large number of social ills plaguing children (UNDP, 2014).

Summary

In this chapter we have seen that Canadian politicians have been well aware of the child poverty problem since at least 1989, when they made a com-mitment to abolish it by the year 2000. Things got worse before they got better. More than two decades later, we are seeing slight improvements, but Canada remains among one the worst of the "rich" countries in regard to abolishing child poverty.

Child poverty is a complex issue that has multiple causes and serious effects. As a result, reducing poverty rates will need to include a range of efforts from a variety of sources and players, including employers, unions, and all levels of government, as well as community and citizens' groups—all of which strategies can be seen in Quebec. We need to create a national anti-poverty strategy and develop a coordinated plan of action aimed at *preventing* poverty and helping those currently in need. This would involve raising the minimum wage rates, improving housing and social assistance, creating a national early learning and child care system, developing and implementing family-friendly workplace practices, and pursuing the eco-nomic and social development of disadvantaged communities and neigh-bourhoods. At present, Canada (excepting Quebec) lags behind many other developed nations on all these initiatives, calling into question its right to be considered "the envy of the world."

Questions for Critical Thought

1. Children are poor because parents are poor, so why do we use the concept "child poverty" and not "family poverty?" Does it help to make the case for more public support? Has this been effective? How else might we draw more public attention to this issue?

2. What would you say are the leading causes of child poverty in this country? How would you propose to deal with these issues? How would you begin to implement your solu-tions? How would you fund your initiatives?

3. Some argue that universalism of services is the answer to child poverty. Do you agree? Why? Why not?

4.   You have been selected to represent Canada at an international forum on child poverty. What would you tell others about child poverty in Canada?

Suggested Readings

MacKinnon, Shauna. 2013. "The Politics of Poverty in Canada," *Social Alternatives* 32, 1: 19–23. The article acknowledges the persistence of poverty in Canada, despite its wealth and reputation. It explains the various ways that poverty is measured, including the low income cut-off (LICO), the low income measure (LIM), and the market basket measure (MBM). It presents some of the politics surrounding public policies developed for poverty reduction.

Sharma, Raghubar. 2012. *Poverty in Canada.* Toronto: Oxford University Press. This book provides a good overview of poverty in Canada, particularly among specific groups including the elderly, recent immigrants, children, and the "working poor." Government demographer Raghubar Sharma explains that in Canada, these groups are often excluded from full participation in our social and economic institutions. Sharma explores the circumstances behind their exclusion.

UNICEF. 2013. *Report Card 11—Child Well-Being in Rich Countries: A Comparative Overview.* Florence, Italy: UNICEF Innocenti Research Centre. *Report Card 11* is a three-part report. Part 1 compares child well-being in 29 of the world's advanced economies; Part 2 includes what children say about their own well-being; and Part 3 examines changes in child well-being over the first decade of the 2000s, looking at each country's progress in educational achievement, childhood obesity levels, the prevalence of bullying, etc.

United Nations Development Program. 2014. *Human Development Report 2014. Sustaining Human Progress: Reducing Vulnerabilities and Building Resilience.* New York: United Nations Development Program. At: http://hdr.undp.org/sites/default/files/hdr14-report-en-1.pdf. This report is the latest in the series of global *Human Development Reports* published by the UNDP since 1990. It provides an independent, empirically grounded analysis of major development issues, trends, and policies. It highlights the importance of social policies as causes and solutions to national and global poverty, and stresses the value of universal programs in promoting resilience among all citizens.

Websites

Campaign 2000
www.campaign2000.ca
Campaign 2000 is a cross-Canada public education movement to build Canadian awareness and support for the 1989 all-party House of Commons resolution to end child poverty in Canada by the year 2000. Campaign 2000 began in 1991 out of concern about the lack of government progress in addressing child poverty. Its website contains links to national "report cards" on child poverty from 2002 to the present. These report cards contain child poverty rates and trends for that year. You can access the *2013 Report Card on Child and Family Poverty in Canada* at www.campaign2000.ca/reportCards/national/2 013C2000NATIONALREPORTCARDNOV26.pdf.

Canadian Council on Social Development

www.ccsd.ca/

> The Canadian Council on Social Development is a nonprofit social policy and research organization focusing on issues such as poverty, social inclusion, disability, cultural diversity, child well-being, employment, and housing. This website contains links to research, publications, policy initiatives, facts, and statistics, as well as access to the Urban Poverty Project: www.ccsd.ca/index.php/research/urban-poverty-project.

Food Banks Canada

www.foodbankscanada.ca/

> Food Banks Canada is the national charitable organization representing and supporting food banks across Canada. Their website gives you access to a range of reports, position papers, and publications on poverty and hunger in Canada. It also gives you access to *Hungercount 2013* a comprehensive report on hunger and food bank use in Canada.

UNICEF: World Summit for Children

www.unicef.org/wsc/

> On 29–30 September 1990 the largest gathering of world leaders in history assembled at the United Nations for the World Summit for Children. The World Summit adopted the Declaration on the Survival, Protection, and Development of Children and a Plan of Action for implementing the Declaration in the 1990s. This website contains a list of attendees, the Summit goals, and its plan of action.

United Way—From Poverty to Possibility

www.unitedway.ca/our-work/poverty-to-possibility

> There are more than 100 United Way Centraides across the country. Each one is an autonomous nonprofit organization governed by a local board of directors. Each United Way Centraide raises money and allocates funds locally to support its community. United Way Centraides invest in numerous programs across the country to give Canadians the ability to avoid or move out of the cycle of poverty. The United Way of Greater Toronto, for example, has also produced a number of reports on poverty, including *Losing Ground: The Persistent Growth of Poverty in Canada's Largest City* (2007) *Decade of Decline* (2002), *Poverty by Postal Code* (2004), and *Strong Neighbourhoods: A Call to Action* (2005).

11 Divorce, Custody, and Child Support in Canada

Learning Objectives

◎ To understand what is meant by "divorce as a process."

◎ To see some of the changing rates and trends in divorce.

◎ To learn about changes in divorce law in Canada over the past few decades.

◎ To examine the Divorce Act of 1985 for changes specifically affecting the lives of children.

◎ To assess recent developments in child support regulations and guidelines, parental compliance, and maintenance enforcement programs.

◎ To understand some of the recent changes in child custody arrangements.

◎ To compare competing explanations and research on the impact of divorce on children.

◎ To find out about research on single-parent families and blended families or stepfamilies.

◎ To consider ways of helping children and families cope with the stress of divorce without stigmatizing and pathologizing them and their experiences.

Introduction

In the middle of a class discussion on the impact of divorce on children, a student raised her hand and made the following statement: "There is no stigma attached to divorce anymore because it is everywhere—divorce is a cancer!" After being asked to explain what she meant, a heated discussion ensued, with numerous students responding, incensed. Reading this, some of you may nod in agreement, in support of this student. Others may be horrified that such views are still held and even openly expressed in a classroom. Needless to say, the incident turned into a valuable teaching and learning moment for most of us in the room, as we began discussing the stigma that continues to be attached to divorce, indicated by the metaphor she used to describe it. It allowed for the opportunity to present the notion of "divorce as a process," which points to the idea that divorce itself is not the cause of family problems but the *product* of them.

In this chapter we will begin with an explanation of what I mean by "divorce as a process." This will be followed by an overview of changing divorce rates and trends, and some explanations for why we have seen some of these changes and fluctuations. Much of the changes have a great deal to do with divorce legislation in Canada, so we will look at divorce law over the past half-century or so. We will spend some time looking at the Divorce Act of 1985, which introduced significant changes in the treatment of children in the divorce process. We look at recent changes to child custody arrangements, new federal child support guidelines, default rates on child support, and government initiatives to counter the problem. This is followed by a discussion of the at-times contradictory literature on the impact of divorce on children. Literature on single-parent families, blended families, and stepfamilies will also be considered. We conclude with some speculation on what can be done to help families, and especially children, better understand and manage the stress associated with divorce, using approaches that can avoid some of the stigma still so often attached to divorce.

Divorce as a Process

Often, when we discuss divorce, we talk about it as a *thing*, like a cold or flu, or disease, or object—something you give, take, receive, or catch. For example, we say things like, "they got *a divorce*," or "divorce should be harder to obtain." While divorce marks the legal end of a marriage, it is in fact, an enduring, dynamic (active), and drawn-out process that is the consequence of a long list of events, feelings, interactions, struggles, etc. that occur long before the official, state-recognized dissolution of a relationship. Divorce is the *product* of conflict, pain, and struggle between two or more people (as children and other adults—lovers, grandparents, siblings—are often involved). Furthermore, while it marks an official end of a relationship, the process itself neither started with the legal proceeding nor ends with the formal signing of divorce papers. The divorce is a mid-point of sorts, and a continuation of many things that have gone on before it—a series of events and interactions that occur in a legal forum, and a set of events and relationships that continue long after that. Having said this, we must also realize that while *some* relationships within that family are officially severed by divorce, others—between adults and between parents and children—continue and may actually improve as a result of the legal termination of a marriage or common-law relationship.

Thinking about divorce as a longer-term process and the consequence of a series of events (affecting different sets of relationships, differently) that came before it may help us to understand it better. In doing this, we may also better understand the impact that parental conflicts and relationship dissolution may and do have on children. Finally, it may help us as a society to assist, through empathy, good policy, and better laws, those who experience the stress and challenges associated with family conflict and relationship breakdown.

Changing Rates and Trends in Divorce

While marriage rates have been declining, divorce rates have increased, particularly since the 1960s (Bélanger et al., 2006). That said, over the past 20 years, the proportion of marriages projected to end in divorce has remained relatively stable, fluctuating between 35 and 42 per cent (Employment and Social Development Canada, 2014). In 2008, there were 211 divorces for every 100,000 people in Canada (Employment and Social Development Canada, 2014). This was about four times higher than the number of divorces in 1968, when there were 55 divorces per 100,000 (Lindsay and Almey, 2006). Some of the biggest increases in the divorce rate came in the 1970s and again in the mid-1980s. Since then, divorce rates have declined or stabilized (see Figure 11.1).

According to the section of the 2011 General Social Survey (GSS) on families, approximately five million Canadians separated or divorced in the previous 20 years (Sinha, 2014). About half of these ended a common-law relationship, 44 per cent a legal marriage, and 7 per cent had ended both a common-law union and a legal marriage at two different points in time. Four in ten had a child together at the time of their separation or divorce (38 per cent), with one-quarter having at least one child under the age of 18 (Sinha, 2014). The GSS estimated that in 2011, 1.2 million Canadian parents were no longer in a spousal or common-law relationship with their child's mother or father (Sinha, 2014).

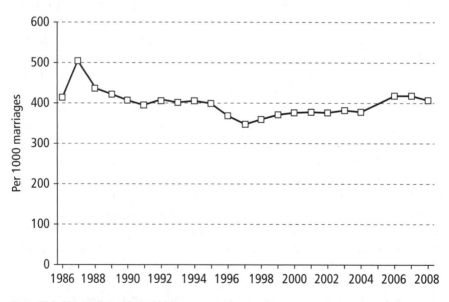

Figure 11.1 Divorce Rate, 1986–2008
Source: Employment and Social Development Canada (2014). Statistics Canada.

Those who divorce are doing so at a later age (Statistics Canada, 2004). According to official figures, in 2008, the average age at divorce was 44.5 for men and 41.9 for women, with the average age at divorce increasing by 5.3 years for both men and women, between 1988 and 2008 (Employment and Social Development Canada, 2014). Having said this, Canadians marrying in their teens were found to face an increased risk of divorce—almost twice as high—compared with those who married between the ages of 25 and 29 (Clark and Crompton, 2006). Numerous studies show that common-law unions also are more likely than marriages to end in dissolution (Milan et al., 2007; Beaupré and Cloutier, 2007; Bouchard, 2006); and most common-law relationships that ended recently were of shorter duration than marriages that ended recently—4.3 years compared with 14.3 years (Beaupré and Cloutier, 2007). Despite this, contrary to popular belief, divorce is not an ever-growing phenomenon "plaguing" young and "individualistic" (selfish) Canadians. As noted above, divorce rates have actually stabilized, with spikes in rates mostly reflecting changes in divorce laws.

Divorce Law in Canada

In the first half of the twentieth century, very few children experienced their parents' divorce because divorce was very difficult to access. In fact, before 1968, Canada did not have a federal divorce law and, while some provinces had their own legislation on divorce, others like Newfoundland and Quebec did not. To become divorced in these latter two provinces, individuals had to seek the passage of a private Act of Parliament to end their marriages. In some other provinces, divorce law incorporated the British Matrimonial Causes Act of 1857 (Douglas, 2001). This Act, which was in place in a number of provinces into the twentieth century, contained a sexual double standard that allowed men to obtain divorce on the grounds of a wife's adultery. Women, on the other hand, could obtain divorce provided they could prove that any incest, rape, sodomy, bestiality, bigamy, or adultery on the part of their husband was coupled with cruelty or desertion (ibid.). Canadian provinces each had separate divorce acts until 1968, when a national Divorce Act was introduced in the federal Parliament.

Divorce Act of 1968

The Divorce Act of 1968 created uniform law across the country, removing the remnants of the previous double standard. As a result, a uniform, longer list of grounds for divorce was laid out in sections 3 and 4 of the Act (Douglas, 2001). Grounds for divorce included mental and physical cruelty, adultery, rape or other sexual offences (including homosexual acts and bigamy), addiction to alcohol or drugs, imprisonment for more than two years, failing to consummate the marriage, or having lived separately (living apart, including disappearance or desertion) for a number of years. The Act also stipulated that decrees for divorce could not be granted unless a trial was held before a judge (ibid.). As a result of these changes, the divorce rate experienced its first major spike (Table 11.1); individuals who had been living in untenable or abusive marriages (for as long as 30 or more years, during a period in which divorce was much harder to obtain, especially for women) were granted more opportunity to end their marriages.

Divorce Act of 1985

Additional significant changes were introduced in the Divorce Act of 1985, which preceded the next major spike in divorce rates. A new, single, and simplified ground for divorce was created in section 8 of the new Act: "marriage breakdown," which could be established by proving a one-year separation or by proving one of the three fault-based criteria—adultery, physical abuse, or mental cruelty (Douglas, 2001). The new Act simplified the divorce process with the introduction of "no-fault" divorces, which allowed uncontested divorces and the ability for couples to avoid the courts whenever possible. In other words, an individual did not have to "sue" for divorce and prove he or she had been wronged. Because most divorces start off uncontested, parties could now file for divorce jointly, with the subsequent development of only a small fraction of divorces—less than 10 per cent —going to trial (ibid.).

Some of the most interesting and significant changes introduced by this Act concern custodial rights and obligations when children are involved. The Divorce Act of 1985 established child support as a priority of the Act and established and applied a set of child support guidelines to assist and simplify the application of child support orders and arrangements (section 15). It also moved away from what was considered the "tender years doctrine" or maternal preference, which almost automatically awarded the custody to mothers on the assumption that they were best-suited for raising children. In its place, the Act adopted the "best interests of the child" as the new principle upon which custody decisions were to be made. Greater emphasis was placed on considerations having to do with the child's relationship with each parent, the child's welfare, the wishes of the child, the avoidance of separating siblings, and the willingness of each parent to facilitate the other parent's access to the child (Douglas, 2001). To help accomplish some of these objectives, joint custody was introduced as an option in child custody decisions. Joint custody, when awarded, allows ex-partners to share in the health, education, and welfare decisions of the child (joint legal custody) as well as shared, but not necessarily equal, living arrangements (joint physical custody) (Juby et al., 2005; Bauserman, 2002). In cases in which one parent is granted custody, the Act underscores the importance of maximum contact for the noncustodial parent. In sum, the Divorce Act of

1985 simplified the procedure for adults, in the hope of reducing conflict, stress, and costly legal procedures, and focused more attention on children. Children again were the focus of the Divorce Act when amendments were introduced in the late 1990s.

Table 11.1 Number of Divorces and Divorce Rate, 1968–2003

Year	Number of Divorces	Divorces per 100,000 Population
1968	11,343	54.8
1969	26,093	124.2
1970	29,775	139.8
1971	29,685	137.6
1972	32,389	148.4
1973	36,704	166.1
1974	45,019	200.6
1975	50,611	222.0
1976	54,207	235.8
1977	55,370	237.7
1978	57,155	243.4
1979	59,474	251.3
1980	62,019	259.1
1981	67,671	278.0
1982	70,430	279.5
1983	68,565	269.3
1984	65,170	253.6
1985	61,976	238.9
1986	78,304	298.6
1987	96,200	362.3
1988	83,507	310.5
1989	80,998	295.3
1990	78,463	282.3
1991	77,020	273.9
1992	79,034	277.9
1993	78,226	270.2
1994	78,880	269.7
1995	77,636	262.2
1996	71,528	241.1
1997	67,406	224.7
1998	69,088	228.4
1999	70,910	232.5
2000	71,144	231.2
2001	71,110	229.2
2002	70,155	223.7
2003	70,828	223.7

Source: Lindsay and Almey (2006: 48, Table 2.5).

The 2011 GSS revealed that despite legal changes, the mother's home was still most often (70 per cent) the child's primary residence after a separation or divorce. Some 15 per cent reported that the child lived mainly with the father, while 9 per cent reported that the child had equal living time between the two parents' homes (the remaining 6 per cent indicated other living arrangements; Sinha, 2014). The 2011 GSS also revealed that 44 per cent of parents whose children lived with their ex-partners most often saw their child less than three months over the course of the previous year, and some 18 per cent had no contact at all with their child (see Figure 11.2). Most often, these were fathers (Sinha, 2014). Close to three-quarters of separated or divorced parents (74 per cent) were satisfied with the amount of time spent with their children; however, 90 per cent of parents whose child mainly lived with them were satisfied compared with only 44 per cent of parents whose child did not primarily live with them (Sinha, 2014).

Children, Divorce, and the Accessing of Services

Couples with dependent children were found to be more likely than couples without children to rely on and use legal, social, and other types of services in the separation process (74 per cent compared with 45 per cent; Beaupré and Cloutier, 2007). When children are involved, parents face additional challenges in the separation process, which often require more supports of various kinds, particularly when arranging their financial well-being, establishing

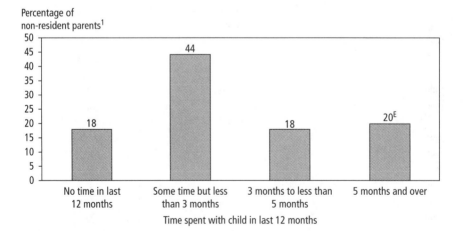

Percentage of non-resident parents[1]

Figure 11.2 Over 60 per cent of Non-Resident Parents Spent No Time or Less Than Three Months with Their Child in the Last 12 Months
Source: Sinha (2014: 10).

[E]use with caution
1. Non-resident parents refer to parents whose children primarily reside with their ex-spouse or partner.
Note: Includes parents with one or more children (aged 18years and under at the time of the survey), who do not all live at the same primary residence and who separated or divorced within the last 20 years. Totals include the "don't know" and "refused" categories, which are not shown in the chart. Percentages may not add to 100%.
Source: Statistics Canada, General Social Survey, 2011.

new living arrangements, finding a suitable approach to decision-making, particularly around health, religion, and education. These agreements had different degrees of legal involvement, with financial agreements most likely to involve legal input from a lawyer, court services, or a judge.[1] Arrangements around major decisions often were decided by the ex-partners themselves, independent of the legal system.

The GSS uncovered that depending on where the child lived, the responsibility for making major child-related decisions on health, education, etc. varied, as did the perception of parents when it came to decision-making. In 2011, 21 per cent of parents whose child primarily resided with them said major child-related decisions were made jointly or on an alternating basis with their ex-partner (Sinha, 2014). In contrast, 49 per cent of parents whose child lived with their ex-partner reported joint or alternating decision-making (Sinha, 2014).

The GSS revealed that financial support for children was in place for about half of separated or divorced parents. Among these, child support payments ranged from under $1,000 to more than $10,000 a year, with the most common amount being between $3,000 and $5,000 a year (Sinha, 2014). Compliance with payments was generally high, with about three-quarters of child support recipients receiving the full amount in the 12 months before the 2011 survey. But this was not always the case.

Regular payment of child support is important to many single-parent families in the post-divorce period, particularly those headed by women, as they tend to be more vulnerable to living on a low income. For these families, a drop in income from a default on a child support payment in any given month may result in economic hardship for the custodial parent and child(ren). Unacceptably high levels of noncompliance with child support orders (high default rates, particularly on the part of noncustodial fathers) throughout the 1990s led to the creation of Bill C-41, An Act to Amend the Divorce Act (the Family Orders and Agreements Enforcement Assistance Act), and the Garnishment, Attachment and Pension Diversion Act—1997. These amendments of the Divorce Act set out the federal child support guidelines—a simplified series of tables specifying the amount of child support to be paid by the noncustodial parent based on the payer's income (Department of Justice, 2006).[2] This federal enforcement legislation was designed to support the efforts of various new provincial enforcement agencies created to help locate spouses in breach of support orders and agreements (so-called deadbeat parents). As part of these efforts, the new legislation gave provincial enforcement agencies access to federal sources of information (Revenue Canada data, for example) to allow the agency to garnish funds from income tax refunds, employment insurance benefits, old age security payments, tax credits, etc. to satisfy support orders in default.[3] It also included a new license denial scheme that permits the denial of certain license applications (such as a passport, pilot and air traffic controller certificates, and other federal licenses) in cases of persistent default on child support (Douglas, 2001). Across the country, between 2001 and 2006, there were 517,000 new cases of divorce or separation with a child support arrangement in place. Just over a third of these cases were enrolled in a maintenance enforcement program (Robinson, 2009). In 2007, for example, nearly 70,000 children and youth under the age of 19, in 50,000 families from five reporting provinces and territories, were enrolled in maintenance enforcement programs, representing 6 per cent of all children in those jurisdictions (Robinson, 2009). In 97 per cent of those families, the recipient of the support payment was the child's mother, on behalf of the child. Despite being enrolled in these enforcement programs, only one-third of families received the full amount of the regular payment due every month in 2007–8. Just over 60 per cent of families received their regular payment in full for at least six months of 2007–8, while 84 per cent received some support during that year (Robinson, 2009). Between 2001 and 2012, the proportion of those fully paying their regular monthly support payments remained stable, with about 65 per cent making the full payment each month (it was 67 per cent in 2011–12; Kelly 2013). As of March 31, 2012, there were more than 88,000 cases enrolled in the nine provinces and territories reporting to maintenance enforcement programs (Kelly, 2013).

Ontario, one of the more aggressive provinces in child support enforcement, created the Family Responsibility Office as part of its Ministry of Community and Social Services.[4] As part of this office, they established a "Good Parents Pay" initiative, which includes a website containing "most wanted"–style profiles or postings of parents who have defaulted on court-ordered child support payments, aimed at getting the public's help in locating missing defaulters on child support. These parents commonly are referred to as "deadbeat dads"; despite changes in custody regulations and arrangements, most noncustodial parents—and so most "defaulters"—are fathers.[5] The individual postings contain the name, alias, age, height, eye and hair colour, photo (where available), occupation, identifying details, and last known whereabouts of the parent, as well as a link for the public to access if they have information to give anonymous tips to help locate the parent (see www.mcss.gov.on.ca/en/goodparentspay/index.aspx).

According to data from the National Longitudinal Survey of Children and Youth (NLSCY), children covered by private child support agreements, arranged by both parents privately, are more likely to receive regular child support payments compared with children whose parents have a court-ordered agreement (Department of Justice, 2002). Children who lived in common-law unions that dissolved were less likely than those whose parents were legally married before the marital breakdown to receive regular child support payments, whether payment arrangements were private agreements or court-ordered (ibid.). A number of analysts have also found a link between the frequency of contact between noncustodial parents (mostly fathers) and their children and the regularity of child support payments (Juby et al., 2005; Department of Justice, 2002; Marcil-Gratton and LeBourdais, 1999). In other words, noncustodial fathers who saw their children weekly were much more likely to make payments regularly and on time than were those who never saw their children (Department of Justice, 2002).

Despite the type of arrangements agreed upon, continuity of contact and care, before and after separation, has been shown to be fundamentally important in ensuring more positive child outcomes following divorce (Juby et al., 2005).

Impact of Divorce on Children

A great deal of emphasis in studies of divorce has been placed on understanding the impact of parental divorce on children. For the most part, researchers have measured children's psychological well-being, quality of interpersonal relationships (including their own likelihood of marriage and other experiences later in life), children's relationship with their parents, and divorce's impact on children's educational attainment (Anthony et al., 2014). Many early studies in this area were based on a *deficit model of divorce*. This deficit model assumed that a heterosexual, two-parent family is necessary for a child's well-being, with all other family forms, particularly single-parent families, seen as deficient or dysfunctional. In this model, divorce is perceived as a traumatic event with severe and enduring (long-term) negative consequences for children (Hetherington and Stanley-Hagan, 1999). In contrast, more recent studies have tended to focus on the diversity of patterns and experiences in adjustment following divorce, with many of these focusing on circumstances, family and individual characteristics, and relations before, during, and after the divorce process (Anthony et al., 2014). Many of these also look at the role of extrafamilial factors and supports to understand how children adjust and cope. Some of these researchers are said to be taking a *life-course approach* or a *risk-and-resiliency perspective* (e.g., Yuk, 2007; Hetherington and Kelly, 2002). This approach understands divorce as a series of family transitions that are undoubtedly stressful, affect individuals, and require adjustment as families negotiate change. They also note that as families move through this transition, risk and protective factors are not static but changing and individual adults and children are affected differently depending on individual, family, and extrafamilial factors (Anthony et al., 2014; Hetherington and Stanley-Hagan, 1999). Finally, proponents of the life course, or risk-and-resiliency, approach recognize that while stressful, divorce can and does present a chance for escape from conflict and discord as well as the possibility for more harmonious relationships in the post-divorce period. Jolivet (2011), for example, notes that studies confirm chronic conflict is often what leads to children's feelings of stress, insecurity, shame, self-blame, sense of rejection, and guilt. She also notes that it is high-conflict divorce that roughly doubles the rate of behavioural and emotional-adjustment problems in children.

Few researchers would deny that divorce negatively affects children, but many researchers also show that a number of mitigating factors, many of which are within the control of parents, can ameliorate the post-separation scenario for children. In fact, some parents have consciously adopted creative solutions and successful parenting arrangements that have made the lives of children experiencing divorce significantly better (Jamison et al., 2014; Clark, 2013). When levels of conflict are low, children are best able to go about their daily lives, succeed in school, and build strong peer relationships (see Box 11.1).

Debate among those who have studied the impact of divorce on children divides researchers and arrays them along a continuum of sorts. Zimiles (2004), for example, summarizes some of this debate in a review essay of two competing American books in the field, pitting Hetherington and Kelly's (2002) *For Better or For Worse* against Wallerstein et al.'s (2000) *The*

Box 11.1   How Children Make Friends in Cases of Joint Physical Custody

Prazen et al. (2011) assessed how joint physical custody arrangements affect an important component of child well-being, children's neighborhood friendships. They interviewed 13 parents and 17 children (ages 5–11) in 10 families, selected via convenience and snowball sampling. Their findings suggest that joint custody arrangements did not overtly affect how children went about making friends. The children provided accounts of making friends that did not seem to have anything to do with their custody arrangements. Children started their friendships differently, with initial invitations initiated by both the children themselves and their parents.

- "I just saw them playing and I went over to say, 'Can I play' and then that's how I got in touch with my friends."
- "There were these two kids, Chelsea and Erika, they were walking by and my mom said, 'Hey, do you want to play with them?' and I said, 'Okay' and then we kind of met." (2011: 253)

Children's accounts of friendship formation appeared to reflect their immediate circumstances, not their custody arrangements.

Source: Prazen et al. (2011).

Unexpected Legacy of Divorce. Each uses (different) longitudinal approaches to understand the effects of divorce on children, and each work arrives at very different conclusions.

Hetherington and Kelly (2002)—proponents of the life-course/risk-and-resiliency approach—focus on the recuperative changes in children at two and six years after a divorce. They explain that almost all children are distressed by their parents' divorce, and that divorce is a high-risk situation, but six years after the divorce the vast majority developed into competent and resilient young people who had adapted to their new life and become reasonably well adjusted. Hetherington's (2003) research found that while some young people who experienced parental divorce were more likely to experience elevated anxiety, depression, and withdrawal, including antisocial and impulsive behaviour (20 per cent in divorced or remarried families, compared with 10 per cent in non-divorced families), others were found to be in high-competency clusters that included high social skills, popularity, and above-average school performance.

Wallerstein et al. (2000), like Wallerstein's other work (1980, 1989), stress that divorce is a profoundly negative and disheartening experience for children. They follow children of divorce from 1971, when Wallerstein began her study, to the present. The longitudinal study shows that although children experience gradual adaptation over time, the negative impact of divorce seldom lightens, with children of divorced parents reaching adulthood as psychologically troubled individuals who find it difficult to maintain stable and satisfying relationships with others (Zimiles, 2004; Amato, 2003; Wallerstein et al., 2000; Wallerstein and Blakeslee, 1989; Wallerstein and Kelly, 1980). Huurre et al. (2006) found this to be especially true among women who experienced parental divorce in their childhood.

Some have argued that due to rising divorce rates, fatherlessness has become one of the most harmful trends of this generation (Blankenhorn, 1996).[6] Some have noted that parental divorce results in children having more difficult childhoods, higher levels of depression, increased rates of delinquent behaviour, lower academic performance and aspirations, earlier and more sexual experiences, lower feelings of closeness to fathers, increased economic instability later in life, and more marital instability (Beckmeyer, Coleman, and Ganong, 2014; Portnoy, 2008; Gloger-Tippelt and König, 2007; Wauterickx et al., 2006; Guttman and Rosenberg, 2003; Kerr and Beaujot, 2002; Williams, 2001).[7] Kerr and Michalski also found that parents living in divorced single-parent and remarried families reported that their children were more hyperactive and inattentive than did parents in **intact families**. The debate continues about whether these effects are long-lasting, inevitable, and widespread. Kerr and Michalski (2007: 104), for example, note that despite the initial disadvantage of children from single-parent families, "they tended to improve quite noticeably over time (with their trajectories moving parallel to those of intact families)."

Interestingly, even those who have found differences in child outcomes between children who experienced parental divorce and those who did not, have found these differences plus long-term effects to be relatively small—not as pervasive or as strong as researchers like Wallerstein and her colleagues have suggested (Amato, 2003). In helping to understand the impact of divorce on children, researchers have increasingly pointed to the importance of moderating factors in the family *before* marital disruption and in the post-divorce family arrangements (ibid.). For example, parents who had less marital conflict in the pre-divorce period had better relationships with their children after separation, which resulted in better child outcomes (Tschann et al., 1989).

Similarly, more recently, Di Stefano and Cyr (2014) explored the role of parental and environmental factors in the relationship between parental separation and child vulnerabilities. They compared results from 358 children from separated families and 1,065 children from non-separated families who were part of the Quebec Longitudinal Study of Child Development. Results demonstrated that parental separation was associated with higher levels of hyperactivity and impulsivity in children over and beyond what was accounted for by child gender, maternal symptoms of depression and anxiety, parenting quality, and household income (Di Stefano and Cyr, 2014). However, parental separation did not predict child anxiety and physical aggression once parental and environmental variables were controlled. Di Stefano and Cyr's results shed light on the importance of considering the quality of the family environment as more predictive of child outcomes than parental separation per se.

In fact, a number of researchers have argued that the single biggest predictor of negative outcomes for children is continuing post-divorce conflict between parents (Portnoy, 2008; Mitcham-Smith and Henry, 2007; Sarrazin and Cyr, 2007). Children are said to be especially negatively affected when they are used to express parents' anger, carry negative messages between parents, and encouraged to think negatively about or not have a relationship with the other parent (Portnoy, 2008). In cases of high-conflict divorces, parents are also found to be less warm towards their children, more withdrawn (disengaged), and more impulsive (inconsistent), often resulting in overly controlling or overly permissive parenting (ibid.). Shared custody and living arrangements have been found to result in more positive child outcomes (Juby et al., 2005; Bausermen, 2002), particularly as most parents who decide to share custody tend to have a better post-divorce relationship with one another. They are often also more likely to hold the belief that a strong relationship with both parents is beneficial to their children's well-being (Juby et al., 2005). Even decades ago, research revealed that regular and frequent visits from noncustodial fathers were found to result in higher self-esteem and lower rates of depression in children (Wallerstein and Kelly, 1980). This, as noted above, also results in increased regularity of payment of child support and decreased default rates.

In sum, although divorce inevitably negatively affects children, the impact is not always or necessarily of long duration, and many intervening factors can ameliorate or aggravate the situation. Many point to the nature of the pre-divorce relationships in order to understand some of the impact (Amato, 2003); others look to the animosity between parents that often continues during the post-divorce period (Zimiles, 2004). Reinforcing the notion of divorce as process, Zimiles reminds us that researchers often have been inclined to assign causality to child outcomes in the divorce experience, but some of the adverse outcomes associated with divorce "also deserve to be viewed as the outgrowth of longstanding personality clashes, incompatibilities and deficiencies/pathologies" that take place before and throughout the actual divorce (ibid., 247–8). Zimiles focuses on personality structures and dynamics among the adults in the marriage, but also reminds us that these long precede and contribute to the marital discord and breakdown.

Canada's Department of Justice (2002: 14) has noted that while some children are harmed into adulthood by their parents' divorce, most come through the changes "fairly well." Troubled relationships between the two parents and economic disadvantages that can and do take place before, during, and after the separation and divorce are clearly factors that most negatively affect children (ibid.). Children who grow up surrounded by conflict (within intact families or following divorce) often are poor achievers in school, have behavioural and psychological problems, and function with reduced social skills (ibid.). In other words, it is not divorce per se but the social and economic relationships before, during, and after divorce that should be included in our analyses.

Single-Parent Families, Repartnering, Stepfamilies, and Blended Families

With the general rise in divorces and separations over the past five decades, we are seeing more step- and lone-parent families (Statistics Canada, 2012; Figure 11.2; Table 11.2; and Table 11.3; see also Chapter 4, Figure 4.2). The number of children born to never-married mothers (not living with a partner) remained stable over the past few decades (until about 2001) at about 5 per cent of all births, while the number of single-parent families as a result of divorce has increased over the past four decades (Statistics Canada, 2012).

By 2006 a growing proportion (29.5 per cent) of lone parents were never married; fewer (19.0 per cent) were alone due to widowhood. About 3 in 10 lone parents (29.9 per cent) were divorced, and this proportion has been

Table 11.2 Distribution (Number and Percentage) and Percentage Change of Census Families by Family Structure, Canada, 2001 to 2011

Census family	2001		2006		2011		% change 2006 to 2011
	Number	%	Number	%	Number	%	
Total census families	8,371,020	100.0	8,896,840	100.0	9,389,700	100.0	5.5
Couple families	7,059,830	84.3	7,482,775	84.1	7,861,860	83.7	5.1
Married	5,901,420	70.5	6,105,910	68.6	6,293,950	67.0	3.1
Common law	1,158,410	13.8	1,376,865	15.5	1,567,910	16.7	13.9
Lone-parent families	1,311,190	15.7	1,414,060	15.9	1,527,840	16.3	8.0
Female parents	1,065,360	12.7	1,132,290	12.7	1,200,295	12.8	6.0
Male parents	245,825	2.9	281,775	3.2	327,545	3.5	16.2

This table displays the results of distribution (number and percentage) and percentage change of census families by family structure. The information is grouped by census family (appearing as row headers), date (2001, 2006, and 2011), and percentage change from 2006 to 2011, calculated using number and percentage units of measure (appearing as column headers). Sources: Statistics Canada, censuses of population, 2001 to 2011.

Source: Statistics Canada (2012b).

decreasing since it peaked in 1996 at 34.3 per cent. As a point of comparison, in 1951, only 3.1 per cent of lone parents were divorced (Milan et al., 2007). This type of information should be useful to adults working with children, particularly if and when they are discussing "family" with children. With this knowledge, we should take care not to assume that all children live with two parents, or that they have one home where they do homework, have permission forms signed, store their clothes, or have their lunches packed.

The 2011 Census recorded a total of 1,527,840 lone-parent families, now making up 16.3 per cent of all families: 12.8 were headed by women, while 3.5 per cent were headed by men (Statistics Canada, 2012b). Between 2001 and 2011, there was a significant increase in the number of lone-father families, while the proportion of female-headed lone-parent families remained about the same (Table 11.2). Most of the increase among the male-headed families has been attributed to the decrease in mothers' being awarded sole custody following a divorce, as well as an increase in joint custody arrangements (ibid.). Nevertheless, women continue to make up the large majority of lone parents, and most have experienced a dramatic drop in family income when they do so (Portnoy, 2008). For example, for children in lone-parent families headed by a woman, the incidence of living in a low-income household in 2011 was 23.0 per cent, while for children living in two-parent families, the incidence was 5.9 per cent (Statistics Canada, 2013i). The economic change that results in the post-divorce period undoubtedly affects children who may have been used to a better standard of living in the pre-divorce period.

Although the situation has been improving for women, past research found that following a divorce, fathers experienced a 10 per cent decline in income, while mothers (who more often are awarded custody of the children) experienced a 25 to 45 per cent drop in family income (Hetherington and Stanley-Hagan, 1999). More recent Canadian data show that women who experience marital dissolution are almost three times as likely as men to experience a significant drop in their household income (Rotermann, 2007). In contrast, nearly 30 per cent of recently divorced and separated men actually experienced an improvement in their (adjusted) household income (ibid.).

Custodial mothers and custodial fathers tend to have significantly different economic resources. Past research revealed that custodial fathers were more likely than custodial mothers to have greater job stability and higher earning power (Hetherington and Stanley-Hagan, 1999). Children living with single mothers, therefore, were often affected by the considerable drop in the family's standard of living, resulting in access to fewer activities, changes in housing location, new schools, and changes in established peer support networks (Portnoy, 2008). Ram and Hou (2005) question whether living in single-parent families following family disruptions has affected all family members to the same degree.

Girls and boys have been found to respond differently to parental divorce and living in single-parent families headed by mothers (Garg et al., 2006). Ram and Hou's (2005) research supports this, noting that living in single-mother households acts to elevate overt aggression more among boys than among girls. Girls scored higher on indirect aggression (internalizing behaviour). Hetherington (2003) includes important additional information to help explain the impact and differences: often, children in female-headed, single-parent families are assigned more responsibility, have less adult supervision, and are more powerful in family decision-making than children in two-parent families. She argues that when these responsibilities are age-appropriate, manageable, and do not interfere too much with other age-appropriate activities with peers and school, and when support from a caring adult is available, children and especially girls have very positive outcomes. They were found to be more independent, caring, and competent. In contrast, when burdens placed on children were inappropriate and excessive, and when children were the main support for an excessively needy parent (in this study, mostly mothers), the effects of lone parenthood were negative (ibid.). This overburdening is associated with depression and anxiety in girls and resistance and antisocial behaviour in boys. In other words, it is not single-parent status per se that affects child outcomes, but a constellation of factors, including the household's economic circumstances and levels of social support available to families and within families, all of which contribute to mothers' emotional well-being and ability to parent on their own.

Stepfamilies

Some women, and even more men, tend to remarry following divorce (Wu and Schimmele, 2005; Beaupré, 2008). That said, stepfamily parents were more than three times more likely to be in a common-law union than non-divorced parents, with about 48 per cent of parents in stepfamilies living common law in 2011 compared with 14 per cent living in intact families (Statistics Canada, 2012d). Because more mothers than fathers continue to be granted custody of children, the most common (heterosexual) step-families include a woman, her biological children, and a stepfather; this configuration is called a *stepfather stepfamily*. A significantly smaller number of families involve a custodial father, his children, and a stepmother: the *stepmother stepfamily*. **Blended families** include children from either of the partners' previous relationships along with a child or children born to their union (also see variation in "complex families" below; Table 11.3). Almost half of all stepfamilies in Canada become blended families with the birth of a child within the (new) family (Juby et al., 2006). In 2011, 11 per cent of all Canadian children aged 24 and under, or about one million children, lived in stepfamilies (Bohnert et al., 2014).

The divorce rate among second marriages is slightly higher than in first marriages and the separation rate among cohabiting stepfamilies is higher still (Juby et al., 2006; Isaacs, 2002; Williams, 2001). Therefore, children living in stepfamilies are potentially exposed to a number of changes and challenges, involving the renegotiation and restructuring of roles and relationships,

Table 11.3 Distribution (Number and Percentage) of Couple Families with Children by Stepfamily Status, Canada, 2011

Couple family with children[a]	Number	%
All couple families with children	3,684,675	100.0
Intact families[b]	3,220,340	87.4
Stepfamilies:	464,335	12.6
Simple stepfamilies	271,930	7.4
Complex stepfamilies:	192,410	5.2
a) Families with child(ren) of both parents and child(ren) of one parent only	149,365	4.1
b) Families with child(ren) of each parent only and no children of both parents	35,765	1.0
c) Families with child(ren) of both parents and child(ren) of each parent only	7,275	0.2

This table displays the results of distribution (number and percentage) of couple families with children by stepfamily status. The information is grouped by couple family with children (appearing as row headers) and number and percentage (appearing as column headers).

[a]Refers to couples with at least one child aged 24 and under. [b]Couple families with at least one child aged 24 and under for whom it cannot be determined if there are stepchildren present are considered intact families.

Source: Statistics Canada (2012b: Table 4).

adjusting to new family arrangements, and more household reorganization (Gibson, 2013; Afifi and Schrodt, 2003). Afifi and Keith (2004) also note that post-divorce stepfamilies can involve a considerable amount of loss: loss of one's previous family, loss of a single-parent bond, and loss of a noncustodial parent–child bond. As a result, a number of studies of stepfamilies tend to focus on or to emphasize the negative effects of stepfamilies on children. Ram and Hou (2005: 334), for example, point out that the stepfamily environment is significantly "more harmful to girls than to boys" (also see Crohn, 2006; Isaacs, 2002). Other studies show that children in remarried families had lower academic achievement scores than children in intact families and single-parent families (Jeynes, 2006). Still others have found that serial attachments and losses and repetitive repartnering that occurs soon after divorce have resulted in difficulty in children's ability to cope with the divorce (Portnoy, 2008). Despite variations, the reality is that there are some expectations and defined roles when it comes to parenting one's own children. In contrast, there are few guidelines for step-parents, and decisions and roles are often negotiated on the fly. In conflicts, biological parents may side with their biological children rather than their new partner, resulting in marital distress (Gibson, 2013). Similarly, a step-parent may choose to withdraw from troubling conversations in order to show that she or he does not intend to replace the child's noncustodial parent (Gibson, 2013).

Due the vast diversity of constellations, social relations, background circumstances, past experiences, and responses to parental remarriage, stepfamilies can either enhance or impede child development (Issacs, 2002). Although many children exhibit problems during the transition period immediately following the remarriage, most children show considerable resilience and do not experience long-term negative effects (ibid.). Isaacs notes that to understand the impact of stepfamilies on children, we need to take a multidimensional approach that accounts for family process, individual risk and vulnerability, and ecological factors (also see Gibson, 2013). The "family process perspective" looks at the impact on children as being mediated by and through the behaviour of family members. For example, new family members can both support and undermine child development. Interestingly, marital satisfaction among stepfathers was positively related to the amount of involvement in child-rearing activities (Adamson et al., 2007; Yuan and Hamilton, 2006). Undoubtedly, less conflictual relations lead to better child outcomes (Isaacs, 2002). Adolescent boys, for example, were found to benefit from close stepfather stepfamily relationships (Yuan and Hamilton, 2006; Isaacs, 2002). We must also keep in mind that child outcomes are affected not only by relationships within the stepfamily but also by relationships across households, between custodial and noncustodial parents. Contact with a supportive noncustodial parent, particularly one of the same sex as the child, can have a positive effect on children (Isaacs, 2002).

The Best Interests of the Child and the Voice of Children

Post-Divorce Parenting

In light of what we know about changing divorce law and the impact of divorce on children, a number of researchers have proposed a new model of post-divorce parenting that includes a *shared parental responsibility framework,* whereby parental responsibilities take precedence over custodial rights and the children's best interests are made central in defining parental and social roles and responsibilities towards meeting the needs of children (Kruk, 2005). Hetherington and Stanley-Hagan (1999) explain that although factors including extrafamilial stress, economic disadvantage, and the physical and psychological health of parents may put children at increased risk following divorce, the impact of these factors can be and is mediated and moderated by the quality of parenting (children's adjustment is associated with the parenting environment). Particularly during the stressful times that precede and follow divorce, children need parents who are consistent, firm, warm, supportive, and responsive to their needs (Beckmeyer et al., 2014; Fritz, 2013; Portnoy, 2008; Nair and Murray, 2005; Hetherington and Stanley-Hagan, 1999). This may be especially difficult for parents, given their own struggles, challenges, and increased rates of depression during and immediately following the divorce process (Jamison et al., 2014; Rotermann, 2007; Nair and Murray, 2005). Positive social supports—from grandparents, siblings, mentors, and other relationships outside of the family—for adults and children tend to help both adjust more quickly (Portnoy, 2008; Ehrenberg et al., 2006; Greef et al., 2006). Furthermore, increased, consistent, and positive (high-quality) involvement by the noncustodial parent has resulted in better outcomes both for children (Portnoy, 2008; Dunn et al., 2004; Fabricius, 2003) and for the adults—especially the fathers (Jenkins and Lyons, 2006; Lehr and MacMillan, 2001).

Federal and provincial governments have gone to considerable lengths to provide parenting advice through handbooks and websites aimed at helping parents recognize and meet the needs of children (see suggested readings).[8] A publication by the province of British Columbia begins by reminding parents that separation is a process that begins long before couples actually separate (Law Courts Education Society of BC, 2006). It outlines some of the feelings that parents experience but also reminds them that children have their own distinctive fears and feelings, and provides suggestions to parents about what children need to hear and what should be avoided. The publication also provides advice on how to relate to the other parent in a respectful and co-operative manner to minimize the conflict to which their children are exposed, and to ensure children are not caught in the middle of parental acrimony. Research shows that divorcing parents need support and access to intervention strategies that place the focus on their children rather than on the issues they have with one another (Fritz, 2013; Mitcham-Smith and Henry, 2007). Mitcham-Smith and Henry explain that parents need to learn to disengage each other and learn how to relate to each other differently for better, more positive child outcomes. They suggest the process needs to include parenting coordinators (other than counsellors and therapists, whose roles are confidential) who are mandated by the court to maintain the necessary focus on the children. Such coordinators can help participants focus and maintain goals essential to the children's well-being (ibid.). This assistance to the parents, of course, should be in addition to other types of supports.

Numerous publications aimed at understanding and coping with divorce also are targeted directly to children (Department of Justice, 2013). Various programs exist for children experiencing parental separation and divorce. Many of these are government-funded and available in most provinces (for more information, see Department of Justice, 2013). In addition to publications, programs, and social services for parents and children, more should be done to inform the general public, educators, and those working with children about some of the challenges associated with divorce—without stigmatizing and pathologizing the children and their experiences—in order to provide more support and understanding through difficult times. We also need to think differently about the role children themselves can play in the divorce process.

Children's Rights and the Voice of Children

Historically, children have been denied the opportunity to participate in custody and access decisions in divorce proceedings. The legal representation of children in family law proceedings is a relatively new phenomenon. Recently, there have been attempts to involve children in the divorce process through the appointment of lawyers to represent children's interest (Office of the Children's Lawyer), the expansion of guardian *ad litem* services (responsible for taking the necessary steps to ascertain the best interests of the child), and private consultation of the child by judges and appointment of child advocates and "friends" (*amicus curae*—"friend of the court") to speak on behalf of children and to ensure their access to other court-appointed services (Bessner, 2002). These are clear shifts towards considering the best interest of the child; however, while seemingly benevolent, they may be less than ideal. Often, these measures do not guarantee that the system is acting according to the child's stated and expressed wishes (Ruddick, 2007; Kushner, 2006). Recently, child advocates have been promoting the reassessment of the child's role in family law, promoting a more child-centred approach, in which children are treated as legal subjects rather than as objects, and their own voices (not those of third parties) and opinions are heard as part of the decision-making process (Bessner, 2002).

Where appropriate, this type of accommodation of children is believed to contribute to better outcomes for both children and families.

Research shows that children want and benefit from having their voices heard in decision-making regarding custody and access (Birnbaum and Saini, 2012). Birnbaum and Saini (2012) note that increasingly, research has recognized the importance of including the voice of the child in both research on divorce and in understanding the impact of issues that affect them during separation and divorce. They conducted a meta-analysis of 35 qualitative studies exploring children's views during decision-making in post-separation and divorce and found that children generally want to be engaged in the decision-making process regarding custody and access. Children wanted the opportunity to have a voice in custody disputes and wanted their views to be represented in discussions about living arrangements. The meta-analysis revealed that children wished that parents had been more sensitive to their needs, particularly surrounding the decision to separate (Birnbaum and Saini, 2012).

Summary

While divorce is a very difficult and common occurrence in society today, forcing people to remain in unhappy, unhealthy, and potentially dangerous environments through restrictive laws and attitudes does not help children, adults, or society. In fact, remaining in abusive or high-conflict relationships is not only problematic for the people within them, but has recently come to be defined as child abuse and may result in children being removed from the parental home by child welfare agencies (Alaggia et al., 2007).

In this chapter, we saw that changing divorce rates are directly linked to changing divorce laws, and that while children are often "caught in the middle" there have been serious attempts on the part of the state and of activists to try to assist families with children in dealing with some of the challenges and hardships that come with family breakdown.

We have suggested that family conflict (caused by intrafamilial and extrafamilial stress) resulting in divorce is best understood as the surgery or therapy that attempts to deal with that problematical relationship. Sometimes divorce is effective in reducing family conflict. At other times divorce itself leads to new complications. However, allowing profound conflicts in a relationship to fester will not make them go away, and may lead to more serious problems. We must recognize that there are families with insurmountable problems that can only be solved with a legal termination of the marital relationship. Couples who find themselves in these situations need support while severing ties with each other so that children can continue their relationships with their parents whenever and wherever possible, desirable, and worthwhile. At the same time, we must make sure that, if physical and emotional contact is not possible between a parent and his or her child or children, economic obligations and responsibilities are nonetheless fulfilled by the estranged parent. Our society has come up with some useful (and some less useful) strategies for dealing with this. We need to continue to seek out creative, thoughtful, and child-friendly solutions that include children as subjects and players in this difficult situation.

Questions for Critical Thought

1. If you were a politician and a proposal is before Parliament that aims to make divorce harder to obtain, how would you vote on this issue? Why? How would you convince others to support your views?

2. You have been hired to write a guide for primary school teachers to help them help their students cope with some of the challenges they may be experiencing during their parents' divorce. What kind of information would you include? In what format? How would it differ if your guide was targeting children?

3. You are a child advocate. Your job at the moment is to advise parents of young children as they work through their divorce proceedings. What would you advise them to do and consider as they make decisions about custody, living arrangements, child support payments, and their attitudes and interactions in light of their changing family circumstances? What specific suggestions might you give that would remind them to act in the best interests of their child or children?

Suggested Readings

Department of Justice. 2013. *Making Plans: A Guide to Parenting Arrangements after Separation or Divorce. How to Put Your Children First.* Ottawa: Department of Justice. At: www.justice. gc.ca/eng/fl-df/parent/mp-fdp/En-Parenting_Guide.pdf.

Department of Justice. 2013. *What Happens Next? Information for Kids about Separation and Divorce.* Ottawa: Department of Justice. At: www.justice.gc.ca/eng/rp-pr/fl-lf/famil/ book-livre/pdf/book-livre.pdf.

These booklets, created and distributed by the Department of Justice Canada, can help parents and children learn about family law, and can also help children realize it is normal for them to have an emotional response to their parents' separation.

Department of Justice. 2012. *The Federal Child Support Guidelines: Step-by-Step.* Ottawa: Department of Justice. At: www.justice.gc.ca/eng/rp-pr/fl-lf/child-enfant/guide/index. html. This publication contains general information aimed at providing convenience and guidance in applying the Federal Child Support Guidelines.

Law Courts Education Society of BC. 2006. *Parenting after Separation for Your Child's Future: A Handbook for Parents.* Victoria: Ministry of Attorney General, 2006. This workbook focuses on the needs of children when parents separate. It provides suggestions as to how parents can better understand and help meet their children's needs. It includes suggestions and information on how parents can inform their children about the separation, how to relate to and negotiate with the other parent, and some of the legal issues they will encounter, including parenting arrangements, the best interests of the child, etc.

Websites

Canadian Children's Rights Council—Canada Child Financial Support in Family Law

www.canadiancrc.com/child_financial_support_famlaw.aspx

> The Canadian Children's Rights Council is a nonprofit, nongovernment educational and advocacy organization concerned with Canadian children's human rights and responsibilities. This website contains information on Federal Child Support Guidelines, among many other things. It also includes access to the Special Joint Committee's report *For the Sake of the Children* presented to the Parliament of Canada in December 1998.

Canadian Council of Child and Youth Advocates (CCCYA)

www.cccya.ca/

> The CCCYA is an alliance of 10 children's advocates from across Canada who have mandates to support the rights of children and youth and to promote youth voice. The organization's goals include increasing the knowledge and understanding of children's advocacy across Canada; identifying areas for common action; influencing policy and practice affecting children; and increasing public awareness of child advocacy and children issues.

Ontario Ministry of the Attorney General—Divorce and Separation

www.attorneygeneral.jus.gov.on.ca/english/family/divorce/default.asp

> This Government of Ontario website contains information and links aimed at helping individuals understand the legal issues and processes of separation and divorce in Ontario, including information on child support, the care and support of children, division of property, etc.

Service Canada—Getting Divorced

www.servicecanada.gc.ca/eng/lifeevents/divorce.shtml

> This Service Canada website contains information to help individuals understand the legal issues and process, rights, and responsibilities related to divorce in Canada. It contains links to legal issues and supports for parents and children.

12 Child Abuse and Child Protection in Canada

Learning Objectives

◎ To explore arguments for and against spanking.

◎ To briefly review the history of parental control over children.

◎ To consider the first legal challenges to parental control in North America.

◎ To learn about section 43 of the Criminal Code of Canada.

◎ To learn how child abuse is currently defined.

◎ To examine child abuse rates and trends.

◎ To better understand child sexual assault and child homicides.

◎ To find out more about common perpetrators and who are the most vulnerable victims.

◎ To explore some theoretical explanations for why children are abused.

Introduction

In March 2014, 10 new charges were laid against convicted child sex offender Christopher Paul Neil after police conducted further investigations into his activities over the past 10 years in Vancouver, Maple Ridge, and Cambodia (Zanocco, 2014). The former teacher, who had at one point aspired to become a priest, was involved in tourism for the purpose of committing sexual offences against children. The charges, both new and old, resulted from a Royal Canadian Mounted Police (RCMP) investigation in collaboration with Interpol (the International Criminal Police Organization). Together, they issued a rare international plea for public assistance in identifying a Canadian man who appeared in photographs of child sexual abuse that were posted on the Internet (RCMP, 2007). The RCMP's National Child Exploitation Coordination Centre (NCECC) had been actively involved in this investigation since 2004. A few days after the worldwide public appeal, the then 32-year-old British Columbia man was arrested for these alleged sex crimes. In 2014, at age 39, he made the news again, as additional charges were laid against him. While this sensational case hit the front pages of newspapers, television screens, and the Internet around the country and the world, twice, hundreds of thousands of cases of child abuse go unreported (Trocmé et al., 2010; Sinha, 2013).

Unlike Halloween, Christmas, or any other commercialized holiday, World Day for Prevention of Child Abuse (19 November), like child abuse itself, often passes unnoticed. We hope to rectify this situation by providing a detailed sketch of the depth and scope of this ongoing problem. The chapter begins with a presentation of the controversial discussion of spanking and of parental use of corporal punishment. We proceed to a brief historical overview of parental control over children and one of the first key legal challenges in North America to parental or adult control over children. We also show that although these early challenges have been in existence for more than 100 years, debate in Canada surrounding Section 43 of the Criminal Code continues. Next, we move to current definitions of child abuse and an examination of rates and trends in child abuse today. We will explore some of the recurring patterns among common perpetrators and victims of violence, and why, as some theorists tell us, these patterns exist and persist.

To Spank or Not to Spank?

When I was an undergraduate student of history (and sociology), I recall reading seventeenth-century accounts by Jesuit priests who came to New France, now Quebec, to help "civilize" and Christianize the "savages." They felt morally righteous compared with many others, because they believed, unlike many others, that "Indians" were human, had a soul, and therefore could be "saved." To help do this, they began to educate Aboriginal communities in Christian morality and Christian ways. While doing this, and to the great horror of many First Nations parents, they used severe forms of **corporal (physical) punishment** to "correct" undesired behaviour and attitudes in First Nations children. At the time, it was seen as the duty of good Christian parents and teachers to beat the sin out of children, because, as the saying went, "spare the rod, spoil the child." Romero (2008) notes that "household government" over women, children, servants, and slaves, which included physical punishment, also was important in English conceptions of order and colonialism (especially among Puritans in the United States).

Today, some continue to use religious explanations for why they spank their children (Davis, 1997). In 2001, seven children from Aylmer, Ontario, were removed from their family by the Children's Aid Society when their parents refused to stop punishing them with switches (slender flexible shoots cut from a tree). The parents were members of the Church of God and believed that the Bible permits the corporal punishment of children (CBC News, 2001). For many other parents, corporal punishment is believed to be an effective tool in correcting bad behaviour, reinforcing respect and obedience, protecting children from harm, teaching life lessons, and preparing them for life's challenges. Some describe spanking as a sign of caring, and if you had asked my parents 30 years ago, they probably would have agreed.

On the other hand, opponents of corporal punishment have argued that spanking is immoral (Turner, 2002), potentially abusive,[1] demoralizing (Durrant, 2012; Durrant et al., 2004), a violation of the Canadian Charter of Rights and Freedoms (Court of Appeal for Ontario, 2002), and ineffective in correcting "misbehavior" (Ackerman et al., 2003; Fritz, 2014; Public Health Agency of Canada, 2008; Pettit et al., 1997; Deator-Deckard et al., 1996; Conger et al., 1994; Durrant, 2012).[2] Durrant et al. (2004), in coalition with the Children's Hospital of Eastern Ontario, in a joint statement on physical punishment, noted that there is no clear evidence of any benefit to using physical punishment with children, that, in fact, it is linked to weaker internalization of moral values. There is also strong evidence that physical punishment places children at increased risk of physical injury, and that few parents actually believe it is effective or constructive (Durrant, 2012).

A study conducted in the United States and Canada noted that most parents want more information on child rearing, including discipline, but few pediatricians discuss such issues with parents (Barkin et al., 2007). The study looked at the types of discipline used by parents and found that just fewer than 40 per cent (38.4 per cent) reported using the same discipline that was used when they were children (just over half, or 54.2 per cent, did not). Parents who experienced spanking and yelling in their childhood were more likely to use those techniques on their own children (ibid.; Durrant et al., 2004; Durrant, 2012; Peltonen et al., 2014). One-third of parents viewed their disciplinary efforts as ineffective (Barkin et al., 2007).

Durrant (2012), among many others (Durrant et al., 2004), recommends that parents receive more, better, and universal parenting education, because studies have shown that parents with knowledge of child development are less likely to interpret a child's drive for independence and testing as "bad behaviour." In contrast, a parent whose sense of control is believed to be threatened by a child's behaviour or who sees the child's behaviour as an intentional challenge to parental authority is more likely to use physical punishment (Durrant et al., 2004). This being the case, increased education on child development (having a parent understand a child's motivation, and assist children with problem-solving, for example) should help parents feel less frustrated and stressed, and be less likely to respond emotionally to a child's (mis)behavior (Durrant, 2012). After all, in most cases, physical punishment results in short-term compliance and, potentially, longer-term, negative behavioural outcomes (see Box 12.1).

A Statistics Canada study of parenting styles found a link between more punitive parenting practices and more aggressive behaviour for girls and boys, for low-income and higher-income households, and across regions of residence (Kong, 2006; Thomas, 2004). The study found that when nonpunitive parenting was used at ages 2–3 and ages 8–9, children had low aggressive behaviour scores at age 8–9 (Thomas, 2004). When punitive parenting was

---

Physical Punishment and Child Behaviour Problems

How does physical punishment contribute to child behaviour problems?

1. Physical punishment serves as a model for rather than an inhibitor of aggression.
2. Physical punishment may interfere with the development of trust in the relationship with the parent, reducing the child's desire to comply.
3. If compliance is controlled by physical punishment, the child's internal motivation to comply in the punisher's absence is weakened.
4. Fear of physical punishment focuses the child's attention on consequences to himself or herself, rather than on the consequences of his or her behaviour for others.

Source: Durrant et al. (2004: 8).

---

used at ages 2–3 and 8–9, children were reported to score high in aggressive behaviour at ages 8–9. However, if punitive parenting was in use at ages 2–3 but changed to nonpunitive parenting at ages 8–9, children scored as low in aggressive behaviour as those whose parenting environment was nonpunitive at both ages (ibid.). While these findings do not prove that there is a causal link between punitive parenting and aggressive behaviour in children, they are consistent with earlier research that showed that harsh or punitive parenting practices can and often do lead to increased aggressive behaviour in children (ibid.; Ackerman et al., 2003; Pettit et al., 1997; Deator-Deckard et al., 1996; Conger et al., 1994) and parental violence against children when they become parents (Peltonen et al., 2014).

A growing number of researchers, pediatricians, service providers, and lawyers suggest that children be afforded the same rights and protection from physical assault that other Canadians and a growing number of children in countries around the world are receiving. That is, Canada should join a growing list of countries that have explicitly prohibited the use of physical punishment against children, including Sweden (1979), Finland (1983), Norway (1987), Austria (1989), Cyprus (1994), Denmark (1997), Latvia (1998), Croatia (1998), and Israel (2000).[3] But this effort represents only about 2.4 per cent of the world's children (UNICEF, 2007c; 2006).

In Canada and around the world, opponents of the use of physical punishment have argued that it is a human rights violation and runs counter to the United Nations Convention on the Rights of the Child. The fact is that we legally protect adults (and pets, for that matter) from physical violence and assault—one cannot legally "correct misbehaviour" of a spouse or partner, employee, coworker, or university student using physical force—but we do not have the same protection for children. If prohibitions were put in place, some proponents of spanking have feared the erosion of parental control over children. In contrast, opponents of the use of corporal punishment have argued that adult or parental power and children's powerlessness are precisely the problem that needs to be eradicated (Durrant, 2012; Moosa-Mitha, 2005; Stasiulis, 2002; Howe, 2001a).

Brief Historical and Cross-Cultural Overview of Parental Control over Children

Historically and across most cultures, parents, and especially fathers, have had almost unquestioned authority over children. That is, children (and often wives) have been treated as chattel or the property of fathers to do with them what they pleased. For example, in the classical period (second century BCE to second century CE) in ancient Rome, the head of a household or *paterfamilias* possessed a unique authority known as *patria potestas*, the legal power and authority of the head, over household religious observance (which made him responsible for the household's appropriate conduct), household property, and its members (Thompson, 2006). *Potestas* (authority) over household members granted him *ius/jus vitae necisque*—"right of life and death." This gave the *paterfamilias* the right to

> (1) expose infant offspring, (2) sell a son into slavery, (3) administer physical punishment to household members, (4) hand over a household member accused of wrong doing for punishment by the wronged party, (5) end the marriages of his children, and (6) violently take the life of his wife (if married in *manu*), child, grandchild, or slave without legal consequences, provided that he had good reason." (ibid., 4)

The right likely was not often used; nonetheless, it existed, as it did in other parts of the world.

In 1646, the General Court of Massachusetts Bay Colony enacted a law mandating that "a stubborn or rebellious son, of sufficient years and understanding," would be brought before the court and "such a son shall be put to death" (Romero, 2008; Sutton, 1988). Needless to say, the Massachusetts Puritans took the disobedience of sons—a violation of the Fifth Commandment—very seriously. In these cases, a son had two options: offer contrition and obedience to his father or face the power of the state (Romero, 2008). Again, death was likely not often the outcome, but fathers had such rights at their disposal.

Lloyd deMause (1975), critical of his social historian peers, noted that there was mass evidence of child abuse and infanticide throughout history that was hidden, distorted, softened, or ignored by the historians who uncovered it. Most of the perpetrators, legally or culturally entitled to "abuse" children, were their parents or other adults committed to their care. Most of this power remained unquestioned for much of human history.

Legal Challenges to Parental/Adult Control in North America

Some have argued that one of the first well-documented challenges to adult control over children in modern North America is the controversial (some have called it a myth [Watkins, 1990]) Mary Ellen Wilson case in New York City in 1874. Although there have been recorded cases of criminal prosecution of parents and masters for excessive punishment of children and apprentices dating as far back as 1655 (ibid.), the Mary Ellen Wilson case was one of the first legal struggles for children's rights in North America (Mallon, 2013).

While there are a number of different versions of this story, there is some agreement that Mary Ellen was the child of Irish immigrants, whose father died and whose mother was unable to care for her (or she was the illegitimate child of the man to whom she later was indentured [ibid., 2]). By the age of two, Mary Ellen wound up in the care of New York City's Department of Charities (Mallon, 2013; Myers, 2002; Lazoritz and Shelman, 1996; Watkins, 1990). She was indentured by the city to a couple, the Connollys, who beat and underfed her, confined her to their home, forced her to do manual labour beyond her strength and age, and did not provide her with warm clothes or shoes in winter or a bed to sleep in.

In 1873, a Methodist caseworker, Etta Wheeler, who often visited the poor, received several complaints about the child and dropped in to find Mary Ellen a prisoner in her own home. Wheeler sought assistance from police and charitable organizations, but was unable to remove Mary Ellen from the home until April 1874. Frustrated by legal restrictions, Wheeler turned to Henry Bergh, president of the New York Society for the Prevention of Cruelty to Animals (NYSPCA). Some say she reasoned that children were members of the animal kingdom and could therefore be protected under the laws governing the mistreatment of animals (Watkins, 1990, debates this). Following an NYSPCA visit, Mary Ellen was removed from the home using a special warrant. There was a trial, resulting in Mrs Connelly's arrest (Mr Connelly had died before this); Mary Ellen was placed in the care of Mrs Wheeler, the caseworker, at Mrs Wheeler's request. Mary Ellen thrived, married, and lived into her eighties.

The case resulted in the foundation of the New York Society for the Prevention of Cruelty to Children (SPCC) in 1874. (The Toronto's Children's

Aid Society was founded 20 years later, in 1894.) The SPCC was the first organization to uphold the legal protection of children's rights in the United States. It also introduced legislation to prevent and punish wrongs to children that occurred in their homes. While the actual details and events surrounding the Mary Ellen Wilson case have been debated (see ibid.), the fact remains that there was an organization to protect animals before there was one to protect children.

In Canada, in 1867, the enactment of the British North America Act included legislation for child welfare, but it was not until 1888, with the passing of the Act for the Protection and Reformation of Neglected Children (commonly known as the Child Protection Act) in Ontario, that children were no longer the exclusive property of parents—the state now had some authority (Child Welfare League of Canada, 2007). Soon after this, Children's Aid Societies emerged to deliver government authority. With the expansion of the welfare state (marked by increased funding for social services) in the post-war period, the child welfare system began to change. By the mid-1960s, the terminology of the child welfare system changed from "child protection" to "child abuse" and "child rescuing"[4] (ibid., 4). With this, the number of children in the care of welfare state agencies, and especially a disproportionate number of First Nations children, increased dramatically. Child welfare remains under provincial jurisdiction, resulting in significant differences across jurisdictions.

The concept of protecting children from abuse in their own homes, and particularly from their own parents, remains controversial to this day. Some critics have argued that the protection of children's rights in this way invades the sanctity of the home and the rights of parents to discipline their children. While it is the responsibility of government and laws to safeguard the rights of children, controversy continues to focus on Section 43 of the Criminal Code of Canada.

Section 43 of the Criminal Code of Canada

Section 43 of the Criminal Code of Canada, enacted in 1892, currently reads as follows:

> Every school teacher, parent or person standing in the place of a parent is justified in using force by way of correction towards a pupil or child, as the case may be, who is under his care, if the force does not exceed what is reasonable under the circumstances.

A number of individuals and organizations have fought unsuccessfully for years for the repeal of this section of the Criminal Code, on the grounds (among others) that it violates children's right to protection from assault—a right granted to adults (Durrant, 2012)—and because what are deemed to be "reasonable force" and "by way of correction" is left to individual judges to interpret and determine. Not long ago, the Canadian Foundation for Children, Youth and the Law challenged the constitutionality of Section 43 in an Ontario Court on violations of Section 7 (on the security of persons) of the Canadian Charter of Rights and Freedoms. In July 2000, the Court upheld Section 43, with the judge dismissing the application (Public Legal Education and Information Services of New Brunswick, 2007). The Foundation turned to the Ontario Court of Appeal, and in September 2001 the Court again upheld the constitutionality of Section 43. The case was then taken to the Supreme Court of Canada. In a 6–3 decision, the Supreme Court ruled that Section 43 does *not* violate the constitutional rights of Canadian children but narrowed the definition of who may use physical punishment, on what ages, body parts, and capacities of children, with what force, and under what circumstances (Durrant et al., 2004).[5]

The Court was not deciding whether corporal punishment was good or bad, right or wrong. However, to ensure the best interests of the child, the Supreme Court stated that

- the force used must be intended to educate or correct the child;
- the force used must be to restrain, control, or express disapproval of the actual behaviour;
- the child must be capable of benefiting from the discipline. In other words, factors such a child's age and disability will influence the child's ability to learn from the use of force; and
- the force used must be "reasonable under the circumstances" and "not offend society's view of decency." (Public Legal Education and Information Services of New Brunswick, 2007: 1)

The Court also interpreted "reasonable force" as "minor corrective force" that is short-lived and not harmful (ibid.). It set limits on what would be considered reasonable force to help reduce the risk that courts will make arbitrary or subjective decisions. The Supreme Court concluded that the following is *not* considered to be reasonable:

- hitting a child under two years of age. It is wrong and harmful because spanking has no value with very young children and can destroy a child's sense of security and self-esteem. Children under two do not have the cognitive ability to understand why someone is spanking them.
- corporal punishment of teenagers. It is not helpful and is potentially harmful to use force on teenagers because it achieves only short-term obedience and may alienate the youth and promote aggressive or other antisocial behaviour.

- using objects to discipline a child such as belts, rulers, etc. This is potentially harmful both physically and emotionally.
- slaps or blows to the head.
- degrading or inhumane treatment.
- corporal punishment which causes injury—causing harm is child abuse. (ibid.)

In reference to teachers, the Court ruled that "teachers may reasonably apply force to remove a child from a classroom or secure compliance with instructions, but not merely as corporal punishment" (ibid.). Since the force used must be corrective, the Court ruled out the use of force stemming from the caregiver's frustration, loss of temper, or abusive personality. The latter use of force would be considered abuse.

Child Abuse Defined

Canada's Department of Justice (2013) has noted that the term *child abuse* refers to the violence, mistreatment, or neglect that a child or adolescent may experience while in the care of someone he or she trusts or depends on (such as a parent, sibling, other relative, caregiver, or guardian). It explains that there are many different forms of abuse and a child may be subjected to more than one. These forms include *physical abuse*, which involves deliberately using force against a child in such a way that the child is either injured or is at risk of being injured. This includes beating, hitting, shaking, pushing, choking, biting, burning, kicking, or assaulting a child with a weapon. It includes holding a child under water or other dangerous or harmful use of force or restraint. Female genital mutilation also is a form of physical abuse (ibid.). Recently, exposing a child to family violence has been grounds for child protection intervention under provincial and territorial child protection laws and so it too is considered a form of child maltreatment (Department of Justice, 2013).

Neglect, according to the Department of Justice, is also a form of child abuse. To be defined as abuse, neglect is chronic, and involves failing to provide what a child needs for physical, psychological, or emotional development and well-being. Neglect includes failing to provide a child with food, clothing, shelter, cleanliness, medical care, or protection from harm. *Emotional neglect* includes failing to provide a child with love, safety, and a sense of worth. This is closely linked to *emotional abuse*, which involves harming a child's sense of self, and includes acts (or omissions) that result in, or place a child at risk of, serious behavioural, cognitive, emotional, or mental health problems. Emotional neglect may include verbal threats, social isolation, intimidation, exploitation, routinely making unreasonable demands, terrorizing a child, or exposing the child to family violence (ibid.).

Sexual abuse and *exploitation* involve using a child for sexual purposes and include fondling, inviting a child to touch or to be touched sexually, intercourse, rape, incest, sodomy, exhibitionism, or involving a child in prostitution or pornography (ibid.). A Statistics Canada report points out that the rate of sexual offences, including sexual assaults, reported to police have been declining (Cotter and Beaupré, 2014). However, sexual offences against children and youth were alarmingly high. A recent Statistics Canada report noted that there were about 14,000 children and youth under the age of 18 who were victims of (police-reported) sexual offence in Canada in 2012, representing a rate of 205 for every 100,000 children and youth (ibid). Police reports and victimization surveys reveal that young women and girls are at the highest risk of sexual assault (ibid; see Box 12.2).

Box 12.2   Girls More Often than Boys the Victims of Family Violence

Girls are disproportionally represented as victims of family violence. In 2011, rates of family violence were 56 per cent higher for girls than boys. This disparity was more muted in the younger age groups, with girls and boys experiencing similar rates before three years of age. However, by age three, girls outnumbered boys as victims of family violence. This gap continued to widen with age, peaking in adolescence. By age 15, the rate for girls was double the rate for boys (566 per 100,000 population versus 281 per 100,000 population).

Girls consistently experienced higher rates of family violence for nearly every type of violent offence. However, this risk was most marked for sexually based offences. Girls were four times more likely than boys to be a victim of police-reported sexual assault or other type of sexual offence at the hands of a family member (129 per 100,000 versus 30 per 100,000).

Table 12.1 Child and Youth Victims (0 to 17 years) of Police-Reported Family Violence, by Sex of the Victim and Type of Offence, Canada, 2011

Type of offence	Female victims		Male victims		Total	
	Number	Rate[a]	Number	Rate	Number	Rate
Homicide	12	0.4	19	0.5	31	0.5
Attempted murder	8	0.2	15	0.4	23	0.3
Physical assault	5,463	163	5,385	153	10,848	158
Sexual offences	4,320	129	1,041	30	5,361	78
Kidnapping/abduction	220	7	147	4	367	5
Other violent crimes	890	27	782	22	1,672	24

[a]Per 100,000.

Source: Sinha (2013).

Child Abuse and Maltreatment Rates and Trends

The *Canadian Incidence Study of Reported Child Abuse and Neglect, 2008,* reported that an estimated 235,842 child-maltreatment-related investigations were conducted in Canada, of which 36 per cent were substantiated (Trocmé et al., 2010). In other words, in 2008 alone, there were an estimated 85,440 substantiated child maltreatment investigations in Canada, with the two most frequently occurring categories of substantiated maltreatment being exposure to intimate partner violence and neglect (Trocmé et al., 2010). Thirty-four per cent of the substantiated investigations were related to exposure to intimate partner violence; another 34 per cent of substantiated investigations involved neglect (ibid). Twenty per cent of substantiated investigations involved maltreatment, with 9 per cent of substantiated investigations being emotional maltreatment (ibid). Sexual abuse was identified as the primary maltreatment category in 3 per cent of substantiated investigations (ibid). There is general agreement that this report (and all others) underestimates the magnitude of the problem, as it includes only cases actually reported to child welfare services. Nonetheless, this report gives us a good indication of what happened to some of Canada's children over the course of one year.

Recent Statistics Canada reports have noted that children and youth are more vulnerable to physical and sexual violence than adults (Cotter and Beaupré, 2014; Sinha, 2013). Children were also most likely to be assaulted in private dwellings, most often in their own homes (Cotter and Beaupré, 2014; Sinha, 2013).

Child Sexual Assault

In 2012, there were approximately 14,000 children and youth who were victims of a police-reported sexual offence in Canada. Despite the slight drop in the rate between 2009 and 2012, children and youth continued to account for more than half (55 per cent) of the victims of sexual offences reported by police, while making up only 20 per cent of the Canadian population (Cotter and Beaupré, 2014). As noted in Box 12.2, female children were victims of police-reported sexual offences at a higher rate than male children (ibid). Around the world, an estimated 150 million girls and 73 million boys under the age of 18 experienced forced sexual intercourse or other forms of sexual violence (UNICEF, 2007c). A survey of 21 countries found that at least 7 per cent of girls (ranging up to 36 per cent in some countries) and 3 per cent of boys (ranging up to 29 per cent in some countries) reported sexual victimization during their childhood (ibid.).

Younger victims were more likely to be sexually assaulted by a family member, while older children were most frequently victimized by an acquaintance or stranger (Sinha, 2013). About 9 in 10 victims knew the accused, while in 12 per cent of cases the accused was a stranger. For 66 per cent of victims up to three years of age, police identified a family member as the perpetrator (Sinha, 2013). Increased attention is being placed on the sexual victimization of children and youth by strangers via the Internet. For example, a Statistics Canada (2009c) study noted that police services across Canada reported 464 incidents of child luring over the Internet during the two-year period of 2006 and 2007. This number will surely increase with increased awareness and reporting of the issue.

Children as Victims of Homicide

Familial homicides against children and youth are relatively rare occurrences that tend to fluctuate widely year-over-year (Sinha, 2013). Around the world, infants under the age of one face about three times the risk of homicide, almost invariably at the hands of their parents, than children ages one to four, and twice the risk of children ages 5–14 (UNICEF, 2007c). In Canada, homicide statistics have shown that every year, children under the age of one are at far greater risk of homicide by a family member than children of any other age (Sinha, 2013). They were most likely to be killed by parents by shaking (shaken baby syndrome) (ibid.).

Beating was the most common cause of death for children ages one to three, along with strangulation and suffocation (this was also the most common for those ages four to six). Teenagers (12 to 17 years) were most often killed as a result of stabbing (Sinha, 2013). For all age groups, a feeling of frustration, anger, and despair was the most common motive in family homicides against children and youth (Sinha, 2013).

Common Perpetrators

Most cases of child abuse go unreported, often because the abused child is in a position of dependence on the abuser (Department of Justice, 2007d). As noted above, children are most likely physically and sexually abused by people they know.

Statistics Canada research shows that just over one-quarter (26 per cent) of those accused of violence against children and youth were family members (including a parent, step-parent, foster parent, sibling, grandparent, or extended family member), while 53 per cent were either acquaintances or friends of the child (Sinha, 2013). Family members were especially named as perpetrators in the most serious forms of violence against children (in 51 per cent of homicide cases and 43 per cent of attempted murder cases). They were also implicated in most cases of abduction, forcible confinement, and kidnapping (ibid). Because of a child's dependency on primary caregivers early in life, it is not surprising to see that infants and toddlers were more likely to be victimized by a member of their family (68 per cent of victimized infants under one and 69 per cent of victimized children one to three years of age were victimized by a family member, most often a parent or step-parent) than any other type of perpetrator. But as children grew older, and entered school, victimization by family members began to drop (at four, five, and six years of age, 67 per cent of cases, 66 per cent of cases, and 59 per cent of cases, respectively, involved family members) (ibid). By the age of nine, family members were replaced by non-family members as those responsible for violence against children, such that by age 12 to 17, 57 per cent of all violent offences were committed by friends or acquaintances, followed by strangers (24 per cent) then family members (18 per cent) (Sinha, 2013).

Common perpetrators were also likely to have experienced one or more of the following stressors over the six months before the reporting of the child abuse: alcohol abuse, drug or solvent abuse, criminal activity, cognitive impairment, mental health issues, physical health issues, lack of social supports, maltreatment as a child, victim of domestic violence, or perpetrator of domestic violence (Kong, 2006; also see Trocmé et al., 2010).

Who Is Most Vulnerable?

Overall, the incidence of substantiated child maltreatment cases was similar for boys (38.69 per 1,000 males) and girls (39.66 per 1,000 females) (Trocmé et al., 2010). Variations, however, were noted when age was factored in. Rates of substantiated maltreatment, as mentioned above, were highest for infants (17.56 substantiated cases per 1,000 females and 16.64 per 1,000 males). Rates of substantiated maltreatment were similar by sex for four to seven year olds; however, there were more affected males reported in the 8- to 11-year-old age range and more affected females reported in the adolescent group (Trocmé et al., 2010).

Police data showed that children ages 6–13 were at greatest risk of physical assault during a four-hour period between 3 and 7 p.m., with 4 of every 10 physical assaults occurring at that time (Statistics Canada, 2005d).

A child's vulnerability to abuse is increased by dislocation, colonization, racism, sexism, homophobia, poverty, and social isolation (Department of Justice, 2007d). For example, throughout our history, children sent to institutions, including children with disabilities, children from ethnic and racial minority groups, Aboriginal children, and children living in poverty were at increased risk of abuse (ibid.). Children living in communities in which inequality, unemployment, and poverty are highly concentrated also are at increased risk (Brzozowski, 2007). Children born during a stressful period in a parent's life, or born with a disability or other health needs (including premature babies), are at increased risk of violence.

Martinello (2014) noted that children with special needs are at an increased risk for sexual assault compared with their peers. She explains that motor delays may limit undressing or dressing and other self-care tasks (requiring others to assist); social delays may inhibit appropriate peer relationships (leaving children isolated and vulnerable); cognitive delays may prevent a child from discerning abuse from care; language delays may prohibit a child from reporting abuse or rejecting an inappropriate advance; and emotional delays may impact a child's self-esteem and potential designation as a "victim" (Martinello, 2014). Not surprising, as in other cases of abuse, caregivers are frequently cited as the most likely perpetrator of sexual abuse against children with intellectual disabilities. Perhaps due to some of the real or perceived challenges associated with receiving ethics approval to do such research, rarely do we have opportunities to understand children's lived experiences with physical abuse, from their own point of view and through their own voices.

Katz and Barnetz (2014), however, compiled 117 Israeli children's narratives during forensic investigations in cases where children are the alleged victims of continuous physical abuse by their biological parents. The study involved 67 boys and 50 girls, ranging in age from 5 to 13 years. All of the children were interviewed following suspected multiple incidents of abuse, but it should be noted that 50 children (42.7 per cent) had disclosed the abuse before the investigation and 67 children (57.3 per cent) disclosed the abuse for the first time during the investigation. In 53 cases, the suspects were the children's fathers; mothers were the suspects in 40 cases; and in 24 cases, both of the parents were the suspects (ibid). During the interviews, the children reported on the physical sensations while being abused. They also spoke about their emotions during the incidents, with some even attempting to understand and explain why their parents hurt them. For example one child said, "My daddy is miserable. It is not his intention to hit us, and he does that only because his father used to hit him all the time" (Katz and Barnetz, 2014: 4). When asked about their future, some recognized the complex realities that they would face following a conviction. For example, children said things like, "I do not want him to leave the house; he is the one that brings the money" and "I don't want my father to be in jail. Sometimes he gives me things, and he gives money to my mother every day" (Katz and Barnetz, 2014: 4–5). But some also recognized that the abuse damaged their well-being: "I want to have a normal life, not the life that I have now. This life is not good for me" (Katz and Barnetz, 2014: 5).

Consequences of Abuse

Depending on the form, duration, and severity of the abuse, a child may experience negative psychological, physical, academic, sexual, interpersonal, self-perceptual, or spiritual effects, which in some cases may surface only later in life (Department of Justice, 2007d). The effects also differ according to the nature of the response to the abuse, if and when the abuse was disclosed or reported.

Exposure to violence, whether as a victim or a witness, can disrupt nervous and immune system development and can lead to social, emotional, and cognitive impairments. It can also result in high-risk health behaviours, including substance abuse and early sexual activity, and lead to anxiety and depressive disorders, impaired work performance, memory disturbances, and aggressive behaviour (UNICEF, 2007c).

The *Canadian Incidence Study* asked child welfare workers to identify any physical, emotional, cognitive, and behavioural issues they saw in child maltreatment cases. Child welfare workers identified more than 15 types of "functioning concerns" in children, including depression and anxiety, alcohol and other drug or solvent abuse, self-harming behaviour, violence towards others, developmental delay, Youth Criminal Justice Act involvement, and academic difficulties (Trocmé et al., 2010). In 46 per cent of substantiated child maltreatment investigations, there was at least one child-functioning issue identified by caseworkers (See Table 12.2). The most frequently reported child functioning issues were academic (in 23 per cent of substantiated maltreatment investigations); depression, anxiety, or withdrawal (19 per cent); aggression (15 per cent); attachment issues (14 per cent); and attention deficit disorder (ADD) or attention deficit hyperactivity disorder (ADHD) (11 per cent of substantiated maltreatment investigations) (Trocmé et al., 2010).

Table 12.2 Child Functioning Concerns in Substantiated Child Maltreatment Investigations in Canada in 2008[a]

Child functioning concern	Number of investigations	Rate per 1,000 children	%
No child functioning concerns	45,980	7.64	54
Type of child functioning concerns			
Depression/anxiety/withdrawal	16,310	2.71	19
Suicidal thoughts	3,511	0.58	4
Self-harming behaviour	5,095	0.85	6
ADD/ADHD	9,101	1.51	11
Attachment issues	11,797	1.96	14
Aggression	13,237	2.20	15
Running (multiple incidents)	3,588	0.60	4
Inappropriate sexual behaviours	3,453	0.57	4
Youth Criminal Justice Act involvement	1,789	0.31	2
Intellectual/developmental disability	9,805	1.63	11
Failure to meet developmental milestones	7,508	1.25	9
Academic difficulties	19,820	3.29	23
Fetal alcohol syndrome/fetal alcohol effect	3,177	0.53	4
Positive toxicology at birth	845	0.14	1
Physical disability	1,428	0.24	2
Alcohol abuse	2,704	0.45	3
Drug/solvent abuse	3,474	0.58	4
Other functioning concern	3,484	0.58	4
At least one child functioning concern	39,460	6.55	46
Total substantiated investigations	85,440	14.19	100

[a]Based on a sample of 6,163 substantiated child maltreatment investigations. Percentages are column percentages. Columns are not additive, as investigating workers could identify more than one.

Source: Trocmé et al. (2010: 39).

Studies indicate that girls and boys are affected differently by abuse. Not unlike other learned responses, girls are more likely to internalize their feelings, which are then manifested in suicidal ideations, eating disorders, low self-esteem, and psychological disorders (Department of Justice, 2007d). Boys are more likely to externalize their feelings, displaying increased aggression, delinquency, and spousal abuse. Boys who experience abuse are more likely to be violent as adolescents and in their adult relationships (ibid.).

Theoretical Explanations for Why Children Are Abused

Due to the complex motivations for child abuse and maltreatment, it is not surprising that numerous theories have been developed to explain why children are abused and why some individuals are more likely to be abusive than others (see Donnelly and Straus, 2005, for a detailed presentation of a wide range of theories surrounding corporal punishment). Here we will consider only a handful of the wide range of explanations available, including social learning theory, social stress-strain theory, and theories derived from combining explanations. Most of these theories aim to help us understand physical abuse. On the other hand, physical and emotional abuses often go hand in hand. Sexual abuse is also most often about power and control, and so some of these theories shed light on that as well.

Theory of Intergenerational Transmission of Violence: Social Learning Theory

Many studies have reported a link between childhood experiences of violence and violent adult behaviour and offences. Some have argued that this is best explained using observational or social learning theory (Bandura, 1973). This theory argues that family violence is learned—children emulate or model behaviour they observe, resulting in the intergenerational transmission of family aggression (Murrell et al., 2007). In other words, abusers have learned to abuse and become abusive parents through *generalized modelling*, their acceptance of aggression as "normal" within families, and *specific modelling*, committing the same types of aggression the individual was exposed to as a child (ibid.).

Murrell et al. tested this theory by studying 1,099 adult men with varying exposure to violence as children and found that men who were abused as children were more likely to abuse than those who were not abused. They also found that the likelihood of committing violence against someone other than an intimate partner increased as the participants' childhood exposure to violence increased.

While this theory is plausible and has been supported by various types of research, it does not adequately explain why some individuals who were abused as children do not abuse as adults (see Letourneau et al., 2007, on resiliency in spite of risk), or why male and female victims of abuse seem to respond differently to abuse they experienced in childhood (Department of Justice, 2007d).

Rodriguez and Richardson (2007) describe what seems to be a variant of social learning theory, called *social information processing theory* (SIP), which encompasses a broader web of cognitive processes. According to SIP theory, parents maintain a collection of parenting-related pre-experiences, including beliefs about discipline, about their child, about the nature of parenting, about locus of control, and about parent–child interactions (ibid.). This collection of beliefs or schema precedes their interactions with their own children. These pre-existing schemas then influence their understanding of their child's behaviour and their own responses to it, particularly when facing a disciplining decision. Parents who have unrealistic expectations about their children's abilities, who lack parental empathy (ability to put themselves in the position of their children), or who do not have positive parental attachment are more likely to use overreactive discipline styles that may lead to abuse (ibid.). This, indeed, sounds plausible.

Social Stress-Strain Theory

Some have argued that parents abuse children in response to stress or strain in their lives. According to general strain theory, individuals who experience strains or stressors are more likely to engage in criminal activity (Froggio and Agnew, 2007; Agnew, 1992). Strains include events and conditions that are disliked by most people (objective strains) or that are specific to the individuals who experience them (subjective strains); both kinds of strain lead to negative emotions and pressure to engage in corrective action (Froggio and Agnew, 2007). Stressors and strains that can lead to crime and violence can include things like loss of valued goals (e.g., money, masculine status, sex, or autonomy) and threats or removal of positively valued stimuli (e.g., loss of nurturer or loss of a sexual partner) (Harper and Voigt, 2007). People who experience subjective strains are particularly susceptible to engaging in criminal activity.

Harper and Voigt (2007) used strain theory coupled with patriarchal power–control explanations (Dobash and Dobash, 1979) to explain domestic lethal violence–suicide. For example, they note that in cases of intimate or domestic murder–suicide, a woman's rejection or abandonment (i.e., challenging his power and control) of her partner threatens his masculine status and the economic stability of the unit (Harper and Voigt, 2007). In other words, the fear of loss of power (dominance–control) can strain (social stress–strain) the male partner into committing acts of violence against family members.

Harper and Voigt note that all of the cases of homicide–suicide that they analyzed, regardless of type, demonstrated some conflict intensity structures, such as dependency or assumed responsibility, unequal relationships, previous jealousy or hostility, and precipitating crises or other triggers (e.g., illness, divorce, impending arrest, job loss, and financial crisis), as well as elements of stress–strain and power dominance. They also found that most of the perpetrators of domestic homicide–suicide in their study were males, and the majority of victims (both adults and children) were females. Of the 45 adult victims, 42 (95.5 per cent) were female. Of the 13 child victims, 12 were female. Children, whether murdered by their fathers or by their mothers, typically were believed to be incapable of taking care of themselves and, therefore, the self-proclaimed caregivers assumed that they must kill them before killing themselves (ibid.). Harper and Voigt note that with regard to homicide–suicide and the extremely high proportion of female victims, there seems to be a powerful patriarchal value system that places the female in a subordinate position, so that she is an object to be controlled by the male as he sees fit. Given the level of powerlessness and subordination of children in our society, this explanation can easily be extended to include children.

Another explanation that brings together power–control (patriarchy) explanations with elements of some of the theories presented above was developed by Dobash and Dobash (1979) and tested by Cavanagh et al. (2007). Cavanagh et al. examined the backgrounds of fathers who fatally abused their children and the contexts in which these homicides occurred. Their findings suggest a number of risk factors were present and interrelated in these cases. The majority of men (62 per cent) who committed these crimes were not the biological fathers of the victims, and most were cohabiting with (81 per cent) rather than married to (15 per cent) the birth mother (ibid.). Their findings highlight the importance of relationships between the perpetrator and the child and between the perpetrator and his intimate partner. They also point out the importance of the individual experiences of perpetrators, including fragmented and disruptive childhoods (as noted in social learning theory above) and adulthoods characterized by minimal education, persistent unemployment, criminal convictions (as noted in social strain theory), and a history of violence. In terms of parenting practices, the analysis of Cavanagh et al. indicates that many men had unreasonable expectations and low tolerance levels of normal childhood behaviours (as identified in SIP theory above). Some fathers viewed children as adults with responsibilities towards *them*; and many were jealous and resentful of the child (ibid.). Interestingly, few of these men intended to kill their child/victim; instead, they wanted to silence, punish, or discipline the child. These men's violence towards the child and the rationalizations they used to mitigate culpability reflected their belief (sense of entitlement) that they had the right to silence the child, and that their time with their intimate partner (the child's mother) had been infringed upon by the child, threatening their power, authority, and control in the relationship (ibid.).

In sum, what we can see in all these theoretical approaches is that child abuse and child homicides are not necessarily committed by crazed or "insane" individuals or parents. Most approaches show that abuse happens at the hands of "normal" men and women who have been challenged or strained by their own past experiences or current social circumstances. Most of the perpetrators, often due to pre-existing schema or experiences, either feel a sense of power and entitlement over those they abuse or fear a loss of power and control. Isolation, frustration, and jealously created or heightened by existing or past circumstances and experiences make matters worse. As a result, we would do well as a society to protect children from abuse by providing understanding, education, and support (emotional and otherwise) to the adults in their lives.

Summary

In May 2014, at the Sixty-seventh World Health Assembly in Geneva, Canada co-sponsored a resolution on strengthening the health sector response to violence, particularly against women and girls and supported its adoption at the World Health Assembly. As a result, the World Health Organization will develop a global plan of action to strengthen the role of national health systems in addressing interpersonal violence against women and girls, and children (Public Health Agency of Canada 2014). While this is clearly a move in the right direction, we should remember that we have yet to repeal section 43 of the Criminal Code of Canada.

Canada's Department of Justice has noted that child abuse is a complex problem linked to inequalities among people in our society, and in particular, the power imbalance between adults and children. If this is so, the problem, while challenging and serious, is not impossible to correct. That is, there is clearly a need for parenting education and the provision of ongoing support to parents. Research and theories in this area, as we have seen above, suggest that parents can learn parenting styles and levels of understanding that could help minimize the risk of abusive responses to children.

In fact, all Canadians can help improve the lives of vulnerable children from maltreatment and abuse through awareness, education, and programs of prevention targeting the adults who have power over them.

Children need to be recognized as equal citizens, with the same powers and rights afforded to all others—and at the very least, the right, like all others in Canadian society, to live free of fear of physical assault. Until this idea becomes embedded in society, a large number of Canada's children face abuse alone and in silence, most often at the hands of those who are expected to love and care for them, and still others will find themselves in the care of child protection services.

Questions for Critical Thought

1. If Government of Canada websites contain pages like "What's Wrong With Spanking?" (Pubic Health Agency of Canada, 2008), why do you think we have yet to repeal section 43 of the Criminal Code of Canada?

2. Were you spanked as a child? Do you feel it "worked"? Will you spank your child? Why? Why not? If you are a proponent of a parent's right to spank children, what arguments would you use to convince others that this is a parental right? Would you allow or mind if "those standing in the position of a parent," like your child's teachers, spank your child? Why? Why not? If you oppose the use of corporal punishment, what arguments would you use to convince others that it should be disallowed?

3. While some children are abused by strangers, most others are abused by people they know. If you were asked to create a training manual for teachers, what kind of information might you include? What information would you include if the manual targeted children three to five years of age?

4. You have been hired to (re)create policy in the area of child abuse. How would you define and document abuse? What would you do to make Canada a safer place for children?

Suggested Readings

Child Welfare League of Canada. 2009. *Be the Best Parent You Can Be. Why Positive Discipline Works*. Ottawa: Child Welfare League of Canada. At: www.cwlc.ca/sites/default/files/ PPES_pamphlet_Eng.pdf. This publication, available online, is directed at parents. In clear and simple language, it distinguishes between discipline and punishment, explains why spanking does not work, and goes on to provide tips on what forms of disciplining children have proven effective.

Department of Justice. 2012. "Child Abuse Is Wrong: What Can I Do?" Ottawa: Department of Justice. At: www.justice.gc.ca/eng/rp-pr/cj-jp/fv-vf/caw-mei/index.html. This is one article in a series of *Public Legal Education and Information* publications produced under the Family Violence Initiative of the Department of Justice Canada. This booklet is for parents, guardians, and anyone concerned about the well-being of children. It provides information about the law on child abuse in Canada, and among other things, outlines types of abuse, what types of discipline are appropriate, and what one should do in cases of suspected abuse.

Donnelly, Michael, and Murray A. Straus, eds. 2005. *Corporal Punishment of Children in Theoretical Perspective*. New Haven: Yale University Press. This comprehensive treatment of theories on corporal punishment includes 20 chapters organized into comparative, psychological, and sociological approaches. Some of the major theories applied and analyzed include ecological perspective, evolutionary biology, rational choice, moral development, conflict, control, social bonds, stress, social control, and family systems theory.

Trocmé, Nico, Barbara Fallon, Bruce MacLaurin, Vandna Sinha, Tara Black, Elizabeth Fast, Caroline Felstiner, Sonia Hélie, Daniel Turcotte, Pamela Weightman, Janet Douglas, and Jill Holroyd (Public Health Agency of Canada). 2010. *Canadian Incidence Study of Reported*

Child Abuse and Neglect 2008 (CIS-2008): Major Findings. Ottawa: Her Majesty the Queen in Right of Canada. At: http://cwrp.ca/sites/default/files/publications/en/CIS-2008-rprt-eng.pdf. This report reflects a national effort by a group of more than 2,000 child welfare service providers, researchers, and policy-makers committed to improving services for abused and neglected children. It presents major findings of the third cycle (data are collected every five years) of the CIS, with analysis of data on child maltreatment reported to and investigated by child welfare agencies in Canada.

UNICEF. 2006. World Report on Violence against Children. New York: UNICEF. At: www.unicef.org/violencestudy/reports.html. This report is the product of the first comprehensive global attempt to describe the scale and impact of violence against children. It approaches the issue of abuse from a combined human rights, public health, and child protection perspective. It argues that violence is a complex problem that takes many forms, and calls for more attention and a multisectoral response.

Websites

Children's Hospital of Eastern Ontario—Child and Youth Abuse
www.cheo.on.ca/en/childyouthabuse

This website contains links to resources on child abuse, including books and pamphlets on physical, sexual, and psychological abuse of children and youth. It also provides links to services and websites for parents and children.

Child Welfare League of Canada (CWLC)
www.cwlc.ca/

The CWLC is a national organization dedicated to promoting the well-being and protection of vulnerable young people. The CWLC promotes best practices among those in the field of child welfare, children's mental health, and youth justice. The website contains links to research and policy initiatives, as well as to other organizations committed to the care and protection of children and youth.

Department of Justice—Family Violence Initiative
www.justice.gc.ca/eng/cj-jp/fv-vf/about-apropos.html

The Department of Justice website contains an entire section on family violence, which includes definitions of abuse, mistreatment, and neglect of children (and adults) at the hands of other members of their family. It provides access to the Family Violence Initiative, which aims to reduce family violence in Canada, as well as access to a pamphlet on spanking, outlining recent court decisions surrounding section 43 of the Criminal Code of Canada, and fact sheets on spousal violence, family violence, child abuse, elder abuse, dating violence, and sexual abuse and exploitation of children.

Ontario Association of Children's Aid Societies (OACAS)
www.oacas.org/

As the self-proclaimed voice of child welfare in Ontario, the OACAS has represented Children's Aid Societies in Ontario since 1912. It provides services in the areas of government relations, communications, information management, education, and training to advocate for the protection and well-being of children. The website contains information on locating one of the 46 Children's Aid Societies in Ontario, as well as a series of publications and documents on child welfare.

Repeal 43 Committee
www.repeal43.org
> The Repeal 43 Committee is a national, voluntary committee of lawyers, pediatricians, social workers, and educators formed in 1994 to advocate repeal of section 43 of the Criminal Code. The site contains an annotated list of selected Canadian studies on corporal punishment, section 43, and child abuse. American, British, and other research can also be accessed through websites linked to this site.

Royal Canadian Mounted Police—Online Child Sexual Exploitation
www.rcmp-grc.gc.ca/ncecc-cncee/index-accueil-eng.htm
> The National Child Exploitation Coordination Centre (NCECC) is a part of Canada's National Police Services. It was created to help protect children from online sexual exploitation. This site provides links to legislation and an overview of key cases in Canada. It also provides a link to research, tips to parents, and a database of missing children.

13 The Disappearance of Childhood?

Learning Objectives

◎ To consider the claim that we are seeing the disappearance of childhood.

◎ To deconstruct what is assumed by the "disappearance of childhood" hypothesis.

◎ To critically assess the notion of "the good old days" of childhood innocence.

◎ To think about "tweening," and the sexualization and commodification of children.

◎ To consider what recent critical thinkers and proponents of children's rights have been saying about the "disappearance of childhood" hypothesis.

◎ To recall that childhood is a social construct and assess what this implies.

◎ To review some of the key themes in this book.

Introduction

In 1982 an author by the name of Neil Postman made headlines by publishing a book called *The Disappearance of Childhood*. The book resonated with popular audiences as it tapped into mass fears that children and childhood today are not like, and worse than, children and childhood in the past because television has turned adult secrets of sex and violence into popular entertainment accessible to children. (Imagine what he would have said about the Internet!) It implied, on one level, that in the not-so-distant past there was a "golden age" of childhood that today is being eroded—stolen by new technology found in modern life. Some of you, like many of my own students at the beginning of my Sociology of Childhood course, may now be nodding in agreement,[1] but let's explore this further. This chapter will present an overview of Postman's hypothesis. The chapter will then raise questions about whether we have reason to worry when we see the advent of the "tween" or the seemingly increasingly sexualized child and commodification of childhood.

Following this is a presentation of views that critically deconstruct some of the assumptions of the disappearance hypothesis. Various thinkers and children's rights activists show us that the hypothesis, while popular, contains a number of shortcomings, particularly when viewed from a children's rights perspective. We will consider again the implications of childhood being a social construct. We conclude by encouraging you to take a more assertive and progressive stand in understanding, including, studying, and theorizing children and childhood.

The Disappearance of Childhood Hypothesis

In *The Disappearance of Childhood* and in a subsequent book, *Building Bridges to the Eighteenth Century* (1999), Postman,[2] like Ariès (1962) before him, argued that the "idea of childhood did not exist in the medieval world" (Postman, 1982: 17). He explained that this was the result of the "absence of literacy, the absence of the idea of education and the absence of the idea of shame" (ibid.). He explained that in pre-industrial societies, before the advent of the printing press, all human communication occurred in a social or oral context; children's lives and adult lives were one, as both worked, both struggled, both lived in close confines, and both were illiterate. Postman states that "that is why there had been no need for the idea of childhood, for everyone shared the same information environment and therefore lived in the same social and intellectual world" (ibid., 36).

Postman argues that we saw the rise of childhood with the rise of the printing press, resulting in the rise of books, literacy, and education, because with the printed book, "another tradition began: the isolated reader and his private eye" (ibid., 27). He explains, "the Literate Man had been created. And in his coming, he left behind the children," adding that "from that point onward, adulthood had to be earned . . . the young would have to *become* adults, and they would have to do it by learning to read" (ibid., 36). Thus, with the rise of books, literacy, and education, the lives of children and adults became increasingly differentiated, with childhood becoming a prolonged apprenticeship towards adulthood. Adults and children increasingly spent time in different worlds, and so developed different symbolic cultures with significantly different sets of expectations. The task of the adult and the role of childhood were to prepare the child for the management of the adult symbolic world. But almost in the same breath and paragraph, Postman adds that "the seeds of childhood's end were being planted" (ibid., 51). Interestingly, some, like Quill (2011), have argued that after the latest electronic turn, we are seeing a disappearance of adulthood as the conception of citizenship grows impoverished, the fundamental connection between education and employment unravels, and education becomes increasingly scrutinized and redefined by cost-effectiveness and value-for-money.

Postman laments that 12- and 13-year-old girls are among the highest paid models in America, that children's clothing has disappeared, and that "even the idea of children's games appears to be slipping from our grasp" (ibid., 3–4). The main culprit, he argues, is television. He postulated that with the rise of television and a changing communications environment, the information hierarchy collapsed, the rigours of a literate education became irrelevant, and children's worlds were no longer protected from adult secrets. He explains that accessing the visual images on television required no preparation or prerequisite training, and as a result the distinction between child and adult became less necessary and obvious. "Children see everything it shows" (ibid., 84), and so "the elders can no longer be relied on as a source of knowledge for the young" (ibid., 89). In being exposed to adult secrets via television, coincidentally, "children develop what may be called adult attitudes—from cynicism to indifference" (ibid., 95). He concludes that innocence is impossible to sustain, and so we are left with the adult child, at first, and next, with the disappearance of childhood. He exclaims that television makes childhood neither desirable nor necessary.[3]

More recently, Kehily (2010) noted that in 2006 a national newspaper in the United Kingdom launched a campaign to halt the "death of childhood." The campaign, "Hold on to Childhood," was supported by academics, writers, and medical experts. Their letter in the *Daily Telegraph* explained that children have been "tainted" by overexposure to electronic media, lack of space to play, and an overemphasis on academic testing in schools (Kehily, 2010; see also Palmer, 2005).

An Illusory Golden Age of Innocence?

When I ask my students, "Are kids today like you when you were a child?" most reply in the negative. Some state that "kids today are mouthy," "they act like adults," "they are less obedient" or "less good" than my students claim to have been as children. Oddly, many find themselves close to uttering such statements like, "in the good old days, when I was a child." And this makes some pause and ponder: "Oh no, I sound like my parents." This is an almost inevitable outcome of Postman's argument, which carries the assumption that while childhood is *now* tainted, tarnished, or destroyed by television, there was a time of childhood innocence that is disappearing before our eyes. He implies that there was a golden age of the child and childhood when children happily and safely enjoyed their separate culture and worlds, before television came along and snatched it from them.

We fear and bemoan the loss of innocence, and loss of a golden age of childhood, but *when* exactly did this age exist? When were children safe from violence, from physical punishment, from domestic conflict? Safe to play freely in the streets? Safe from poverty and from discrimination? Safe from the stigma of being a child whose parents divorced or from sexism and sexual abuse? Safe from the isolation and discrimination that results from the stigma associated with having a disability (see Box 13.1)? Were Aboriginal children safe and carefree in residential schools? We need also to reflect on whether we believe it is wrong that some children today are aware of some of their rights, and refuse to be talked down to, spanked, or marginalized, and whether we believe it is wrong for children today to know more than we did when we were kids. Is ignorance truly equivalent to bliss? Must ignorance and innocence go hand in hand?

Postman's hypothesis is simply unsubstantiated and seemingly ideologically driven. Buckingham (1998: 558), for example, condemns Postman as a technological determinist, who appears to "offer little more than a form of anguished conservatism, a nostalgia for an illusory golden age in which childhood remained unsullied by the corrupting force of the electronic media."

In his critique of the "loss of innocence" thesis, Henry Giroux (1998) explains that the myth of innocence not only erases the complexities of childhood and the wide range of experiences children encounter, but also offers an excuse for adults to evade responsibility for how children are constrained

---

Box 13.1   Editorial Published by the Office of the Provincial Advocate for Children and Youth, 23 September 2014.

Demographic profile

Children aged 5 to 14 have a disability rate of 4.6%. Across Canada, 174 810 children between the ages of 5 and 14 have an identified disability. As children enter the school system, barriers and challenges are more likely to be encountered and disability is more likely to be identified. Whereas only four specific disability types were identified for children aged 0 to 4, nine specific disability types are identified for children aged 5 to 14. The five additional types measured are emotional/psychological, communication and learning disabilities and disabilities related to agility and mobility.

The most common types of disability reported for children aged 5 to 14 are chronic conditions and learning and/or communication limitations. Boys were more likely to experience each of these disability types than were girls, in addition to most other types of disability as well...

...Among children aged 5 to 14 with disabilities, 57.6% have mild to moderate disabilities and 42.4% have severe to very severe disabilities.

As children grow older, they encounter more areas of life where they may experience disadvantage. As is the case with children aged 0 to 4, the majority of parents of older children with disabilities reported their child is at a disadvantage in home life and at play, but now also report that their child can be at a disadvantage at school and in other areas. 77.4% of parents reported their child was at a disadvantage in life at school, and 44.3% reported their child was at a disadvantage in areas such as transportation or leisure...

Education

Access to the education system is one of the most important issues for older children with disabilities. Among children with disabilities aged 5 to 14, 94.0% attend school. Of

and affected by political, social, cultural, and economic institutions run by adults. He adds that the notion of childhood innocence also makes children invisible as social agents and real people, except as projections of adult fantasies about childhood, a nostalgic reflection on the part of adults over the disappearance of their own childhood as they age (Vanobbergen, 2004) or else a last source of enchantment in an otherwise disenchanted world (Beck, 1992; Duschinsky, 2013). These fantasies of childhood innocence allow adults to ignore the fact that children suffer from adult greed, power, and recklessness so often found in adult policies and practice (Giroux, 1998; Livingstone, 2009; Hill, 2011).

Giroux states that the notion of innocence emerges less as a way of highlighting the disappearance of childhood than as a metaphor for advancing

---

children aged 5 to 14 with a disability, 90 590 attend mainstream schools with no special education classes, 55 650 attend mainstream schools with at least some special education classes and 12 880 attend special education schools.

Disability severity can have an impact on what type of school children with disabilities attend. Among those who attend mainstream or special schools, 14.5% of children with severe or very severe disabilities attend special schools, while only 3.0% of children with mild or moderate disabilities attend special schools.

In addition to special education classes, many schools throughout Canada now practice inclusive education, where children who have special education requirements are able to participate fully in regular classroom settings with the help of aides such as tutors:

- 35 100 children with disabilities who attend only regular classes have tutors or teachers' aides;
- 10 470 children who attend only regular classes have note-takers or readers;
- 4 020 receive attendant care;
- 3 480 use talking books.

Children with disabilities are in general reported to be doing well at school. 73.9% of parents report that their children did average, well or very well on their latest report card.

Schoolyard violence can be a reality for children with disabilities. 30.1% of parents of school-aged children with disabilities reported their child had been physically assaulted or attacked by another child at school within the twelve months prior to being surveyed. Disability severity is a significant factor with respect to violence: for children with severe or very severe disabilities, the reported rate of assault by other children is 38.2%.

Source: Office of the Provincial Advocate for Children and Youth of Ontario. 2014 Report to the Legislature. Toronto: Office of the Provincial Advocate for Children and Youth of Ontario, 2014. Print.

a conservative political agenda aimed at promoting "family values" and the views and goals of dominant, Western, capitalist ideology.[4] Through this political and ideological prism, innocence is not only selective about which children are endangered and deserving of help and "protection," but it is also used to signal who and what constitutes the threat (ibid.). As you might expect, the finger of blame is never pointing in the direction of political and economic powers, which have failed to provide children with a voice, space, or resources necessary to advance their well-being, but at individual pathology—the few bad apples, molesters, or corruptors that immorally threaten "innocent children." Giroux, like Livingstone (2009), Hill (2011), Egan (2013), and Hawkes and Dune (2013) more recently, however, does not deny that children are increasingly subjected to social and economic forces that exploit them through sexualization, commodification, and commercialization.

Are Children Growing Up Too Fast? Tweening, Sexualization, and the Commodification of Childhood

A very brief, popular piece by Cynthia Kopkowski (2008) captures the views and fears of a number of adults working with, or observing, (mostly female) children today. In "Lolita in the Classroom," an epistle lamenting the sexualization and looming disappearance of girlhood, Kopkowski suggests that "maybe it was when stores began stocking thongs embroidered with 'wink wink' in sizes for 7- to 10-year-olds, to be covered by sweatpants with 'Juicy' stitched across the rear. That's about the time it became apparent that there is less sand in the hourglass for girlhood than there used to be" (ibid., 36). Kopkowski recommends that teachers lead by example by dressing appropriately (read conservatively), while at the same time supporting the introduction of dress codes in schools and seminars for parents. In short, she implies that we return sex to the bedroom, where it belongs—hidden, mystified, and taboo, inevitably arousing children's interest all the more.[5]

This critique is not meant to undermine research that has linked the sexualization of children, and especially girls, to eating disorders, depression, and low self-esteem (American Psychological Association Task Force on the Sexualization of Girls, 2007),[6] but Kopkowski's own invoking of Lolita, the fictional, sexualized child character in the 1955 novel by Vladimir Nabokov, must lead us to ask, when were children *not* sexualized? And beyond this, when were children ever not curious about sex?

Middle girlhood, because of its ambiguity regarding sexuality, maturity, and gender, has become a site for discourse about lost childhood (Cook and Kaiser, 2004; Livingstone, 2009; Hill, 2011; Egan, 2013; Hawkes and Dune; 2013). Cook and Kaiser, drawing on trade discourses from the children's clothing industry, interviews with children, and views of children's market observers, demonstrate that the "tween" has been constructed and maintained as an ambiguous, gendered, and age-delineated marketing and merchandising category.[7] They add that the notion of the "tween" cannot be fully understood "apart from its inception in and articulation with the market exigencies" of girlhood (ibid., 204). They explain that the term "tween" appeared in 1987 in an article by Carol Hall in a marketing journal to describe a market made up of children ages 9–15. By 1998, the term was entrenched in marketing circles, yet it is not a term youth themselves use or may even know (ibid.). And while tweening involves the sexualization of girls (as objects of the sexual gaze and in anticipation of girls' sexual personae), Cook and Kaiser note that it also allows girls to exhibit agency in their appropriation of style, and this inevitably evokes uncertainty and fear in some adults. Parents, for one, have had reason to fear and feel discomfort with this, as have those who are increasingly critical of and concerned with the commodification of childhood.

Livingstone (2009) notes that childhood is undergoing a radical transformation in ways that are complex and multifaceted. The reality is that "childhood" has always been dynamic, but children and tweens today are indeed complex. For example, Jackson et al. (2013) examined 71 narratives from a media video diary component of a "tween" popular culture project. They assessed how engaged or disengaged tween girls were from postfeminist identities promoted via "girlie" and "sexy" clothing. They found a fluidity of girls' subjectivities—tween girls in some instances positioned themselves in media-influenced discourses of girlhood femininity, and at other times as critical consumers, rejecting the marketing ploys and "sexy" identifiers that they are constantly bombarded with (see Box 13.2).

Box 13.2   "The Whole Playboy Mansion Image": Girls' Negotiating "Sexy" Clothing

A New Zealand study, examining narratives extracted from a media video diary component of a "tween" popular culture project with 71 preteen girls, found girls' positioning around sexiness complex and negotiated. Girls were both profoundly influenced by the media but at the same time critical of it. For example, one 13-year-old girl's video diary contained a narrative about her purchase of a "Playboy bunny" duvet. She told researchers, "Ooh, here's my Playboy be-ed! Playboy! [zooming in on bed] Makes me feel much more grown up!"

On the other hand, researchers found girls to be cautious about identifying with products that frame them as sexual. For example, as 12-year-old Elodie, expressed,

Continued

a lot of girls at my school are influenced by the whole [contemptuous expression] Playboy Mansion image, that whole miniskirts and tank-tops and crap [exasperated laugh]. It's, it's sick, like, it's seriously sick! Like the whole (puts on a "bimbo" voice) "I wanna impress guys so I'm gonna wear a padded bra today!" Or, or "I'm gonna make up my face so I look prettier for the guys today." And the guys are not at the [makes quotation marks] mature status that we're at right now and so obviously, they're still kids . . . I mean they wouldn't notice any kind of that stuff (Jackson et al., 2013: 153).

Jackson et al. conclude by suggesting,

as do Renold and Ringrose (2011) in their discussion of "schizoid subjectivities," that these "pushes and pulls" organise around the requirement to negotiate contradicting girlhood femininity discourses that constitute them as passive and asexual on the one hand ("media influence"/"child innocence") and "savvy," agentic and "sexy" on the other ("postfeminist discourse"). Examining the girls' narratives here we have not ended up at a place of "influenced" passivity or "agentic" savvy-ness, but a more nuanced point where neither possibility is straightforward. Rather, the binary is complicated: we found "agency" embedded in regulatory discourses, "influenced" selves rubbing up against "savvy" ones, "sexy" identities being both refused and carefully negotiated. Girls' social identities as middle class "tween-children" worked with and through discursive constructions of the binary, establishing boundaries of appropriateness around age and sexuality that constrained possibilities for girls' embodied identities. Indeed, we must underline the specificity of our findings to the particular pre-teen age and social class of the girls, as well as to their location in a New Zealand culture that both shares much in common with Anglo-American societies but also has its own unique features. (2013: 157)

Source: Jackson et al. (2013).

Vanobbergen (2004), like many others, confirms that within the last couple of decades we have seen the rapid rise of a consumer childhood, with retailers becoming more child-oriented and promotional activities aimed at more and younger children. The commodification of childhood has included convincing parents that they need to have or to purchase specific goods and services for "normal" child development (see Cook, 2004) and convincing children that they have power and choice, as arbiters of their own identities and fashions.

McKendrick et al. (2000), while writing on the commercialization of children's play space, make an important observation about the commodification of childhood in general. They conclude that new commercial endeavours, like commercial playgrounds, are primarily about satisfying adult needs (for themselves, and with respect to how they want their children to play), rather than about the needs, desires, and choices of children. Marketers have also been keenly aware of the growing power of peer influence in children's purchases (Murray, 2005). Because of the incredible purchasing power of children, preteens, and parents (because of or on behalf of children), and the big business of children's dress and play, we may never see the disappearance of childhood. We certainly don't see evidence of it in advertising targeting children or in the ever-growing marketing strategies that have developed online.

Are we not right back to Postman's condemnation of television, advertising, the new media, and the changing information environment? As Hoikkala et al. (1987) remark, Postman does not consider electronic media, including television, to be instruments of social control, but instead, simply a threat to values, norms, and traditions. "Postman is not a social critic; he is a moral technologist" (ibid., 93). Hoikkala et al. explain that Postman relies on a single theoretical tool—the changing information environment—ignoring that the information environment is always set in a social and cultural context, audiences are differentiated, and children's lives differ according to variations in their age, sex, and living environments. Postman treats television as being separate from the world, people, and interests that control it. Postman asks, "What do the media do to people?" Others suggest that we ask, "What do people do with the media?" (ibid.).

In contrast to Postman, some, like Herbert Marcuse, have tried to show that we should pay more attention to capitalists' dependency on television and advertising to create and deliver an ever-mounting number of false needs in order to sells more goods. Marcuse (1964: 7–8) reminds us that "free choice among a wide variety of goods or services does not signify freedom, if these goods and services sustain social controls over a life of toil and fear." He adds that the indoctrinating power of the media did not start, nor will it end, with the mass production or decline of television. With billions of dollars to be made, the commodification of childhood is but part of a larger picture that includes the infantilization of adulthood, which is accompanied by notions of instant gratification and adult indulgence in the purchase of their own "toys" (in the form of electronic gadgets, fancy cars, etc.).

As we saw in Chapter 6, children's purchasing power and power over adult purchases—"kidfluence"—are simply too massive to allow childhood to disappear. So, if childhood is not being annihilated by the media, why are Postman and others so fearful and morally outraged? Hoikkala et al. (1987) argue that more than anything else, it is plausible that Postman, like many others, actually dreaded the prospect of adults losing control over children.

Deconstructing and Debunking the Disappearance Hypothesis

Children's rights advocates are not a new breed. In fact, Postman's (1982) book includes a section in which he is critical of the Children's Rights Movement. He notes that under this banner there are two separate movements: one that he seemingly approves of, which believes that childhood is desirable and fragile and in need of protection, and another that he does not, which includes the conception of children's rights that reject adult control over children. He calls this second position "reactionary," and in part blames it for contributing to some of the disappearance of childhood, by promoting the idea that children don't have to earn the right to adulthood.

James et al. (1998) are very likely the type that Postman would have placed in his second "reactionary" camp—the camp that questions and rejects adult control over children. James et al. have criticized the notion of separating children from adults and situating them in an autonomous world of their own ("children's culture," "children's play," "children's spaces"), as this exoticizes and "others" children, and decontextualizes their social worlds and relationships. Separating children into their own world, or lamenting the loss of children's separate and "innocent" world, also assumes that these separate "children's worlds" have not themselves been constructed and constrained by adults. James et al. remind us that this "separate worlds/separate sphere" approach inevitably leads to moralizing discourses about lost, stolen, or disappearing childhoods, threatened or invaded by adults. In other words, in talking about children as separate, helpless, and different, we also inevitably end up in discussions about "child protection" rather than about child empowerment. Children are not a homogeneous mass, and are neither sweet, innocent, and naive nor simply mini-adults. Stasiulis (2002: 511) notes that

> underlying virtually all analyses of lost or stolen childhood is a discourse on the "innocence" and "vulnerability" of childhood with a complex and contradictory genealogy that layers among others: the Romantic sentimental exaltation of children, Evangelical alarmism concerning the corrupt nature of children, and American Progressive Era celebration of childhood freedom and advocacy for adult supervision.

She believes that the implementation of the United Nations (UN) Convention on the Rights of the Child, which has advanced a model of active citizenry for children, has been obstructed by these still dominant Western notions that fetishize childhood innocence and passivity.

Given the tenacity of this discourse, Stasiulis puts forth an alternative model of children's citizenship that seeks to implement the participation rights of children and supports a view of children as empowered, knowledgeable, compassionate, and global citizens, but at the same time recognizes that children are marginalized and in need of group-differentiated protections (like other marginalized groups, avoiding the conventional victimization of children; also see Lansdown et al., 2014).

Like Stasiulis, Moosa-Mitha (2005) notes that while "the rights revolution" is a central feature of modern political consciousness, children and children's rights have not been taken seriously in theories and practice of citizenship. She is critical of the normative practices and assumptions, built on real and constructed differences between adults and children, which continue to marginalize and exclude children's citizenship rights. According to Moosa-Mitha, by pushing aside myths of childhood innocence, and its loss, we can move towards a more difference-centred approach and understanding of children's rights and citizenship, which involves recognizing that children are not adults, nor are they simply not-yet adults; and that children themselves are different from one another.

Childhood Still a Social Construct

Childhood, as we personally experienced it and as we as a society have known it, has been and is changing (see Livingstone, 2009). You are probably not incorrect in thinking that children today are different from you as a child. You can probably also expect that children of the future are likely to say the same about those who came before them. This should come as no surprise because culture is malleable and ever changing, as are the institutions, objects, and concepts that compose it—including childhood. But also, and importantly, people change as they grow up and take on some of the responsibilities of adulthood.

One of Postman's underlying assumptions is that as a social construct, if childhood can be created, it can also be destroyed. On the other hand, we may want to conceive of childhood as always having existed, because children have always existed, only dynamically taking on different shapes and forms across cultures and history, and within and across subcultures within any one culture and time. To deny this would be to deny every adult his or her past, which many nostalgically cling to in their own personal conceptions of loss of innocence and childhood.

In recognizing this, we should also note that in any given culture and point in time, we are really talking about childhoods, as race, gender, class, family and immigration status, and many other factors intersect to result in diverse lived experiences. Adults cannot assume that because they know their own childhood they know all children and all childhoods; they need to involve children themselves in the deconstruction, understanding, and (re)construction of their unique worlds. We can better acknowledge their abilities and strengths, legitimize their experiences, and give them the power and voice to reasonably participate in civil society.

Conclusion

R. Gordon Kelly (1974) pointed out that studying childhood and the culture surrounding it provides crucial insights into core values and practices of a society. While there is still a long way to go to fight sexism, racism, classism, ableism, etc. among adults, we have at least made attempts to recognize that these inequalities in power and treatment exist. We have also paid some attention to "ageism" as it applies to aging Canadians marginalized by discriminatory policies and practices such as mandatory retirement. But we continue to conceptualize and treat children as "less-thans" and "not-yets," as needy, powerless, and incapable—patiently waiting, in an apprenticeship towards adulthood. In Canada, adults continue to be allowed to physically discipline children, even though they are not allowed to physically discipline each other. Adults are allowed to sever their relationships with each other, but children are not allowed to do the same to adults. Adults are granted the right to "do" while children are expected to "wait" and be "done to."

We have allowed adults to mystify, ideologize, and define childhood in ways that make sense to and benefit themselves. This has made it possible for goods producers, advertisers, and retailers, as well as service providers, policy-makers, and politicians, to manipulate and marginalize children for adult purposes. When relegated the status of "special," children have been disempowered and marginalized. In keeping children "othered" and powerless, we have allowed adults, no matter how powerless themselves, to have control over them.

It would be simplistic to believe that the growing attention placed on the "power" of the child consumer is anything but smoke and mirrors, and it has very little to do with gains in children's rights. Children continue to play very marginal roles in real decision-making. As Marcuse (1964) has reminded us, free choice among a range of goods does not signify freedom if exercising that "choice" effectively maintains control over other aspects of our lives.

Western culture has used ideas within developmental psychology and democratic notions of "free choice" to market goods to children, allowing them to circumvent parental control over purchases (Cook, 2004), but we rarely have allowed this to move beyond material possessions—into granting them rights and choice in other matters that affect their lives. So, if in the marketplace children have been allowed to act as arbiters of their own fashions (Cook, 2004), why not in other aspects of everyday life?

Because children cannot formally participate in governing and larger decision-making, most of the world's countries have ratified the Convention on the Rights of the Child and have made a commitment to meeting children's needs, protecting them from violence and abuse, and allowing them to play a more active role in community life. Many countries, including Canada, continue to routinely violate the Convention through their actions and inactions. Governments need to be held accountable.

What does studying children and childhood teach us? It teaches us that the social world is very complex. What is obvious and before our eyes—like the seemingly plausible argument that childhood is disappearing as a consequence of consumerism and the media, or that childhood is threatened by children's rights activists—is not simple and easy to understand. By accepting the obvious are we missing the deeper and more complex reality? Studying children also reminds us that we need to dig deeper, ask critical questions, and reach beyond what seem to be obvious and common-sense assumptions and observations of the world. We are reminded in all this to critically ask *cui godet* (Latin for "who benefits"). We should also remember to ask what children think, how they experience their worlds, and how best we can help them navigate their social spaces before we jump to conclusions and create more rules and less freedom.

Canadian sociology can learn much about our society through a better understanding of children and childhood. Children need to be thought of as citizens, rights-bearers, and autonomous, thinking beings. There is much work yet to be done in this area—but this may bode well for you, the future scholars, activists, parents, teachers, policy-makers, and service providers working with and for children in this country.

Questions for Critical Thought

1. Are children today like you were when you were a child? What do you think accounts for differences, if any?

2. Why do you think Neil Postman's hypothesis has popular appeal? Are you convinced by his argument? Why or why not?

3. Should children be protected from the adult world? What should we protect them from—sex? violence? consumerism? individualism? How would/should we do that?

4. Is there such a thing as too many rights? Explain your answer.

5. What is the single most important thing that you have learned from this book? How do you anticipate it will affect your behaviour and future practice?

Suggested Readings

Egan, R. Danielle. 2013. *Becoming Sexual: A Critical Appraisal of the Sexualization of Girls.* Cambridge: Polity Press. Egan notes that we have seen a rise in moral panics regarding children, and particularly tween-aged girls, who have been presented as innocent, vulnerable, *and* dangerous. Egan's aim is to "complicate" reductionist thinking on the sexual child. She argues that the evidence underlying the fears that fuel anti-sexualization arguments is meagre and based on personal opinions. The voices of children, and especially girls, are also ignored.

Epstein, D., M.J. Kehily, and E. Renold. 2012. "Culture, policy and the un/marked child: fragments of the sexualisation debates," *Gender and Education* 24 (3): 249–54. The editors of *Gender and Education* have published a special issue devoted to public debates driven by concerns over the premature sexualization of children, as part of a wider fear that childhood is in crisis. This introduction pulls together a multiplicity of ideas generated by responses to the sexualization of girls.

Postman, Neil. 1982. *The Disappearance of Childhood*. New York: Vintage Books. Postman suggests that childhood is a relatively recent and quickly disappearing social invention. He explains that it came to be with the rise of the printing press, literacy, and education, but began its downward spiral and disappearance with the rise of television. Using psychology, history, McLuhanology, and common sense, Postman, in simple language and style, writes to convince his readers that almost without obstruction childhood will "continue on its journey to oblivion." (1982: 150)

Websites

Canadian Children's Rights Council
www.canadiancrc.com/index.aspx

The Canadian Children's Rights Council is a nonprofit educational and advocacy organization concerned with Canadian children's human rights and responsibilities. Its website contains links to the UN Convention on the Rights of the Child and various other UN documents and study results, and includes information and links to sources on child poverty in Canada.

Defence for Children International—Canada
www.dci-canada.org/

Defence for Children International (DCI) is a worldwide movement in support of children's rights. Founded in Geneva, Switzerland, in 1979 (the International Year of the Child), DCI is an independent, grassroots organization that played a significant role in the creation and ratification of the UN Convention on the Rights of the Child. This website contains links to international news, events, and political campaigns that are linked to children's rights.

Office of the Provincial Advocate for Children and Youth—Ontario
www.provincialadvocate.on.ca

The Office of the Provincial Advocate for Children and Youth was established in 2007 to promote the voice of children and youth in Ontario. In 2008 the Legislature of Ontario appointed Irwin Elman as the new Provincial Advocate. The duty of the Office is to provide a voice for children and youth and to educate Ontarians on the rights of children and youth. This website contains information about the services it provides and children's rights in the province.

Notes

Chapter 1

1. Rousseau writes on "Sophy" as well as "Emile" (a popular boy's name in France), in Book 4 of *Emile*. He opens by saying that "Sophy should be as truly a woman as Emile is a man.... But for her sex, a woman is a man; she has the same organs, the same needs, the same faculties. The machine is the same in its construction; its parts, its working, and its appearance are similar. Regard it as you will the difference is only in degree" (Rousseau, 1974 [1762]: 321).
2. Ironically, Rousseau and his lifelong companion, Therese Levasseur, abandoned their own five children at the Paris orphanage soon after their births.
3. We should be careful to note that there are hundreds of culturally diverse groups across Africa; there has been a tendency among Western academics to inaccurately talk about Africa as culturally homogeneous.
4. My goal is not to undermine human rights and the work of humanitarian organizations, but rather to demonstrate the variability in views surrounding age and childhood.

Chapter 2

1. Human ethologists (those who study animal behaviour to better understand human behaviour) like John Bowlby (1969), for example, believed that children display a variety of preprogrammed behaviours that help individuals to survive.
2. There are also interactionist theories of socialization, feminist theories of socialization, class-based theories of socialization, etc. See Handel et al. (2007) and Wyness (2006).
3. Some have argued that part of the problem in implementing the CRC is related to Canada's political organization. Canada is a federation of provinces (10) and territories (three), within which the federal government is responsible for the development and maintenance of the national body through its control of foreign policy, defence, citizenship and immigration, currency, trade and commerce, criminal law, and the administration of the lives of Canada's First Nations who are governed and recognized by the Indian Act. The provinces, since Confederation, have retained control of the preservation of regional differences and the functioning of everyday life through their control of education, social services (social welfare), health care, labour regulations and standards (minimum wage, etc.), language rights, and the regular administration of the criminal justice system. While there have been efforts to maintain "universal," cross-Canada standards (such as in health care), this has amounted to a patchwork of policies and practices across the country that makes studying something like "childhood in Canada" very difficult and implementing Canada-wide reforms virtually impossible. These jurisdictional complexities have been identified as part of the problem when implementing policies and programs aimed at assisting children and in fulfilling Canada's international obligations.

Chapter 3

1. For example, Cait (2005) writes about how the death of a parent when young women were between the ages of 11 and 17 affected their identity development later in life; Teram et al. (2005) speak to female survivors of child sexual abuse.

2. Orellana (2001: 367) declared that "their daily experiences are not simply preparation for the future, when they can begin 'productive' lives, and they are not problems to be diagnosed and fixed."
3. For a copy of the questions, see www.statcan.ca/english/sdds/instrument/4450_Q2_V5_E.pdf, which is published by Statistics Canada (2006).
4. Morgan et al. (2002) found focus groups to be an effective way of engaging 7-to 11-year-old children in discussions about their experiences of living with asthma.

Chapter 4

1. Fridkin and Kenney (2007), in a study of boys' and girls' views of politics, found a gender gap in policy and partisanship among eighth-grade students—a product of gender differences during early childhood socialization.
2. For example, Lareau's (2000) model was tested in child care settings by Nelson and Schutz (2007), who found that children raised by "concerted cultivation" were less accustomed to managing their own time and interactions, while children raised according to the "natural growth" model developed skills at entertaining themselves and demonstrated social competence with children of many different ages.
3. Authoritative parenting is not to be confused with **authoritarian parenting**, which is typically associated with low acceptance of children (children should be seen and not heard, few rights, low responsiveness on the part of parents) and high levels of control (many rules and obedience is strictly enforced).

Chapter 5

1. Private, independent, and home schooling options are available in all provinces and territories as long as they meet the general standards prescribed in the jurisdiction (Statistics Canada, 1996).
2. For example, see Robert McIntosh's (2003) work on educating boys of the Nova Scotia coal mines.
3. For example, see Tim Stanley's (2003) work on Chinese schooling and segregation in Victoria.
4. For example, see Theodore Rand's (2003) work on schooling in Nova Scotia. Also see Davey (2003).
5. The last residential school closed in 1996 (Dickason with McNab, 2009: 312).
6. According to Davis and Moore (1945) every society has and needs social stratification (inequality, layering of people along class lines), as it needs to differently motivate, place, and reward individuals within the social structure. Davis and Moore imply that the most highly rewarded (most highly paid, in most cases) in any society are those who have the most skills, have sacrificed the most (more years of schooling, for example), or are willing to fill the most important or most difficult positions in any society. They also assume we all start off on a level playing field, and those who are the most motivated, hard-working, talented, etc. are the ones most likely to achieve success and rewards—underscoring the existence of a meritocracy.
7. A 2001 Participation and Activity Limitation Survey (PALS) estimated that 155,000 Canadian children between the ages of 5 and 14 (about 4 per cent of all children in this age group) have some form of activity limitation (physical, cognitive, or emotional disability or chronic condition) (Kohen et al., 2007). This number varied across provinces,

from a low of 2.5 per cent in Quebec to a high of 4.8 per cent in Alberta and Nova Scotia. Of these 155,000, about 38 per cent were receiving special education services in 2001. According to Statistics Canada data, males account for almost two-thirds of all elementary school special needs students. Children from low socioeconomic status families and from single-parent families are also more likely to be overrepresented among children requiring special education (Bohatyretz and Lipps, 1999).

8. George Dei has written extensively on race and schooling and has noted that we often associate "at risk," "dropout," and "disadvantaged" with black/African-Canadian children in the public school system. He recently called for a revisioning of public schools to (1) introduce a more effective method of teaching diverse youth; (2) create spaces where the needs of the most disadvantaged are seriously and concretely addressed; (3) promote schools with strong community ties; and (4) help learners build their self, collective, and cultural identities within an environment of excellence (Dei, 2008: 346).

9. For example, Schopenhauer (1987), writing in the 1800s, said that women were "mental myopics" (mentally short-sighted, and incapable of profound and worldly thought).

10. Women who were "hysterical" (or thought to be overstepping traditional gender roles and boundaries) at times underwent hysterectomy on the belief that the womb controlled the mind and its removal would end the hysteria; this is why we still call the surgical removal of a woman's womb a "hysterectomy."

11. Swain's work also showed that whereas neither the boys nor the girls at Highwoods (the private, upper-class school) and Petersfield (the public, middle-class school) were teased for working hard or achieving high academic performance, girls at Westmoor Abbey (the public, working-class school) were maligned and disparaged just as much as boys if they were thought to be either working too hard or attaining (academically) too much.

12. They also note that gender has much less influence on academic performance than do other background characteristics such as socioeconomic status and race (Gilbert and Gilbert, 1998).

13. Chen and French (2008) remind us that there are cultural variations when it comes to children's normative social competence. For example, different societies place different value on social initiative and shyness; the meaning of developmental patterns associated with social functioning varies by culture; peer involvement and function vary by culture; socialization goals and practices (including those by and with peers) also vary by culture.

14. They also identify key features of friendship across developmental stages. For example, infants and toddlers reflect interest in peers by looking, smiling, touching, and showing a desire to be near a preferred social partner; older toddlers typically display mutual affect, engage in coordinated social play, and may exclude other children who may try to join in the play; pre-kindergartners are likely to have at least one friend they can name, are more likely to have stable friendships, and are more likely to engage in "we talk" ("we're making a tunnel together"); children in early elementary grades spend a significant amount of time with their friends and seek proximity, and turn to friends as an important source of instrumental and emotional support (Buysse et al., 2008).

15. For research on romantic relationships, see Thorne and Luria (1986); Thorne (1993); Epstein (1997); Adler and Adler (1998); Renold (2000).

16. A study of peer comforting strategies, designed to measure the kind of social support children give each other, found that companionship was the most positively evaluated strategy tested (others included sympathy, advice, account giving/explaining the event, minimization, and optimism (Clark et al., 2008).

Chapter 7

1. Although I critique developmental theories for their rigidity and assumptions about "normal" developmental stages, when it comes to early learning and care, understanding the mental/cognitive, emotional, and physical needs of children has been found to be extremely beneficial for children in the same way that well-trained medical doctors and well-trained high school teachers are better equipped to deal with the needs of those they work with.

2. Quebec's eligibility criteria are more equitable than the national Employment Insurance plan (EI eligibility is 600 hours of employment, compared with $2,000 in earnings in the Quebec plans; Phipps, 2006). Quebec's replacement rate is also more generous compared with the national plan (EI basic rate is 55 per cent for 15 weeks maternity and 35 weeks of parental leave to a maximum of $39,000, while Quebec's "basic plan" offers 70 per cent for the first 25 weeks and 55 per cent for the next 25, for a maximum of $57,000; the "special plan" offers 75 per cent for 15 weeks maternity, 25 weeks parental, and 3 weeks fathers-only leave, for a maximum of $57,000 (Phipps, 2006; Albanese, 2011).

Chapter 8

1. The "economic class" is made up of permanent residents admitted (based on their occupation, skill level, level of education, etc.) with the aim of contributing to the country's economic development. It includes skilled workers, business immigrants and their immediate families, as well as live-in caregivers. The "family class" includes spouses/partners, children, parents, and grandparents of Canadian sponsors, which aims to reunite families living across international borders. Finally, the "protected persons" category includes government-assisted and sponsored refugees selected abroad and recognized in Canada as "Convention Refugees" or persons in need of protection (see also CIC, 2007d).

2. In contrast, many others have very negative experiences, which then affect their desire to learn. For example, when asked why she was not interested in school, a 14-year-old girl replied, "I don't have any friends in the classroom. . . . They [classmates] know that I am not very good in English. If I was Canadian and speak English, I will have friends. . . . If I know English it would be better. I can never know English like Canadian people" (Quaicoe, 2007).

Chapter 10

1. The Quebec government agrees with the basic principles of the NCB, but chooses not to participate because it wants to assume control over income support for children in that province (Government of Canada, 2007).

2. Median income marks the centre point of a ranked distribution, so that half of all family incomes within a particular grouping are above the median and half are below.

3. One measure that some have claimed is not relative is the market-basket measure, which determines the cost of the basic necessities (food, shelter, transportation, etc.) for, say, a family of four in a specific locale. The problem with this approach is that it easily becomes a subjective measure, depending on how conservatively the researcher or institution defines "basic" and "necessities." In other words, a group like the Canadian Centre for Policy Alternatives, were it to devise such a market basket, would do so with greater generosity than would, for instance, the Fraser Institute. For more details, see Mendelson (2005: 36–9) and Webber (1998).

Chapter 11

1. For an inventory of government-based (provincial and territorial) family services, including mediation, parent education, and family court services, see Department of Justice (2006b).
2. The federal child support guidelines were amended on 1 May 2006. Amendments include updated federal child support tables to reflect changes to provincial, territorial, and federal tax rates (Department of Justice, 2006).
3. Default refers to no payments, partial payments, late payments, and late partial payments of child support.
4. For a detailed overview of provincial and territorial guidelines, see Department of Justice (2002). For a more detailed description of maintenance enforcement services, see Robinson (2006).
5. In response to the use of terms like "deadbeat dads" and some of the legal changes and challenges to divorce laws, there has been a rise in fathers' rights groups and movements in Canada. For an informal listing of Canadian men's/fathers' rights groups, see www.canadian.net/~fact/fact/groupdta.htm. Many such websites are available across the country.
6. The earliest studies on the impact of divorce and marital breakdown on children tended to assume that the absence of the father resulted in adverse effects for children (Juby et al., 2006).
7. Strohschein (2007) found that children living in single-parent and stepfamilies were more likely than those in two- (biological) parent households to be prescribed methylphenidate, a drug commonly prescribed for the treatment of attention deficit hyperactivity disorder (which is presumed to be caused by increased stress from divorce and/or increased contact by children of divorced parents with medical professionals).
8. Publications are considerably cheaper and easier to develop and administer than the creation of other types of community-based services and supports.

Chapter 12

1. Durrant et al. (2004) explain that there is no clear distinction between physical punishment and abuse (when does one become the other?), as degree of force, parental intent, and even extent of injury have not been found to be useful and clear-cut distinctions.
2. One should note that most opponents of physical punishment are not propagating a ban on discipline (encompassing a wide range of philosophies and methods aimed at protecting, socializing, and guiding children towards self-control, independence, and respect for others). Most would argue that discipline is necessary and beneficial, while physical punishment is not.
3. With similar developments towards this in Italy, Belgium, and South Africa, among others (Durrant et al., 2004).
4. "Child rescuing" particularly targeted First Nations children, placing them in non-Aboriginal homes. For a detailed account of some of the problems encountered by First Nations children, see Blackstock et al. (2006), Bunting (2004), Trocmé et al. (2004), and Timpson (1995).
5. Despite setbacks, organizations such as the Repeal 43 Committee (www.repeal43.org) continue to advocate for change.

Chapter 13

1. And for this reason, I felt it was important to close this book with a discussion of an older book (1982). I believe that now, more than ever, his claim has popular appeal—and again, now more than ever, the argument requires serious scrutiny and assessment.
2. Postman is not alone in this. Winn (1984), for example, accused the sexual revolution, the women's movement, and growth of television for the "loss of childhood." For variations on this theme, also see Elkind (1981), Suransky (1982), and Packard (1983). Interestingly, the Walt Disney Corporation, in the 1950s, marketed itself as the creator of "good" movies, set to counter the perceived negative effects of television (Sammond, 2005).
3. Hoikkala et al. (1987) note that if indeed television gives children access to adult worlds, why does a strict and persistent division of society along age lines continue to marginalize children?
4. Postman has been identified as a "spokesman for conservative media policy and conservative social policy" (Hoikkala et al., 1987: 88).
5. We should not forget that children *are* sexual beings, after all, and childhood sexuality is common and "normal."
6. We seem considerably less concerned about the less sexy and less moral panic–inducing negative health risks associated with the increasingly sedentary lives of Canadian "tweens" (see Jones, 2002).
7. And this is not very different from the preteen (or "sub"-teen) of years past. In fact, advice columns of the 1940s reveal that some girls wanted to wear adult-like clothing and makeup by the age of 12, while mothers preferred that they wait until ages 14–16 (Cook and Kaiser, 2004). What differs, perhaps, is that "tween" has become a marketable identity in itself.

Glossary

Acculturation Changes in an individual who is a participant in a culture contact situation; the process by which a person is influenced directly by the external culture and by the changing culture of which the individual is a member.

Adaptation The process through which an individual becomes suited to an environment, including internal, psychological (emotional and affective) change, and/or external sociocultural (behavioural) change.

Agents of socialization The institutions and relations that help to produce, enforce, and maintain socially accepted expectations and roles; these include: *family*, one of the most important (and personal) agents, with whom we learn cultural and religious values, social expectations, gender socialization, etc; *school*, which is responsible for raising "good citizens" by teaching social values: punctuality, competition, hard work, success, rewards, meritocracy, hierarchy; *peer group*, the first "egalitarian" agent, among whom children learn to "fit in," belong, interact with people their own age; *media*, from which children learn, among other things, to be consumers (imitation, wants and needs).

Allophone An individual whose mother tongue is neither English nor French.

Assimilation The process whereby minorities begin to lose their distinctiveness through the absorption into the activities and objectives of the dominant society or culture.

Authoritarian parenting Parenting that is low on acceptance (children seen and not heard, low responsiveness on the part of parents) and high on control (many rules, enforcement of obedience result in dependency, low responsibility, situational compliance).

Authoritative parenting Parenting that is high on acceptance (children have rights), high on responsiveness by parents, high on control (clear rules, and obedience is enforced), and that results in more independence in children; generally associated with positive child outcomes.

Baby boom A period characterized by relatively high birth rates (typically, when the birth rate exceeds 2 per cent of the population); most often associated with the two decades immediately following the World War II in North America and parts of Europe, marked by economic growth and stability.

Blended family Includes one or more children from the current union and one or more children from the previous unions; a blended stepfamily contains children of both spouses/partners from one or more previous unions.

Colonization At a basic level, it refers to the act of sending settlers to a geographic location and establishing political control; however, it often involves invasion, dispossession, and subjugation of people. The result is the dispossession of land from the original inhabitants, often legalized after the fact.

Corporal (physical) punishment An action intended to cause physical discomfort or pain to correct behaviour, to "teach a lesson," or to deter someone from repeating the behaviour. Some physical punishments do not involve hitting (e.g., washing a child's mouth with soap or having a child kneel on the floor).

Cross-sectional design Involves making observations on a subset of a population (people or things), at one cross-section or point in time.

Cultural capital The "inherited" values of one's group or social class reinforced in schools though curriculum and pedagogy.

Deficit model The practice of focusing on an individual or social group as the "problem," without considering the role of the social environment or the institutional practices that are rooted in injustice and inequality.

Descriptive research Research that answers the questions who, what, where, and when. "Why" is excluded from this list (*see* explanatory research). It describes data or characteristics about a population or phenomenon.

Discrimination The denial of equal treatment to some group(s) or members of a group because of race, ethnicity, gender, disability, etc. The behavioural part of prejudice.

Ethnic enclaves Business/job opportunities that are established within ethnic neighbourhoods and communities that are usually owned, operated, or controlled by members of the ethnic group.

Ethnic group A group of people who share ancestral origins, customs, and beliefs, who are separated from others by social boundaries.

Evaluation research Studies that examine projects and programs to decide whether they have had the predicted effects, and if not, to determine why not.

Explanatory research Research that answers the question "why"? (*see* descriptive research). It includes attempts to understand cause and effect.

Exploratory research Research that breaks new ground, conducted because a problem has not been clearly defined; it helps to determine the best research design, data collection method, etc. One is often left with more questions than answers.

First Nations A term that came into common usage in the 1970s to replace the word "Indian," which many people found offensive. Although the term is widely used, no legal definition of it exists. The term "First Nations peoples" refers to both Status and non-Status Indians in Canada.

Gender schema Organized knowledge structures (schema) that are gendered. These schema then influence behaviour (choice of friends, toys, clothes, activities, judgement of others).

Gender socialization The ongoing process through which we learn to conform to socially accepted and desired gender norms—a constellation of gender-differentiated expectations and experiences.

Genocide The deliberate and systematic intent, or act, of extermination of a national, racial, political, or cultural group.

Globalization A term used to describe a process by which local or national people and things are transformed into global or worldwide forms. It involves change at the economic, technological, sociocultural, and political levels. Most often it refers to the integration of national economies into an international economy through changes in production, trade, investment, flow of capital, migrations, and technological change.

Grounded theory A research method that intentionally operates counter to traditional approaches that embrace the scientific method. Researchers begin "on the ground" by collecting data, information, biographies, etc., then grouping information into concepts and categories, and finally deriving theory from observations. It is the reverse of more traditional "scientific" approaches, which begin by researching and developing a hypothesis, then collecting data, etc.

Indian A highly contested term used in the Indian Act to refer to a person who is entitled (according to the state) to be registered as an Indian (Justice Canada, 2014).

Indian Act Canadian federal legislation, first passed in 1876, that regulates the management of indigenous populations and Indian reserve lands. The Act has been amended several times, with one of the most famous revisions occurring in 1985, which saw the introduction of Bill C-31.

Intact family Statistics Canada's term to refer to a family in which all children in the household are the biological and/or adopted offspring of both members of the couple.

Intensive parenting (also **Intensive mothering**) A popular neoliberal and demanding form of parenting that includes the following notions: caring for children is primarily the responsibility of mothers; parenting should be child-centred; children are sacred; and mothers should intellectually stimulate children to ensure appropriate brain development, so that children, who are always monitored, can reach their full potential.

Inuit Aboriginal people in northern Canada, who live north of the treeline, in Nunavut, the Northwest Territories, northern Quebec, and Labrador. The word means "people" in the Inuit language, Inuktitut. The singular of Inuit is Inuk.

Kidfluence The power and influence today's children have over adult and household spending and parental purchases (including family vacations, cars, and groceries).

Licensed/regulated child care spaces Operators or agencies that meet minimum requirements for the legal operation of a child care centre, a family child care home, or a family child care agency.

Longitudinal studies/research Repeated observations of the same factors within the same population group over longer periods of time, so that data collection or observation takes place at multiple points in time (*see* cross-sectional research).

Median family/household income The midpoint of all incomes within a population, so that half earn more and half earn less; not to be confused with average income, which is derived by summing all incomes then dividing by the total number of incomes. Many statisticians consider median income a better indicator than the average or mean household income as it is not dramatically affected by unusually high or low values that distort the calculation of any mathematical average.

Meritocracy A social system that gives opportunities and advantages to people on the basis of their ability rather than, e.g., their wealth or seniority.

Métis People of mixed—Aboriginal and European—ancestry who have a unique culture that draws upon their diverse ancestral origins; originally, a culture developed from the offspring of Scots and French fur trader fathers and Aboriginal mothers in lands under the nominal control of the Hudson's Bay Company and the North West Company.

National Longitudinal Survey of Children and Youth A long-term study of Canadian children that follows their development and well-being from birth to early adulthood. The study is designed to collect information about factors influencing a child's social, emotional, and behavioural development and to monitor the impact of these factors on the child's development over time.

Neoliberalism The re-emergence of economic liberalism from the 1970s to the present. It embraces conservative characteristics such as anti-unionism, free-market economics, and welfare reform (cuts to social welfare programs and spending).

OECD countries Founded in 1948, the Organisation for Economic

Co-operation and Development is made up of 30 of the most economically developed countries in the world, all of which accept the principles of representative democracy and a free-market economy.

Population A group of people or things that share a particular characteristic of interest.

Prescriptive/prescribed role Socially mandated ideas that are suggestive of how we should behave.

Primary socialization Social learning that takes place in childhood and involves learning about larger social roles, values, and action.

Privatization The process of transferring ownership from the public sector (government) to the private sector (business); the transfer of any government function to the private (often, for-profit) sector.

Pronatalism An ideology promoting child-bearing (high birth rates), which at times includes policies and programs limiting access to abortion and contraception, as well as financial and social incentives for the population (often only a select, "desired" or "desirable" segment) to reproduce.

Prosocial programs/behaviour The modelling of behaviour believed to be "good" for individuals and society, which may include lessons on social values such as sharing, co-operation, self-control, understanding differences, etc.

Punitive parenting The parenting style or practice that involves or approves of the use of physical/corporal or more severe verbal punishment to enforce rules and discourage undesired behaviour.

Qualitative research Nonstatistical examination and interpretation of observations, for the purpose of discovering underlying meaning, patterns, and relationships.

Quantitative research The statistical representation and manipulation of observations for the purpose of describing and explaining social phenomena.

Racial/racialized group An arbitrary and socially constructed classification of people into categories based on real or imagined physical characteristics. Racialization is a process of attributing racial meaning to people or their behaviour.

Resiliency Springing back, or the ability to readily recover from shock, depression, trauma, etc.

Secondary socialization The "recalibrating" that typically takes place later in life that involves learning very specific roles (sometimes in subcultures, or in work, parenting, retirement).

Service (sector) economy Also known as the "tertiary sector" of an economy (after the primary/resource extraction and secondary/manufacturing sectors). It involves the provision of services by people to and for people, businesses, and consumers (e.g., repair, customer support, medical, entertainment, hospitality, education, accommodation, etc.).

Social construct Any theoretical or heuristic concept (mental image/idea or thing) that has been invented or created.

Socialization Process through which we learn to conform to social norms; become social beings;

become participants in society. The imposition of social expectations and patterns of behaviour (the learning of socially accepted ways); *see* primary socialization and secondary socialization.

Social reproduction The daily and generational production and maintenance of a population; this has proven to be work predominantly done by women; it continues to be undervalued compared with traditional paid work.

Status (registered) Indian A First Nations person who is registered under the Indian Act, Canadian federal legislation that sets out the requirements for determining who is a Status Indian, among many other things. *Non-Status* refers to a First Nations person who is not registered as an Indian under the Indian Act. This may be because his or her ancestors were never registered or because he or she lost Indian status under former provisions of the Act.

Stepfamily A family in which at least one of the children in the household is from a previous relationship of one of the parents. In a simple stepfamily, the child(ren) of one of the spouses or partners lives in the household.

Traditional nuclear family The term *nuclear family* was developed to refer to a family group consisting of two parents and one or more of their children living in the same household; in its traditional form, men are expected to fill the instrumental, public, breadwinner role and women are expected to fill the expressive, private, emotional, domestic role.

Tweens Preteens or children between the ages of 9 and 12 (or 14); a relatively new definition for the phase in the life cycle that includes those believed to be neither fully "children" and not yet "adolescents."

Uninvolved/unengaged parenting Parenting that is low on responsiveness and low in demands or control.

Visible minority Racial or cultural groups that can be identified as members of a minority group by their skin colour, facial features, or manner of speaking. Although the term's use is contested, the concept is Canada's official designation for persons other than Aboriginal peoples who are non-Caucasian in race or non-white in colour. The term originated with the Employment Equity Act of 1986.

Welfare state A model of governance in which the state assumes primary responsibility of the welfare of its citizens through the provision of social services aimed at protecting their safety and well-being. This often includes the provision of a range of (universally applied) social programs including unemployment insurance, minimum wage, maternity leave, health benefits, etc.; these are usually assumed to be applied to citizens as a right.

References

Canadian Economic Observer (Statistics Canada Catalogue no. 11-010)

Canadian Social Trends (Statistics Canada Catalogue no. 11-008)

Education Matters (Statistics Canada Catalogue no. 81-004-XIE)

Health Reports (Statistics Canada Catalogue no. 82-003)

Juristat (Statistics Canada Catalogue no. 85-002-XIE)

Perspectives (Statistics Canada Catalogue no. 75-001-XIE)

Perspectives on Labour and Income (Statistics Canada Catalogue no. 75-011-XIE)

Abner, Kristin, Rachel Gordon, Robert Kaestner, and Sanders Korenman. 2013. "Does Child-Care Quality Mediate Associations between Type of Care and Development?" *Journal of Marriage and Family* 75, 5: 1203–17.

Aboriginal Affairs and Northern Development Canada. 2014. Residential Schools. Ottawa: Government of Canada. At: www.aadnc-aandc.gc.ca/eng/1302882353814/1302882592498.

Aboriginal and Northern Affairs Canada. 2013. Jordan's Principle. Ottawa: Government of Canada. At: www.aadnc-aandc.gc.ca/eng/1334329827982/1334329861879.

Aboud, Frances, and Lior Miller. 2007. "Promoting Peer Intervention in Name-Calling," *South African Journal of Psychology* 37, 4: 803–19.

Ackerman, B., E. Brown, and C. Izard. 2003. "Continuity and Change in Levels of Externalizing Behaviour in School of Children from Economically Disadvantaged Families," *Child Development* 74: 694–709.

Ackroyd, Judith, and Andrew Pilkington. 1999. "Childhood and the Construction of Ethnic Identities in a Global Age: A Dramatic Encounter," *Childhood* 6, 4: 443–54.

Adamson, Kari, Marion O'Brien, and Kay Pasley. 2007. "An Ecological Approach to Father Involvement in Biological and Stepfather Families," *Fathering* 5, 2: 129–47.

Adelson, Joseph. 1997. "What We Know about Day Care," *Commentary* 104, 5: 52–4.

Adler, Peter, and Patricia Adler. 1998. *Peer Power: Preadolescent Culture and Identity.* New Brunswick, NJ: Rutgers University Press.

Advertising Standards Canada. 2014. Broadcast Code for Advertising to Children—The Code. At: www.adstandards.com/en/clearance/childrens/broadcastCodeForAdvertisingToChildren-TheCode.aspx.

Afifi, Tamara, and Stacia Keith. 2004. "A Risk and Resiliency Model of Ambiguous Loss in Postdivorce Stepfamilies," *Journal of Family Communication* 4, 2: 65–98.

——— and Paul Schrodt. 2003. "Uncertainty and the Avoidance of the State of One's Family in Stepfamilies, Postdivorce Single-parent Families, and First Marriage Families," *Human Communication Research* 29, 4: 516–32.

Agnew, Robert. 1992. "Foundation for a General Strain Theory of Crime and Delinquency," *Criminology* 30: 47–87.

Ahmed, Nina. 2005. *Intergenerational Impact of Immigrants' Selection and Assimilation on Health Outcomes of Children.* Ottawa: Statistics Canada Analytical Studies Branch Research Paper Series (Catalogue no. 11F0019MIE—No. 247).

Akyeampong, Ernest B. 2005. "Business Support Services," *Perspectives on Labour and Income* 6, 5: 5–9.

———. 2007. "Canada's Unemployment Mosaic, 2000 to 2006," *Perspectives on Labour and Income* 20, 2: 5–12.

Alaggia, Ramona, Angelique Jenney, Josephine Mazzuca, and Melissa Redmond. 2007. "In Whose Best Interest? A Canadian Case Study of the Impact of Child Welfare Policies in Cases of Domestic Violence," *Brief Treatment and Crisis Intervention* 7, 4: 275–89.

Alanen, Leena. 2000. "'Review Essay': Visions of a Social Theory of Childhood," *Childhood* 7, 4: 493–505.

Albanese, Patrizia. 2006. "Small Town, Big Benefits: The Ripple Effect of $7/day Child Care," *Canadian Review of Sociology and Anthropology* 43, 2: 125–40.

———. 2007. "(Under)Valuing Care Work: The Case of Child-Care Workers in Small-Town Quebec," *International Journal of Early Years Education* 15, 2: 125–39.

———. 2009. "Ethnicity, Immigration and Family Life" in M. Baker, ed., *Families: Changing Trends in Canada*. Toronto: McGraw-Hill Ryerson Ltd, pp.130–53.

———. 2009. "$7/Day, $7/Hour, 7 Days a Week: Juggling Communities, Shift Work and Child Care in a Changing ('New') Economy," in Jeffery Klaehn, ed., *Roadblocks to Equality*. Toronto: Black Rose Books, pp. 26–40.

———. 2011. "Addressing the Interlocking Complexity of Paid Work and Care: Lessons From Changing Family Policy in Quebec" in C. Krull and J. Sempruch, eds, *A Life in Balance? Reopening the Family-Work Debate*. Vancouver: UBC Press, pp. 130–43.

———. 2011. "Balancing Paid Work and Family Responsibilities: Lessons on Family Policy from Quebec," in Catherine Krull and Justyna Sempruch, eds, *The Family/Paid Work Contradiction: Challenges and Possibilities*. Vancouver: University of British Columbia Press.

Alexander, Allison. 1997. "Children and Television," in Newcomb (1997). At: www.museum.tv/archives/etv/C/htmlC/childrenand/childrenand.htm.

Ali, Mehrunnisa, and Kenise Kilbride. 2004. *Forging New Ties: Improving Parenting and Family Support Services for New Canadians with Young Children*. Ottawa: Human Resources and Skills Development Canada.

Ali, Mehrunnisa, with Sviltana Taraban and Jagjeet Kaur Gill. 2003. "Unaccompanied/Separated Children Seeking Refugee Status in Ontario: A Review of Documented Policies and Practices." Toronto: Joint Centres of Excellence for Research on Immigration and Settlement, CERIS Working Paper No. 27.

Amato, Paul. 2003. "Reconciling Divergent Perspectives: Judith Wallerstein, Quantitative Family Research and Children of Divorce," *Family Relations* 52, 4: 332–9.

Amato, Paul, and Frieda Fowler. 2002. "Parenting Practices, Child Adjustment and Family Diversity," *Journal of Marriage and Family* 64: 703–16.

Ambert, Anne-Marie. 1997. *Parents, Children and Adolescents*. Binghamton, NY: Hawthorne Press.

———. 2006. "Same-Sex Couples and Same-Sex Parent Families: Relationships, Parenting and Issues of Marriage," Ottawa: Vanier Institute of the Family. At: www.vifamily.ca/library/cft/samesex_05.html.

American Psychological Association Task Force on the Sexualization of Girls (Zurbringgen, Eileen, Rebecca Collins, Sharon Lamb, Tomi-Ann Roberts, Deborah Tolman, L. Monique Ward, and Jeanne Blake). 2007. *Report of the APA Task Force on the Sexualization of Girls*. Washington: APA.

Anderson, Sara, Tama Leventhal, and Véronique Dupéré. 2014. "Exposure to Neighborhood Affluence and Poverty in Childhood and Adolescence and Academic Achievement and Behavior," *Applied Developmental Science* 18, 3: 123–38.

Andreychuk, Raynell (Chair), and Joan Fraser (Deputy Chair). 2007. *Children: The Silenced Citizens: Effective Implementation of Canada's International Obligations with Respect to the Rights of Children*. Final Report of the Standing Senate Committee on Human Rights. Ottawa: Senate Committees Directorate. At: www.fncfcs.com/docs/Children_TheSilentCitizens_April2007.pdf.

Anisef, Paul, and Kenise Murphy Kilbride. 2001. "Study on Parenting Issues of Newcomer Families in Ontario" (8 files). Toronto: Joint Centre of Excellence for Research on Immigration and Settlement and Citizenship and Immigration Canada.

Anthony, Christopher, James DiPerna, and Paul Amato. 2014. "Divorce, Approaches to Learning, and Children's Academic Achievement: A Longitudinal Analysis of Mediated and Moderated Effects," *Journal of School Psychology* 52, 3: 249–61.

Archard, David. 2004. *Children: Rights and Childhood*. London: Routledge.

Ardila-Rey, Alicia, Beth Richman, and Susan McCann Brown. 2001. "The World of *Sesame Street* Research," in Fisch and Truglio (2001: 141–79).

Arendell, T. 2001. "The New Care Work of Middle Class Mothers", in K. Daly, ed., *Minding the Time in Family Experience: Emerging Perspectives and Issues.* Contemporary Perspectives in Family Research, vol. 3. New York: JAI Press, 163–204.

Ariès, Philippe. 1962. *Centuries of Childhood: A Social History of Family Life.* New York: Alfred A. Knopf.

Armstrong, Robin. 2000. "Mapping the Conditions of First Nations Communities," *Canadian Social Trends* 3. Toronto: Thompson Educational, 28–32.

Arpino, Bruno, and Valeria Bordone. 2014. "Does Grandparenting Pay Off? The Effect of Child Care on Grandparents' Cognitive Functioning." *Journal of Marriage and Family* 76, 2: 337–51.

Assembly of First Nations. 2007a. "The $9 Billion Myth Exposed: Why First Nations Poverty Endures." At: www.afn. ca/cmslib/general/M-Ex.pdf.

———. 2007b. "Indian Residential Schools Settlement Update," *Assembly of First Nations Bulletin* 7 Feb. At: www.afn.ca/cmslib/general/IRS-Update.pdf.

AuCoin, Kathy. 2005. "Children and Youth as Victims of Violent Crime," in *Juristat* 25, 1. Ottawa, Statistics Canada.

Aycan, Zeynep, and Rabindra Kanungo. 1998. "Impact of Acculturation on Socialization Beliefs and Behavioral Occurrences among Indo-Canadian Immigrants," *Journal of Comparative Family Studies* 29, 3: 451–67.

Bailey, J.M., D. Bobrow, M. Wolf, and S. Mikach. 1995. "Sexual Orientation of Adult Sons of Gay Fathers," *Developmental Psychology* 31, 1: 124–9.

Baker, Kaysee, and Arthur Raney. 2007. "Equally Super? Gender-Role Stereotyping of Superheroes in Children's Animated Programs," *Mass Communication and Society* 10, 1: 25–41.

Baker, Maureen. 2006. *Restructuring Family Policies: Convergences and Divergences.* Toronto: University of Toronto Press.

Baker, Maureen, Jonathan Gruber, and Kevin Milligan. 2005. *Universal Childcare, Maternal Labor Supply and Family Well-Being.* Cambridge, MA: National Bureau of Economic Research.

Ball, J. 2004. "As If Indigenous Knowledge and Communities Mattered: Transformative Education in First Nations Communities in Canada," *American Indian Quarterly* 28, 3 and 4: 454–79.

Bandura, Albert. 1973. *Aggression: A Social Learning Analysis.* Englewood Cliffs, NJ: Prentice-Hall.

———. 1977. *Social Learning Theory.* Englewood Cliffs, NJ: Prentice-Hall.

———. 2002. "Social Cognitive Theory of Mass Communications," in J. Bryant and D. Zillmann, eds, *Media Effects: Advances in Theory and Research.* Mahwah, NJ: Erlbaum, pp. 121–54.

Barakett, Joyce, and Ailie Cleghorn. 2008. *Sociology of Education.* Toronto: Pearson Prentice-Hall.

Barkin, Shari, Benjamin Scheindlin, Edward Ip, Irma Richardson, and Stacia Finch. 2007. "Determinants of Parental Discipline Practices: A National Sample from Primary Care Practices," *Clinical Pediatrics* 46: 64–9.

Barman, Jean. 2003. "Schooled for Inequality: The Education of British Columbia Aboriginal Children," in Janovicek and Parr (2003: 212–35).

Barrett, H., and F. Tasker. 2001. "Growing Up with a Gay Parent: Views of 101 Gay Fathers on Their Sons' and Daughters' Experiences," *Educational and Child Psychology* 18: 62–77.

Battle, Ken. 2007. "Child Poverty: The Evolution and Impact of Child Benefits," in R. Brian Howe and Katherine Covell, eds, *A Question of Commitment: Children's Rights in Canada.* Waterloo, ON: Wilfrid Laurier University Press, pp. 21–44.

———. 2008. *Bigger and Better Child Benefit: A $5,000 Canada Child Tax Benefit.* Ottawa: Caledon Institute of Social Policy.

Bauer, Patricia, and Molly Coyne. 1997. "When the Name Says It All: Preschoolers' Recognition and Use of the Gendered Nature of Common Proper Names," *Social Development* 6, 3: 271–91.

Bauserman, Robert. 2002. "Child Adjustment in Joint-Custody versus Sole-Custody Arrangements: A Meta-Analytic Review," *Journal of Family Psychology* 16, 1: 91–102.

Beaupré, Pascale. 2008. "I do . . . Take Two? Changes in Intentions to Remarry among Divorced Canadians During the Past 20 years," in *Matter of Fact*. Ottawa: Statistics Canada (Catalogue no. 890-630-X). At: http://www.statcan.gc.ca/pub/89-630-x/2008001/article/10659-eng.htm.

Beaupré, Pascale, and Elisabeth Cloutier. 2007. *Navigating Family Transitions: Evidence from the General Social Survey, 2006*. Ottawa: Statistics Canada (GSS, Cycle 20: Family Transitions Survey—Catalogue no. 89-625-XIE-No. 002).

Béchard, Marcel. 2007. *GSS, Cycle 20: Family Transitions Survey—Family Structure by Region, 2006 (Revised)*. Ottawa: Social and Aboriginal Statistics Division, Statistics Canada (Catalogue no. 89-625-XIE).

Béchard, Marcel. 2011. *General Social Survey, 2010: Overview of the Time Use of Canadians*. Ottawa: Statistics Canada (Catalogue no. 89-647-X).

Beck, U. 1992. *Risk Society: Towards a New Modernity*. London: Sage.

Beckmeyer, Jonathon, Marilyn Coleman, and Lawrence Ganong. 2014. "Postdivorce Coparenting Typologies and Children's Adjustment," *Family Relations* 63, 4: 526–37.

Bégin, Louise, L. Ferland, G. Girard, and C. Gougeon. 2002. *School Daycare Services*. Québec: Gouvernement du Québec (Catalogue no. 2002-02-00121).

Behrman, Richard. E., and Lisa Markham. 2005. "The Contribution of Parenting to Ethnic and Racial Gaps in School Readiness," *Future of Children* 15, 1: 139–68. At: www.futureofchildren.org/information2826/information_show.htm?doc_id=255990.

Beiser, M., A. Goodwill, P. Albanese, K. McShane, and M. Nowakowski. 2014. "Predictors of Immigrant Children's Mental Health in Canada: Selection, Settlement Contingencies, Culture, or All of the Above?" *Social Psychiatry and Psychiatric Epidemiology* 49, 5: 743–56.

Beiser, M., A. Goodwill, V. Kaspar, and S. Noh. 2000. *Changes in Poverty Status and Developmental Behaviours: A Comparison of Immigrant and Non-Immigrant Children in Canada*. Ottawa: Human Resources Development Canada, Applied Research Branch Strategic Policy. At: www.hrsdc. gc.ca/en/cs/sp/sdc/pkrf/publications/research/2000-001332/2000-001332.pdf.

Beiser, M., Angela Shik, and Monika Curyk. 1999. *New Canadian Children and Youth Study: Literature Review*. Ottawa: Health Canada.

Beiser, Morton, Feng Hou, Ilene Hyman, and Michel Tousignant. 2002. "Poverty, Family Process, and the Mental Health of Immigrant Children in Canada," *American Journal of Public Health* 92, 2: 220–7.

Béland, Daniel, and André Lecours. 2006. "Sub-state Nationalism and the Welfare State: Québec and Canadian Federalism," *Nations and Nationalism* 12, 1: 77–96.

Bélanger, Alain. 2006. *Report on the Demographic Situation in Canada, 2002*. Ottawa: Statistics Canada, Demography Division (Catalogue no. 91-209-XIE).

———, Yves Carrière, and Stephanie Gilbert. 2006. *Report on the Demographic Situations in Canada—2000*. Ottawa: Minister of Industry (Catalogue no. 91-209-XIE).

Bell, Daniel. 1973. *The Coming of Post-Industrial Society: A Venture in Social Forecasting*. New York: Basic Books.

———. 1976. "Welcome to the Post-Industrial Society," *Physics Today* 28, 2: 46–9.

Bem, S.L. 1981. "Gender Schema Theory: A Cognitive Account of Sex Typing," *Psychological Review* 88: 354–64.

Bentley, Kristina Anne. 2005. "Can There Be Any Universal Children's Rights?" *International Journal of Human Rights* 9, 1: 107–23.

Beran, Tanya. 2008. "Stability of Harassment in Children: Analysis of the Canadian National Longitudinal Survey of Children and Youth," *Journal of Psychology* 142, 2: 131–46.

Beran, Tanya, Ginger Hughes, and Judy Lupart. 2008. "A Model of Achievement and Bullying: Analyses of the Canadian National Longitudinal Survey of Children and Youth," *Educational Research* 50, 1: 25–39.

Bernard, André, and Jeannine Usalcas. 2014. "The Labour Market in Canada and the United States since the Last Recession," in *Economic Insights* (11-626X-No.036). Ottawa: Statistics Canada.

Bernhard, Judith, Patricia Landolt, and Luin Goldring. 2006. "Transnational, Multi-local Motherhood: Experiences of Separation and Reunification among Latin American Families in Canada," *Policy Matters* 24: 1–6.

Bernhard, Judith, M.L. Lefebvre, G. Chud, and R. Lange. 1996. "Linguistic Match between Children and Caregivers in Canadian Early Childhood Education," *Canadian Journal of Research in Early Childhood Education* 5, 2: 202–22.

Berry, Brent. 2007. "Disparities in Free Time Activity in the United States: Trends and Explanations," *Sociological Perspectives* 50, 2: 177–208.

Berry, Daniel, Clancy Blair, Alexandra Ursache, Michael Willoughby, Patricia Garrett-Peters, Lynne Vernon-Feagans, Mary Bratsch-Hines, W. Roger Mills-Koonce, and Douglas Granger. 2014. "Child Care and Cortisol Across Early Childhood: Context Matters," *Developmental Psychology* 50, 2: 514–25.

Bessner, Ronda. 2002. *The Voice of Children in Divorce, Custody and Access Proceedings.* Ottawa: Family, Children and Youth Section of the Department of Justice.

Bezanson, Kate. 2006. *Gender, the State and Social Reproduction: Household Insecurities in Neoliberal Times.* Toronto: University of Toronto Press.

Bezanson, Kate, and Meg Luxton, eds. 2006. *Social Reproduction: Feminist Political Economy Challenges Neoliberalism.* Montreal and Kingston: McGill-Queen's University Press.

Bigner, J.J. 1999. "Raising Our Sons: Gay Men as Fathers," *Journal of Gay and Lesbian Social Services* 10, 1: 61–77.

Bigner, J.J., and R.B. Jacobson. 1989a. "Parenting Behaviours of Homosexual and Heterosexual Fathers," *Journal of Homosexuality* 18: 173–86.

———. 1989b. "The Value of Children to Gay and Heterosexual Fathers," *Journal of Homosexuality* 18: 163–72.

Birnbaum, Rachel, and Michael Saini. 2012. "A Qualitative Synthesis of Children's Participation in Custody Disputes," *Research on Social Work Practice* 22, 4: 400–9.

Bittman, Michael, Leonie Rutherford, Jude Brown, and Leonard Unsworth. 2012. "Digital Natives? New and Old Media and Children's Language Acquisition," *Family Matters* 91: 18 –26.

Bittman, Michael, Leonie Rutherford, Jude Brown, and Lens Unsworth. 2011. "Digital Natives? New and Old Media and Children's Outcomes," *Australian Journal of Education* 55, 2: 161–75.

Blackstock, Cindy. 2009. "Jordan's Story: How One Boy Inspired a World of Change," in *Aboriginal Children's Health: Leaving No Child Behind. Canadian Supplement to The State of the World's Children.* Toronto: UNICEF Canada, pp. 46–51. At: http://www.unicef.ca/sites/default/files/imce_uploads/DISCOVER/OUR%20WORK/ADVOCACY/DOMESTIC/POLICY%20ADVOCACY/DOCS/Leaving%20no%20child%20behind%202009.pdf.

Blackstock, C., T. Cross, J. George, I. Brown, and J. Formsma. 2006. *Reconciliation in Child Welfare: Touchstones of Hope for Indigenous Children, Youth and Families.* Ottawa: Centre of Excellence for Child Welfare and National Indian Child Welfare Association. At: www.reconciliation-movement.org/docs/Touchstones_of_Hope.pdf.

Bland, Douglas. 2013. *Canada and the First Nations: Cooperation or Conflict?* Ottawa: Macdonald-Laurier Institute for Public Policy. At: http://site.ebrary.com.ezproxy.lib.ryerson.ca/lib/oculryerson/docDetail.action?docID=10708569.

Blankenhorn, David. 1996. *Fatherless America: Confronting Our Most Urgent Social Problem.* New York: Basic Books.

Blau, D.M. 1999. "The Effect of Income on Child Development," *Review of Economics and Statistics* 81, 2: 261–76.

Blouin, Patric, and Marie-Josée Courchesne. 2007. *Summary of Public School Indicators for the Provinces and Territories, 1998/1999 to 2004/2005.* Ottawa: Culture, Tourism and the Centre for Education Statistics Division (Catalogue no. 81-595-MIE—No. 050).

Bobet, Ellen. 1994. "Indian Mortality," in *Canadian Social Trends* 2. Toronto: Thompson Educational, pp. 57–60.

Bohatyretz, Sandra, and Garth Lipps. 1999. "Diversity in the Classroom, Characteristics of Elementary Students

Receiving Special Education," *Education Quarterly Review* 6, 2: 7–19.

Bohnert, Nora, Anne Milan, and Heather Lathe. 2014. "Enduring Diversity: Living Arrangements of Children in Canada over 100 Years of the Census," in *Demographic Documents*. Ottawa: Statistics Canada (Catalogue no. 91F0015M —No. 11).

Bollmer, Julie, Monica Harris, and Richard Milich. 2006. "Reactions to Bullying and Peer Vicimization: Narratives, Physiological Arousal and Personality," *Journal of Research in Personality* 40, 5: 803–28.

Bombay, Amy, Kimberly Matheson, and Hymie Anisman. 2013. "Expectations among Aboriginal Peoples in Canada Regarding the Potential Impacts of a Government Apology." *Political Psychology* 34, 3: 443–60.

Bombay, Amy, Kimberly Matheson, and Hymie Anisman. 2014. "The Intergenerational Effects of Indian Residential Schools: Implications for the Concept of Historical Trauma." *Transcultural Psychiatry* 51, 3: 320–38.

Bos, H., F. van Balen, and D. van den Boom. 2004. "Experience of Parenthood, Couple Relationship, Social Support and Child-Rearing Goals in Planned Lesbian Mother Families," *Journal of Child Psychology and Psychiatry* 45, 4: 755–64.

Bosacki, Sandra, Zopito Marini, and Andrew Dane. 2006. "'Voices from the Classroom': Pictorial and Narrative Representations of Children's Bullying Experiences," *Journal of Moral Education* 35, 2: 231–45.

Bouchard, Genevieve. 2006. "Cohabitation versus Marriage: The Role of Dyadic Adjustment in Relationship Dissolution," *Journal of Divorce and Remarriage* 46, 1 and 2: 107–17.

Bourdieu, Pierre, and Jean Claude Passeron. 1977. *Reproduction in Education, Culture and Society*. Beverly Hills, CA: Sage.

Bouvier, Luc. 2002. *Les sacrifies de la bonne entente: histoire des francophones du Pontiac*. Montreal: L'Action Nationale.

Bowlby, John. 1958. "The Child's Attachment to His Mother," *International Journal of Psycho-Analysis* 39: 1–23.

———. 1969. *Attachment and Loss*, vol. 1— *Attachment*. New York: Basic Books.

Bowles, Samuel, and Herbert Gintis. 1976. *Schooling in Capitalist America*. New York: Basic Books.

Boyd, Monica. 2000. "Ethnicity and Immigrant Offspring," in Madeline A. Kalbach and Warren E. Kalbach, eds, *Perspectives on Ethnicity in Canada*. Toronto: Harcourt Canada, pp. 137–54.

Bradshaw, Jonathan. 2002. "Child Poverty and Child Outcomes," *Children and Society* 16: 131–40.

Bretherton, Inge, David Lambert, and Barbara Golby. 2005. "Involved Fathers of Preschool Children as Seen by Themselves and Their Wives: Accounts of Attachment, Socialization and Companionship," *Attachment and Human Development* 7, 3: 229–51.

Bricheno, Patricia, and Mary Thornton. 2007. "Role Model, Hero or Champion? Children's Views Concerning Role Models," *Educational Research* 49, 4: 383–96.

Bronfenbrenner, Urie. 1977. "Towards an Experimental Ecology of Human Development," *American Psychologist* 32, 7: 513–31.

———. 1995. "The Bioecological Model from a Life Course Perspective: Reflections from a Participant Observer," in P. Moen, G.H. Elder Jr, and K. Luscher, eds, *Examining Lives in Context: Perspectives on the Ecology of Human Development*. Washington: APA Books, 599–618.

Bronfenbrenner, Urie, and Stephen Ceci. 1994. "Nature–Nurture Reconceptualized in Developmental Perspective: A Bioecological Model," *Psychological Review* 101: 568–86.

Bronfenbrenner, Urie, and P.A. Morris. 1998. "The Ecology of Developmental Processes," in R.M. Lerner, ed., *Handbook of Child Psychology*. New York: Wiley, pp. 993–1028.

Brooks-Gunn, Jeanne, and Greg J. Duncan. 1997. "The Effects of Poverty on Children," in Richard. E. Behrman, ed., *Children and Poverty: The Future of Children*, vol. 7. Los Altos, CA: Centre for Future of Children, David and Lucile Packard Foundation, pp. 55–71.

Brown, Larry. 1991. "The Mary Ellen Myth: Readers Respond," *Social Work* 36, 6: 553.

Brown, Tony, Emily Tanner-Smith, Chase Lesane-Brown, and Michael Ezell.

2007. "Child, Parent, and Situational Correlates of Familial Ethnic/Race Socialization," *Journal of Marriage and Family* 69: 14–25.

Brunod, Regis, and Solange Cook-Darzens. 2002. "Men's Role and Fatherhood in French Caribbean Families: A Multi-Systemic 'Resource' Approach," *Clinical Child Psychology and Psychiatry* 7, 4: 559–69.

Brzozowski, Jodi-Anne. 2007. "Family Violence against Children and Youth," in *Family Violence in Canada: A Statistical Profile 2007*. Ottawa: Statistics Canada (Catalogue no. 85-224-XIE), pp. 20–31.

Buchbinder, Mara, Jeffrey Longhofer, Thomas Barrett, Peter Lawson, and Jerry Floersch. 2006. "Ethnographic Approaches to Child Care Research: A Review of the Literature," *Journal of Early Childhood Research* 4, 1: 45–63.

Buckingham, David. 1998. "Review Essay: Children of the Electronic Age? Digital Media and the New Generation Rhetoric," *European Journal of Communication* 13, 4: 557–65.

Bühler-Niederberger, Doris. 2010a. "Introduction: Childhood Sociology—Defining the State of the Art and Ensuring Reflection," *Current Sociology* 58, 2: 155–64.

Bühler-Niederberger, Doris. 2010b. "Childhood Sociology in Ten Countries: Current Outcomes and Future Directions," *Current Sociology* 58, 2: 369–84.

Bunting, Annie. 2004. "Complicating Culture in Child Placements Decisions," *Canadian Journal of Women and the Law* 16, 10: 137–64.

Burdette, Hillary L., and Robert C. Whitaker. 2005. "A National Study of Neighborhood Safety, Outdoor Play, Television Viewing and Obesity in Preschool Children," *Pediatrics* 116, 3: 657–62.

Burke, Catherine. 2005. "'Play in Focus': Children Researching Their Own Spaces and Places for Play," *Children, Youth and Environments* 15, 1: 27–53.

Burton, Peter, Shelley Phipps, and Lori Curtis. 2005. *All in the Family: A Simultaneous Model of Parenting Style and Child Outcomes*. Research Paper Series, No. 261. Ottawa: Statistics Canada.

Burton, Peter, Shelley Phipps, and Lihui Zhang. 2014. "The Prince and the Pauper: Movement of Children Up and Down the Canadian Income Distribution," *Canadian Public Policy* 40, 2: 111–25.

Bushnik, Tracey. 2006. *Child Care in Canada*. Ottawa: Statistics Canada (Catalogue no. 89-599-MIE-No. 003).

Buysse, Virginia, Barbara Davis Goldman, Tracey West, and Heidi Hollingsworth. 2008. "Friendships in Early Childhood: Implications for Early Education and Intervention," in William Brown, Samuel Odom, and Scott McConnell, eds, *Social Competence of Young Children: Risk, Disability and Intervention*. Baltimore, MD: Paul H. Brookes, pp. 77–97.

Byrne, Bronagh. 2012. "Minding the Gap: Children with Disabilities and the United Nations Convention on the Rights of Persons with Disabilities," in Michael Freeman, ed., *Law and Childhood Studies—Current Legal Issues*, vol. 14. Oxford: Oxford University Press, pp. 419–37.

Cait, Cheryl-Anne. 2005. "Parental Death, Shifting Family Dynamics and Female Identity Development," *Omega* 51, 2: 87–105.

Calvert, Sandra, Jennifer Kotler, Sean Zehnder, and Erin Shockey. 2003. "Gender Stereotyping in Children's Reports about Educational and Informational Television," *Media Psychology* 5, 2: 139–62.

Calvert, Sandra, Bonnie Strong, Eliza Jacobs, and Emily Conger. 2007. "Interaction and Participation for Young Hispanic and Caucasian Girls' and Boys' Learning of Media Content," *Media Psychology* 9: 431–45.

Campaign 2000. 2000. *Child Poverty in Canada—Report Card 2000*. Toronto: Campaign 2000. At: http://www.campaign2000.ca/reportCards/national/2000NationalReportCardEnglish.pdf.

———. 2002. *UN Special Session on Children—Putting Promises into Action: A Report on Decade of Child and Family Poverty in Canada*. Toronto: Campaign 2000. At: www.campaign2000.ca/rc/unsscMAY02/MAY02statusreport.pdf.

———. 2005. *Decisions Time for Canada: Let's Make Poverty History—2005 Report Card on Child Poverty in*

Canada. Toronto: Campaign 2000. At: www.campaign2000.ca/rc/rc05/05NationalReportCard.pdf.

———. 2007a. *Oh Canada! Too Many Children in Poverty for Too Long: 2006 Report Card on Child and Family Poverty in Canada.* Toronto: Campaign 2000. At: www.campaign2000.ca/rc/rc06/06_C2000NationalReportCard.pdf.

———. 2007b. *2007 Report Card on Child and Family Poverty in Canada—It Takes a Nation to Raise a Generation: Time for a National Poverty Reduction Strategy.* Toronto: Campaign 2000. At: www.campaign2000.ca/rc/rc07/2007_C2000_NationalReportCard.pdf.

———. 2011. *Revisiting Family Security in Insecure Times—2011 Report Card on Child and Family Poverty in Canada.* Toronto: Campaign 2000. At: www.campaign2000.ca/reportCards/national/2011EnglishRreportCard.pdf.

———. 2013. *Canada's Real Economic Action Plan Begins with Poverty Eradication—2013 Report Card on Child and Family Poverty in Canada.* Toronto: Campaign 2000. At: www.campaign2000.ca/reportCards/national/2013C2000NATIONALREPORTCARDNOV26.pdf.

Campbell, Darren, and Warren Eaton. 1999. "Sex Differences in the Activity Level of Infants," *Infant and Child Development* 8: 1–17.

Campbell, Frances, Gabriella Conti, James J. Heckman, Moon Seong Hyeok, Rodrigo Pinto, Elizabeth Pungello, and Pan Yi. 2014. "Early Childhood Investments Substantially Boost Adult Health," *Science* 343, 6178: 1478–85.

Canadian Broadcasting Corporation. 2000, November 10. "Canada #1 in UN Survey—Again." At: www.cbc.ca/world/story/2000/06/29/UN_report000629.html.

Canadian Broadcast Standards Council. 2007. Voluntary Code Regarding Violence in Television Programming. At http://www.sfu.ca/cmns/faculty/kline_s/320/2010Summer/Resources/Canadian%20Broadcast%20Standards%20Council.pdf.

Canadian Cadet Organizations. 2013. What Cadets Do—Army Cadet. Ottawa: Government of Canada. At: www.cadets.ca/en/what-cadets-do/army.page.

Canadian Centre for Child Protection. 2011, December 13. "First Survey of Quebec Parents on Internet Use by Children Aged 3 to 12 [news release]." At: https://protectchildren.ca/app/en/media_release_marie_vincent_foundation.

Canadian Institute of Health Research, Natural Sciences and Engineering Research Council of Canada, and Social Sciences and Humanities Research Council of Canada. 1998. *Tri-Council Policy Statement: Ethical Conduct for Research Involving Humans* (with 2000, 2002, 2005 amendments). Ottawa.

Canadian Radio-Television and Telecommunications Commission (CRTC). 1995, April 3. "CRTC Announces Public Hearing and Regional Consultations on Approaches to Better Protect Children against Violence [news release]." Ottawa: CRTC/Government of Canada. At: www.crtc.gc.ca/ENG/NEWS/RELEASES/1995/r950403.

———. 1996. Policy on Violence in Television Programming—Public Notice CRTC 1996-36. Ottawa: CRTC/Government of Canada. At: www.crtc.gc.ca/archive/ENG/Notices/1996/Pb96-36.htm.

———. 2014. TV and Radio Advertising Basics. At: http://www.crtc.gc.ca/eng/info_sht/b300.htm.

Canadian Teachers' Federation. 2003. *Kids' Take on Media.* At: http://www.ctf-fce.ca/Research-Library/KidsEnglish.pdf.

———. 2006. *Commercialism in Canadian Schools: Who Calls the Shots?* Ottawa: Canadian Teachers' Federation, Canadian Centre for Policy Alternatives, and Federation des Syndicats de L'Enseignment.

———. 2008. *Child Poverty and Schools: CTF Brief Presented to the Senate Committee on Social Affairs, Science and Technology.* At: http://www.ctf-fce.ca/Research-Library/Brief-reChildPovertyandSchools-eng.pdf.

———. 2014. Poverty: Professional Knowledge on Key Issues Affecting Education. At: http://www.ctf-fce.ca/en/Pages/Issues/Poverty.aspx.

Caraher, Martin, Jane Landon, and Kath Dalmeny. 2006. "Television Advertising and Children: Lessons from Policy Development," *Public Health Nutrition* 9, 5: 596–605.

Cavanagh, Kate, R. Emerson Dobash, and Russell Dobash. 2007. "The Murder of Children by Fathers in the Context of Child Abuse," *Child Abuse and Neglect* 31, 7: 731–46.

CBC News. 2001, July 9. "Spanking Parents Refused Custody." At: www.cbc.ca/news/story/2001/07/09/spanking_parents010709.html.

———. 2007, Nov 2. "Canadian Accused of Thai Sex Crimes Nabbed in Vancouver Airport." At: www.cbc.ca/world/story/2007/11/02/cdnsuspect-thailand.html.

Ceglowski, Deborah. 1997. "Understanding and Building Upon Children's Perceptions of Play Activities in Early Childhood Programs," *Early Childhood Education Journal* 25, 2: 107–12.

Chawla, Raj and Sharanjit Uppal. 2012. "Household Debt in Canada," *Perspectives on Labour and Income* 24, 2: 1–15.

Cheadle, Jacob, and Paul Amato. 2011. "A Quantitative Assessment of Lareau's Qualitative Conclusions about Class, Race, and Parenting," *Journal of Family Issues* 32, 5: 679–706.

Chen, Gina Masullo. 2013. "Don't Call Me That: A Techno-Feminist Critique of the Term Mommy Blogger," *Mass Communication and Society* 16, 4: 510–32.

Chen, Jen-Hao. 2014. "Asthma and Child Behavioral Skills: Does Family Socioeconomic Status Matter?" *Social Science and Medicine* 115, 38–48.

Chen, Wei-Wei. 2014. "The Relationship between Perceived Parenting Style, Filial Piety, and Life Satisfaction in Hong Kong," *Journal of Family Psychology* 28, 3: 308–14.

Chen, Xinyin, and Doran French. 2007. "Children's Social Competence in Cultural Context," *Annual Review of Psychology* 59: 591–616.

Cherney, Isabelle D. 2003. "Children's and Adults' Recall of Sex-Stereotyped Toy Pictures: Effects of Presentation and Memory Task," *Infant and Child Development* 14: 11–27.

Chiang, Lan-Hung Nora. 2008. "'Astronaut families': Transnational Lives of Middle-Class Taiwanese Married Women in Canada," *Social & Cultural Geography* 9, 5: 505–18.

Child Soldiers International. 2014. Straight-18. At: http://www.child-soldiers.org/theme_reader.php?id=1.

Child Welfare League of Canada. 2007. *The Welfare of Canadian Children: It's Our Business—A Collection of Resource Papers for a Healthy Future for Canadian Children and Families*. Ottawa: Child Welfare League.

Christensen, Pia Haudrup. 2004. "Children's Participation in Ethnographic Research: Issues of Power and Representation," *Children and Society* 18: 165–76.

Chung, Angie. 2013. "From Caregivers to Caretakers: The Impact of Family Roles on Ethnicity among Children of Korean and Chinese Immigrant Families," *Qualitative Sociology* 36, 3: 279–302.

Chung, Haejoo, and Carles Muntaner. 2006. "Political and Welfare State Determinants of Infant and Child Health Indicators: An Analysis of Wealthy Countries," *Social Science and Medicine* 63, 3: 829–42.

Citizenship and Immigration Canada (CIC). 2007a. *Welcome to Canada. What You Should Know*. At: https://www.linchsnational.ca/docs/WhatsNew/welcome.pdf.

———. 2007b. Facts and Figures 2006—Immigration Overview. Canada, Permanent Residents Less than 15 Years of Age by Gender and Age. At: www.cic.gc.ca/english/resources/statistics/facts2006/permanent/06.asp.

———. 2007c. Facts and Figures 2006—Immigration Overview. Canada, Permanent Residents Less than 15 Years of Age by Gender, Age and Category. At: www.cic.gc.ca/english/resources/statistics/facts2006/permanent/07.asp.

———. 2007d. Facts and Figures 2006—Immigration Overview. Permanent and Temporary Residents, Overview—Annual Immigration. At: www.cic.gc.ca/english/resources/statistics/facts2006/overview/index.asp.

———. 2007e. Facts and Figures 2006—Immigration Overview. Canada—Permanent Residents by Top Source Countries. At: www.cic.gc.ca/english/resources/statistics/facts2006/permanent/12.asp.

———. 2007f. Facts and Figures 2006—Immigration Overview. Canada—Permanent Residents by Mother Tongue. At: www.cic.gc.ca/english/resources/statistics/facts2006/permanent/28.asp.

———. 2007g. Facts and Figures 2006—Immigration Overview. Canada—Permanent Residents by Province or Territory and Urban Area. At: www.cic.gc.ca/english/resources/statistics/facts2006/permanent/18.asp.

———. 2007h. Recent Immigrants in Metropolitan Areas. Canada—A Comparative Profile Based on 2001 Census, Part C: Families and Households. At: www.cic.gc.ca/english/resources/research/census2001/canada/partc.asp.

———. 2007i. Recent Immigrants in Metropolitan Areas. Canada—A Comparative Profile Based on 2001 Census, Part F: Housing. At: www.cic.gc.ca/english/resources/research/census2001/canada/partf.asp.

———. 2007j. Recent Immigrants in Metropolitan Areas. Canada—A Comparative Profile Based on 2001 Census, Part D: Participation in the Economy. At: www.cic.gc.ca/english/resources/research/census2001/canada/partd.asp.

———. 2014a. Your Rights and Freedoms in Canada. At: http://www.cic.gc.ca/english/newcomers/before-rights-all.asp.

———. 2014b. Facts and Figures 2013—Immigration Overview: Permanent Residents. Canada—Permanent Residents 15 Years of Age or Older by Age and Category. At: http://www.cic.gc.ca/english/resources/statistics/facts2013/permanent/06.asp.

———. 2014c. Facts and Figures 2013—Immigration Overview: Permanent Residents. Canada—Permanent Residents Less than 15 Years of Age by Gender, Age and Category. At: http://www.cic.gc.ca/english/resources/statistics/facts2013/permanent/05.asp.

———. 2014d. Facts and Figures 2013—Immigration Overview: Permanent Residents. Canada—Permanent Residents by Category and Source Area. At: http://www.cic.gc.ca/english/resources/statistics/facts2013/permanent/08.asp.

———. 2014e. Facts and Figures 2013—Immigration Overview: Permanent Residents. Canada—Permanent Residents by Province or Territory and Urban Area. At: http://www.cic.gc.ca/english/resources/statistics/facts2013/permanent/11.asp.

City of Toronto. 2005. *Toronto 2005–2009—Child Care Service Plan.* Toronto: Children's Services Division. At: www.toronto.ca/children/pdf/splan05.pdf.

Clark, Brenda. 2013. "Supporting the Mental Health of Children and Youth of Separating Parents," *Paediatrics and Child Health* 18, 7: 373–7.

Clark, Ruth Anne, Erina MacGeorge, and Lakesha Robinson. 2008. "Evaluation of Peer Comforting Strategies by Children and Adolescents," *Human Communication Research* 34: 319–45.

Clark, Warren, and Susan Crompton. 2006. "Till Death Do Us Part? The Risk of First and Second Marriage Dissolution," *Canadian Social Trends* 81: 24–31.

Classen, Albrecht. 2005. "Philippe Ariès and the Consequences: History of Childhood, Family Relations, and Personal Emotions: Where Do We Stand Today?" in Classen, ed., *Childhood in the Middle Ages and the Renaissance: The Results of a Paradigm Shift in the History of Mentality.* Berlin: Walter de Gruyter.

Coad, Jane, and Ruth Evans. 2008. "Reflections on Practical Approaches to Involving Children and Young People in the Data Analysis Process," *Children and Society* 22: 41–52.

Coates, Elizabeth. 2002. "'I Forgot the Sky!' Children's Stories Contained within Their Drawings," *International Journal of Early Years Education* 10, 1: 21–35.

Cohen, Lynn. 2008. "Foucault and the Early Childhood Classroom," *Educational Studies* 44, 1: 7–21.

Colbert, Judith. 2010. *Welcoming Newcomer Children: The Settlement of Young Immigrants and Refugees.* Toronto: Fairmeadow.

Colbert, Judith. 2014. *Child Health Across Cultures.* Toronto: Fairmeadow.

Cole, Charlotte, Cairo Arafat, Chava Tidhar, Wafa Zidan Tafesh, Nathan Fox, Melane Killen, Alicia Ardila-Rey, Lewis Leavitt, Gerry Lesser, Beth Richman, and Fiona Yung. 2003. "The Educational Impact of Rechov SumSum/Shara's Simsim: A Sesame Street Television Series to Promote Respect and Understanding among Children Living in Israel, The West Bank and Gaza," *International Journal of Behavior Development* 27, 5: 409–22.

Collins, Randall. 2006. "Comparative and Historical Patterns of Education," in

Maureen Hallinan, ed., *The Handbook of the Sociology of Education*. Boston: Springer Science and Business Media, pp. 213–39.

Collins, Rebecca, Terry Schell, Phyllis Ellickson, and Daniel McCaffrey. 2003. "Predictors of Beer Advertising Awareness among Eighth Graders," *Addiction* 98, 9: 1297–306.

Colón, A.R., with P.A. Colón. 2001. *A History of Children: A Socio-Cultural Survey across Millennia*. Westport, CT: Greenwood Press.

Commission on Elementary Education. 2006. "School Daycare Services: Placing Quality at the Heart of Priorities." Québec: Government of Quebec.

Condry, John, and Sandra Condry. 1976. "Sex Differences: A Study of the Eye of the Beholder," *Child Development* 47: 812–19.

Conger, R., X. Ge, G. Elder, F. Lorenz, and R. Simons. 1994. "Economic Stress, Coercive Family Process and Developmental Problems of Adolescents," *Child Development* 65: 541–61.

Connell, Raewyn. 2000. *The Men and the Boys*. Cambridge: Polity.

———. 2010. "Kartini's Children: On the Need for Thinking Gender and Education Together on a World Scale," *Gender and Education* 22, 6: 603–15.

Connolly, Paul. 1998. *Racism, Gender Identities and Young Children: Social Relations in a Multi-ethnic, Inner-City Primary School*. London: Routledge.

Connor, Susan. 2006. "Food-Related Advertising on Preschool Television: Building Brand Recognition in Young Viewers," *Pediatrics* 118, 4: 1478–85.

Cook, Daniel Thomas. 2004. *The Commodification of Childhood: The Children's Clothing Industry and the Rise of the Child Consumer*. Durham, NC: Duke University Press.

Cook, Daniel Thomas, and Susan Kaiser. 2004. "Betwixt and Be Tween: Age Ambiguity and the Sexualization of the Female Consuming Subject," *Journal of Consumer Culture* 4, 2: 203–27.

Cool, Julie. 2007. *Childcare in Canada: The Federal Role*. Ottawa: Library of Parliament. At: http://www.parl.gc.ca/content/lop/researchpublications/prb0420-e.pdf.

Cooley, Charles. 1956 [1922]. *Human Nature and the Social Order*. Glencoe, IL: Free Press.

Corak, Miles. 2011. "Age at Immigration and the Education Outcomes of Children," in *Analytical Studies Branch Research Paper Series*. Ottawa: Statistics Canada (Catalogue no. 11F0019M—No. 336). At: www.statcan.gc.ca/pub/11f0019m/11f0019m2011336-eng.pdf.

Cornock, Marc, and Heather Montgomery. 2011. "Children's Rights In and Out of the Womb," *International Journal of Children's Rights* 19, 1: 3-19.

Corsaro, William. 2005. *The Sociology of Childhood*, 2nd edn. London: Sage.

Corsaro, William. 2015. *The Sociology of Childhood*, 4th edn. Los Angeles: Sage.

Cote, Mark, Richard Day, and Grieg de Peuter, eds. 2007. *Utopian Pedagogy: Radical Experiments against Neoliberal Globalization*. Toronto: University of Toronto Press.

Cotter, Adam, and Pascale Beaupré. 2014. "Police-Reported Sexual Offences against Children and Youth in Canada," in *Juristat* 34, 1: 1–29. Ottawa: Statistics Canada.

Courage, Mary, Greg Reynolds, and John Richards. 2006. "Infants' Attention to Patterned Stimuli: Developmental Change from 3 to 12 Months of Age," *Child Development* 77, 3: 680–95.

Court of Appeal for Ontario. 2002. Section 43 of the Criminal Code (Date: 20020115; Docket: C34749). At: http://www.ontariocourts.on.ca/decisions/2002/january/canadianC34749.htm.

Couture, Ernest. 1940. *The Canadian Mother and Child*. Ottawa: Department of Health.

Craig, Wendy, Debra Pepler, and Julie Blias. 2007. "Responding to Bullying: What Works," *Social Psychology International* 28, 4: 465–77.

Crawford, Sara K. Karen N. Stafford, Sarah M. Phillips, Kathleen J. Scott, and Patricia Tucker. 2014. "Strategies for Inclusion in Play among Children with Physical Disabilities in Childcare Centers: An Integrative Review," *Physical and Occupational Therapy in Pediatrics* 34, 4: 404–23.

Cressey, Daniel. 2007. "Is Baby DVD Research Mickey Mouse Science?" *Nature* 448, 23: 848–9.

Crohn, Helen. 2006. "Five Styles of Positive Stepmothering from the Perspective of Young Adult Stepdaughters," *Journal of Divorce and Remarriage* 46, 1 and 2: 119–34.

Cross, P. 2006. "Emerging Patterns in the Labour Market: A Reversal from the 1990s," *Canadian Economic Observer* 3: 1–13.

Cunningham, Charles E., Lesley Cunningham, Jenna Ratcliffe, and Tracey Vaillancourt. 2010. "A Qualitative Analysis of the Bullying Prevention and Intervention Recommendations of Students in Grades 5 to 8," *Journal of School Violence* 9, 4: 321–38.

Cunningham, Mick. 2001. "The Influence of Parental Attitudes and Behaviors on Children's Attitudes towards Gender and Household Labor in Early Adulthood," *Journal of Marriage and Family* 63: 111–22.

da Fonseca, Marcia. 2014. "Eat or Heat? The Effects of Poverty on Children's Behavior," *Pediatric Dentistry* 36, 2: 132–7.

Dahl, Gordon, and Erico Moretti. 2004. *The Demand for Sons: Evidence from Divorce, Fertility and Shotgun Marriage*. Cambridge, MA: National Bureau of Economic Research, Working Paper Series No. W10281.

Daly, Kerry. 1993. "Reshaping Fatherhood: Finding the Models," *Journal of Family Issues* 14, 4: 510–30.

———. 2004. *The Changing Culture of Parenting*. Ottawa: Vanier Institute of the Family.

Daly, Kerry, Lynda Ashbourne, and Jaime Brown. 2013. "A Reorientation of Worldview: Children's Influence on Fathers," *Journal of Family Issues* 34, 10: 1401–24.

Danby, Susan. 2009. "Childhood and Social Interaction in Everyday Life: An Epilogue," *Journal of Pragmatics* 41, 8: 1596–9.

Danby, Susan, Lynette Ewing, and Karen Thorpe. 2011. "The Novice Researcher: Interviewing Young Children," *Qualitative Inquiry* 17, 1: 74–84.

Danby, Susan, and Ann Farrell. 2004. "Accounting for Young People's Competence in Educational Research: New Perspectives on Research Ethics," *Australian Educational Researcher* 31, 3: 35–49.

Darwin, Charles. 1994 [1859]. *The Origin of Species by Means of Natural Selection*. London: Studio Editions.

Davey, Ian. 2003. "The Rhythm of Work and the Rhythm of School," in Janovicek and Parr (2003: 108–21).

Davin, Delia D. 1991. "The Early Childhood Education of the Only Child Generation in Urban China," in Irving Epstein, ed., *Chinese Education: Problems, Policies, and Prospects*. New York: Garland, pp. 42–65.

Davis, Kingsley, and Wilbert Moore. 1945. "Some Principles of Stratification," *American Sociology Association* 10, 2: 242–9.

Davis, Phillip W. 1997. "The Changing Meaning of Spanking," in A.S. Skolnick and J. Skolnick, eds, *Families in Transition*, 9th edn. New York: HarperCollins, pp. 278–89.

Davis, Shannon. 2002. "Sex Stereotypes in Commercials Targeted towards Children: A Content Analysis," *Sociological Spectrum* 23: 407–24.

Day, David, Michele Peterson-Badali, and Martin Ruck. 2006. "The Relationship between Maternal Attitudes and Young People's Attitudes towards Children's Rights," *Journal of Adolescence* 29: 193–207.

Dean, Hartley. 2007. "Tipping the Balance: The Problematic Nature of Work–Life Balance in a Low Income Neighborhood," *Journal of Social Policy* 36, 2: 519–37.

Deator-Deckard, K., K. Dodge, J. Bates, and G. Pettit. 1996. "Physical Discipline among African American and European American Mothers: Links to Children's Externalizing Behaviours," *Developmental Psychology* 32: 1065–72.

Dei, George J. Sefa. 2008. "Schooling as Community: Race, Schooling, and the Education of African Youth," *Journal of Black Studies* 38, 3: 346–66.

de Leeuw, Sarah. 2009. "'If Anything Is to Be Done with the Indian, We Must Catch Him Very Young': Colonial Constructions of Aboriginal Children and the Geographies of Indian Residential Schooling in British Columbia, Canada," *Children's Geographies* 7, 2: 123–40.

deMause, Lloyd, ed. 1975. *The History of Childhood: The Evolution of Parent–Child Relationships as a Factor in History*. New York: Harper and Row.

Denison, Jacqueline, Colleen Varcoe, and Annette Browne. 2014. "Aboriginal Women's Experiences of Accessing Health Care When State Apprehension of Children Is Being Threatened," *Journal of Advanced Nursing* 70, 5: 1105–16.

Dennison, Barbara, Tara A. Erb, and Paul L. Jenkins. 2002. "Television Viewing and Television in Bedroom Associated with Overweight Risk among Low-Income Preschool Children," *Pediatrics* 109, 6: 1028–35.

Department of Justice. 1985. Divorce Act, 1985, c. 3 (2nd Supp.) D-3.4. [Assented to 13 Feb. 1986]. At: laws.justice.gc.ca/en/ShowFullDoc/cs/D-3.4//20080321/en?command=HOME&caller=SI&fragment=divorce%20Act%20of%201968&search_type=all&day=21&month=3&year=2008&search_domain=cs&showall=L&statuteyear=all&lengthannual=50&length=50.

———. 2002. *Children Come First: A Report to Parliament Reviewing the Provisions and Operation of the Federal Child Support Guidelines*, 2 vols. Ottawa: Minister of Justice and Attorney General of Canada.

———. 2004. *Voice and Support: Programs for Children Experiencing Parental Separation and Divorce* (Background Paper). Ottawa: Department of Justice. At: www.justice.gc.ca/en/ps/pad/reports/2004-FCY-2/chapter_3.html.

———. 2006a. *Federal Child Support Guidelines: Step-By-Step*. Ottawa: Minister of Justice and the Attorney General of Canada. At: www.justice.gc.ca/en/ps/sup/pub/guide/guide.pdf.

———. 2006b. *Inventory of Government-Based Family Justice Services*. Ottawa: Department of Justice. At: www.justice.gc.ca/en/ps/pad/resources/fjis/report/section2.asp.

———. 2007a. *Sexual Abuse and the Exploitation of Children and Youth: A Fact Sheet from the Department of Justice Canada*. Ottawa: Department of Justice. At: www.justice.gc.ca/en/ps/fm/sexabuse_fs.pdf.

———. 2007b. "Part V—Sexual Offences, Public Morals and Disorderly Conduct—Definition of Child Pornography," in *Criminal Code of Canada*. Ottawa: Department of Justice. At: laws.justice.gc.ca/en/showdoc/cs/C-46.

———. 2007c. *What Happens Next? Information for Kids about Separation and Divorce*. Ottawa: Department of Justice.

———. 2007d. *Child Abuse: A Fact Sheet from the Department of Justice Canada*. Ottawa: Department of Justice. At: www.justice.gc.ca/en/ps/fm/child_abuse_fact_sheet.pdf.

———. 2012. *Child Abuse Is Wrong: What Can I Do?* Ottawa: Department of Justice. At: http://www.justice.gc.ca/eng/rp-pr/cj-jp/fv-vf/caw-mei/index.html.

———. 2013. About Family Violence. Ottawa: Department of Justice. At: http://www.justice.gc.ca/eng/cj-jp/fv-vf/about-apropos.html.

Dethloff, Nina. 2005. "Same-Sex Parents in a Comparative Perspective," *International Law Forum du droit international* 7: 195–205.

Dickason, Olive Patricia, with David T. McNab. 2009. *Canada's First Nations: A History of Founding Peoples from Earliest Times*, 4th edn. Toronto: Oxford University Press.

Diekmann, Andreas, and Kurt Schmidheiny. 2004. "Do Parents of Girls Have a Higher Risk of Divorce? An Eighteen-Country Study," *Journal of Marriage and Family* 66: 651–60.

Dinerman, Miriam. 2001. "Editorial: Counting, Costs and the Value of Caring Work," *Affilia* 6, 2: 133–7.

Di Stefano, Gessica, and Francine Cyr. 2014. "Child Adjustment Following Parental Separation: The Role of Maternal Well-Being, Parenting Quality, and Household Income," *Journal of Child Custody* 11, 1: 5–24.

Dittrick, Crystal, Tanya Beran, Faye Mishna, Ross Hetherington, and Shaheen Shariff. 2013. "Do Children Who Bully Their Peers Also Play Violent Video Games? A Canadian National Study," *Journal of School Violence* 12, 4: 297–318.

Dobash, R E, and Russell Dobash. 1979. *Violence against Wives: A Case against the Patriarchy*. New York: Free Press.

Dobson, Jarod, Hélène Maheux, and Tina Chui. 2013. Generation Status: Canadian-Born Children of Immigrants. Ottawa: Statistics Canada (Catalogue no. 99-010-X2011003). At: http://www12.statcan.gc.ca/nhs-enm/2011/as-sa/99-010-x/99-010-x2011003_2-eng.pdf.

Dockett, Sue, and Bob Perry. 2005. "Researching with Children: Insights from the Starting School Research Project," Early Child Development and Care 175, 6: 507–21.

———. 2005. "'You Need to Know How to Play Safe': Children's Experiences with Starting School," Contemporary Issues in Early Childhood 6, 1: 4–18.

Doherty, Gillian, Martha Friendly, and Jane Beach. 2003. OECD Thematic Review of Early Childhood Education and Care: Canadian Background Report. Ottawa: Her Majesty the Queen in Right of Canada.

Doherty, Gillian, Donna Lero, Hillel Goelman, Annette LaGrange, and Jocelyne Tougas. 2000. You Bet I Care! Wages, Working Conditions, and Practices in Child Care Centres. Guelph: Centre for Families, Work and Wellbeing.

Dolev, R., and M. Suzanne Zeedyk. 2006. "How To Be a Good Parent in Bad Times: Constructing Parenting Advice about Terrorism," Child: Care, Health and Development 32, 4: 467–76.

Donne, David. 1997. "Radio Corporation of America," in Newcomb (1997). At: www.museum.tv/archives/etv/R/htmlR/radiocorpora/radiocorpora.htm.

Donnelly, Michael, and Murray A. Straus, eds. 2005. Corporal Punishment of Children in Theoretical Perspective. New Haven: Yale University Press.

Dooley, Martin, and Jennifer Stewart. 2007. "Family Income, Parenting Styles and Child Behavioural-Emotional Outcomes," Health Econ.16, 2: 145–62.

Doucet, Andrea. 2006. Do Men Mother? Toronto: University of Toronto Press.

Douglas, Kristen. 2001. Divorce Law in Canada. Ottawa: Law and Government Division, Government of Canada.

Duindam, Vincent, and Ed Spruijt. 2002. "The Reproduction of Fatherhood," Feminism and Psychology 12, 1: 28–32.

Dumont, Micheline, Michèle Jean, Marie Lavigne, and Jennifer Stoddart. 1987. Quebec Women—A History. Toronto: Women's Press.

Dunn, Judy, Helen Cheng, Thomas O'Connor, and Laura Bridges. 2004. "Children's Perspectives on Their Relationships with Their Nonresident Fathers: Influences, Outcomes and Implications," Journal of Child Psychology and Psychiatry 45, 3: 553–66.

Durkin, Kevin, and Bradley Nugent. 1998. "Kindergarten Children's Gender-Role Expectations for Television Actors," Sex Roles 38, 5 and 6: 387–402.

Durrant, Joan. 2012. "Physical Punishment of Children: Lessons from 20 Years of Research," Canadian Medical Association Journal 184, 12: 1373–7.

Durrant, Joan E., Ron Ensom, and Coalition on Physical Punishment of Children and Youth. 2004. Joint Statement on Physical Punishment of Children and Youth. Ottawa: Coalition on Physical Punishment of Children and Youth. At: www.nospank.net/joint_statement_e.pdf.

Duschinsky, Robbie. 2013. "Augustine, Rousseau, and the Idea of Childhood," Heythrop Journal 54, 1: 77–88.

Dyson, Lily L. 2005. "The Lives of Recent Chinese Immigrant Children in Canadian Society: Values, Aspirations and Social Experiences," Canadian Ethnic Studies 37, 2: 49–66.

Edelbrock, Craig, Richard Rende, Robert Plomin, and Lee Anne Thompson. 1995. "A Twin Study of Competence and Problem Behaviour in Childhood and Early Adolescence," Journal of Child Psychology and Psychiatry 36, 5: 775–85.

Edwards, Rosalind, and Pam Alldred. 1999. "Children and Young People's Views of Social Research—The Case of Research on Home–School Relations," Childhood 6, 2: 261–81.

Edwards, Rosalind, and Val Gillies. 2013. "The Moral Context for Parenting: 'Where Are The Parents?' Changing Parenting Responsibilities Between the 1960s and the 2010s," in Charlotte Faircloth, Diane Hoffman and Linda Layne, eds, Parenting in Global Perspective: Negotiating Ideologies of Kinship, Self and Politics. London: Routledge, pp. 21–35.

Egan, R. Danielle. 2013. *Becoming Sexual: A Critical Appraisal of the Sexualization of Girls*. Cambridge: Polity Press.

Egeland, Grace, Angela Pacey, Zirong Cao, and Isaac Sobol. 2010. "Food Insecurity among Inuit Preschoolers: Nunavut Inuit Child Health Survey, 2007–2008," *Canadian Medical Association Journal* 182, 3: 243-248.

Ehrenberg, Marion, Laura-Lynn Stewart, Diane Roche, Jennifer Pringle, and Jacqueline Bush. 2006. "Adolescents in Divorcing Families: Perspectives of What Helps and Hinders," *Journal of Divorce and Remarriage* 45, 3 and 4: 69–91.

Eley, Thalia C., Derek Bolton, Thomas O'Connor, Sean Perrin, Patrick Smith, and Robert Plomin. 2003. "A Twin Study of Anxiety-Related Behaviours in Pre-school Children," *Journal of Child Psychology and Psychiatry & Allied Disciplines* 44, 7: 945–60.

Elkin, Frederick. 1960. *The Child and Society: The Process of Socialization*. New York: Random House.

Elkind, David. 1981. *The Hurried Child: Growing Up Too Fast Too Soon*. Reading, MA: Addison-Wesley.

Elliott, William. 2013. "The effects of economic instability on children's educational outcomes," *Children and Youth Services Review* 35, 3: 461–71.

Emmen, Rosanneke, Maike Malda, Judi Mesman, Hatice Ekmekci, and Marinus van IJzendoorn. 2012. "Sensitive Parenting as a Cross-Cultural Ideal: Sensitivity Beliefs of Dutch, Moroccan, and Turkish Mothers in the Netherlands," *Attachment and Human Development* 14, 6: 601–19.

Employment and Social Development Canada. 2014. Family Life—Divorce. Ottawa: Employment and Social Development Canada. At: http://www4.hrsdc.gc.ca/.3ndic.1t.4r@-eng.jsp?iid=76.

Eni, Rachel. 2009. "Health Disparities in Canada: A Focus on First Nations Children," in UNICEF Canada. 2009. *Canadian Supplement to The State of the World's Children. Aboriginal Children's Health: Leaving No Child Behind*. Toronto: UNICEF Canada, pp: 10–20. At: www.unicef.ca/sites/default/files/imce_uploads/DISCOVER/OUR%20WORK/ADVOCACY/DOMESTIC/POLICY%20ADVOCACY/DOCS/Leaving%20no%20child%20behind%2009.pdf.

Enkhtor, Dulamdary. 2007. "Paving a Two-Way Street: Encouraging Children's Participation in a Study on the Physical and Emotional Punishment of Children in Vietnam," *Children, Youth and Environments* 17, 1: 88–104.

Ennemoser, Marco, and Wolfgang Schneider. 2007. "Relations of Television Viewing and Reading: Findings from a 4-Year Longitudinal Study," *Journal of Educational Psychology* 99, 2: 349–68.

Epstein, Debbie. 1997. "Cultures of Schooling/Cultures of Sexuality," *International Journal of Inclusive Education* 1: 37–53.

Epstein, D., M.J. Kehily, and E. Renold. 2012. "Culture, Policy and the Unmarked Child: Fragments of the Sexualisation Debates," *Gender and Education* 24, 3: 249–54.

Epstein, Rachel, ed. 2009. *Who's Your Daddy? And Other Writings on Queer Parenting*. Toronto: Sumach Press.

Erwin, Elizabeth, and Naomi Morton. 2008. "Exposure to Media Violence and Young Children with and without Disabilities: Powerful Opportunities for Family-Professional Partnerships," *Early Childhood Education Journal* 36, 2: 105–12.

Esping-Andersen, Gøsta. 2007. "Sociological Explanations of Changing Income Distributions," *American Behavioral Scientist* 50, 5: 639–58.

Evans, Andrea, Alexander Caudarella, Savithiri Ratnapalan, and Kevin Chan. 2014. "The Cost and Impact of the Interim Federal Health Program Cuts on Child Refugees in Canada," *PLoS ONE* 9, 5: 1–4.

Fabricius, William. 2003. "Listening to Children of Divorce: New Findings That Diverge from Wallerstein, Lewis and Blakeslee," *Family Relations* 52, 4: 385–96.

Fagot, B.I. 1986. "Beyond the Reinforcement Principle: Another Step towards Understanding Sex Role Development," *Developmental Psychology* 21: 1097–104.

Faircloth, Charlotte, Diane Hoffman, and Linda Layne, eds. 2013. *Parenting in Global Perspective: Negotiating Ideologies of Kinship, Self and Politics.* New York: Routledge.

Fallon, Barbara, Martin Chabot, John Fluke, Cindy Blackstock, Bruce MacLaurin, and Lil Tonmyr. 2013. "Placement Decisions and Disparities among Aboriginal Children: Further Analysis of the Canadian Incidence Study of Reported Child Abuse and Neglect Part A: Comparisons of the 1998 and 2003 Surveys," *Child Abuse and Neglect* 37, 1: 47–60.

Fantino, Ana Marie, and Alice Colak. 2001. "Refugee Children in Canada: Searching for Identity," *Child Welfare* 80, 5: 587–96.

Farber, Susan. 1981. *Identical Twins Reared Apart: A Re-Analysis.* New York: Basic Books.

Farrell, Ann, Collette Taylor, and Lee Tennent. 2002. "Early Childhood Services: What Can Children Tell Us?" *Australian Journal of Early Childhood* 27, 3: 13–17.

Fauth, Rebecca, Tama Leventhal, and Jeanne Brooks-Gunn. 2007. "Welcome to the Neighborhood? Long-Term Impacts of Moving to Low-Poverty Neighborhoods on Poor Children's and Adolescents' Outcomes," *Journal of Research on Adolescence* 17, 2: 249–84.

Ferguson, Christopher, Cheryl Olson, Lawrence Kutner, and Dorothy Warner. 2014. "Violent Video Games, Catharsis Seeking, Bullying, and Delinquency: A Multivariate Analysis of Effects," *Crime and Delinquency* 60, 5: 764–84.

Fergusson, Emma, Barbara Maughan, and Jean Golding. 2008. "Which Children Receive Grandparental Care and What Effect Does It Have?" *Journal of Child Psychology and Psychiatry* 49, 2: 161–9.

Ferns, C., and M. Friendly. 2014. *The State of Early Childhood Education and Care in Canada 2012.* Toronto: Movingchildcareforward.ca.

Ferrao, Vincent. 2010. "Paid Work," in *Women in Canada: A Gender-Based Statistical Report.* Ottawa: Statistics Canada (Catalogue no. 89-503-X). http://www.statcan.gc.ca/pub/89-503-x/2010001/article/11387-eng.pdf.

Findlay, Leanne, Dafna Kohen, and Anton Miller. 2014. "Developmental Milestones among Aboriginal Children in Canada," *Paediatrics and Child Health* 19, 5: 241–6.

Fisch, Shalom, and Rosemarie Truglio, eds. 2001. *"G" is for Growing: Thirty Years of Research on Children and Sesame Street.* Mahwah, NJ: Erlbaum.

Fitzgerald, H., T. Mann, and M. Barratt. 1999. "Fathers and Infants," *Infant Mental Health Journal* 20, 3: 213–21.

Flaks, D.K., I. Ficher, F. Masterpsqua, and G. Joseph. 1995. "Lesbians Choosing Motherhood: A Comparative Study of Lesbian and Heterosexual Parents and Their Children," *Developmental Psychology* 31, 1: 105–14.

Flanagan, K., J.P. Beach, and P. Varmuza 2013. *You Bet We Still Care. A Survey of Centre-Based Early Childhood Education and Care in Canada: Highlights Report.* Ottawa: Child Care Human Resources Sector Council. At: www.wstcoast.org/pdf/YouBetSurveyReport_Final.pdf.

Folta, Sara, Jeanne Goldberg, Christina Economos, Rick Bell, and Rachel Meltzer. 2006. "Food Advertising Targeting at School-Age Children: A Content Analysis," *Journal of Nutrition Education and Behaviour* 38, 4: 244–8.

Fortier, Sandra. 2006. "On Being a Poor Child in America: Views of Poverty from 7–12-Year-Olds," *Journal of Children and Poverty* 12, 2: 113–28.

Foucault, Michel. 1977. *Discipline and Punishment: The Birth of the Prison.* London: Allen Lane.

Frederick, John, and Chris Goddard. 2007. "Exploring the Relationship between Poverty, Childhood Adversity and Child Abuse from the Perspective of Adulthood," *Child Abuse Review* 16: 323–41.

Free the Children. 2015. Our Story. At: http://www.freethechildren.com/about-us/our-story.

Freedman, Alisa. 2014. "Sesame Street's Place in Japan: Marketing Multicultural New York in Cosmopolitan Tokyo," *Japan Forum* 26: 144–63.

Freeman, Nancy. 2007. "Preschoolers' Perception of Gender Appropriate Toys and Their Parents' Beliefs about Genderized Behaviors: Misconceptions, Mixed Messages or Hidden Truths?" *Early Childhood Education Journal* 34, 5: 357–66.

Freiler, Christa, and Judy Cerny. 1998. *Benefiting Canada's Children: Perspectives on Gender and Social Responsibility.* Ottawa: Status of Women Canada.

Freiler, Christa, Laurel Rothman, and Pedro Barata. 2004. *Pathways to Progress: Structural Solutions to Address Child Poverty.* Toronto: Campaign 2000. At: www.campaign2000.ca/res/dispapers/PathwaysENG.pdf.

Frerichs, Leah, Julie Andsager, Shelly Campo, Mary Aquilino, and Carolyn Stewart Dyer. 2006. "Framing Breastfeeding and Formula-Feeding Messages in Popular US Magazines," *Women and Health* 44, 1: 95–118.

Freud, Sigmund. 1971. *New Introductory Lectures on Psychoanalysis.* London: Allen and Unwin.

———. 2003. *An Outline of Psychoanalysis.* London: Penguin.

Frideres, James S., and René R. Gadacz. 2001. *Aboriginal Peoples in Canada: Contemporary Conflicts,* 6th edn. Toronto: Prentice-Hall.

Fridkin, Kim, and Patrick Kenny. 2007. "Examining the Gender Gap in Children's Attitudes towards Politics," *Sex Roles* 56, 3 and 4: 133–40.

Friendly, Martha. 2006. "Early Learning and Child Care: How Does Canada Measure Up?" in *Briefing Notes.* Toronto: Childcare Resource and Research Unit.

Fritz, Gregory K., ed. 2013. "Co-Parenting: A Guide for Parents," *Brown University Child and Adolescent Behavior Letter* 29, S12: 1: 1–II.

Fritz, Gregory K., ed. 2014. "Discipline: A Guide for Parents," *Brown University Child and Adolescent Behavior Letter* 30, S11: I–II.

Froggio, Giacinto, and Robert Agnew. 2007. "The Relationship between Crime and 'Objective' versus 'Subjective' Strains," *Journal of Criminal Justice* 35: 81–7.

Fukkink, Ruben, and Anna Lont. 2007. "Does Training Matter? A Meta-analysis and Review of Caregiver Training Studies," *Early Childhood Research Quarterly* 22, 3: 294–311.

Funk, Jeanne, Heidi Bechtoldt Baldacci, Tracie Pasold, and Jennifer Baumgardner. 2004. "Violence Exposure in Real-Life, Video Games, Television, Movies and the Internet: Is There Desensitization?" *Journal of Adolescence* 27: 23–39.

Furedi, F. 2001. *Paranoid Parenting.* London: Allen Lane.

Furnham, Adrian, and L. Gasson. 1998. "Sex Differences in Parental Estimates of Their Children's Intelligence," *Sex Roles* 38: 151–62.

Gådin, Katja Gillander. 2012. "Sexual Harassment of Girls in Elementary School: A Concealed Phenomenon within a Heterosexual Romantic Discourse," *Journal of Interpersonal Violence* 27, 9: 1762–79.

Galarneau, Diane. 2010. "Temporary Employment in the Downturn," *Perspectives on Labour and Income* 11, 11: 1–15.

Gannon, Susanne. 2007. "Laptops and Lipstick: Feminising Technology," *Learning, Media and Technology* 32, 1: 53–67.

Gassman-Pines, Anna, and Hirokazu Yoshikawa. 2006. "The Effects of Antipoverty Programs on Children's Cumulative Level of Poverty-Related Risk," *Developmental Psychology* 42, 6: 981–99.

Gennetian, Lisa, and Cynthia Miller. 2002. "Children and Welfare Reform: A View from an Experimental Welfare Program in Minnesota," *Child Development* 73, 2: 601–21.

Gera, Surendra, and Kurt Mang. 1998. "The Knowledge-Based Economy: Shifts in Industrial Output," *Canadian Public Policy* 24, 2: 149–84.

Gerbner, G., L. Gross, M. Morgan, N. Signorelli, and J. Shanahan. 2002. "Growing Up with Television: Cultivation Processes," in J. Bryant and D. Zillmann, eds, *Media Effects: Advances in Theory and Research.* Mahwah, NJ: Erlbaum, pp. 43–68.

Ghiglieri, Michael. 2000. *The Dark Side of Man: Tracing the Origins of Male Violence.* Cambridge, MA: Helix Books.

Gibson, Diane. 2013. "Ambiguous Roles in a Stepfamily: Using Maps of Narrative Practices to Develop a New Family Story with Adolescents and Parents," *Contemporary Family Therapy: An International Journal* 35, 4: 793–805.

Giddens, A. 1997. *Sociology*, 3rd edn. Oxford: Polity Press in association with Blackwell Publishers.

Gilbert, Rob, and Pam Gilbert. 1998. *Masculinity Goes to School*. London: Routledge.

Gill, Stephen, and Isabella Bakker. 2003. *Power, Production and Social Reproduction: Human Insecurity in the Global Political Economy*. London: Palgrave.

Gillies, Val. 2005. "'Raising the 'Meritocracy': Parenting and the Individualization of Social Class," *Sociology* 39, 5: 835–53.

Giroux, Henry. 1998. "Nymphet Fantasies: Child Beauty Pageants and the Politics of Innocence," *Social Text* 16, 4: 31–53.

Gloger-Tippelt, Gabriele, and Lilith König. 2007. "Attachment Representations in 6-year-old Children from One and Two Parent Families in Germany," *School Psychology International* 28, 3: 313–30.

Goelman, Hillel, Bozena Zdaniuk, W. Thomas Boyce, Jeffrey Armstrong, and Marilyn Essex. 2014. "Maternal Mental Health, Child Care Quality, and Children's Behavior," *Journal of Applied Developmental Psychology* 35, 4: 347–56.

Goldberg, Abbie, and Katherine Allen. 2007. "Imagining Men: Lesbian Mothers' Perceptions of Male Involvement during the Transition to Parenthood," *Journal of Marriage and Family* 69: 352–65.

Goldberg, Abbie, and Maureen Perry-Jenkins. 2007. "The Division of Labor and Perception of Parental Roles: Lesbian Couples across the Transition to Parenthood," *Journal of Social and Personal Relationships* 24, 2: 297–318.

Golombok, S., B. Perry, A. Burston, C. Murray, J. Mooney-Somers, and M. Stevens. 2003. "Children with Lesbian Parents: A Community Study," *Developmental Psychology* 39, 1: 20–33.

Golombok, Susan, Laura Mellish, Sarah Jennings, Polly Casey, Fiona Tasker, and Michael Lamb. 2014. "Adoptive Gay Father Families: Parent-Child Relationships and Children's Psychological Adjustment," *Child Development* 85, 2: 456–68.

Gómez Espino, Juan Miguel. 2013. "Two Sides of Intensive Parenting: Present and Future Dimensions in Contemporary Relations Between Parents and Children in Spain," *Childhood* 20, 1: 22–36.

Government of British Columbia. 2007. Child, Family and Community Service Act. At: www.qp.gov.bc.ca/statreg/stat/C/96046_01.htm.

Government of Canada. 1997. National Children's Agenda. At: www.socialunion.ca/nca/June21-2000/english/index_e.html.

———. 2004. *Multilateral Framework on Early Learning and Child Care*. Gatineau: Early Learning and Child Care. At: http://www.ecd-elcc.ca/eng/elcc/elcc_multiframe.shtml.

———. 2005. Canada–Quebec Agreement on Early Learning and Child Care. Funding Agreement. At: action.web.ca/home/crru/rsrcs_crru_full.shtml?x=82553.

———. 2006. Universal Child Care Plan. At: www.universalchildcare.ca/en/faqs_benefit.shtml.

———. 2007. *The National Child Benefit—Progress Report 2005*. Ottawa. Her Majesty the Queen in Right of Canada (Catalogue no. HS1-3/2005E). At: www.nationalchildbenefit.ca.

———. 2010. *Tri-Council Policy Statement 2—Ethical Conduct for Research Involving Humans*. Ottawa: Canadian Institutes for Health Research, Natural Sciences and Engineering Research Council of Canada, and Social Sciences and Humanities Research Council of Canada. At: http://www.pre.ethics.gc.ca/pdf/eng/tcps2/TCPS_2_FINAL_Web.pdf.

———. 2014. An Act Respecting the Mandatory Reporting of Internet Child Pornography by Persons Who Provide an Internet Service. S.C. 2011, c. 4. Ottawa: Justice Laws Website. At: http://laws-lois.justice.gc.ca/eng/acts/I-20.7/page-1.html.

———. 2015. Universal Child Care Benefit. Ottawa: Canadian Revenue Agency. http://www.cra-arc.gc.ca/uccb/.

Government of Manitoba. 2007. The Child and Family Services Act. At: web2.gov.mb.ca/laws/statutes/ccsm/c080e.php.

Government of Ontario. 2014. Child and Family Services Act, R.S.O. 1990, c. C. 11. Toronto: Government of Ontario. At: http://www.e-laws.gov.on.ca/html/statutes/english/elaws_statutes_90c11_e.htm.

Government of Quebec. 2003. *Development and Funding Scenarios to Ensure the Permanence, Accessibility and Quality of Childcare Services: Consultations 2003*. Québec: Ministère de l'Emploi, de la Solidarité Sociale et de la Famille.

———. 2004. *Reconciling Freedom and Social Justice: A Challenge for the Future— Government Action Plan to Combat Poverty and Social Exclusion*. Québec: Ministère de l'Emploi, de la Solidarité sociale et de la Famille. At: www.mess. gouv.qc.ca/publications/index_en.asp?ca tegorie=portail|cr|saca|sr|SRport|jeune s&type=MG#liste.

Graff, Kaitlin, Sarah Murnen, and Anne Krause. 2013. "Low-Cut Shirts and High-Heeled Shoes: Increased Sexualization across Time in Magazine Depictions of Girls," *Sex Roles* 69, 11/12: 571–82.

Graham, Linda. 2007. "Out of Sight, Out of Mind/Out of Mind, Out of Site: Schooling and Attention Deficit Hyperactivity Disorder," *International Journal of Qualitative Studies in Education* 20, 5: 585–602.

Gray, Colette, and Joanne Donnelly. 2013. "Unheard Voices: The Views of Traveller and Non-traveller Mothers and Children with ASD," *International Journal of Early Years Education* 21, 4: 268–85.

Greef, Abraham, Alfons Vansteenwegen, and Liesbeth DeMot. 2006. "Resiliency in Divorced Families," *Social Work in Mental Health* 4, 4: 67–81.

Green, Joyce. 2006. "From Stonechild to Social Cohesion: Anti-racist Challenges for Saskatchewan." *Canadian Journal of Political Science* 39, 3: 507–27

Green, R., J. Mandel, M.E. Hotvedt, J. Gray, and L. Smith. 1986. "Lesbian Mothers and Their Children: A Comparison with Solo Parent Heterosexual Mothers and Their Children," *Archives of Sexual Behaviour* 15, 2: 167–84.

Greenwood, Margo Lianne, and Sarah Naomi de Leeuw. 2012. "Social Determinants of Health and the Future Well-Being of Aboriginal Children in Canada." *Paediatrics and Child Health*, 17, 7: 381–4.

Groebel, Jo. 1998. "Media Violence and Children," *Educational Media International* 35, 3: 216–27.

Grover, Sonja. 2004. "Why Won't They Listen To Us? On Giving Power and Voice to Children Participating in Social Research," *Childhood* 11, 1: 81–93.

Grusec, Joan. 1992. "Social Learning Theory and Developmental Psychology: The Legacies of Robert Sears and Albert Bandura," *Developmental Psychology* 28, 5: 776–86.

Guan, Shu-Sha, Patricia Greenfield, and Marjorie Orellana. 2014. "Translating Into Understanding: Language Brokering and Prosocial Development in Emerging Adults From Immigrant Families," *Journal of Adolescent Research* 29, 3: 331–55.

Guèvremont, Anne. 2010a. "The Early Learning Experiences of Off-Reserve First Nations Children in Canada," Ottawa: Statistics Canada (Catalogue no. 89-644-X). http://www.stat-can.gc.ca/pub/89-644-x/2010001/article/11279-eng.htm.

———. 2010b. The Early Learning Experiences of Metis Children in Canada. Ottawa: Statistics Canada (Catalogue no. 89-644-X). At: http://www.statcan.gc.ca/pub/89-644-x/2010001/article/11280-eng.htm.

———. 2010c. The Early Learning Experiences of Inuit Children in Canada. Ottawa: Statistics Canada (Catalogue no. 89-644-X). At: http://www.statcan.gc.ca/pub/89-644-x/2010001/article/11281-eng.htm.

Gutnick, Aviva Lucas, Michael Robb, Lori Takeuchi, and Jennifer Kotler. 2011. *Always Connected: The New Digital Media Habits of Young Children*. New York: The Joan Ganz Cooney Center at Sesame Workshop. At: http://www.joanganzcooneycenter.org/wp-content/uploads/2011/03/jgcc_alwayscon-nected.pdf.

Guttmann, Joseph, and Michael Rosenberg. 2003. "Emotional Intimacy and Children's Adjustment: A Comparison between Single-Parent Divorced and Intact Families," *Educational Psychology* 23, 4: 457–72.

Haas, Louis. 1998. *The Renaissance Man and His Children: Childbirth and Early Childhood in Florence, 1300–1600*. New York: St Martin's Press.

Hagan, Lisa Kindleberger, and Janet Kuebli. 2006. "Mothers' and Fathers'

Socialization of Preschoolers' Physical Risk Taking," *Journal of Applied Developmental Psychology* 28: 2–12.

Hall, Carol. 1987. "Tween PowerZ: Youth's Middle Tier Comes of Age," *Marketing and Media Decisions* (Oct.): 56–62. ·

Handel, Gerald, Spencer Cahill, and Frederick Elkin. 2007. *Children and Society: The Sociology of Children and Childhood Socialization*. Los Angeles: Roxbury Publishing.

Hare, Jan. 2012. "'They Tell a Story and There's Meaning Behind That Story': Indigenous Knowledge and Young Indigenous Children's Literacy Learning," *Journal of Early Childhood Literacy* 12, 4: 389–14.

Hargreaves, Duane, and Marika Tiggermann. 2003. "The Effect of 'Thin Ideal' Television Commercials on Body Dissatisfaction and Schema Activation during Early Adolescence," *Journal of Youth and Adolescence* 32, 5: 367–73.

Harper, Dee Wood, and Lydia Voigt. 2007. "Homicide Followed by Suicide: An Integrated Theoretical Perspective," *Homicide Studies* 11, 4: 295–318.

Harris, Judith Rich. 1998. *The Nurturing Assumption: Why Children Turn Out the Way They Do: Parents Matter Less Than You Think and Peers Matter More*. New York: Free Press.

Harrison, Kristen. 2006. "Fast and Sweet: Nutritional Attributes of Television Food Advertisements with and without Black Characters," *Howard Journal of Communications* 17, 4: 249–64.

Hastings, Paul, Kelly McShane, Richard Parker, and Farriola Ladha. 2007. "Ready to Make Nice: Parental Socialization of Young Sons' and Daughters' Prosocial Behaviors with Peers," *Journal of Genetic Psychology* 168, 2: 177–200.

Hawkes, Gail, and Tinashe Dune. 2013. "Introduction. Narratives of the Sexual Child: Shared Themes and Shared Challenges," *Sexualities* 16, 5/6: 622–34.

Health Canada. 2011. Aboriginal Head Start on Reserve. Ottawa: Government of Canada. At: http://www.hc-sc.gc.ca/fniah-spnia/famil/develop/ahsor-papa_intro-eng.php.

Healthy Child Manitoba. 2003. *A New Generation of Canadian Families: Raising Young Children—A New Look at Data from National Surveys*. Ottawa: Human Resources Development Canada. At: www.gov.mb.ca/healthychild/ecd/raising_young_children.pdf.

Heath, D. Terri. 2001. "The Impact of Delayed Fatherhood on the Father–Child Relationship," *Journal of Genetic Psychology* 155, 4: 511–30.

Helwig, Charles, Sharon To, Qian Wang, Chunqiong Liu, and Shaogang Yang. 2014. "Judgments and Reasoning About Parental Discipline Involving Induction and Psychological Control in China and Canada," *Child Development* 85, 3: 1150–67.

Hetherington, E. Mavis. 2003. "Social Support and the Adjustment of Children in Divorced and Remarried Families," *Childhood* 10, 2: 217–36.

Hetherington, E. Mavis, and John Kelly. 2002. *For Better or For Worse: Divorce Reconsidered*. New York: Norton.

Hetherington, E. Mavis, and Margaret Stanley-Hagan. 1999. "The Adjustment of Children with Divorced Parents: A Risk and Resiliency Perspective," *Journal of Child Psychology and Psychiatry* 40, 1: 129–40.

Heywood, Colin. 2001. *A History of Childhood*. Cambridge: Polity Press.

Hill, Jennifer Ann. 2011. "Endangered Childhoods: How Consumerism Is Impacting Child and Youth Identity," *Media, Culture and Society* 33, 3: 347–62.

Hill, Malcolm. 2006. "Children's Voices on Ways of Having a Voice—Children's and Young People's Perspectives on Methods Used in Research and Consultation," *Childhood* 13, 1: 69–89.

Hill, Shirley. 2002. "Teaching and Doing Gender in African American Families," *Sex Roles* 47, 11 and 12: 493–506.

Ho, Grace W.K. 2014. "Acculturation and Its Implications on Parenting for Chinese Immigrants: A Systematic Review," *Journal of Transcultural Nursing* 25, 2: 145–58.

Hoffman, Diane, and Guoping Zhao. 2007. "Global Convergence and Divergence in Childhood Ideologies and the Marginalization of Children," *Education and Society* 25, 1: 57–75.

Hoikkala, Tommi, Ossi Rahkonen, Christoffer Tigerstedt, and Jussi Tuormaa. 1987. "Wait a Minute, Mr Postman!—Some Critical Remarks on

Neil Postman's Childhood Theory," *Acta Sociologica* 30, 1: 87–99.

Holloway, Sarah, and Helena Pimlott-Wilson. 2014. "Any Advice Is Welcome Isn't It? Neoliberal Parenting Education, Local Mothering Cultures, and Social Class," *Environment and Planning* 46, 1: 94–111.

Holton, Avery. 2013. "What's Wrong with Max? Parenthood and the Portrayal of Autism Spectrum Disorders," *Journal of Communication Inquiry* 37, 1: 45–63.

Howard, J. and K. McInnes. 2013. "The Impact of Children's Perception of an Activity as Play Rather than Not Play on Emotional Well-Being," *Child: Care, Health and Development* 39, 5: 737–42.

Howe, R. Brian. 2001a. "Do Parents Have Fundamental Rights?" *Journal of Canadian Studies* 36, 3: 61–78.

———. 2001b. "Implementing Children's Rights in a Federal State: The Case of Canada's Child Protection System," *International Journal of Children's Rights* 9: 361–82.

Howe, R. Brian, and Katherine Covell, eds. 2007. *A Question of Commitment: Children's Rights in Canada*. Waterloo, ON: Wilfrid Laurier University Press.

Howe, R.B., and K. Covell. 2009. "Engaging Children in Citizenship Education: A Children's Rights Perspective," *Journal of Educational Thought*, 43, 1: 21–44.

Howe, R.B., and K. Covell. 2010. "Miseducating Children about Their Rights," *Education, Citizenship and Social Justice* 5, 2: 91–102.

Howe, R.B., and K. Covell. 2010. "Toward Education in the Best Interests of the Child," *Education and Law Journal* 20, 1: 17–33.

Howe, R.B., and K. Covell. 2011. "Countering Disadvantage, Promoting Health: The Value of Children's Human Rights Education," *Journal of Educational Thought* 45, 1: 59–85.

Hsiung, Ping-chen. 2005. *A Tender Voyage: Children and Childhood in Late Imperial China*. Stanford, CA: Stanford University Press.

Hua, Josephine, and Catherine Costigan. 2012. "The Familial Context of Adolescent Language Brokering within Immigrant Chinese Families in Canada," *Journal of Youth and Adolescence* 41, 7: 894–906.

Hübenthal, Maksim, and Anna Maria Ifland. 2011. "Risks for Children? Recent Developments in Early Childcare Policy in Germany," *Childhood* 8, 1: 114–27.

Hudson, Pete. 1997. "First Nations Child and Family Services: Breaking the Silence," *Canadian Ethnic Studies* 29, 1: 161–72.

Hughes, K., and G. Lowe. 2000. "Surveying the 'Post-Industrial' Landscape: Information Technologies and Labour Market Polarization in Canada," *Canadian Review of Sociology and Anthropology* 37, 1: 29–53.

Hughes, Mary, Linda Waite, Tracey LaPierre, and Ye Luo. 2007. "All in the Family: The Impact of Caring for Grandchildren on Grandparents' Health," *Journals of Gerontology Series B: Psychological Sciences & Social Sciences* 62B, 2: S108–19.

Human Rights Watch. 2009. *Lost in Transit: Insufficient Protection for Unaccompanied Migrant Children at Roissy Charles de Gaulle Airport*. New York: Human Rights Watch.

Huurre, Taina, Hanna Junkkari, and Hillevi Aro. 2006. "Long-Term Psychosocial Effects of Parental Divorce: A Follow-Up Study from Adolescence to Adulthood," *European Archives of Psychiatry and Clinical Neurosciences* 256, 4: 256–63.

Immervoll, Herwig, and David Barber. 2005. "Can Parents Afford to Work? Childcare Costs, Tax-Benefit Policies and Work Incentives," in *OECD Social, Employment and Migration Working Papers,* no. 31. Paris: Directorate for Employment, Labour and Social Affairs. At: www.oecd.org/social/soc/35862266.pdf.

Ingleby, David, and Charles Watters. 2002. "Refugee Children at School: Good Practices in Mental Health and Social Care," *Education and Health* 20, 3: 43–5.

Irving, Howard, Shirley Chau, A. Ka Tat Tsang, and Michael Benjamin. 1998. *Satellite Children: An Exploratory Study of Their Experience and Perception*. Toronto: Centre of Excellence for Research on Immigration and Settlement (CERIS).

Irwin, Lori, and Joy Johnson. 2005. "Interviewing Young Children:

Explicating Our Practices and Dilemmas," *Qualitative Health Research* 15, 6: 821–31.

Isaacs, Ar. 2002. "Children's Adjustment to Their Divorced Parents' New Relationships," *Journal of Paediatric Child Health* 38: 329–31.

Isajiw, Wsevolod W. 1999. *Understanding Diversity: Ethnicity and Race in the Canadian Context*. Toronto: Thompson Educational.

Ismael, Shereen Tareq. 2006. *Child Poverty and the Canadian Welfare State: From Entitlement to Charity*. Edmonton: University of Alberta Press.

Jaccoud, Mylene, and Renee Brassard. 2003. "The Marginalization of Aboriginal Women in Montreal," in David Newhouse and Evelyn Peters, eds., *Not Strangers in These Parts: Urban Aboriginal Peoples*. Ottawa: Policy Research Initiative, pp. 131–45.

Jackson, Sue, Tiina Vares, and Rosalind Gill. 2013. "'The Whole Playboy Mansion Image': Girls' Fashioning and Fashioned Selves within a Postfeminist Culture," *Feminism and Psychology* 23, 2: 143–62.

Jalongo, Mary Renck. 2002. "Editorial: On Behalf of Children," *Early Childhood Education Journal* 30, 1: 1–2.

James, Allison, Chris Jenks, and Alan Prout. 1998. *Theorizing Childhood*. Oxford: Polity Press.

Jamison, Tyler, Marilyn Coleman, Lawrence Ganong, and Richard Feistman. 2014. "Transitioning to Post-divorce Family Life: A Grounded Theory Investigation of Resilience in Coparenting," *Family Relations* 63, 3: 411–23.

Janovicek, Nancy. 2003. "How Do We Know the Histories of Children and Youth?" in Janovicek and Parr (2003: 9).

Janovicek, Nancy, and Joy Parr, eds. 2003. *Histories of Canadian Children and Youth*. Toronto: Oxford University Press.

Japel, Christa, Richard E. Tremblay, and Sylvana Côtè. 2005. "Quality Counts: Assessing the Quality of Day Services Based on Quebec Longitudinal Study of Child Development," *IRPP Choices* 11, 5: 1–42.

Jenkins, John, and Kevin Lyons. 2006. "Non-Resident Fathers' Leisure with Their Children," *Leisure Studies* 25, 2: 219–32.

Jennings, Sheila, Nazilla Khanlou, and Chang Su. 2014. "Public Health Policy and Social Support for Immigrant Mothers Raising Disabled Children in Canada," *Disability and Society* 29, 10: 1645–57.

Jenson, Jane. 2001. "Family Policy, Child Care and Social Solidarity—The Case of Quebec," in Prentice (2001: 39–62).

———. 2004. "Changing the Paradigm: Family Responsibility or Investing in Children," *Canadian Journal of Sociology* 29, 2: 169–92.

Jenvey, Vickii. 2007. "The Relationship between Television Viewing and Obesity in Young Children: A Review of Existing Explanations," *Early Childhood Development and Care* 177, 8: 809–20.

Jeynes, William. 2006. "The Impact of Parental Remarriage on Children: A Meta-Analysis," *Marriage and Family Review* 40, 4: 75–102.

Jimack, P.D. 1974. "Introduction," in Jean Jacques Rousseau, *Emile*. London: Dent/Everyman's Library.

Johnson, Fern L., and Karren Young. 2002. "Gendered Voices in Children's Television Advertising," *Critical Studies in Media Communication* 19, 4: 461–80.

Johnson, Genevieve Marie. 2010. "Internet Use and Child Development: Validation of the Ecological Techno-Subsystem," *Journal of Educational Technology and Society* 13, 1: 176–85.

Johnson, Genevieve Marie. 2013. "Traditional Literacy Skills and Internet Use among 8- to 12-Year-Old Children," *Reading Psychology* 34, 5: 486–506.

Johnson, Holly. 2005. "Assessing the Prevalence of Violence against Women in Canada," *Statistical Journal of the United Nations ECE* 22: 225–38.

Johnson, Peter. 1983. *Native Children and the Child Welfare System*. Ottawa: The Canadian Council on Social Development.

Johnsson-Smaragdi, Ulla, and Annelis Jonsson. 2006. "Book Reading in Leisure Time: Long-Term Changes in Young Peoples' Book Reading Habits," *Scandinavian Journal of Educational Research* 50, 5: 519–40.

Jolivet, Kendra Randall. 2011. "The
Psychological Impact of Divorce on
Children: What Is a Family Lawyer to
Do?" *American Journal of Family Law* 25,
4: 175–83.

Jones, Charles, Linn Clark, Joan Grusec,
Randle Hart, Gabriele Plickert, and
Lorne Tepperman. 2002. *Poverty, Social
Capital, Parenting and Child Outcomes
in Canada.* Ottawa: Human Resources
Development Canada, Working Paper
Series of the Applied Research Branch of
Strategic Policy.

Jones, Jennifer. 2002. "Sedentary 'Tweens'
at Higher Risk for Heart Disease,"
Canadian Medical Association Journal
166, 8: 1075.

Jose, Paul E., Carol S. Huntsinger, Phillip
R. Huntsinger, and Fong-Ruey Liaw.
2000. "Parental Values and Practices
Relevant to Young Children's Social
Development in Taiwan and the United
States," *Journal of Cross-Cultural
Psychology* 31, 6: 677–702.

Joyette, Donna. 2014. *Newcomer Engagement
in Early Childhood Development
Services and Supports in the Region of
Peel.* Region of Peel: Peer Children
and Youth Initiative. At: http://
www.pcyi.org/uploads/File/Reports/
NewcomerEngagement_ECD_
FinalReport_April30.pdf.

Juby, Heather, C. Le Bourdais, and N.
Marcil-Gratton. 2005. "Sharing
Roles, Sharing Custody? Couples'
Characteristics and Children's Living
Arrangements at Separation," *Journal of
Marriage and Family* 67: 157–72.

Juby, Heather, Nicole Marcil-Gratton,
Celine Le Bourdais, with Paul-Marie
Huot. 2006. "A Step Further in
Family Life: The Emergence of the
Blended Family," in Alain Bélanger,
Yves Carrière, and Stephanie Gilbert,
*Report on the Demographic Situations in
Canada—2000.* Ottawa: Minister of
Industry (Catalogue no. 91-209-XIE),
pp. 167–203.

Justice Canada. 2014. Indian Act. Ottawa:
Minister of Justice. At: http://laws-lois.
justice.gc.ca/eng/acts/i-5.

Kaare, Birgit, Petter Bae Brandtzaeg,
Jan Heim, and Tor Endestad. 2007.
"In the Borderland between Family
Orientation and Peer Culture: The Use

of Communication Technologies among
Norwegian Tweens," *New Media and
Society* 9, 4: 603–24.

Kaibara, E. 1976 [1710]. "Wazoku doji-
kun (Precepts on Childrearing and
Education)," in Masami Yamazumi
and Kazue Nakae, eds, *Kosodate no sh
(Documents on Childrearing).* Tokyo:
Heibon-sha 2: 3–57.

Kane, Emily. 2006. "'No Way My Boys
Are Going to be Like That!' Parents'
Responses to Children's Gender Nonconformity," *Gender and Society* 20, 2:
149–76.

Katz, C., and Z. Barnetz, 2014. "'Love
Covereth All Transgressions": Children's
Experiences with Physical Abuse As
Portrayed in Their Narratives During
Forensic Investigations," *Children and
Youth Services Review* 43: 1-7.

Kee, Daniel, Alicia Gregory-Domingue,
Kathryn Rice, and Katie Tone. 2005.
"A Release from Proactive Interference
Analysis of Gender Schema Encoding
for Occupations in Adults and
Children," *Learning and Individual
Differences* 15: 203–11.

Kehily, Mary Jane. 2010. "Childhood in
Crisis? Tracing the Contours of 'Crisis'
and Its Impact upon Contemporary
Parenting Practices," *Media, Culture and
Society* 32, 2: 171–85.

Kehily, Mary Jane. 2012. "Contextualising
the Sexualisation of Girls Debate:
Innocence, Experience and Young
Female Sexuality," *Gender and Education*
24, 3: 255–68.

Keith-Lucas, Alan. 1991. "The Mary Ellen
Myth: Readers Respond," *Social Work*
36, 6: 553.

Kellner, Florence. 2002. "Yet Another
Coming Crisis? Coping with Guidelines
from the Tri-council," in Will C.
Van den Hoonaard, ed., *Walking the
Tightrope: Ethical Issues for Qualitative
Researchers.* Toronto: University of
Toronto Press, pp. 26–33.

Kelly, Mary Bess. 2013. "Payment Patterns
of Child and Spousal Support," in
Juristat. Ottawa: Statistics Canada
(Catalogue no. 85-002-X). At:
http://www.statcan.gc.ca/pub/85-
002-x/2013001/article/11780-eng.htm.

Kelly, R. Gordon. 1974. "Literature and the Historian," *American Quarterly* 26, 2: 141–59.

Kendeou, Panayiota, Julie Lynch, Paul van den Broek, Chris Espin, Mary Jane White, and Kathleen Kremer. 2005. "Developing Successful Readers: Building Early Comprehension Skills through Television Viewing and Listening," *Early Childhood Education Journal* 33, 2: 91–8.

Kerr, Don. 2004. "Family Transformations and the Well-Being of Children: Recent Evidence from Canadian Longitudinal Data," *Journal of Comparative Family Studies* 35, 10: 73–90.

Kerr, Don, and Roderic Beaujot. 2002. "Family Relations, Low Income and Child Outcomes: A Comparison of Canadian Children in Intact-, Step-, and Lone-Parent Families," *International Journal of Comparative Sociology* 43, 2: 134–52.

Kerr, Don, and Joseph Michalski. 2007. "Family Structure and Children's Hyperactivity Problems: A Longitudinal Analysis," *Canadian Journal of Sociology* 32, 1: 85–112.

Keung, Nicholas. 2014. "Ryerson Researcher Finds Drawings Open a Window to an Immigrant Child's World," *Toronto Star Online* 4 March. At: www.thestar.com/news/immigration/2014/03/04/ryerson_researcher_finds_draw-ings_open_a_window_to_an_immi-grant_childs_world.html.

Key, Ellen. 1907. *The Century of the Child*. New York: Putnam's Sons.

Kids Media Centre. 2013. *An Ethical Framework for Content Creators in the Children's Digital Space*. Toronto: Kids Media Centre (Centennial College and Ontario Media Development Corporation). At: http://kids-mediacentre.ca/downloads/Ethical-Framework-Best-Practices-kmc.pdf.

Killoran, Isabel, Dorothy Tymon, and George Frempong. 2007. "Disabilities and Inclusive Practices within Toronto Preschools," *International Journal of Inclusive Education* 11, 1: 81–95.

Kim, Jaemin, Branka Agic, and Kwame McKenzie. 2014. "The Mental Health of Korean Transnational Mothers: A Scoping Review," *International Journal of Social Psychiatry* 60, 8: 783–94.

Kim, Mi Song. 2013. "Technology-Mediated Collaborative Learning Environments for Young Culturally and Linguistically Diverse Children: Vygotsky Revisited," *British Journal of Educational Studies* 61, 2: 221–46.

King, Michael. 2007. "The Sociology of Childhood as Scientific Communication: Observations from a Social Systems Perspective," *Childhood* 14, 2: 193–213.

Kirsh, Steven. 2006. *Children, Adolescents and Media Violence: A Critical Look at the Research*. Thousand Oaks, CA: Sage.

Kline, Stephen. 1993. *Out of the Garden: Toys and Children's Culture in the Age of TV Marketing*. Toronto: Garamond Press.

Klinger, Lori, James Hamilton, and Peggy Cantrell. 2001. "Children's Perceptions of Aggressive and Gender-Specific Content in Toy Commercials," *Social Behavior and Personality* 29, 1: 11–20.

Knowles, Valerie. 1992. *Strangers at Our Gates: Canadian Immigration and Immigration Policy 1540–1990*. Toronto: Dundurn Press.

Kohen, Dafna, and Anne Guèvremont. 2014. "Income Disparities in Preschool Outcomes and the Role Of Family, Child, and Parenting Factors," *Early Child Development and Care* 184, 2: 266–292.

Kohen, Dafna, Sharanjit Uppal, Anne Guevremont, and Fernando Cartwright. 2008. Children with Disabilities and the Educational System—A Provincial Perspective. Ottawa: Statistics Canada. At: http://www.statcan.gc.ca/pub/81-004-x/2007001/9631-eng.htm.

Kohn, Melvin. 1977. *Class and Conformity: A Study of Values*. Chicago: University of Chicago Press.

Kojima, Hideo. 1986. "Japanese Concepts of Child Development from the Mid-seventeenth to Mid-nineteenth Century," *International Journal of Behavioral Development* 9: 315–29.

Kong, Rebecca. 2006. "Family Violence against Children and Youth," in *Family Violence in Canada: A Statistical Profile 2006*. Ottawa: Statistics Canada (Catalogue no. 85-224-XIE), pp. 29–43.

Kong, Rebecca, Holly Johnson, Sara Beattie, and Andrea Cardillo. 2003. "Sexual Offences in Canada," in

Juristat 23, 6. Ottawa: Statistics Canada (Catalogue no. 85-002-XIE). At: http://www.statcan.gc.ca/pub/85-002-x/85-002-x2003006-eng.pdf.

Koolstra, Cees, Juliette van Zanten, Nicole Lucassen, and Nazreen Ishaak. 2004. "The Formal Pace of Sesame Street over 26 Years," *Perceptual and Motor Skills* 99, 1: 354–60.

Koops, Willem. 2003. "Imagining Childhood," in Koops and Michael Zuckerman, eds, *Beyond the Century of the Child*. Philadelphia: University of Pennsylvania Press, pp. 1–18.

Kopkowski, Cynthia. 2008. "Lolita in the Classroom: Dolls in Fishnets, Hair Extensions for Kids, and Pole-Dancing Tween TV Stars—Girlhood Isn't What It Used to Be, and That Means Teaching Girls Isn't Either," *NEA Today* 26, 6: 36–7.

Korteweg, Lisa, Ismel Gonzalez, and Jojo Guillet. 2010. "The Stories Are the People and the Land: Three Educators Respond to Environmental Teachings in Indigenous Children's Literature," *Environmental Education Research* 16, 3 and 4: 331–50.

Kotrla, Bowie. 2007. "Sex and Violence: Is Exposure to Media Content Harmful to Children?" *Children and Libraries: Journal of the Association for Library Services to Children* 5, 2: 50–2.

Kowalchuk, Krista, and Susan Crompton. 2009. "Social Participation of Children with Disabilities." Ottawa: Statistics Canada (Catalogue no. 11-008-X).

Kruk, Edward. 2005. "Shared Parental Responsibility: A Harm Reduction-Based Approach to Divorce Law Reform," *Journal of Divorce and Remarriage* 43, 3 and 4: 119–40.

Krull, Catherine. 2007. "Families and the State: Family Policy in Canada," in David Cheal, ed., *Canadian Families Today: New Perspectives*. Toronto: Oxford University Press, pp. 254–72.

Kushner, Margo. 2006. "Whose Best Interests: The Ruling or the Children?" *Journal of Divorce and Remarriage* 44, 3 and 4: 17–29.

Lagoni, Laurel, and Alicia Skinner Cook. 1985. "Stepfamilies: A Content Analysis of Popular Literature, 1961–1982," *Family Relations* 34, 4: 521–25.

Lahikainen, Anja, Tiina Kirmanen, Inger Kraav, and Merle Taimalu. 2003. "Studying Fears in Young Children: Two Interview Methods," *Childhood* 10, 1: 83–104.

Lamarche, Veronique, Mara Brendgen, Michel Boivin, Frank Vitaro, Ginette Dionne, and Daniel Perusse. 2007. "Do Friends' Characteristics Moderate the Prospective Links between Peer Victimization and Reactive and Proactive Aggression," *Journal of Abnormal Child Psychology* 35: 665–80.

Lamb, M.E., ed. 1987. *The Father's Role: Cross-Cultural Perspectives*. Hillsdale, NJ: Erlbaum.

Lamb, Sharon, Kelly Graling, and Emily Wheeler. 2013. "Pole-arized' Discourse: An Analysis of Responses to Miley Cyrus's Teen Choice Awards Pole Dance," *Feminism and Psychology* 23, 2: 163–83.

Lansdown, Gerison, Shane Jimerson, and Reza Shahroozi. 2014. "Children's Rights and School Psychology: Children's Right to Participation," *Journal of School Psychology* 52, 1: 3–12.

Lareau, Annette. 2000. "Social Class and the Daily Lives of Children: A Study from the United States," *Childhood* 7, 2: 155–71.

———. 2003. *Unequal Childhoods: Class, Race and Family Life*. Berkeley: University of California Press.

LaRochelle-Côté, Sébastien, and Sharanjit Uppal. 2011. "The Financial Well-Being of the Self-Employed," *Perspectives on Labour and Income* 23, 4: 3–15.

Larouche, Marie-Noelle, Benoit Galand, and Therese Bouffard. 2008. "The Illusion of Scholastic Incompetence and Peer Acceptance in Primary School," *European Journal of Psychology of Education* 23, 1: 25–39.

Larson, Mary Strom. 2001. "Interactions, Activities and Gender in Children's Television Commercials: A Content Analysis," *Journal of Broadcasting and Electronic Media* 45, 1: 41–56.

Larson, R.W., and S. Verma. 1999. "How Children and Adolescents Spend Time across the World: Work, Play and Developmental Opportunities," *Psychological Bulletin* 125: 701–36.

Law Courts Education Society of BC. 2006. *Parenting after Separation for Your Child's Future: A Handbook for Parents*. Victoria: Ministry of Attorney General.

Lazoritz, Stephen, and Eric Shelman. 1996. "Before Mary Ellen," *Child Abuse and Neglect* 20, 3: 235–7.

Leach, Penelope, Jacqueline Barnes, Lars-Erik Malmberg, Kathy Sylva, and Alan Stein. 2008. "The Quality of Different Types of Child Care at 10 and 18 Months: A Comparison between Types and Factors Related to Quality," *Early Child Development and Care* 178, 2: 177–209.

Leadbeater, Bonnie, and Paweena Sukhawathanakul. 2011. "Multicomponent Programs for Reducing Peer Victimization in Early Elementary School: A Longitudinal Evaluation of the WITS Primary Program," *Journal of Community Psychology* 39, 5: 606–20.

Leaper, Campbell, Lisa Breed, Laurie Hoffman, and Carly Ann Perlman. 2002. "Variations in the Gender-Stereotyped Content of Children's Television Cartoons across Genres," *Journal of Applied Social Psychology* 32, 8: 1653–62.

Lee, Nick. 1998. "Towards an Immature Sociology," *Sociological Review* 46, 3: 458–82.

———. 2001. *Childhood and Society: Growing Up in an Age of Uncertainty.* Buckingham, UK: Open University Press.

Lehr, Ron, and Peter MacMillan. 2001. "The Psychological and Emotional Impact of Divorce: The Non-custodial Father's Perspective," *Families in Society: The Journal of Contemporary Human Services* 82, 4: 373–82.

Leon, Margarita. 2007. "Speeding Up or Holding Back? Institutional Factors in the Development of Childcare Provision in Spain," *European Societies* 9, 3: 315–37.

Lesnick, Alice. 2005. "On the Job: Performing Gender and Inequality at Work, Home and School," *Journal of Education and Work* 18, 2: 187–200.

Letourneau, N.L., C.B. Fedick, and J.D. Willms. 2007. "Mothering and Domestic Violence: A Longitudinal Analysis," *Journal of Family Violence* 22: 649–59.

Levin, Diane, and Nancy Carlsson-Paige. 2007. "Marketing Violence: The Special Toll on Young Children of Color," *Journal of Negro Education* 72, 4: 427–37.

LeVine, Robert. 2003. *Childhood Socialization: Comparative Studies of Parenting, Learning and Educational Change.* Hong Kong: Comparative Education Research Centre/University of Hong Kong.

Lewis, Ann. 2004. "'And When Did You Last See Your Father?' Exploring the Views of Children with Learning Difficulties/Disabilities," *British Journal of Special Education* 31, 1: 3–9.

Lewis, M.K., and A.J. Hill. 1998. "Food Advertising on British Children's Television: A Content Analysis and Experimental Study with Nine-Year Olds," *International Journal of Obesity* 22: 206–14.

Lieberson, Stanley, and Eleanor Bell. 1992. "Children's First Names: An Empirical Study of Social Taste," *American Journal of Sociology* 98, 3: 511–54.

Lin, Jane. 2006. "The Teaching Profession: Trends from 1999 to 2005," *Education Matters* 3, 4. At: www.statcan.ca/english/freepub/81-004-XIE/2006004/teach.htm.

Lindsay, Colin, and Marcia Almey. 2006. "Family Status," in Statistics Canada, *Women in Canada: A Gender-Based Statistics Report, 2006,* 5th edn. Ottawa: Minister of Industry (Catalogue no. 89-503-XPE), pp. 35–52.

Lindsay, Sally, Gillian King, Anne Klassen, Victoria Esses, and Melissa Stachel. 2012. "Working with Immigrant Families Raising a Child with a Disability: Challenges and Recommendations for Healthcare and Community Service Providers," *Disability and Rehabilitation* 34, 23: 2007–17.

Lindsay, Sally, Amy Mcpherson, Henna Aslam, Patricia Mckeever, and Virginia Wright. 2013. "Exploring Children's Perceptions of Two School-Based Social Inclusion Programs: A Pilot Study," *Child and Youth Care Forum* 42, 1: 1–18.

Lindsey, Eric, and Yvonne Caldera. 2006. "Mother–Father–Child Triadic Interaction and Mother–Child Dyadic Interaction: Gender Differences within and between Contexts," *Sex Roles* 55: 511–21.

Linebarger, Deborah, Anjelika Kosanic, Charles Greenwood, and Nii Sai Doku. 2004. "Effects of Viewing the

Television Program *Between the Lions* on the Emergent Literacy Skills of Young Children," *Journal of Educational Psychology* 96, 2: 297–308.

Lisosky, Joanne. 2001. "For *All* Kids' Sakes: Comparing Children's Television Policy-Making in Australia, Canada and the United States," *Media, Culture and Society* 23: 821–42.

Liu, Mowei, Xinyin Chen, Kenneth Rubin, Shujie Zheng, Liying Cui, Dan Li, Huichang Chen, and Li Wang. 2005. "Autonomy- vs. Connectedness-Oriented Parenting Behaviours in Chinese and Canadian Mothers," *International Journal of Behavioral Development* 29, 6: 489–95.

Liu, Mowei, and Feng Guo. 2010. "Parenting Practices and Their Relevance to Child Behaviors in Canada and China," *Scandinavian Journal of Psychology* 51, 2: 109–14.

Livingstone, Sonia M. 2009. *Children and the Internet: Great Expectations, Challenging Realities*. Cambridge: Polity.

Locke, John. 1937 [1690]. *Treatise of Civil Government and a Letter Concerning Toleration*. New York: D. Appleton-Century Company.

———. 1964 [1693]. *Some Thoughts Concerning Education*. London: Heinemann.

———. 1975 [1697]. *Of the Conduct of the Understanding*. Oxford: Oxford University Press.

Lolichen, P.J. 2007. "Children in the Driver's Seat: Children Conducting a Study of Their Transport and Mobility Problems," *Children, Youth and Environments* 17, 1: 236–56.

Lowe, G. 2000. *The Quality of Work—A People-Centred Agenda*. Toronto: Oxford University Press.

Luffman, Jacqueline. 2006. "Core-Age Labour Force," *Perspectives on Labour and Income* 7, 9: 5–11.

Lumpkin, James. 2008. "Grandparents in a Parental or Near-Parental Role," *Journal of Family Issues* 29, 3: 357–72.

Luxton, Meg. 2002. *Feminist Perspectives on Social Inclusion and Children's Well-Being*. Perspectives on Social Inclusions Working Paper Series. Toronto: Laidlaw Foundation. At: www.laidlawfdn.org/cms/file/children/luxton.pdf.

Lyttle, Melanie. 2014. "Technology in Children's Programming," *Children and Libraries: The Journal of the Association for Library Service to Children* 12, 2: 34–35.

Ma, Xin. 2002. "The First Ten Years in Canada: A Multi-level Assessment of Behavioural and Emotional Problems of Immigrant Children," *Canadian Public Policy* 28, 3: 395–418.

MacDonald, Martha, Shelley Phipps, and Lynn Lethbridge. 2005. "Taking Its Toll: The Influence of Paid and Unpaid Work in Women's Well-being," *Feminist Economics* 11, 1: 63–94.

MacDonnell, Susan. 2007. *Losing Ground: The Persistent Growth of Poverty in Canada's Largest City*. Toronto: United Way of Greater Toronto. At: www.uwgt.org/whoWeHelp/reports/pdf/LosingGround-fullReport.pdf.

MacDonnell, Susan, Don Embuldeniya, and Fawzia Ratanshi. 2004. *Poverty by Postal Code: The Geography of Neighbourhood Poverty, City of Toronto, 1981–2001*. Toronto: United Way of Greater Toronto.

MacKay, Robin. 2005. "Bill C-2: An Act to Amend the Criminal Code (Protection of Children and Other Vulnerable Persons) and the Canada Evidence Act," in *Law and Government Division*. Ottawa: Government of Canada. At: www.parl.gc.ca/common/bills_ls.asp?lang=E&ls=c2&source=library_prb&Parl=38&Ses=1#byoungpersonstxt.

MacKinnon, Shauna. 2013. "The Politics of Poverty in Canada," *Social Alternatives* 32, 1: 19–23.

MacNaughton, Glenda. 2001. "Silences and Subtexts of Immigrant and Non-immigrant Children," *Childhood Education* 78, 1: 30–6.

Mahon, Ann, Caroline Glendinning, Karen Clarke, and Gary Craig. 1996. "Researching Children: Methods and Ethics," *Children and Society* 10: 145–54.

Mahon, Rianne. 2005. "Rescaling Social Reproduction: Childcare in Toronto/Canada and Stockholm/Sweden," *International Journal of Urban and Regional Research* 29, 2: 341–57.

Mallon, Gerald. 2013. "From the Editor: The Legend of Mary Ellen Wilson and Etta Wheeler: Child Maltreatment and

Protection Today," *Child Welfare* 92, 2: 9–11.

Mandell, Nancy. 1988. "The Least-Adult Role in Studying Children," *Journal of Contemporary Ethnography* 16, 4: 433–67.

Marcil-Gratton, N., and C. Le Bourdais. 1999. *Custody, Access and Child Support: Findings from the National Longitudinal Survey of Children and Youth* (CSR 1999-3E). Ottawa: Department of Justice.

Marcuse, Herbert. 1964. *One Dimensional Man*. Boston: Beacon Press.

Marie-Vincent Foundation. 2011, December 13. "First Survey of Québec Parents on Internet Use by Children Aged 3 to 12 [news release]." Montreal: Marie-Vincent Foundation. At: http://marie-vincent.org/wp-content/uploads/2012/12/Survey-December-13.pdf.

Marshall, Katherine. 2006. "Converging Gender Roles," *Perspectives on Labour and Income* 7, 7: 6–17.

Martin, Carol Lynn, and Diane Ruble. 2004. "Children's Search for Gender Cues: Cognitive Perspectives on Gender Development," *Current Directions in Psychological Science* 13, 2: 67–70.

Martin, Jacqueline, and Hildy Ross. 2005. "Sibling Aggression: Sex Differences and Parents' Reactions," *International Journal of Behavioral Developments* 29, 2: 129–38.

Martin, Karin A., and Jennifer Torres. 2014. "Where Did I Come From? US Parents' and Preschool Children's Participation in Sexual Socialisation," *Sex Education* 14, 2: 174–90.

Martinello, Emily. 2014. "Reviewing Strategies for Risk Reduction of Sexual Abuse of Children with Intellectual Disabilities: A Focus on Early Intervention," *Sexuality and Disability* 32, 2: 167–74.

Mascheroni, Giovanna, Ana Jorge, and Lorleen Farrugia. 2014. "Media Representations and Children's Discourses on Online Risks: Findings from Qualitative Research in Nine European Countries," *Cyberpsychology: Journal of Psychosocial Research on Cyberspace* 8, 2: 24–37.

Mason, Jan, and Susan Danby. 2011. "Children as Experts in their Lives: Child Inclusive Research," *Child Indicators Research* 4, 2: 185–9.

Mayall, Barry. 2000. "The Sociology of Childhood in Relation to Children's Rights," *International Journal of Children's Rights* 8, 3: 243–59.

Mayall, Berry. 2002. *Towards a Sociology for Children: Thinking from Children's Lives*. Buckingham, UK: Open University Press.

Mayall, Berry. 2013. *A History of the Sociology of Childhood*. London, UK: Institute of Education Press.

McCain, Margaret, and J. Fraser Mustard. 1999. *Reversing the Real Brain Drain: Early Years Study—Final Report*. Toronto: Ontario Children's Secretariat.

McCartney, Kathleen, Eric Dearing, Beck Taylor, and Kristen Bub. 2007. "Quality Child Care Supports the Achievement of Low-Income Children: Direct and Indirect Pathways through Caregiving and Home Environment," *Journal of Applied Developmental Psychology* 28, 5 and 6: 411–26.

McClelland, Daphne. 2001. "The "Other Mother" and Second Parent Adoption," *Journal of Gay and Lesbian Social Services* 13, 3: 1–21.

McDaniel, Susan. 2002. "Women's Changing Relations to the State and Citizenship: Caring and Intergenerational Relations," *Canadian Review of Sociology and Anthropology* 39, 2: 125–49.

McDonald, Ryan J. 1994. "Canada's Off-Reserve Aboriginal Population," in *Canadian Social Trends* 2. Toronto: Thompson Educational, pp. 51–6.

McEwen, Annie, and Jennifer Stewart. 2014. "The Relationship between Income and Children's Outcomes: A Synthesis of Canadian Evidence," *Canadian Public Policy* 40, 1: 99–109.

McGill, Brittany. 2014. "Navigating New Norms of Involved Fatherhood: Employment, Fathering Attitudes, and Father Involvement," *Journal of Family Issues* 35, 8: 1089–106.

McIntosh, Robert. 2003. "The Boys of the Nova Scotia Coal Mines: 1873–1923," in Janovicek and Parr (2003: 77–87).

McKendrick, John, Michael Bradford, and Anna Fielder. 2000. "Kid Customer? Commercialization of Playspace and the Commodification of Childhood," *Childhood* 7, 3: 295–314.

McKie, Craig. 2000. "A History of Emigration from Canada," in *Canadian Social Trends* 3. Toronto: Thompson Educational, pp. 11–14.

McLaughlin, Janice, Emma Clavering. 2011. "Questions of Kinship and Inheritance in Pediatric Genetics: Substance and Responsibility," *New Genetics and Society* 30, 4: 399–413.

McLoyd, V.C. 1998. "Socioeconomic Disadvantage and Child Development," *American Psychologist* 53: 185–204.

McMullen, Kathryn. 2004. "Children of Immigrants: How Well Do They Do In School?" in *Education Matters*. Ottawa: Statistics Canada (Catalogue no. 81-004-XIE). At: http://www.statcan.gc.ca/pub/81-004-x/200410/7422-eng.htm.

McRoberts, Kenneth. 1988. *Quebec: Social Change and Political Crisis*. Toronto: McClelland and Stewart.

Mead, George Herbert. 1962 [1934]. *Mind, Self and Society*. Chicago: University of Chicago Press.

Media Awareness Network. 2001. *Canada's Children in a Wired World: The Parents' View*. Ottawa: Industry Canada, Health Canada and Human Resources Development Canada. At: http://mediasmarts.ca/sites/default/files/pdfs/publication-report/full/YCWWI-parents-view.pdf.

Media Awareness Network. 2005. *Young Canadians in a Wired World—Phase II*. Ottawa: Industry. At: http://mediasmarts.ca/sites/mediasmarts/files/pdfs/publication-report/full/YCWWII-trends-recomm.pdf.

Mehrabian, Albert. 2001. "Characteristics Attributed to Individuals on the Basis of Their First Names," *Genetic, Social and General Psychology Monographs* 127, 1: 59–88.

Mendelson, Michael. 2005. *Measuring Child Benefits, Measuring Child Poverty*. Ottawa: Caledon Institute of Social Policy. At: www.caledoninst.org/Publications/PDF/525ENG%2Epdf.

Menzies, Charles R. 1999. "First Nations, Inequality, and the Legacy of Colonialism," in James Curtis, Edward Grabb, and Neil Guppy, eds, *Social Inequality in Canada: Patterns, Problems, Policies*, 3rd edn. Toronto: Prentice-Hall, pp. 236–44.

Menzies, Peter, and Adje van de Sande. 2003. "A Formative Evaluation of the Customary Care Program: Native Child and Family Services of Toronto," *Native Social Work Journal*, 4, 1: 30–50.

Meyers, Michael. 1993. "An Argument against Educating Young Children," *Education* 113, 3: 485–88.

Miall, C., and K. March. 2005. "Social Support for Changes in Adoption Practice: Gay Adoptions, Open Adoption, Birth Reunions and the Release of Confidential Information," *Family in Society: Journal of Contemporary Social Services* 86, 1: 83–92.

Milan, Anne. 2013. *Fertility: Overview, 2009 to 2011*. Ottawa: Statistics Canada (Catalogue no. 91-209-X). http://www.statcan.gc.ca/pub/91-209-x/2013001/article/11784-eng.pdf.

Milan, Anne, Leslie-Anne Keown, and Covadonga Robles Urquijo. 2011. "Families, Living Arrangements and Unpaid Work," in *Women in Canada: A Gender-Based Statistical Report*. Ottawa: Statistics Canada (Catalogue no. 89-503-X). At: http://www.statcan.gc.ca/pub/89-503-x/2010001/article/11546-eng.pdf.

Milan, Anne, Mireille Vézina, and Carrie Wells. 2007. *Family Portrait: Continuity and Change in Canadian Families and Households in 2006*. Ottawa: Statistics Canada (Catalogue no. 97-553-XIE). At: www12.statcan.ca/english/census06/analysis/famhouse/pdf/97-553-XIE2006001.pdf.

Ming-Sum, Tsui. 1997. "A Child's Conception of Another World: A Chinese Boy's View of Canada," *Child and Adolescent Social Work Journal* 14, 2: 79–93.

Ministère de l'Emploi, de la Solidarité sociale et de la Famille. 2007. Quebec Parental Insurance Plan. At: www.rqap.gouv.qc.ca/a-propos-regime/caracteristiques_en.asp.

Ministry of Community and Social Services. 2007. Good Parents Pay. Toronto: Family Responsibility Office. At: http://www.mcss.gov.on.ca/en/good-parentspay/gpp_index.aspx.

Mishna, Faye, and Ramona Alaggia. 2005. "Weighing the Risks: A Child's Decision to Disclose Peer Victimization," *Children and Schools* 27, 4: 217–26.

Mishna, Faye, Beverley Antle, and Cheryl Regehr. 2004. "Tapping the Perspectives of Children: Emerging Ethical Issues in Qualitative Research," *Qualitative Social Work* 3, 4: 449–68.

Missall, Kristen, and Robin Hojnoski. 2008. "The Critical Nature of Young Children's Emerging Peer-Related Social Competence for Transition to School," in William Brown, Samuel Odom, and Scott McConnell, eds, *Social Competence of Young Children: Risk, Disability and Intervention*. Baltimore: Paul H. Brookes, pp. 117–37.

Mitcham-Smith, Michelle, and Wilma Henry. 2007. "High-Conflict Divorce Solutions: Parenting Coordination as an Innovative Co-Parenting Intervention," *The Family Journal: Counseling and Therapy for Couples and Families* 15, 4: 368–73.

Momirov, Julianne, and Kenise Murphy Kilbride. 2005. "Family Lives of Native Peoples, Immigrants and Visible Minorities," in Nancy Mandel and Ann Duffy, eds, *Canadian Families: Diversity, Conflict and Change*. Toronto: Harcourt Brace, pp. 87–110.

Montgomery, Heather. 2009. *An Introduction to Childhood: Anthropological Perspectives on Children's Lives*. West Sussex, UK: Wiley-Blackwell.

Montgomery, Kathryn. 2007. *Generation Digital: Politics, Commerce and Childhood in the Age of the Internet*. Cambridge, MA: MIT Press.

Moosa-Mitha, Mehmoona. 2005. "A Difference-Centred Alternative to Theorization of Children's Citizenship Rights," *Citizenship Studies* 9, 4: 369–88.

Moran, Kristin. 2006. "The Global Expansion of Children's Television: A Case Study of the Adoption of Sesame Street in Spain," *Learning, Media and Technology* 31, 3: 287–300.

Moran-Ellis, Jo. 2010. "Reflections on the Sociology of Childhood in the UK," *Current Sociology* 58, 2: 186–205.

Morgan, Myfanwy, Sara Gibbs, Krista Maxwell, and Nicky Britten. 2002. "Hearing Children's Voices: Methodological Issues in Conducting Focus Groups with Children Aged 7–11 Years," *Qualitative Research* 2, 1: 5–20.

Morgan, S.P., D.N. Lye, and G.A. Condran. 1988. "Sons, Daughters, and the Risk of Marital Disruptions," *American Journal of Sociology* 94: 110–29.

Morgan, S.P., and Michael Pollard. 2002. "Do Parents of Girls Really Have a Higher Risk of Divorce?" Paper presented at the 2002 Annual Meeting of the Population Association of America, Atlanta, GA, 8–10 May.

Morissette, René, and Yuri Ostrovsky. 2005. *The Instability of Family Earnings and Family Income in Canada, 1986 to 1991 and 1996 to 2001*. Ottawa: Statistics Canada, Analytical Studies Branch Research Paper Series (11F0019MIE—No. 265).

Morissette, René, Xuelin Zhang, and Marie Drolet. 2002. "Are Families Getting Richer?" *Canadian Social Trends* 66: 15–19.

Morrison, Todd, Melanie A Morrison, and Tomas Borsa. 2014. "A Legacy of Derogation: Prejudice toward Aboriginal Persons in Canada," *Psychology*, 5, 9: 1001-1010.

Morrongiello, Barbara, and Kerri Hogg. 2004. "Mothers' Reactions to Children Misbehaving in Ways That Can Lead to Injury: Implications for Gender Difference in Children's Risk Taking and Injuries," *Sex Roles* 50, 1 and 2: 103–18.

Morrongiello, Barbara, Daniel Zdzieborski, and Jackie Normand. 2010. "Understanding Gender Differences in Children's Risk Taking and Injury: A Comparison of Mothers' and Fathers' Reactions to Sons and Daughters Misbehaving in Ways that Lead to Injury," *Journal of Applied Developmental Psychology* 31, 4: 322–9.

Morrow, Virginia, and Martin Richards. 1996. "The Ethics of Social Research with Children: An Overview," *Children and Society* 10, 2: 90–115.

Moss, Kathleen. 2004. "Kids Witnessing Family Violence," *Canadian Social Trends* 73: 12–16.

Murray, Gail. 2005. "The Long History of Children as Consumers," *Reviews in American History* 33, 1: 84–8.

Murrell, Amy, Karen A. Christoff, and Kris R. Henning. 2007. "Characteristics of Domestic Violence Offenders: Associations with Childhood Exposure to Violence," *Journal of Family Violence* 22: 523–32.

Myers, John E.B. 2002. "Keep the Lifeboat Afloat," *Child Abuse and Neglect* 26: 561–7.

Myles, John, and F. Hou. 2003. *Neighbourhood Attainment and Residential Segregation among Toronto's Visible Minorities*. Ottawa: Statistics Canada, Analytical Studies Branch Research Paper Series (Catalogue no. 11F0019MIE—No. 206).

Nair, Hira, and Ann Murray. 2005. "Predictors of Attachment Security in Preschool Children from Intact and Divorced Families," *Journal of Genetic Psychology* 166, 3: 245–63.

National Council of Welfare. 2007. *Solving Poverty: Four Cornerstones of Workable National Strategy for Canada*. Ottawa: Her Majesty the Queen in Right of Canada. At: www.ncwcnbes. net/documents/researchpublications/ ResearchProjects/NationalAntiPovert yStrategy/2007Report-SolvingPoverty/ ReportENG.pdf.

National Council of Welfare. 2013. *Poverty Profile: Special Edition*. Ottawa: Her Majesty the Queen in Right of Canada. At: http://www.esdc.gc.ca/eng/commun- ities/reports/poverty_profile/snapshot.pdf.

National Institute of Child Health and Human Development Early Child Care Research Network. 2005. "Duration and Developmental Timing of Poverty and Children's Cognitive and Social Development from Birth through Third Grade," *Child Development* 76, 4: 795–810.

Nelson, E.D. (Adie). 2001. "The Things That Dreams Are Made On: Dreamwork and the Socialization of 'Stage Mothers,'" *Qualitative Sociology* 24, 4: 439–58.

Nelson, E.D. (Adie), and Barrie Robinson. 2002. *Gender in Canada*. Toronto: Prentice-Hall.

Nelson, Fiona. 1996. *Lesbian Motherhood: An Exploration of Canadian Lesbian Families*. Toronto: University of Toronto Press.

Nelson, Margaret. 2010. *Parenting Out of Control: Anxious Parents in Uncertain Times*. New York: NYU Press.

Nelson, Margaret, and Rebecca Schultz. 2007. "Day Care Differences and the Reproduction of Social Class," *Journal of Contemporary Ethnography* 36, 3: 281–317.

Nesdale, Drew, Judith Griffiths, Kevin Durkin, and Anne Maass. 2005. "Group Norms, Threat and Children's Racial Prejudice," *Child Development* 76, 3: 652–63.

———. 2007. "Effects of Group Membership, Intergroup Competition and Out-Group Ethnicity on Children's Ratings of In-Group and Out-Group Similarity and Positivity," *British Journal of Developmental Psychology* 25, 3: 359–73.

Newcomb, Horace, ed. 1997. *Encyclopedia of Television*. Chicago: Museum of Broadcast Communications.

Newhouse, David, and Evelyn Peters. 2003. "Introduction," in David Newhouse and Evelyn Peters, eds, *Not Strangers in These Parts: Urban Aboriginal Peoples*. Ottawa: Policy Research Initiative, pp. 5-13. At: http://publications.gc.ca/collections/ Collection/CP22-71-2003E.pdf

Newhouse, David, and Evelyn Peters. 2003b. "Definitions of Aboriginal Peoples," in David Newhouse and Evelyn Peters, eds, *Not Strangers in These Parts: Urban Aboriginal Peoples*. Ottawa: Policy Research Initiative, pp. 20–1. At: http://publications.gc.ca/collections/ Collection/CP22-71-2003E.pdf.

New York Times. 1874, April 11. "Mary Ellen Wilson," p. 2.

Nickerson, Amanda, Dewey Cornell, J. David Smith, and Michael Furlong. 2013. "School Antibullying Efforts: Advice for Education Policymakers," *Journal of School Violence* 12, 3: 268–82.

Noël, Alain. 2002. *A Law against Poverty: Quebec's New Approach to Combating Poverty and Social Exclusion*. Ottawa: Canadian Policy Research Networks.

Nowicki, Elizabeth. 2008. "The Interaction of Attitudes toward Racial Membership and Learning Ability in School-Aged Children," *Educational Psychology* 28, 3: 229–44.

Nowicki, Elizabeth, Jason Brown. 2013. "'A Kid Way': Strategies for Including Classmates with Learning or Intellectual Disabilities," *Intellectual and Developmental Disabilities* 51, 4: 253–62.

Nowicki, Elizabeth, J. Brown, and M. Stepien, 2014. "Children's Thoughts on the Social Exclusion of Peers with

Intellectual or Learning Disabilities," *Journal of Intellectual Disability Research* 58, 4, 346–57.

Ochocka, Joanna, and Rich Janzen. 2008. "Immigrant Parenting: A New Framework of Understanding," *Journal of Immigrant and Refugee Studies* 6, 1: 85–111.

Ogrodnik, Lucie, ed. 2008. *Family Violence in Canada: A Statistical Profile*. Ottawa: Statistics Canada (Catalogue no. 85-224-X).

Oh, Wonjung, Kenneth Rubin, Julie Bowker, Cathryn Booth-LaForce, Linda Rose-Krasnor, and Brett Laursen. 2008. "Trajectories of Social Withdrawal from Middle Childhood to Early Adolescence," *Journal of Abnormal Child Psychology* 36: 553–66.

Ohri-Vachaspati, Punam, Zeynep Isgor, Leah Rimkus, Lisa Powell, Dianne Barker, and Frank Chaloupka. 2015. "Child-Directed Marketing Inside and on the Exterior of Fast Food Restaurants," *American Journal of Preventive Medicine* 48, 1: 22–30.

Orellana, Marjorie Faulstich. 2001. "The Work Kids Do: Mexican and Central American Immigrant Children's Contributions to Households and Schools in California," *Harvard Educational Review* 71, 3: 366–89.

Organisation for Economic Co-operation and Development (OECD). 2005. *Society at a Glance: OECD Social Indicators 2005 Edition*. Paris: OECD.

———. 2006. *Starting Strong II—Early Childhood Education and Care*. Paris: OECD. At: www.oecd.org/dataoecd/14/32/37425999.pdf.

———. 2007a. *Education at a Glance—2007*. Paris: OECD.

———. 2007b. *Country Profile for Canada 2007—Education at a Glance, OECD Indicators*. Paris: OECD and Council of Ministers of Education, Canada.

———. 2011. *Doing Better for Families*. Paris, OECD.

———. 2012. *Starting Strong III—A Quality Toolbox for Early Childhood Education and Care*. Paris: OECD. www.oecd.org/edu/school/startingstrongiiiaqualitytoolboxforearlychildhoodeducationandcare.htm.

———. 2013. *Education at a Glance—Canada*. Paris: OECD.

———. 2013. "Country Note," in *Education at a Glance—Canada*. Paris: OECD. At: http://www.oecd.org/edu/Canada_EAG2013%20Country%20Note.pdf.

Office of the Provincial Advocate for Children and Youth [website]. 2014. At http://provincialadvocate.on.ca.

Oswell, David. 2013. *The Agency of Children: From Family to Global Human Rights*, Cambridge, UK: Cambridge University Press.

Otnes, Cele, Young Chan Kim, and Kyungseung Kim. 1994a. "All I Want for Christmas: An Analysis of Children's Brand Requests to Santa Claus," *Journal of Popular Culture* 27, 4: 183–94.

———. 1994b. "Yes, Virginia, There Is a Gender Difference: Analyzing Children's Requests to Santa," *Journal of Popular Culture* 28, 1: 17–29.

Oxman-Martinez, Jacqueline, and Ye Ri Choi. 2014. "Newcomer Children: Experiences of Inclusion and Exclusion, and Their Outcomes," *Social Inclusion* 2, 4: 23–37.

Paat, Yok-Fong. 2013. "Working with Immigrant Children and Their Families: An Application of Bronfenbrenner's Ecological Systems Theory," *Journal of Human Behavior in the Social Environment*. 23, 8: 954–66.

Pacini-Ketchabaw, Veronica, and Ana-Elisa Armstrong de Almeida. 2006. "Language Discourses and Ideologies as the Heart of Early Childhood Education," *International Journal of Bilingual Education and Bilingualism* 9, 3: 310–41.

Pacini-Ketchabaw, Veronica, J.K. Bernhard, and M. Freire. 2001. "Struggling to Preserve Home Language: The Experiences of Latino Students and Families in the Canadian School System," *Bilingual Research Journal* 25, 1 and 2: 115–46.

Packard, Vance. 1983. *Our Endangered Children*. Boston: Little, Brown.

Packer, Martin. 2008. "Is Vygotsky Relevant? Vygotsky's Marxist Psychology," *Mind, Culture and Activity* 15, 1: 8–31.

Palacio-Quintin, Ercilia. 2000. "Impact of Day Care on Child Development," *Isuma* 1, 2: 17–22.

Palameta, Boris. 2004. "Low Income among Immigrants and Visible Minorities," *Perspectives* 5, 4: 12–17.

Palmer, Sue. 2005, July 22. "Put the Children Back at the Centre," *TES: Times Educational Supplement* 4644: 20.

Paquet, Nicole, n.d. "Toward a Policy on Work–Family Balance—Discussion Paper. Abridged Edition." Québec: Ministère de l'Emploi, de la Solidarité sociale et de la Famille.

Parliament of Canada. 2007. Bill C-22: An Act to amend the Criminal Code (age of protection) and to make consequential amendments to the Criminal Records Act. Ottawa: Parliament of Canada. At: http://www.parl.gc.ca/About/Parliament/LegislativeSummaries/bills_ls.asp?ls=c22&parl=39&ses=1.

Parsons, Talcott. 1966. *Societies: Evolutionary and Comparative Perspectives.* Englewood Cliffs, NJ: Prentice-Hall.

———. 1975. "The School Class as a Social System: Some Functions in American Society," in R.S. Holger, ed., *The Sociology of Education: A Sourcebook.* Homewood, Ill.: Dorsey Press.

Patterson, Charlotte. 1996. "Lesbian Mothers and Their Children: Findings from the Bay Area Families Study," in J. Laird and R.J. Green, eds, *Lesbians and Gays in Couples and Families: A Handbook for Therapists.* San Francisco: Jossey-Bass, pp. 20–37.

———. 2006. "Children of Lesbian and Gay Parents," *Current Directions in Psychological Science* 15, 5: 241–4.

Pawlowski, Charlotte Skau, Tine Tjørnhøj-Thomsen, Jasper Schipperijn, and Jens Troelsen. 2014. "Barriers for Recess Physical Activity: A Gender Specific Qualitative Focus Group Exploration," *BMC Public Health* 14, 1: 1484–502.

Pellegrini, Anthony, Jeffrey Long, Cary Roseth, Catherine Bohn, and Mark Van Ryzin. 2007. "A Short-Term Longitudinal Study of Pre-schoolers' Sex Segregation: The Role of Physical Activity, Sex and Time," *Journal of Cognitive Psychology* 121, 3: 282–9.

Peltonen, Kirsi, Noora Ellonen, Tarja Pösö, and Steven Lucas. 2014. "Mothers' Self-Reported Violence toward Their Children: A Multifaceted Risk Analysis," *Child Abuse and Neglect* 38, 12: 1923–33.

Penn, Helen. 2004. *Child Care and Early Childhood Development Programmes and Policies: The Relationship to Eradicating Child Poverty.* London: Childhood Poverty Research and Policy Centre.

Perrons, Diane. 2000. "Care, Paid Work, and Leisure: Rounding the Triangle," *Feminist Economics* 6, 1: 105–14.

Persky, Susan, and Jim Blascovich. 2007. "Immersive Virtual Environments versus Traditional Platforms: Effects of Violent and Non-violent Video Game Play," *Media Psychology* 10, 1: 135–65.

Petrenchik, Theresa M. 2008. *Childhood Disability in the Context of Poverty. A Discussion Paper Prepared for the Ontario Ministry of Children and Youth Services.* Hamilton: CanChild Centre for Childhood Disability Research. At: http://www.canchild.ca/en/ourresearch/resources/ChildhoodDisabilityintheContextof Poverty_CanChild.pdf.

Pettit, G., J. Bates, and K. Dodge. 1997. "Supportive Parenting, Ecological Context and Children's Adjustment: A Seven-Year Longitudinal Study," *Child Development* 68: 908–23.

Phipps, Shelley. 2006. "Working for Working Parents: The Evolution of Maternity and Parental Benefits in Canada," *IRPP Choices* 12, 2: 1–40.

Phipps, Shelley, and Lori Curtis. 2000. *Poverty and Child Well-Being in Canada and the United States: Does It Matter How We Measure Poverty?* Gatineau, QC: Human Resources Development Canada, Working Paper Series, Applied Research Branch of Strategic Policy.

Phipps, Shelley, and Lynn Lethbridge. 2006. *Income and the Outcomes of Children.* Ottawa: Statistics Canada, Analytical Studies Branch Research Paper Series. At: www.statcan.ca/english/research/11F0019MIE/11F0019 MIE2006281.pdf.

Pigford, Ashlee-Ann, Noreen Willows, Nicholas Holt, Amanda Newton, and Geoff Ball. 2012. "Using First Nations Children's Perceptions of Food and Activity to Inform an Obesity Prevention Strategy," *Qualitative Health Research* 22, 7: 986–96.

Pike, Jennifer J., and Nancy A. Jennings. 2005. "The Effects of Commercials on Children's Perceptions of Gender Appropriate Toy Use," *Sex Roles* 52, 1 and 2: 83–91.

Pinker, Steven. 2002. *The Blank Slate: The Modern Denial of Human Nature.* London: Penguin.

Piquemal, Nathalie. 2005. "Cultural Loyalty: Aboriginal Students Take an Ethical Stance," *Reflective Practice* 6, 4: 523–38.

Ploeger, Annemie, Han L.J. van der Maas, and Maartje Raijmakers. 2008. "Is Evolutionary Psychology a Metatheory for Psychology? A Discussion of Four Major Issues in Psychology from an Evolutionary Developmental Perspective," *Psychological Inquiry* 19, 1: 1–18.

Pohan, Cathy, and Carla Mathison. 2007. "Advancing the Conversation: Television—Providing Powerful Multicultural Lessons Inside and Outside the Classroom," *Multicultural Perspectives* 9, 1: 19–25.

Pollard, Juliet. 2003. "A Most Remarkable Phenomenon: Growing Up Métis: Fur Traders' Children in the Pacific Northwest," in Janovicek and Parr (2003: 57–70).

———. 1983. *Forgotten Children: Parent–Child Relations from 1500 to 1900.* New York: Cambridge University Press.

Pollock, Linda. 1987. *A Lasting Relationship: Parents and Children over Three Centuries.* Hanover, NH: University Press of New England.

Polman, Hanneke, Bram Orobio de Castro, and Marcel A.G. van Aken. 2008. "Experimental Study of the Differential Effects of Playing versus Watching Violent Video Games on Children's Aggressive Behavior," *Aggressive Behavior* 34, 3: 256–64.

Portnoy, Sandford. 2008. "The Psychological Effects of Divorce: A Lawyer's Primer, Part 2: The Effects of Divorce on Children," *American Journal of Family Law* 21, 4: 126–34.

Postman, Neil. 1982. *The Disappearance of Childhood.* New York: Vintage Books.

———. 1999. *Building Bridges to the Eighteenth Century.* New York: Alfred A. Knopf.

Potvin Kent, and A. Wanless. 2014. "The Influence of the Children's Food and Beverage Advertising Initiative: Change in Children's Exposure to Food Advertising on Television in Canada between 2006–2009," *International Journal of Obesity* 38, 4: 558–62.

Poulton, Terry. 2008. "'Kidfluence' on family spending strong: YTV Report," *Media in Canada* 22 February. At: http://mediaincanada.com/2008/02/22/tweenreport-20080222.

Powell, Kimberly, and Lori Abels. 2002. "Sex-Role Stereotyping in TV Programs Aimed at the Preschool Audience: An Analysis of *Teletubbies* and *Barney and Friends,*" *Women and Language* 25, 2: 14–22.

Pratt, Michael, Henry Danso, Mary Louise Arnold, Joan Norris, and Rebecca Filyer. 2001. "Adult Generativity and the Socialization of Adolescents: Relations to Mothers' and Fathers' Parenting Beliefs, Styles and Practices," *Journal of Personality* 69, 1: 89–120.

Prazen, Ariana, Nicholas Wolfinger, Caitlin Cahill, and Lori Kowaleski-Jones. 2011. "Joint Physical Custody and Neighborhood Friendships in Middle Childhood," *Sociological Inquiry* 81, 2: 247–59.

Prensky, M. 2001. "Digital Natives, Digital Immigrants," *On the Horizon,* 9, 5: 1–6.

Prentice, Alison, Paula Bourne, Gail Cuthbert Brandt, Beth Light, Wendy Mitchinson, and Naomi Black. 1988. *Canadian Women: A History.* Toronto: Harcourt Brace Jovanovich.

Prentice, Susan, ed. 2001. *Changing Child Care: Five Decades of Child Care Advocacy and Policy in Canada.* Halifax: Fernwood.

———. 2007. "Less Access, Worse Quality," *Journal of Children and Poverty* 13, 1: 57–73.

Prusank, Diane, and Robert Duran. 2014. "Walking the Tightrope: Parenting Advice in Essence Magazine," *Journal of Communications* 25, 1: 77–97.

Public Health Agency of Canada. 2008. What's Wrong with Spanking? Ottawa: Government of Canada. At: http://www.phac-aspc.gc.ca/hp-ps/dca-dea/publications/spanking-fessee/.

Public Health Agency of Canada. 2013. Aboriginal Head Start In Urban and Northern Communities. Ottawa: Government of Canada. At: http://www.

phac-aspc.gc.ca/hp-ps/dca-dea/prog-ini/ahsunc-papacun/index-eng.php.

Public Health Agency of Canada. 2014. "In the Spotlight." Ottawa: Government of Canada. At: http://www.phac-aspc.gc.ca/sfv-avf/spotlight-vedette-eng.php#actionplan.

Public Legal Education and Information Services of New Brunswick. 2007. Spanking and Disciplining Children. Frederickon: PLEIS-NB. At: http://www.legal-info-legale.nb.ca/en/spanking_disciplining_children.

Punch, Samantha. 2002. "Research with Children: The Same or Different from Research with Adults?" *Childhood* 9, 3: 321–41.

Quaicoe, Lloydetta. 2007. "Wanting to Belong: Schooling Experiences of New Immigrant and Refugee Children." Presented at 9th National Metropolis Conference, Exploring Canada's Diversity, Today and Tomorrow, Toronto, 1–4 March 2007.

Quill, Lawrence. 2011. "The Disappearance of Adulthood," *Studies in Philosophy and Education* 30, 4: 327–41.

Quirke, Linda. 2006. "'Keeping Young Minds Sharp': Children's Cognitive Stimulation and the Rise of Parenting Magazines, 1959–2003," *Canadian Review of Sociology and Anthropology* 43, 4: 387–406.

Qvortrup, Jens. 1994. "Childhood Matters: An Introduction," in J. Qvortrup, M. Bardy, G. Sgritta, and H. Winterberger, eds, *Childhood Matters: Social Theory, Practice and Politics*. Aldershot: Avebury.

———. 2004. "The Waiting Child," *Childhood* 11, 3: 267–73.

Qvortrup, Jens, William A. Corsaro, and Michael-Sebastian Honig, eds. 2009. *The Palgrave Handbook of Childhood Studies*. Basinstoke: Palgrave Macmillan.

Raby, R. 2012. *School Rules: Obedience, Discipline and Elusive Democracy*. Toronto: University of Toronto Press.

Ram, Bali, and Feng Hou. 2005. "Sex Difference in the Effects of Family Structure on Children's Aggressive Behavior," *Journal of Comparative Family Studies* 36, 2: 329–41.

Rand, Theodore. 2003. "An Argument for Assessment and Free Schools (Nova Scotia)," in Janovicek and Parr (2003: 122–5).

Reading, Charlotte Loppie, and Fred Wien. 2009. "Health Inequalities and Social Determinants of Aboriginal Peoples' Health." Prince George: National Collaborating Centre for Aboriginal Health. At http://www.nccah-ccnsa.ca/docs/social%20determinates/nccah-loppie-wien_report.pdf.

Renold, Emma. 2000. "'Coming Out': Gender, (Hetero)Sexuality and the Primary School," *Gender and Education* 12: 309–26.

———. 2007. "Primary School 'Studs': (De)constructing Young Boys' Heterosexual Masculinities," *Men and Masculinities* 9, 3: 275–97.

Reynaert, Didier, Maria Bouverne-De Bie, and Stijn Vandevelde. 2009. "A Review of Children's Rights Literature Since the Adoption of the United Nations Convention on the Rights of the Child," *Childhood* 16, 4: 518–34.

Rizzo, Kathryn, Holly Schiffrin, and Miriam Liss. 2013. "Insight into the Parenthood Paradox: Mental Health Outcomes of Intensive Mothering," *Journal of Child and Family Studies* 22, 5: 614-620.

Roberts, Donald, and Ulla Foehr. 2004. *Kids and Media in America*. Cambridge: Cambridge University Press.

Robertson, Eleanor. 2008. "Promoting Acceptance of Sexual Diversity in a Class of Fifth Grade Boys," *Journal of LGBT Youth* 5, 1: 15–26.

Robinson, Paul. 2006. *Child and Spousal Support: Maintenance Enforcement Survey Statistics, 2003/2004*. Ottawa: Statistics Canada (Catalogue no. 85-228-XIE).

Robinson, Paul. 2009. "Profile of Child Support Beneficiaries," in *Juristat*. Ottawa: Statistics Canada (Cat. # 85-022-X). At: http://www.statcan.gc.ca/pub/85-002-x/2009001/article/10784-eng.htm.

Robson-Haddow, Jennifer. 2004. *Key to Tackling Child Poverty: Income Support for Immediate Needs and Assets for Their Future*. Ottawa: Caledon Institute of Social Policy.

Rodriguez, Christina, and Michael Richardson. 2007. "Stress and Anger as Contextual Factors and Preexisting Cognitive Schemas: Predicting Parental Child Maltreatment," *Child Maltreatment* 12, 4: 325–37.

Roe, Amy, Laura Bridges, Judy Dunn, and Thomas O'Connor. 2006. "Young Children's Representations of Their Families: A Longitudinal Follow-Up Study of Family Drawings by Children Living in Different Family Settings," *International Journal of Behavioral Development* 30, 6: 529–36.

Romagnoli, Amy, and Glenda Wall. 2014. "'I Know I'm a Good Mom': Young, Low-Income Mothers' Experiences with Risk Perception, Intensive Parenting Ideology and Parenting Education Programmes," *Health, Risk and Society* 14, 3: 273–89.

Romano, Elisa, Richard Tremblay, Bernard Boulerice, and Raymond Swisher. 2005. "Multilevel Correlates of Childhood Physical Aggression and Prosocial Behavior," *Journal of Abnormal Child Psychology* 33, 5: 565–78.

Romero, R. Todd. 2008. "Totherswamp's Lament: Christian Indian Fathers and Sons in Early Massachusetts," *Journal of Family History* 33, 1: 5–12.

Rose, Donald, and Nicholas Bodor. 2006. "Household Food Insecurity and Overweight Status in Young School Children: Results from the Early Childhood Longitudinal Study," *Pediatrics* 117, 2: 464–73.

Rose, Gregory M., Vassilis Dalakas, and Fredric Kropp. 2003. "Consumer Socialization and Parental Style across Cultures: Findings from Australia, Greece, and India," *Journal of Consumer Psychology* 13, 4: 366–76.

Rose, Katherine, Brigitte Vittrup, Tinney Leveridge. 2013. "Parental Decision Making About Technology and Quality in Child Care Programs," *Child and Youth Care Forum* 42, 5: 475–88.

Rosen, David. 2007. "Child Soldiers, International Humanitarian Law and the Globalization of Childhood," *American Anthropologist* 109, 2: 296–306.

Ross, David, and Paul Roberts. 1999. *Income and Child Well-Being: A New Perspective on the Poverty Debate*. Ottawa: Canadian Council on Social Development. At: www.ccsd.ca/pubs/inckids/index.htm.

Ross, David, and Paul Roberts, and Katherine Scott. 2000. "Family Income and Child Well-Being," *Isuma* 1, 2: 51–4.

Ross, H., and H. Taylor. 1989. "Do Boys Prefer Daddy or His Physical Style of Play?" *Sex Roles* 20, 1 and 2: 23–31.

Rotermann, Michelle. 2007. "Marital Breakdown and Subsequent Depression," *Health Reports* 16, 2: 33–44.

Rothstein, Richard. 2004. *Social Class and Schools: Using Social, Economic and Educational Reform to Close the Black–White Achievement Gap*. New York: Columbia University Press.

Rousseau, Cécile, Aline Drapeau, Louise Lacroix, Déogratias Bagilishya, and Nicole Heusch. 2005. "Evaluation of a Classroom Program of Creative Expression Workshops for Refugee and Immigrant Children," *Journal of Child Psychology and Psychiatry* 46, 2: 180–5.

Rousseau, Jean-Jacques. 1974 [1762]. *Emile*. London: Dent/Everyman's Library.

———. 1994 [1762]. "On the Social Contract," in Roger D. Masters and Christopher Kelly, eds, *Collected Writings of Rousseau*, vol. 4. Hanover, NH: Dartmouth College/University Press of New England.

Roy, Francine. 2006. "From She to She: Changing Patterns of Women in the Canadian Labour Force," *Canadian Economic Observer* 3.1–3.10.

Roy, Laurent, and Jean Bernier. 2007. *Family Policy, Social Trends and Fertility in Quebec: Experimenting with the Nordic Model?* Québec: Ministère de la Famille, des Aînés et de la Condition Féminine.

Royal Canadian Mounted Police. 2007, October 16. "International Child Sexual Abuse Investigation [news release]." Ottawa: RCMP Media Relations. At: www.rcmp-grc.gc.ca/news/2007/2007_10_16_abuse_e.htm.

Royal Commission on Aboriginal Peoples. 1996a. People to People, Nation to Nation: Highlights from the Royal Commission on Aboriginal Peoples. Ottawa, ON: Minister of Supply and Services Canada.

Royal Commission on Aboriginal Peoples. 1996. "Part 2: False Assumptions and a Failed Relationship," in *Report of the Royal Commission on Aboriginal Peoples*. Ottawa: Indian and Northern Affairs Canada. At: www.ainc-inac.gc.ca/ch/rcap/sg/sgmm_e.html.

Royal Commission on the Status of Women in Canada. 1970. *Report of the Royal Commission on the Status of Women.* Ottawa: Crown Copyrights/Information Canada.

Ruddick, Sue. 2007. "At the Horizons of the Subject: Neo-Liberalism, Neo-Conservatism and the Rights of the Child. Part One: From 'Knowing' Fetus to 'Confused' Child," *Gender, Place and Culture* 14, 5: 513–26.

Rutherford, Paul. 1997. "Advertising," in Newcomb (1997). At: www.museum.tv/archives/etv/A/htmlA/advertising/advertising.htm.

Sadeghi, Shiva. 2008. "Minority Language Students' Perceptions of Multiculturalism, Democratic Values, and Citizenship." PowerPoint presentation for the Centre for Excellence in Research on Immigration and Settlement, Toronto, 4 April 2008. At: ceris.metropolis.net/frameset_e.html.

Sadker, M.P., and D.M. Sadker. 1991. *Teachers, Schools and Society.* New York: McGraw-Hill.

Sadoway, Geraldine. 2001. "Canada's Treatment of Separated Refugee Children," *European Journal of Migration and Law* 3, 3 and 4: 347–81.

Sahakian, Mabel Lewis, and William S. Sahakian. 1974. *Rousseau as Educator.* New York: Twayne Publishers.

Sammond, Nicholas. 2005. *Babes in Tomorrowland: Walt Disney and the Making of the American Child, 1930–1960.* Durham, NC: Duke University Press.

Samuel, T., John Verma, and B.P. Ravi. 1992. "Immigrant Children in Canada: A Demographic Analysis," *Canadian Ethnic Studies* 24, 3: 51–8.

Sanders, Jackie, and Robyn Munford. 2008. "Conformity and Resistance in Self-Management Strategies of 'Good Girls,'" *Childhood* 15, 4: 481–97.

Sankaran, Priya, Carmen Whyte, and Erin Sufrin. 1998. *There's Always the Fine Print.* Toronto: Schools of Radio and Television Arts and Early Childhood Education, Ryerson University.

Sarrazin, Janie, and Francine Cyr. 2007. "Parental Conflicts and Their Damaging Effects on Children," *Journal of Divorce and Remarriage* 47, 1 and 2: 77–93.

Sayer, L., S. Bianchi, and J. Robinson. 2004. "Are Parents Investing Less in Children? Trends in Mothers' and Fathers' Time with Children," *American Journal of Sociology* 110, 1: 1–43.

Schiffrin, Holly, Miriam Liss, Katherine Geary, Haley Miles-McLean, Taryn Tashner, Charlotte Hagerman, and Kathryn Rizzo. 2014. "Mother, Father, or Parent? College Students' Intensive Parenting Attitudes Differ by Referent," *Journal of Child and Family Studies* 23, 6: 1073–80.

Schoenbach, Klaus. 2001. "Myths of Media and Audiences," *European Journal of Communication* 16, 3: 361–76.

Schopenhauer, Arthur. 1987. *Essays and Aphorisms.* New York: Penguin.

Schor, Juliet. 2004. *Born to Buy.* New York: Scribner.

Segal, Nancy. 2012. *Born Together—Reared Apart: The Landmark Minnesota Twin Study.* Boston, MA: Harvard University Press.

Senechal, Monique, and Joanne LeFevre. 2002. "Parental Involvement in the Development of Children's Reading Skills: A Five Year Longitudinal Study," *Child Development* 73, 2: 445–60.

Shanahan, Suzanne. 2007. "Lost and Found: The Sociological Ambivalence Toward Childhood," *Annual Review of Sociology* 33, 1: 407–28.

Sharma, Raghubar. 2012. *Poverty in Canada.* Toronto: Oxford University Press.

Shaw, Catherine, Louca-Mai Brady, and Ciara Davey. 2011. *Guidelines for Research with Children and Young People.* London: National Children's Bureau Research Centre. At: http://www.nfer.ac.uk/nfer/schools/developing-young-researchers/ncbguidelines.pdf.

Sheridan, Sonja, and Ingrid Pramling Samuelsson. 2013. "Preschool a Source for Young Children's Learning and Well-Being," *International Journal of Early Years Education* 21, 2/3: 207–22.

Sherman, Aurora, and Eileen Zurbriggen. 2014. "'Boys Can Be Anything': Effect of Barbie Play on Girls' Career Cognitions," *Sex Roles* 70, 5/6: 195–208.

Shimoni, R., David Este, and Dawne E. Clark. 2003. "Paternal Engagement in Immigrant and Refugee Families,"

Journal of Comparative Family Studies 34, 4: 555–68.

Short, Liz. 2007. "Lesbian Mothers Living Well in the Context of Heterosexism and Discrimination: Resources, Strategies and Legislative Change," *Feminism and Psychology* 17, 1: 57–74.

Siegenthaler, Amanda, and Jerry Bigner. 2000. "The Value of Children to Lesbian and Non-lesbian Mothers," *Journal of Homosexuality* 39, 2: 73–91.

Sigle-Rushton, Wendy, and Jane Waldfogel. 2007. "Incomes of Families with Children: A Cross-National Comparison," *Journal of European Social Policy* 17, 4: 299–318.

Simich, Laura, H. Hamilton, H. Fenta, L. Marshall. 2009. "Immigrant Parents' Settlement Experiences and Contributions to Children's Health: Analysis, Knowledge Transfer and Exchange," in *Research Report to the Ontario Metropolis Centre*. Toronto: CERIS. At: http://ceris.ca/wp-content/uploads/virtual-library/Simich_et_al_2007.pdf.

Simmons, Noreen, and Judith Johnson. 2006. "Cross-Cultural Differences in Beliefs and Practices That Affect the Language Spoken to Children: Mothers with Indian and Western Heritage," *International Journal of Language and Communication Disorders* 42, 4: 445–65.

Singh, Gopal, and Reem Ghandour. 2012. "Impact of Neighborhood Social Conditions and Household Socioeconomic Status on Behavioral Problems among US Children," *Maternal and Child Health Journal* 16, 158–169.

Sinha, Maire. 2013. *Family Violence in Canada: A Statistical Profile, 2011.* Ottawa: Statistics Canada (Catalogue no. 85-002-X). At: http://www.statcan.gc.ca/pub/85-002-x/2013001/article/11805/11805-4-eng.htm#a6.

———. 2013. "Section 4: Family Violence against Children and Youth," in *Family Violence in Canada: A Statistical Profile, 2011.* Ottawa: Statistics Canada (Catalogue no. 85-002-X). At: http://www.statcan.gc.ca/pub/85-002-x/2013001/article/11805/11805-4-eng.htm#a6.

———. 2014. *Parenting and Child Support after Separation or Divorce.* Ottawa:

Statistics Canada (Catalogue no. 89-652-X).

Skinner, B.F. 1953. *Science and Human Behavior.* New York: Macmillan.

Smith, Anne. 2007. "Children and Young People's Participation Rights in Education," *International Journal of Children's Rights* 15: 147–64.

Smith, Stacy, Katherine Pieper, Amy Granados, and Marc Choueiti. 2010. "Assessing Gender-Related Portrayals in Top-Grossing G-Rated Films," *Sex Roles* 62, 11/12: 774–86.

Sørensen, Kaspar, Annette Mouritsen, Lise Aksglaede, Casper Hagen, Signe Sloth Mogensen, and Anders Juul. 2012. "Recent Secular Trends in Pubertal Timing: Implications for Evaluation and Diagnosis of Precocious Puberty," *Hormone Research in Paediatrics* 77, 3: 137–45.

Spees, Jennifer Greve, and Toni Schindler Zimmerman. 2002. "Gender Messages in Parenting Magazines: A Content Analysis," *Journal of Family Therapy* 14, 3 and 4: 73–100.

Spence, Adam. 2008. *A Gathering Storm. The Cost of Food, Gasoline and Energy and Changing Economic Conditions in Ontario.* Toronto: Ontario Association of Food Banks (OAFB). At: http://www.oafb.ca/assets/pdfs/A_Gathering_Storm.pdf.

Spies, Tracy, Joseph Morgan, and Miki Matsuura. 2014. "Faces of Hunger: The Educational Impact of Hunger on Students with Disabilities," *Intervention in School and Clinic* 50, 1: 5–14.

Spock, Benjamin. 2004 [1946]. *Baby and Child Care*, 8th edn. New York: Pocket Books.

Stafford, Janine. 2002. *A Profile of the Childcare Services Industry.* Ottawa: Statistics Canada (Catalogue no. 63-016-XPB).

Stafseng, O. 1993. "A Sociology of Childhood and Youth—the Need of Both?" in J. Qvortrup, ed., *Childhood as a Social Phenomenon: Lessons from an International Project.* Vienna: European Centre for Social Welfare Policy and Research.

Stanbridge, Karen. 2007. "Framing Children in the Newfoundland Confederation Debate, 1948," *Canadian Journal of Sociology* 32, 2: 177–201.

Standing Senate Committee on Human Rights. 2007. *Children: The Silenced Citizens.* At: http://www.parl.gc.ca/ Content/SEN/Committee/391/huma/ rep/rep10apr07-e.pdf.

Stanley, Tim. 2003. "White Supremacy, Chinese Schooling, and School Segregation in Victoria: The Case of the Chinese Students' Strike, 1922–1923," in Janovicek and Parr (2003: 126–42).

Stanwick, Richard. 2006. "Canada Gets a Marginal Grade in Childhood Injury," *Canadian Medical Association Journal* 175, 8: 845.

Starr, Christine, and Gail Ferguson. 2012. "Sexy Dolls, Sexy Grade-Schoolers? Media and Maternal Influences on Young Girls' Self-Sexualization," *Sex Roles* 67, 7/8: 463–76.

Stasiulis, Daiva. 2002. "The Active Child Citizen: Lessons from Canadian Policy and the Children's Movement," *Citizenship Studies* 6, 4: 507–38.

Statistics Canada. 1996a. *A Statistical Portrait of Elementary Education in Canada.* Ottawa: Statistics Canada and Council of Ministers of Education.

———. 1996b. "Family Incomes, 1995," *The Daily* 11 December.

———. 1998. "1996 Census: Labour Force Activity, Occupation and Industry, Place of Work, Mode of Transportation to Work, Unpaid Work," *The Daily* 17 March.

———. 1999. "National Longitudinal Survey of Children and Youth: Transition into Adolescence," *The Daily* 6 July.

———. 2000. *Women in Canada—2000: A Gender-Based Statistical Report.* Ottawa: Statistics Canada.

———. 2001. "School Performance of Children from Immigrant Families," *The Daily* 14 November

———. 2002. *Profile of Canadian Families and Households: Diversification Continues.* Ottawa: Statistics Canada (Catalogue no. 96F0030XIE2001003).

———. 2003. *2001 Census: Analysis Series—Education in Canada: Raising the Standard.* Ottawa: Minister of Industry.

———. 2004a. "Youth Smoking Survey," *The Daily* 14 June.

———. 2004b. "Average Hours per Week of Television Viewing—2002," CANSIM tables 502-0002 and 502-0003. At:

statscan.ca/english/kits/winner/2004/ grade9/TVwatching/Canadian%20.

———. 2004c. Update on Economic Analysis. Ottawa: Statistics Canada (Catalogue no. 11-623.XIE). At: www. statcan.ca/english/freepub/11-623-XIE/2003001/trdescrip.htm.

———. 2004d. "Divorces," *The Daily* 4 May.

———. 2005a. "National Longitudinal Survey of Children and Youth: Home Environment, Income and Child Behaviour—1994/95 to 2002/03," *The Daily* 21 February.

———. 2005b. "Canadian Community Health Survey: Obesity among Children and Adults," *The Daily* 6 July.

———. 2005c. "The Socio-economic Progress of the Children of Immigrants," *The Daily* 25 Oct.

———. 2005d. "Children and Youth as Victims of Violent Crime," *The Daily* 20 Apr.

———. 2005e. "Family Violence in Canada: A Statistical Profile," *The Daily* 14 July.

———. 2005f. "Television Viewing," *The Daily* 31 March.

———. 2006b. "Back to School Fact Book," *Education Matters* 3, 3. At: www.statcan. ca/english/freepub/81-004-XIE/81-004-XIE2006003.htm.

———. 2006c. "Television Viewing, by Age and Sex, by Province—2004," CANSIM tables 502-0002 and 502-0003 (Catalogue no. 87F0006XIE). At: www40.statcan.ca/101/cst01/arts23.htm.

———. 2006d. "Table: Population by Sex and Age Group, 2006," CANSIM, table 051-0001. Ottawa: Statistics Canada. At: www40.statcan.ca/l01/cst01/ demo10a.htm.

———. 2006e. "Child Care: An Eight Year Profile," *The Daily* 5 Apr.

———. 2007b. *Births—2005.* Ottawa: Health Statistics Division, Minister of Industry (Catalogue no. 84F0210XIE).

———. 2007c. *Educational Indicators in Canada: Report of the Pan-Canadian Education Indicators Program 2007.* Ottawa: Canadian Education Statistics Council.

———. 2007d. "Study: Time with Family," *The Daily* 13 February.

———. 2007e. *Labour Force Information.* Ottawa: Minister of Industry (Catalogue no. 71-001-XIE).

————. 2007f. "Leading Indicators," *The Daily* 21 August.

————. 2007g. *Income in Canada—2005.* Ottawa: Statistics Canada (Catalogue no. 75-202-XIE). At: www.statcan.ca/english/freepub/75-202-XIE/75-202-XIE2005000.pdf.

————. 2007h. "Incomes of Canadians," *The Daily* 3 May.

————. 2008. *Participation and Activity Limitation Survey (2001 and 2006).* Ottawa: Statistics Canada. At: http://www.statcan.gc.ca/pub/89-628-x/2008004/t/5201211-eng.htm.

————. 2008b. Income Trends in Canada 1980–2005. Ottawa: Statistics Canada (Catalogue no. 13F0022XIE).

————. 2009a. "Table 21: Percentage of First Nations and Non-Aboriginal Populations Living in Crowded Dwellings, Canada, 1996 and 2006." Ottawa: Statistics Canada. At: http://www12.statcan.ca/census-recensement/2006/as-sa/97-558/table/t21-eng.cfm.

————. 2009b. School-Age Population Living in Low-Income Circumstances. Cat. # 81-599-X Issue no. 004. Ottawa: Statistics Canada. http://www.statcan.gc.ca/pub/81-599-x/81-599-x2009004-eng.pdf.

————. 2009c. "Study: Child Luring through the Internet," *The Daily* 12 March.

————. 2010. *National Longitudinal Survey of Children and Youth—Cycle 8 Survey.* Ottawa: Statistics Canada and Human Resources and Social Development Canada. At: http://www23.statcan.gc.ca/imdb/p2SV.pl?Function=getSurvey&SDDS=4450.

————. 2011. "Elementary and Secondary Public School Indicators," *The Daily* 30 November.

————. 2012. Census Dictionary: Census Year, 2011. Ottawa: Minister of Industry. At: http://www12.statcan.gc.ca/census-recensement/2011/ref/dict/98-301-X2011001-eng.pdf.

————. 2012b. *Portrait of Families and Living Arrangements in Canada. Families, Households and Marital Status, 2011 Census of Population.* Ottawa: Minister of Industry (Catalogue no. 98-312-X2011001). At: http://www12.statcan.gc.ca/census-recensement/2011/as-sa/98-312-x/98-312-x2011001-eng.pdf.

————. 2012c. *The Canadian Population in 2011: Age and Sex.* Ottawa: Minister of Industry (Catalogue no. 98-311-X2011001).

————. 2012d. "Study: Profile of Parents in Stepfamilies, 2011," *The Daily* 18 October.

————. 2013a. "Elementary-Secondary Education Survey for Canada, the Provinces and Territories, 2012," *The Daily* 4 December. At: http://www.statcan.gc.ca/daily-quotidien/131204/dq131204c-eng.pdf.

————. 2013b. "Summary Elementary and Secondary School Indicators for Canada, the Provinces and Territories, 2006/2007 to 2010/2011." Ottawa: Tourism and Centre for Education Statistics (Catalogue no. 81-595-M—No. 099).

————. 2013c. "Labour Force Survey, February 2013," *The Daily* 8 March.

————. 2013d. "2011 National Household Survey: Portrait of Canada's Labour Force," *The Daily* 26 June.

————. 2013e. *Aboriginal Peoples in Canada: First Nations People, Métis and Inuit-National Household Survey.* Ottawa: Statistics Canada. At: http://www12.statcan.gc.ca/nhs-enm/2011/as-sa/99-011-x/99-011-x2011001-eng.pdf.

————. 2013f. "Table 202-0801: Low Income Cut-Offs Before and After Tax by Community and Family Size, 2011 Constant Dollars Annual (dollars)." Ottawa: Statistics Canada. At: http://www5.statcan.gc.ca/cansim/a26?lang=eng&retrLang=eng&id=2020801&paSer=&pattern=&stByVal=1&p1=1&p2=-1&tabMode=dataTable&csid=.

————. 2013g. Low Income Lines, 2011–2012. Ottawa: Statistics Canada (Catalogue no. 75F0002M—No. 002).

————. 2013h. 2011 "National Household Survey: Income of Canadians," *The Daily* 11 September.

————. 2013i. "Income of Canadians, 2011," *The Daily* 27 June.

————. 2013j. "Canadian Internet Use Survey, 2012," *The Daily* 26 November.

————. 2014a. "Study: Occupational Profile and Overqualification of Young Workers in Canada, 1991 to 2011," *The Daily* 2 April.

————. 2014b. "Labour Force Survey, June 2014," *The Daily* 11 July.

————. 2014c. *Aboriginal Peoples Reference Guide, National Household Survey, 2011.* Ottawa: Statistics Canada. At: http://www12.statcan.gc.ca/nhs-enm/2011/ref/guides/99-011-x/99-011-x2011006-eng.cfm.

Stearns, Peter. 2005. *Growing Up: The History of Childhood in a Global Context.* Waco, Texas: Baylor University Press.

———. 2005b. "Conclusion: Change, Globalization and Childhood," *Journal of Social History,* 38, 4: 1041–6.

———. 2006. *Childhood in World History.* New York: Routledge.

———. 2009. "Analyzing the Role of Culture in Shaping American Childhood: A Twentieth-Century Case," *European Journal of Developmental Psychology.* 6, 1: 34–52.

———. 2014. "Obedience and Emotion: A Challenge in the Emotional History of Childhood," *Journal of Social History* 47, 3: 593–611.

Steeves, Valerie. 2014a. *Young Canadians in a Wired World, Phase III: Experts or Amateurs? Gauging Young Canadians' Digital Literacy Skills.* Ottawa: Media Smarts.

Steeves, Valerie. 2014b. *Young Canadians in a Wired World, Phase III: Encountering Racist and Sexist Content Online.* Ottawa: Media Smarts. At: http://mediasmarts. ca/sites/mediasmarts/files/publication-report/full/ycwwiii_encountering_ racist_sexist_content_online.pdf.

Steeves, Valerie. 2005. *Young Canadians in a Wired World—Phase II—Trends and Recommendations.* Ottawa: Media Awareness Network. At: www.media-awareness.ca/english/research/YCWW.

Stevens, Tara, and Miriam Mulsow. 2006. "There Is No Meaningful Relationship between Television Exposure and Symptoms of Attention Deficit/ Hyperactivity Disorder," *Pediatrics* 117, 3: 665–72.

Stevenson, Garth. 2006. *Parallel Paths: The Development of Nationalism in Ireland and Quebec.* Montreal and Kingston: McGill-Queen's University Press.

Stinson, Jane. 2006. "Impact of Privatization on Women," *Canadian Dimension* 40, 3: 27–32.

Straus, Murray. 1994. *Beating the Devil Out of Them: Corporal Punishment in American Families.* New York: Lexington Books.

Strohschein, Lisa. 2005. "Parental Divorce and Child Mental Health Trajectories," *Journal of Marriage and Family* 67: 1286–1300.

———. 2007. "Prevalence of Methylphenidate Use among Children Following Parental Divorce," *Canadian Medical Association Journal* 176, 12: 1711–14.

"Study Finds Girls Overexposed to Alcohol Advertising," 2004. *Alcoholism and Drug Abuse Weekly* 16, 28: 2.

Suransky, Valerie. 1982. *The Erosion of Childhood.* Chicago: University of Chicago Press.

Sussman, Deborah, and Stephanie Bonnell. 2006. "Wives as Primary Breadwinners," *Perspectives* 7, 8: 10–17. At: http://www.statcan.gc.ca/pub/75-001-x/10806/9291-eng.htm.

Suter, Elizabeth, Karen Daas, and Karla Mason Bergen. 2008. "Negotiating Lesbian Family Identity via Symbols and Rituals," *Journal of Family Issues* 29, 1: 26–47.

Sutherland, Anne, and Beth Thompson. 2001. *Kidfluence: Why Kids Today Mean Business.* Toronto: McGraw-Hill Ryerson.

Sutherland, Neil. 2003. "When You Listen to the Winds of Childhood, How Much Can You Believe?" in Janovicek and Parr (2003: 19–34).

Sutton, John R. 1988. *Stubborn Children: Controlling Delinquency in the United States, 1640–1981.* Berkeley: University of California Press.

Suziedelytea, Agne. 2015. "The Effects of Old and New Media on Children's Weight," *Applied Economics* 47, 10: 1008–18.

Swain, Jon. 2005. "Sharing the Same World: Boys' Relations with Girls during Their Last Year of Primary School," *Gender & Education* 17, 1: 75–91.

Tay-Lim, Joanna, and Sirene Lim. 2013. "Privileging Younger Children's Voices in Research: Use of Drawings and a Co-construction Process," *International Journal of Qualitative Methods* 12, 1: 65–84.

Taylor, Gerald. 1994. "Sociological Interpretations of Schooling: The Functional Perspective," in Lorna Erwin and David MacLennan, eds, *Sociology of Education in Canada: Critical Perspectives on Theory, Research and Practice.* Toronto: Copp Clark Longman, pp. 32–54.

Taylor, Yvette. 2009. *Lesbian and Gay Parenting: Securing Social and Educational Capital.* New York: Palgrave Macmillan.

Teachman, Gail, and Barbara Gibson. 2013. "Children and Youth with Disabilities:

Innovative Methods for Single Qualitative Interviews," *Qualitative Health Research* 23, 2: 264–74.

Tenenbaum, Harriet, and Campbell Leaper. 2002. "Are Parents' Gender Schemas Related to Their Children's Gender-Related Cognitions? A Meta-Analysis," *Developmental Psychology* 38, 4: 615–30.

Te One, Sarah, Rebecca Blaikie, Michelle Egan-Bitran, and Zoey Henley. 2014. "You Can Ask Me If You Really Want to Know What I Think," *Educational Philosophy and Theory* 46, 9: 1052–68.

Teram, Eli, Candice Schachter, and Carol Stalker. 2005. "The Case for Integrating Grounded Theory and Participatory Action Research: Empowering Clients to Inform Professional Practice," *Qualitative Health Research* 15, 8: 1129–40.

Tétreault, Sylvie, Sophie Blais-Michaud, Pascale Marier Deschênes, Pauline Beaupré, Hubert Gascon, Normand Boucher, and Monique Carrière. 2014. "How to Support Families of Children with Disabilities? An Exploratory Study of Social Support Services," *Child and Family Social Work* 19, 3: 272–81.

Thomas, Eleanor. 2004. *Aggressive Behaviour Outcomes for Young Children: Change in Parenting Environment Predicts Change in Behaviour.* Ottawa: Statistics Canada (Catalogue no. 89-599-MIE—No. 001).

———. 2006. "Readiness to Learn at School among Five-Year-Old Children in Canada." Ottawa: Statistics Canada, Children and Youth Research Paper Series.

———. 2009. "Canadian Nine-Year-Olds at School." Ottawa: Statistics Canada, Children and Youth Research Paper Series. At: http://www.statcan.gc.ca/pub/89-599-m/89-599-m2009006-eng.pdf.

Thomas, Nigel, and Claire O'Kane. 1998. "The Ethics of Participatory Research with Children," *Children and Society* 12: 336–48.

Thomas, Susan Gregory. 2007. *Buy, Buy, Baby.* New York: Houghton Mifflin.

Thompson, Steven. 2006. "Was Ancient Rome a Dead Wives Society? What Did the Roman Paterfamilias Get Away With?" *Journal of Family History* 31, 1: 3–27.

Thorne, Barrie. 1990. "Girls and Boys Together . . . But Mostly Apart: Gender Arrangements in Elementary School," in M.S. Kimmel and M.A. Messner, eds, *Men's Lives*, 3rd edn. Boston: Allyn and Bacon, pp. 61–73.

———. 1993. *Gender Play: Girls and Boys in School.* New Brunswick, NJ: Rutgers University Press.

Thorne, Barrie, and Z. Luria. 1986. "Sexuality and Gender in Children's Daily Worlds," *Social Problems* 33: 176–90.

Timpson, J. 1995. "Four Decades of Literature on Native Canadian Child Welfare: Changing Themes," *Child Welfare* 74, 3: 525–46.

Torjman, Sherri. 2010. *Poverty Reduction in Québec: The First Five Years.* Ottawa: Caledon Institute of Social Policy.

Tougas, Jocelyne. 2001a. "What We Can Learn from the Quebec Experience," in Gordon Cleveland and Michael Krashinsky, eds, *Our Children's Future: Child Care Policy in Canada.* Toronto: University of Toronto Press, pp. 92–105.

———. 2001b. "Child Care in Quebec: Where There's Will, There's a Way." Ottawa, Ontario: Child Care Advocacy Association of Canada.

———. 2002. *Reforming Quebec's Early Childhood Care and Education: The First Five Years.* Toronto: Childcare Resource and Research Unit. At: http://www.childcarecanada.org/publications/occasional-paper-series/02/05/reforming-québecs-early-childhood-care-and-education-firs.

Tremblay, Stephane, Nancy Ross, and Jean-Marie Berthelot. 2001. "Factors Affecting Grade 3 Student Performance in Ontario: A Multilevel Analysis," *Education Quarterly Review* 7, 4: 25–36.

Trocmé, Nico, Barbara Fallon, Bruce MacLaurin, Vandna Sinha, Tara Black, Elizabeth Fast, Caroline Felstiner, Sonia Hélie, Daniel Turcotte, Pamela Weightman, Janet Douglas, and Jill Holroyd. 2010. *Canadian Incidence Study of Reported Child Abuse and Neglect 2008 (CIS-2008): Major Findings.* Ottawa: Public Health Agency of Canada. At: http://cwrp.ca/sites/default/files/publications/en/CIS-2008-rprt-eng.pdf.

Trocmé, Nico, D. Knoke, and C. Blackstock. 2004. "Pathways to the

Overrepresentation of Aboriginal Children in Canada's Child Welfare System," *Social Service Review* 78, 4: 577–600.

Tschann, Jeanne, Janet Johnston, Marsha Kline, and Judith Wallerstein. 1989. "Family Process and Child Functioning during Divorce," *Journal of Marriage and Family* 51: 431–44.

Turcotte, Martin. 2006. "Passing on the Ancestral Language," *Canadian Social Trends* 80: 20–6.

———. 2007. "Time Spent with Family During a Typical Workday, 1986 to 2005," *Canadian Social Trends* 83: 2–11.

Turmel, Andre. 2008. *A Historical Sociology of Childhood: Developmental Thinking, Categorization and Graphic Visualization.* New York: Cambridge University Press.

Uchikoshi, Yuuko. 2005. "Narrative Development in Bilingual Kindergartens: Can Arthur Help?" *Developmental Psychology* 41, 3: 464–78.

———. "Early Reading in Bilingual Kindergarteners: Can Educational Television Help?" *Scientific Studies of Reading* 10, 1: 89–120.

UNICEF. 1990a. Convention on the Rights of the Child. New York: United Nations.

———. 1990b. *World Summit for Children.* New York: United Nations. At: www.unicef.org/wsc/>.

———. 2006. *World Report on Violence against Children.* New York: UNICEF.

———. 2007a. "The Oslo Challenge." At: www.unicef.org/magic/briefing/oslo.html.

———. 2007b. *Report Card 7—Child Poverty in Perspective: An Overview of Child Well-Being in Rich Countries.* Florence, Italy: UNICEF Innocenti Research Centre. At: www.unicef-irc.org/publications/article.php?type=3&id_article=49.

———. 2007c. *Eliminating Violence against Children—A Handbook for Parliamentarians.* New York: United Nations (no. 13-2007).

———. 2009. *Canadian Supplement to The State of the World's Children. Aboriginal Children's Health: Leaving No Child Behind.* Toronto: UNICEF Canada. http://www.unicef.ca/sites/default/files/imce_uploads/DISCOVER/OUR%20WORK/ADVOCACY/DOMESTIC/POLICY%20ADVOCACY/DOCS/

Leaving%20no%20child%20behind%2009.pdf.

———. (Peter Adamson). 2013. *Innocenti Report Card No. 11— Child Well-Being Poverty in Rich Countries: A Comparative Overview.* Florence: United Nations Children's Fund.

———. 2013. *Report Card 11—Child Well-Being in Rich Countries: A Comparative Overview.* Florence, Italy: UNICEF Innocenti Research Centre. At: http://www.unicef.ca/sites/default/files/imce_uploads/DISCOVER/OUR%20WORK/ADVOCACY/DOMESTIC/POLICY%20ADVOCACY/DOCS/unicef_report_card_11.pdf.

United Nations Development Programme (UNDP). 2014. *Human Development Report 2014: Sustaining Human Progress: Reducing Vulnerabilities and Building Resilience.* New York: United Nations Development Programme. At: http://hdr.undp.org/sites/default/files/hdr14-report-en-1.pdf

United Nations High Commission for Refugees (UNHCR). 1994. *Refugee Children: Guidelines on Protection and Care.* Geneva: UNHCR.

Urquia, Marcelo, John Frank, Richard Glazier, and Rahim Moineddin. 2007. "Birth Outcomes by Neighbourhood Income and Recent Immigration in Toronto," *Health Reports* 18, 4: 1–10.

Utter, Jennifer, Robert Scragg, and David Schaff. 2006. "Association between Television Viewing and Commonly Advertised Foods among New Zealand Children and Youth," *Public Health Nutrition* 9, 5: 606–12.

Vandell, Deborah Lowe. 2000. "Parents, Peer Groups and Other Socializing Influences," *Developmental Psychology* 36, 6: 699–710.

Van Lier, Pol, Frank Vitaro, Brigitte Wanner, Patricia Vuijk, and Alfons Crijnen. 2005. "Gender Differences in Developmental Links among Antisocial Behavior, Friends' Antisocial Behavior, and Peer Rejection in Childhood: Results from Two Cultures," *Child Development* 76, 4: 841–85.

Van Ngo, Hieu, and Barbara Scleifer. 2007. "Immigrant Children and Youth in Focus," *CITC* 29–33.

Vanobbergen, Bruno. 2004. "Wanted: *Real* Children: About Innocence and Nostalgia in a Commodified Childhood," *Studies in Philosophy of Education* 23: 161–76.

Vares, Tiina, Sue Jackson, and Rosalind Gill. 2011. "Preteen Girls Read 'Tween' Popular Culture: Diversity, Complexity and Contradiction," *International Journal of Media and Cultural Politics* 7, 2: 139–154.

Verdon, Lisa. 2007. "Are 5-Year-Old Children Ready to Learn at School? Family Income and Home Environment Contexts," *Education Matters* 4, 1.

Vermeer, Harriet, and Marinus van Ijzendoorn. 2006. "Children's Elevated Cortisol Levels at Daycare: A Review and Meta-analysis," *Early Childhood Research Quarterly* 21, 3: 390–401.

Vygotsky, L.S. 1967 [1933]. "Play and Its Role in the Mental Development of the Child," *Soviet Psychology* 5: 6–18.

———. 1998 [1931]. "The History of the Development of Higher Mental Functions," in R. Rieber, ed., *The Collected Works of L.S. Vygotsky*, vol. F, *The History of the Development of Higher Mental Functions*. New York: Springer.

Wainright, J.L., S.T. Russell, and C.J. Patterson. 2004. "Psychosocial Adjustment, School Outcomes, and Romantic Relationships of Adolescents with Same-Sex Parents," *Child Development* 75, 6: 1886–98.

Waldram, J.B., D.A. Herring, and T.K. Young. 2006. *Aboriginal Health in Canada: Historical, Cultural, and Epidemiological Perspectives*. Toronto: University of Toronto Press

Walker, Sheila, Stephen Petrill, Frank Spinath, and Robert Plomin. 2004. "Nature, Nurture and Academic Achievement: A Twin Study of Teacher Assessments of 7-Year-Olds," *British Journal of Educational Psychology* 74, 3: 323–42.

Wallerstein, Judith, and S. Blakeslee. 1989. *Second Chances: Men, Women and Children a Decade after Divorce*. Boston: Houghton Mifflin.

Wallerstein, Judith, and John Kelly. 1980. *Surviving the Breakup: How Children and Parents Cope with Divorce*. New York: Basic Books.

Wallerstein, Judith, J.M. Lewis, and S. Blakeslee. 2000. *The Unexpected Legacy of Divorce: A 25 Year Landmark Study*. New York: Hyperion.

Warner, Mildred, and Susan Prentice. 2013. "Regional Economic Development, and Child Care: Toward Social Rights," *Journal of Urban Affairs* 35, 2: 195–217.

Wasterfors, David. 2011. "Stretching Capabilities: Children with Disabilities Playing TV and Computer Games," *Disability and Society* 26, 3: 337–49.

Watabe, Akiko, and David Hibbard. 2014. "The Influence of Authoritarian and Authoritative Parenting on Children's Academic Achievement Motivation: A Comparison between the United States and Japan," *North American Journal of Psychology* 16, 2: 359–82.

Watkins, Sallie. 1990. "The Mary Ellen Myth: Correcting Child Welfare History," *Social Work* 35, 6: 500–3.

Watson, John B. 1925. *Behaviorism*. New York: Norton.

Wauterickx, Naomi, Anneleen Gouwy, and Piet Bracke. 2006. "Parental Divorce and Depression: Long-Term Effects in Adult Children," *Journal of Divorce and Remarriage* 45, 3 and 4: 43–68.

Webber, Maryanne. 1998. *Measuring Low Income and Poverty in Canada: An Update*. Ottawa: Statistics Canada (Catalogue no. 98-13, 75F0002M).

Weininger, Elliot, and Annette Lareau. 2003. "Translating Bourdieu into the American Context: The Question of Social Class and Family–School Relations," *Poetics* 31, 5 and 6: 375–402.

Wendelborg, Christian, and Borgunn Ytterhus. 2013. "Development and Change in Disabled Children's Social Participation Assessed by Parents in Norwegian Daycare Centres: 1999–2009," *European Journal of Special Needs Education* 28, 3: 288–304.

Whattam, Tracy. 2003. "Reflections on Residential School and Our Future: 'Daylight in our Minds.'" *International Journal of Qualitative Studies in Education* (QSE) 16, 3: 435–9.

White, M. 2003. "Retraining Programs for Displaced Workers in the Post-Industrial Era: An Exploration of Government Policies and Programs in Canada and England," *Compare* 33, 4: 497–505.

Wiart, Lesley, Heather Kehler, Gwen Rempel, and Suzanne Tough. 2014. "Current State of Inclusion of Children with Special Needs in Child Care Programmes in One Canadian

Province," *International Journal of Inclusive Education* 18, 4: 345–58.

Wiegers, Wanda. 2002. *The Framing of Poverty as "Child Poverty" and Its Implications for Women.* Ottawa: Status of Women Canada.

Wilkinson, Richard G. 2005. *The Impact of Inequality: How to Make Sick Societies Healthier.* New York: New Press.

Williams, Cara. 2001. "Family Disruptions and Childhood Happiness," *Canadian Social Trends* 62: 2–4.

Williamson, Deanna, and Fiona Salkie. 2005. "Welfare Reforms in Canada: Implications for the Well-Being of Pre-school Children in Poverty," *Journal of Children & Poverty* 11, 1: 55–76.

Winn, Marie. 1984. *Children without Childhood.* Harmondsworth, UK: Penguin.

Wong, Janelle, and Vivian Tseng. 2008. "Political Socialization in Immigrant Families: Challenging Top-Down Parental Socialization Models," *Journal of Ethnic and Migration Studies* 34, 1: 151–68.

World Bank. 2011. Choosing and Estimating Poverty Indicators. Washington, DC: World Bank Group. At: http://web.worldbank.org/WBSITE/EXTERNAL/TOPICS/EXTPOVERTY/EXTPA/0,,contentMDK:20242881~isCURL:Y~menuPK:492130~pagePK:148956~piPK:216618~theSitePK:430367,00.html.

Woronov, T.E. 2007. "Performing the Nation: China's Children as Little Red Pioneers," *Anthropological Quarterly* 80, 3: 647–72.

Worswick, Christopher. 2001. *School Performance of the Children of Immigrants in Canada, 1994–1998.* Ottawa: Statistics Canada, Analytical Studies Branch Research Paper Series (Catalogue no. 11F0019MIE, No. 78).

Wotherspoon, Terry. 2009. *The Sociology of Education in Canada: Critical Perspectives,* 3rd edn. Toronto: Oxford University Press.

Wu, Zheng, and Christopher Schimmele. 2005. "Repartnering after First Union Disruption," *Journal of Marriage and Family* 67: 27–36.

Wyness, Michael. 2006. *Childhood and Society: An Introduction to the Sociology of Childhood.* Houndsmills, UK: Palgrave Macmillan.

Wyness, Michael. 2013. "Children's Participation and Intergenerational Dialogue: Bringing Adults Back into the Analysis," *Childhood* 20, 4: 429–42.

Yeung, Jean, Miriam Linver, and Jeanne Brooks-Gunn. 2002. "How Money Matters for Young Children's Development: Parental Investment and Family Processes," *Child Development* 73, 6: 1861–79.

Yi-Ping, Shih, and Yi Chin-Chun. 2014. "Cultivating the Difference: Social Class, Parental Values, Cultural Capital and Children's After-School Activities in Taiwan," *Journal of Comparative Family Studies* 44, 2: 55–75.

Yuk King Lau. 2007. "Parent-Child Relationships, Parental Relationships and Children's Self-Esteem in Post-Divorce Families in Hong Kong," *Marriage and Family Review* 42, 4: 87–103.

YTV. 2002. "Wave 8, 2002 Tween Report: Special Kidfluence Edition." Toronto: Ifop-Canada Market Research.

———. 2007. "2006 Tween Report: Special Media Usage Edition." Toronto: Solutions Research Group.

Yuan, Anastasia, and Hayley Hamilton. 2006. "Stepfather Involvement and Adolescent Well-Being: Do Mothers and Nonresidential Fathers Matter?" *Journal of Family Issues* 27, 9: 1191–213.

Zanocco, Vivian. 2014. "Christopher Paul Neil, Convicted Sex Offender, Faces 10 New Charges in BC," *CBC News Online* 28 March. At: http://www.cbc.ca/news/canada/british-columbia/christopher-paul-neil-convicted-sex-offender-faces-10-new-charges-in-b-c-1.2590785.

Zeytinoglu, I.U., B. Seaton, W. Lillevik, and J. Moruz. 2005. "Working in the Margins: Women's Experiences of Stress and Occupational Health Problems in Part-Time and Casual Retail Jobs," *Women and Health* 41, 1: 87–107.

Zimiles, Herbert. 2004. "Schismatic Studies of Divorce," *Human Development* 47: 239–50.

Zimmerman, Frederick, Dimitri A. Christakis, and Andrew N. Meltzoff. 2007. "Associations between Media Viewing and Language Development in Children under Age 2 Years," *Journal of Pediatrics* 151, 4: 364–8.

Zuckerman, Diane, and Barry Zuckerman. 1985. "Television's Impact on Children," *Pediatrics* 75, 2: 233–40.

Index

punishment: corporal/physical, 224–7, 229–31; *see also* child abuse

Quebec: anti-poverty strategy in, 196; child care in, 122, 124, 129, 131–2, 138, 196; education in, 85–6; family policy in, 195–6
Quiet Revolution, 86, 132
Quill, Lawrence, 246
Qvortrup, Jens, 33, 39

Raby, Rebecca, 36
race: media and, 104–5; prejudice and, 96
racial/racialized groups, 144, 146, 187
racism: immigrants and, 150–1; institutional, 161, 170
Ram, Bali, and Feng Hou, 215, 217
refugees, 145, 155–6, 187
relational approaches, 35
religion, 85–6, 164, 224
remarriage, 216
Renold, Emma, 95
research, 41–60; by children, 43–4, 55–8; children's vulnerability and, 53–5; confidentiality and, 54–5; deductive, 46–7; ethnographic, 45–6, 50–1; exploratory, 46; inductive, 48; process of, 44–52; qualitative/quantitative, 45–8; time dimension of, 48
Research Ethics Boards, 52
residential schools, 86, 163–5
rights: child protection and, 226–7, 241; children's, 3–4, 57, 254–5, 256–7; divorce and, 219–20; theories and, 20, 29–33, 34, 36
risk-and-resiliency perspective, 209–10, 211
Rodriguez, C., and M. Richardson, 239
Romagnoli, A., and G. Wall, 68
Romero, R. Todd, 224
Rose, Katherine, et al., 117
Rosen, David, 14
Rothstein, Richard, 88
Rousseau, Jean-Jacques, 8, 9–10, 139
Royal Canadian Mounted Police, 223
Royal Commission on Aboriginal Peoples, 170–1
Royal Commission on the Status of Women, 129
Ryerson, Egerton, 85, 86

schools: "common," 85; enrolment in, 83; "grammar," 85; Internet and, 117; residential, 86, 163–5; *see also* education
Schor, Juliet, 119
self, "looking-glass," 25, 26
Senate Committee on Human Rights, 33
separation, 206, 218; *see also* divorce

service economy, 122–3
Sesame Street, 115–17
sexualization, 250–2; media and, 107–10; self-, 107, 109, 110
sexual offences, 232, 233–4; *see also* abuse, sexual
Shanahan, Suzanne, *x*, 1–2
shared parental responsibility framework, 218
Sharma, Raghubar, 198
Shaw, Catherine, et al., 49, 59
Sherman, A., and E. Zurbriggen, 92
Shimoni, R., et al., 148–9
Sigle-Rushton, W., and J. Waldfogel, 192
Simich, Laura, et al., 153
"Sixties Scoop," 164
Skinner, B.F., 24–5
Smith, Anne, 94
Smith, Stacy, et al., 110
social actors: children as, 34
social artifacts, 49
social cognitive theory, 26
social constructs, 1, 255–6
Social Darwinism, 21
social inclusion/exclusion, 96–8
social information processing theory, 239
socialization, 27–9; agents of, 28; education and, 87; families and, 62–3; gender, 72–4; primary, 28; same-sex parents and, 77–9; secondary, 28
social learning theory, 26, 113, 238–9
social reproduction, 124
social role theory, 28
social skills: peers and, 94–5
social stress-strain theory, 239–41
societies: agricultural, 11; nomadic, 10–11; post-industrial, 122
sociocultural theory, 27
sociology, *x*, 19–40; "adding" children to, 26–9; new, 33–5, 94
soldiers, child, 13–16
spanking, 224–7; *see also* child abuse
Spock, Benjamin, 65, 80
Stanbridge, Karen, 36–7
standpoint theory, 35
Starr, C., and G. Ferguson, 108–10
Stasiulis, Daiva, 36, 94, 254–5
Statistics Canada, 2–3, 48, 89; Aboriginal peoples and, 178; employment and, 123, 192; parenting styles and, 225–6; poverty and, 183, 186; violence and, 232, 233, 234
Stearns, Peter, *x*, 4, 5, 7, 10–11, 17
Steeves, Valerie, 119
stepfamilies, 67, 216–17
stereotypes: media and, 111, 113
Strachan, John, 85
"Straight-18," 14, 15–16